Discipleship in the Ancient World and Matthew's Gospel

Second Edition

Michael J. Wilkins

Baker Books
A Division of Baker Book House Co
Grand Rapids, Michigan 49516

Library of Congress Cataloging-in-Publication Data

Wilkins, Michael J.
    [Concept of disciple in Matthew's Gospel]
    Discipleship in the ancient world and Matthew's Gospel / Michael J. Wilkins.—2nd ed.
       p.   cm.
    Originally published: The concept of disciple in Matthew's Gospel. Leiden, the Netherlands ; New York : E. J. Brill, 1988, in series: Supplements to Novum Testamentum, 0167–9732 ; v. 59.
      Includes bibliographical references and indexes.
      ISBN 0-8010-2007-7 (pbk.)
      1. Bible. N. T. Matthew—Criticism, interpretation, etc. 2. Christian life—Biblical teaching. I. Title.
    [BS2575.2.W55   1995]
    226.2'06—dc20   95-32137

The epilogue originally appeared as "Named and Unnamed Disciples in Matthew: A Literary-Theological Study," *SBL Seminar Papers* 30 (1991). Used with permission.

CONTENTS

PREFACE

The end of one road, the beginning of many others. Almost sixteen years ago my wife and I began our long and winding road together, and as a team we have explored the essence of discipleship. We have had many wonderful moments and many difficult moments, but the Lord has always been there to see us through. With the publication of this dissertation we come to the end of one path. We, above all, give thanks to our Lord Jesus Christ for enabling us to accomplish the task He set before us; but we would also like to give special thanks to the host of family and friends who have stood by us.

To our wonderful daughters, Michelle and Wendy, we love you and dedicate even more time to developing and to enjoying our family. To our parents, John and Margaret Melia and Reverend Stuart and Barbara Campbell, thank you for loving us and believing in us. A special thanks to Mom and Dad Melia for your loving, sacrificial, financial support in some real times of crisis.

To the two churches we had the privilege to pastor, the Carlsbad (North County) Evangelical Free Church and the Cayucos Community Evangelical Free Church, thank you for your prayers and encouragement. We give very special thanks to the secretaries of those churches, Mrs. Jan Statzer and Mrs. Margaret Allen, who gave of their personal time to type several papers leading to this dissertation. To our close friends, Norman and Vondell Jakeway, thank you for always being there to help and to be a real part of our family.

To a wonderful friend and surfing partner, Mr. Kenneth Verheyen, thank you for your unfailing encouragement and friendship. Thank you also for the financial help you gave which made possible the publication of the book. The Lord is certainly using you in significant ways of ministry.

To the editors of *Novum Testamentum* we are profoundly grateful for your willingness to include this book in the series *Supplements to Novum Testamentum*. We consider this one of the rare honors of our lives. To Mr. Julian Deahl of E. J. Brill, thank you for your kind assistance in the tedious task of intercontinental editorial supervision.

To my mentors in the doctoral program at Fuller Theological Seminary, Professors Ralph Martin and Donald Hagner, and the external reader, Professor Jack Dean Kingsbury, Union Theological Seminary (Virginia), thank you for your wise guidance and advice. Professor Martin, even while you were going through many personal crises you provided encouragement, and although our paths may take different directions in the future, we will continue to be grateful for your example of scholarly integrity and persevering trust in the goodness of God. The final manuscript was submitted to the faculty at Fuller Theological Seminary in March, 1986, and is offered here in essentially the same form. I now look forward to cordial interaction with the wider scholarly community.

The publication of the book in this series was made possible by a financial subsidy from Biola University, La Mirada, California, USA, at which I am presently Chair and Associate Professor in the department of New Testament Language and Literature, Talbot School of Theology. To my colleagues and to the administration of Biola University, thank you for the many ways you have given us help.

My best friend and wife, Lynne, thank you. What we have in our marriage has given us the the stability and endurance to pursue and accomplish our dreams. Now we go on to pursue other dreams, down other roads. I can never thank you enough for your unwavering confidence, support, and love. You are indeed the wind beneath my wings.

San Clemente, California, USA
September, 1987   MICHAEL J. WILKINS

PREFACE TO THE SECOND EDITION

My thanks to Baker Book House for negotiating a second edition of my book on discipleship. The book was originally published by E. J. Brill (The Netherlands) in the *Novum Testamentum Supplements* series. I appreciate this second edition because 1) it allows a wider distribution at a lesser cost, and 2) it allows me to include an epilogue which updates the discussion of discipleship in Matthew's gospel.

This second edition also carries a new title: *Discipleship in the Ancient World and Matthew's Gospel.* The new title expresses more accurately the contents of the book. Several reviewers of the first edition mentioned that some of the most important contributions of the book could be overlooked because the title did not adequately emphasize the contents.

The research originally moved in two directions and comprises the five primary chapters of the book. First, I undertook an analysis of master-disciple relationships as they were found in the ancient world leading up to the time of Christ, including classical and Hellenistic Greek literature, all ancient Jewish literature, including Philo and the Qumran community, and then on into the early church and Talmudic Judaism. Second, I undertook a comparative study of Matthew's use of the most common term for "disciple," μαθητής, and then a study of Matthew's theological perspective of Simon Peter. These five chapters have been received with widespread appreciation; hence they remain here as in the first edition.

The epilogue looks at recent developments in Matthean discipleship. I touched briefly on the recent history of Matthean discipleship studies, then displayed the prominent characteristics of Matthean disciples which form something of a consensus in modern scholarship. I then looked at recent historical/social-critical and literary-critical approaches to the disciples in Matthew, concluding with my own reflections on the recent status of study.

I would like to express my appreciation to Mr. Jim Weaver at Baker Book House for spearheading this second edition. It has been a pleasure and privilege getting to know you, Jim. Thanks for your support and encouragement.

San Clemente, California, USA
May, 1995

MICHAEL J. WILKINS

ABBREVIATIONS

AASOR	Annual of the American Schools of Oriental Research
AB	Anchor Bible
AGJU	Arbeiten zur Geschichte des antiken Judentums und des Urchristentums
AnBib	Analecta biblica
ANET	J. B. Pritchard (ed.), *Ancient Near Eastern Texts*
ANQ	*Andover Newton Quarterly*
APOT	R. H. Charles (ed.), *Apocrypha and Pseudepigrapha of the Old Testament*
ATAbh	Alttestamentliche Abhandlungen
ATANT	Abhandlungen zur Theologie des Alten und Neuen Testaments
ATR	*Anglican Theological Review*
BDB	E. Brown, S. R. Driver, and C. A. Briggs, *Hebrew and English Lexicon of the Old Testament*
BDF	F. Blass, A. Debrunner, and R. W. Funk, *A Greek Grammar of the New Testament*
BETL	Bibliotheca ephemeridum theologicarum lovaniensium
BGD	W. Bauer, F. W. Gingrich, and F. Danker, *Greek-English Lexicon of the New Testament*
BHK	R. Kittel, *Biblia hebraica*
BHT	Beiträge zur historischen Theologie
Bib	*Biblica*
BJRL	*Bulletin of the John Rylands University Library of Manchester*
BTB	*Biblical Theology Bulletin*
BWANT	Beiträge zur Wissenschaft vom Alten und Neuen Testament
BZAW	Beihefte zur *ZAW*
BZNW	Beihefte zur *ZNW*
CBQ	*Catholic Biblical Quarterly*
CBQMS	Catholic Biblical Quarterly Monograph Series
CNT	Commentaire du Nouveau Testament
ConB OTS	Coniectanea biblica, Old Testament Series
CRINT	Compendia Rerum Iudaicarum ad Novum Testamentum
EWNT	Exegetisches Wörterbuch zum Neuen Testament
GBSNTS	Guides to Biblical Scholarship: New Testament Series
GBSOTS	Guides to Biblical Scholarship: Old Testament Series
HALAT	W. Baumgartner et al., *Hebräisches und aramäisches Lexikon zum Alten Testament*
HKAT	Handkommentar zum Alten Testament
HKNT	Handkommentar zum Neuen Testament
HNT	Handbuch zum Neuen Testament
HNTC	Harper's New Testament Commentaries
ICC	International Critical Commentary
Int	*Interpretation*
IRT	Issues in Religion and Theology
ITQ	*Irish Theological Quarterly*
JAAR	*Journal of the American Academy of Religion*
JBL	*Journal of Biblical Literature*
JETS	*Journal of the Evangelical Theological Society*
JNSL	*Journal of Northwest Semitic Languages*
JNES	*Journel of Near Eastern Studies*
JQR	*Jewish Quarterly Review*
JQRMS	Jewish Quarterly Review Monograph Series

JSNT	*Journal for the Study of the New Testament*
JSOT	*Journal for the Study of the Old Testament*
JSS	*Journal of Semitic Studies*
JTS	*Journal of Theological Studie*
Judaica	*Judaica: Beiträge zum Verständnis. . . .*
KB	L. Koehler and W. Baumgartner, iLexicon in Veteris Testamenti libros
KJV	King James Version
LCL	Loeb Classical Library
MeyerK	H. A. W. Meyer, Kritisch-exegetischer Kommentar über das Neue Testament
MM	J. H. Moulton and G. Milligan, *The Vocabulary of the Greek Testament*
NASB	New American Standard Bible
NCB	New Century Bible (new edit.)
NClB	New Clarendon Bible
NEB	New English Bible
NICNT	New International Commentary on the New Testament
NICOT	New International Commentary on the Old Testament
NIDNTT	C. Brown (ed.), *The New International Dictionary of New Testament Theology*
NIGNTC	New International Greek Testament Commentary
NovT	*Novum Testamentum*
NovTSup	Novum Testamentum, Supplement Series
NTA	*New Testament Abstracts*
NTAbh	Neutestamentliche Abhandlungen
NTS	*New Testament Studies Numen*
Numen:	*International Review for the History of Religions*
OCD	*Oxford Classical Dictionary*
RB	*Revue biblique*
RQ	*Revue de Qumrân*
RSR	*Recherches de science religieuse*
RSV	Revised Standard Version
SANT	Studien zum Alten und Neuen Testament
SBLAS	Society of Biblical Literature Aramaic Studies
SBLASP	SBL Abstracts and Seminar Papers
SBLDS	SBL Dissertation Series
SBLMS	SBL Monograph Series
SBLSBS	SBL Sources for Biblical Study
SBLSCS	SBL Septuagint and Cognate Studies
SBLST	SBL Semeia Studies
SBLTT	SBL Texts and Translations
SBS	Stuttgarter Bibelstudien
SBT	Studies in Biblical Theology
SNTSMS	Society for New Testament Studies Monograph Series
SOTSMS	Society for Old Testament Studies Monograph Series
ST	*Studia theologica*
Str-B	[H. Strack and] P. Billerbeck, *Kommentar zum Neuen Testament*
SUNT	Studien zur Umwelt des Neuen Testaments
TP	Palestinian Talmud
TB	Babylonian Talmud
TDNT	G. Kittel and G. Friedrich (eds.), *Theological Dictionary of the New Testament*
THKNT	Theologischer Handkommentar zum Neuen Testament
TLG	Thesaurus Linguae Graecae, University of California, Irvine
TNTC	Tyndale New Testament Commentary
TOTC	Tyndale Old Testament Commentary
TynB	*Tyndale Bulletin*
TWAT	G. J. Botterweck and H. Ringgren (eds), *Theologisches Wörterbuch zum Alten Testament*

TWNT	G. Kittel and G. Friedrich (eds), *Theologisches Wörterbuch zum Neuen Testament*
TZ	Theologische Zeitschrift
TWOT	R. Laird Harris, Gleason L. Archer, Jr., and Bruce K. Waltke (eds.), *Theological Wordbook of the Old Testament*
UBSGNT	United Bible Societies Greek New Testament
UNT	Untersuchungen zum Neuen Testament
USQR	*Union Seminary Quarterly Review*
VKGNT	K. Aland (ed.), *Vollständige Konkordanz zum griechischen Neuen Testament*
VT	*Vetus Testamentum*
VTSup	Vetus Testamentum, Supplement Series
WBC	Word Biblical Commentary
WC	Westminster Commentary
WMANT	Wissenschaftliche Monographien zum Alten und Neuen Testament
WTJ	*Westminster Theological Journal*
WUNT	Wissenschaftliche Untersuchungen zum Neuen Testament
ZAW	*Zeitschrift für die alttestamentliche Wissenschaft*
ZNW	*Zeitschrift für die neutestamentliche Wissenschaft*
ZPEB	Zondervan Pictorial Encyclopedia of the Bible
ZTK	*Zeitschrift für Theologie und Kirche*

INTRODUCTION

The student of the New Testament is much like a student of classical music. For years the student is privileged to listen to various experts offer renditions of a master composer. Each rendition differed somewhat and each recaptured important features of the master which the others were not able to express. Some experts focused on technical features, others on the esoteric. Some experts were creatively contemporary, while others were conservatively cautious. But the student listened to all until the day finally arrived when he was given the privilege of offering his own rendition. This dissertation marks the arrival of that day in the life of this student of the New Testament. The master composer is Matthew, the composition studied is the gospel according to Matthew, and the movement is the orchestration of the disciples of Jesus as viewed through the eyes of the composer. The experts have been studied; careful thought has been given to their attempts to recapture the intent of the composer. While this student is cognizant that he can never perfectly reproduce the original intent, the humble, yet diligent purpose is to attempt to recreate that first beautiful rhapsody.

The clearest sound of the rhapsody is to be found in the genre of the composition. Matthew's composition is a "gospel,"[1] an interpreted history of God's activities in Jesus Christ; his intent was to move his audience to faith.[2] While John explicitly declares this motive as he concludes his gospel (Jn 20:31), Matthew subtly weaves it into his introductory scenes (Mt 1). But the rhapsody did not stop in Matthew's introduction. His story of the gospel is given artistically,[3] and variegated refrains

---

[1] Graham Stanton, "Matthew as a Creative Interpreter of the Sayings of Jesus," *Das Evangelium und die Evangelien*, ed. Peter Stuhlmacher, WUNT 28 (Tübingen: J. C. B. Mohr [Paul Siebeck], 1983), p. 287; Stanton demonstrates why he believes Matthew would have accepted εὐαγγέλιον as a title for his writing.

[2] Although found elsewhere, the phrase "interpreted history" is borrowed from Ralph Martin, *New Testament Foundations: A Guide for Christian Students*, I (Grand Rapids: Eerdmans, 1975), p. 43. For a recent discussion of the literary genre "gospel" as it relates to the 'intent' of the evangelist, see Robert Guelich, "The Gospel Genre," *Das Evangelium und die Evangelien*, ed. Peter Stuhlmacher, WUNT 28 (Tübingen: J. C. B. Mohr [Paul Siebeck], 1983), pp. 183-219. "Moving to faith" implies initial faith, but here it especially signifies increasing faith.

[3] One of the most recent trends in Matthean study is the emphasis on Matthew's gospel as a "story" which the author skillfully weaves; e.g., R. A. Edwards, *Matthew's Story of Jesus* (Philadelphia: Fortress, 1985). For an example of this type of direction in Markan studies, see Ernest Best, *Mark: The Gospel as Story*, Studies of the New Testament and its World, ed. John Riches (Edinburgh: T. & T. Clark, 1983). This trend is found in gospel studies as a whole, discussed below with "composition criticism" and "reader-response criticism."

are to be found in the many themes which he clarions. One of those
themes is discipleship. More clearly than any other gospel writer, Matthew records the programmatic nature of discipleship by concluding his
gospel with the great commission "to make disciples." None would
dispute the special focus Matthew gives to this theme, but "discipleship"
admits of a narrow as well as a broader definition. Discipleship can be
narrowly understood as a technical discussion of the historical master-
disciple relationship, but it can also be understood in a broader way as
Christian experience, that is, "the self-understanding of the early Christian believers as believers: what such a way of life requires, implies, and
entails."[4] Matthew presents a faithful record of the tradition of the
master-disciple relationship which was established between Jesus and his
followers, but he also interpreted that tradition so that his readers would
be moved to faith. The narrow definition of discipleship to Jesus is
discovered in a study of the tradition; the broad definition of discipleship
to Jesus is discovered in a study of Matthew's interpretation of the
traditon.[5] For Matthew's readers the harmony of the two definitions was
found by standing on the foundation of the tradition while they lived out
their faith. The goal of this study is to add to a greater understanding of
both definitions of discipleship in Matthew's gospel.

Matthean experts have not restrained themselves in their efforts to
explicate the message of this gospel. In a recent survey of Matthean
study, G. Stanton confesses that he concentrated on the origin and purpose of the gospel of Matthew because "in the past fifteen years there has
been such a flood of scholarly literature that a comprehensive survey
would become a mere catalogue."[6] The study of discipleship in general,
and in Matthew's gospel in particular, has such an ancient and a modern
history that it demands specialization today. The modern history of
discipleship studies[7] reveals an increasing refinement in methodologies,

---

[4] Fernando F. Segovia, "Introduction: Call and Discipleship—Toward a Reexamination of the Shape and Character of Christian Existence in the New Testament,"
in *Discipleship in the New Testament*, ed. Fernando F. Segovia (Philadelphia: Fortress,
1985), p. 2.

[5] A careful delineation of these two features is presented in Stanton, "Matthew as a
Creative Interpreter of the Sayings of Jesus," pp. 273-287.

[6] Graham Stanton, "The Origin and Purpose of Matthew's Gospel: Matthean
Scholarship from 1945 to 1980," *Aufstieg und Niedergang der Römischen Welt* II, 25, 3, ed.
H. Temporini und W. Haase (Berlin: Walter de Gruyter, 1985), p. 1891.

[7] The major studies in chronological order are: Eduard Schweizer, *Lordship and
Discipleship*, trans. and rev. by the author, SBT 28 (1955; London: SCM, 1960); Anselm
Schulz, *Nachfolgen und Nachahmen: Studien über das Verhältnis der neutestamentlichen Jüngerschaft
zur urchristlichen Vorbildethik*, SANT 6 (Munich: Kösel-Verlag, 1962); Hans Dieter Betz,
Nachfolge und Nachahmung Jesu Christi im Neuen Testament, BHT 37 (Tübingen:
Mohr/Siebeck, 1967); Martin Hengel, *The Charismatic Leader and His Followers*, trans. J.

each leading to a greater understanding.[8] Applying a narrower methodology to the discipleship passages in Matthew, the present study intends to explicate Matthew's concept of discipleship from his use of the most common term for disciple, μαθητής.

But on the other hand, the Matthean student cannot be so narrowly focused that he overlooks assistance from other fields. Scholarly activities in many other domains have opened new avenues for approaching the gospel of Matthew, and when they are traveled by the Matthean student they offer possibilites of greater understanding of the gospel message. Therefore, the narrow search for Matthew's understanding of discipleship needs to be enhanced by the application of broader research tools. This study will employ three research tools in the quest for greater understanding of the Matthean disciples.

One research tool which helps clarify the Matthean portrait of Jesus' disciples is modern linguistics, specifically as linguistics relates to a study of the term μαθητής. Although word studies have historically been a common means for attempting to clarify the meaning of the biblical literature, modern lexicological and semantical analysis has revolutionized such studies. The work of J. Barr has facilitated that revolution, beginning with his book *The Semantics of Biblical Language*. He points out that many linguistic arguments about New Testament terms are often based upon unsystematic and haphazard approaches to the integration of the biblical languages and linguistic science.[9] In particular, he criticizes the approach to lexicography which characterizes much of the *Theological Dictionary of the New Testament (TDNT)*.[10] Barr's primary criticism of *TDNT* is lodged against the undefined relation of "concept history" and the "history of words."[11] Although K. Rengstorf's article on μαθητής in *TDNT*[12] is excellent at many points, it displays the very characteristic

---

Greig (1968; New York: Crossroad, 1981). The most influential work focusing on Matthew exclusively is Ulrich Luz, "The Disciples in the Gospel according to Matthew," trans. Graham Stanton and Robert Morgan, in *The Interpretation of Matthew*, ed. G. Stanton, IRT 3 (1971; London / Philadelphia: SPCK / Fortress, 1983); and the most recent direction is taken by Richard A. Edwards, "Uncertain Faith: Matthew's Portrait of the Disciples," in *Discipleship in the New Testament*, ed. Fernando F. Segovia (Philadelphia: Fortress, 1985).

[8] Segovia gives a perceptive analysis of the advance in methodologies in discipleship studies; cf. Fernando F. Segovia, "Introduction: Call and Discipleship," in *Discipleship in the New Testament*, ed. Fernando F. Segovia (Philadelphia: Fortress, 1985), pp. 3-4.

[9] James Barr, *The Semantics of Biblical Language* (Oxford: Oxford University Press, 1961), pp. 21ff.

[10] Ibid., pp. 206-262.

[11] Ibid., p. 207.

[12] Karl H. Rengstorf, "μαθητής," *TDNT*, ed. Gerhard Kittel, trans. and ed. Geoffrey W. Bromiley, IV (Grand Rapids: Eerdmans, 1967), pp. 415-460.

criticized by Barr. Even so, scholarly[13] and popular[14] treatments of the history of μαθητής are still guided by the rather imprecise conclusions reached about the *history of the concept of discipleship* and the relation of that historical concept to the *history of the term.*[15]

Many New Testament scholars have begun employing modern linguistics as an aid to understanding biblical words and they have helped clarify how word studies can be even more effective when guided by lexical semantics.[16] In a recent popular level work, D. Carson shows how even the non-specialist can avoid common exegetical fallacies which stem from unsound word studies by employing sound principles of lexical semantics.[17] Although the New Testament student does not have to be an expert in linguistics, he must diligently employ basic principles of lexical semantics in order to understand clearly the biblical use of words. Had Rengstorf written his article in the waning years, instead of the middle, of the twentieth century he would have been able to reap the benefits of linguistics as an aid to New Testament research, and might have avoided some of the conclusions he reached.

Therefore, this work will seek to employ the basic principles of lexical semantics in order to gain a better understanding of the history of the term μαθητής in various contextual uses. A secondary purpose, which will direct the study, is to clarify why Rengstorf's linguistic conclusions are invalid. For example, although its primary purpose is to classify the various ways μαθητής is used in the classical and Hellenistic Greek

[13] E.g., Dietrich Müller, "μαθητής," *NIDNTT*, I, trans. and ed. Colin Brown (Grand Rapids: Zondervan, 1975), pp. 483f. The treatment of the historical background of μαθητής in *EWNT* is too brief to evaluate the overall influence Rengstorf had on it; cf. P. Nepper-Christensen, "μαθητής," *Exegetisches Wörterbuch zum Neuen Testament*, ed. Horst Balz and Gerhard Schneider, II (Stuttgart: W. Kohlhammer, 1982), col. 915-921.

[14] E.g., Michael Griffiths, *The Example of Jesus*, The Jesus Library (Downers Grove, Illinois: InterVarsity, 1985), p. 21.

[15] One of the avowed purposes of *The New International Dictionary of New Testament Theology* has been to heed some of the corrective warnings of Barr (cf. the remaks by the editor in the preface, p. 10), yet the article by Müller on "μαθητής," shows no major advances in linguistic precision over Rengstorf. Griffiths' book (*The Example of Jesus*, p. 21) is one of the most recent popular treatments of discipleship, and is abreast of much scholarly work, but still follows the lead of Rengstorf's article on the history of μαθητής and the Hebrew equivalent *talmidhim*, and so confuses the history of the concept and the term.

[16] E.g., Eugene A. Nida, *Language Structure and Translation*, essays selected and introduced by Anwar S. Dil (Stanford, California: Stanford University Press, 1975); David Hill, *Greek Words and Hebrew Meanings: Studies in the Semantics of Soteriological Terms*, SNTSMS 5 (Cambridge: At the University Press, 1967); G. B. Caird, *The Language and Imagery of the Bible* (Philadelphia: Westminster, 1980); J. P. Louw, *Semantics of New Testament Greek*, SBLSS (Philadelphia / Chico: Fortress / Scholars, 1982); Moisés Silva, *Biblical Words and Their Meaning: An Introduction to Lexical Semantics* (Grand Rapids: Zondervan, 1983).

[17] D. A. Carson, *Exegetical Fallacies* (Grand Rapids: Baker, 1984), pp. 25-66.

literature, the first chapter will respond to Rengstorf's argument that μαθητής was a disreputable term among the Socratic-Platonic-Aristotelian philosophers and that this attitude permanently affected its use wherever Greek was used. This conclusion opens the field of semantics, since he suggests that the term itself actually referred to a Sophistic student in common Greek usage. The investigation in chapter one will lead to an exhaustive study of the contextual usage of μαθητής in selected classical and Hellenistic authors, made possible through access to the *Thesaurus Linguae Graecae* computer database. The various uses of the term will be categorized and conclusions suggested as to its "common" and "technical" usage by classical and Hellenistic authors. Chapter Two will also be guided by linguistic concerns, as it attempts to trace the use of Hebrew equivalents of μαθητής. Chapter Three will continue to trace the history of the use of μαθητής, here in the Jewish literature outside of the Old Testament up to the compilation of the Rabbinical writings. Chapters four and five will complete the historical analysis of the uses of μαθητής up to the time of Matthew. The term will be analyzed in its contextual usage in Matthew's gospel, especially as compared to the use in the other synoptic gospels. This historical survey of μαθητής will help clarify the use of the term in the gospel of Matthew and hopefully will correct some of the invalid linguistic conclusions reached by Rengstorf.

Sociological investigation is another modern research tool which is proving valuable as an aid to the student of the biblical literature.[18] This tool is just now beginning to exert its influence on biblical research, but already the influence is significant. Rengstorf wrote his article at a time prior to the employment of sociological investigation by biblical scholars, and, as with linguistics, he might not have made some of his claims about the history of μαθητής if he had been able to compare modern linguistic analysis with modern sociological analysis. For example, he declares that since the terminology for discipleship is absent from the Old Testament, the "concept" of discipleship between human masters and disciples is absent as well. This conclusion will be discussed in chapter two from a semantical point of view, because Rengstorf automatically connects the

---

[18] E.g., in the Old Testament: Roland de Vaux, *Ancient Israel: Its Life and Institutions,* trans. John McHugh (New York: McGraw-Hill, 1961); Robert R. Wilson, *Sociological Approaches to the Old Testament,* GBS: OTS (Philadelphia: Fortress, 1984); Norman K. Gottwald, *The Hebrew Bible—A Socio-Literary Introduction* (Philadelphia: Fortress, 1985); in the New Testament: John G. Gager, *Kingdom and Community: The Social World of Early Christianity,* Prentice-Hall Studies in Religion Series (Englewood Cliffs, New Jersey: Prentice-Hall, 1975); Abraham J. Malherbe, *Social Aspects of Early Christianity* (Baton Rouge, Louisiana: Louisiana State University Press, 1977); Gerd Theissen, *Sociology of Early Palestinian Christianity,* trans. John Bowden (1977; Philadelphia: Fortress, 1978); Derek Tidball, *The Social Context of the New Testament: A Sociological Analysis* (Exeter, Devon / Grand Rapids: Paternoster / Zondervan, 1984).

concept of discipleship with certain terms, but the conclusion will also be
analyzed from a sociological point of view. Various sociological structures and organizations revealed in the Old Testament will be analyzed
to see if they yield evidence of master-disciple relationships. Chapter
three will include a sociological analysis of various types of discipleship
structures revealed in the Jewish literature outside of the Old Testament.
These relationships will be compared to the disciples of Jesus in order to
understand more fully the similarities with, and differences from, other
master-disciple relationships in existence at the time.

A third research tool which is profitably applied to biblical studies is
modern literary analysis. One may analyze the biblical literature simply
as literature,[19] or one may investigate the text in order to explicate the
intention and achievements of the author through analysis of the compo-
nent elements and structure of the text itself. The latter investigation may
either seek to answer the what and how of a writing or it may seek to
answer the whence and why.[20] Two of the most recent literary
approaches to Matthew are redaction criticism and composition
criticism. Since these disciplines are sometimes confused, S. Smalley
clarifies their differences:

> One (redaction criticism) is the study of the observable changes introduced
> by the Gospel writers into the traditional material they received and used.
> The other (composition criticism) examines the *arrangement* of this material,
> an arrangement which is motived by the theological understanding and
> intention of the evangelists.[21]

Recently, these two literary tools have been recognized to be complementary processes of one methodology, and both have made a significant
impact on studies in the gospel of Matthew.

The appearance of G. Bornkamm's extremely influential essay, "Die
Sturmstillung im Matthäusevangelium," in 1948[22] commonly marks the
beginning of redaction critical approaches to Matthean studies.[23] Redaction critical techniques have affected all major Matthean works in the last

---

[19] E.g., Leland Ryken, *The Literature of the Bible* (Grand Rapids: Zondervan, 1974);
Kenneth Dauber, "The Bible as Literature: Reading Like the Rabbis," *Reader-Response
Approaches to Biblical and Secular Texts*, ed. Robert Detweiler, *Semeia* 31 (1985) 27-47.
[20] Richard N. Soulen, "Literary Criticism," *Handbook of Biblical Criticism*, (1976; 2d.
ed.; Atlanta, Georgia: John Knox, 1981), p. 113.
[21] Stephen S. Smalley, "Redaction Criticism," *New Testament Interpretation: Essays on
Principles and Methods*, ed. I. Howard Marshall (Exeter, England / Grand Rapids: Paternoster / Eerdmans, 1977), p. 181.
[22] The real impact of Bornkamm's work was not felt in the English-speaking world
until 1963 when it was translated and published as "End-Expectation and Church in
Matthew," along with the redaction-critical works of his students; cf. Günther Bornkamm, Gerhard Barth, and Heinz Joachim Held, *Tradition and Interpretation in Matthew*,
trans. Percy Scott (1963; rpt.; Philadelphia: Westminster, n.d.).
[23] The most important, recent, and perceptive analysis of the state of Matthean studies

two to three decades, whether the writer has employed or decried the use of the tool, but recent stirrings in synoptic studies have caused most students of Matthew's gospel to re-evaluate the techniques used.

Various approaches to composition criticism have attempted to provide more objectivity by emphasizing the gospel of Matthew as a whole, a self-contained entity. W. Thompson suggests that many redaction critical approaches simply compare the gospel with its parallel sources in order to identify redactional material, but overlook the gospel in relation to itself as a means of identifying the evangelist's interpretation.[24] Many Matthean scholars are urging a more objective approach to the use of redaction-critical techniques,[25] and several suggest that one means of providing that objectivity is the employment of a variety of holistic literary approaches. In a recent attempt at reconstructing the *Sitz im Leben* of the gospel of Matthew, D. Hagner suggests that

> The final test of a reconstructed *Sitz im Leben* is how well it enables us to understand the varied contents of a Gospel as a whole. It is the Gospel as it stands that must finally be explained, for it is this that the author put into the hands of his readers. The better sense we can make of the particular emphases and distinctives of the Gospel, its content and organization, the more satisfactory will be the hypothetical *Sitz im Leben*.[26]

Hagner's statement speaks of the need for seeing the gospel as a whole in order to arrive at a hypothetical *Sitz im Leben*, but the same need is required for the study of discipleship in Matthew. The goal to understand Matthew's purpose in his use of the term μαθητής can be realized only by examining all occurrences of the term in the gospel, searching for features unique to Matthew and common to the tradition, and then focusing on the development of the theme as a part of Matthew's story of his gospel.[27]

---

is by Stanton, "Origin and Purpose of Matthew's Gospel," pp. 1890-1951. To see the explosion of Matthean studies, and also to see an earlier analysis which perceptively foresaw many current developments, cf. Ralph P. Martin, "St. Matthew's Gospel in Recent Study," *ExpTim* LXXX (1968-1969) 132-136.

[24] W. G. Thompson has been at the forefront of those advocating a holistic approach to Matthew's gospel. He suggests that the exegete first do a "vertical analysis" (take the gospel as a whole), and then a "horizontal analysis" (compare the gospel to its sources): William G. Thompson, *Matthew's Advice to a Divided Community: Mt 17:22—18:35*, AnBib 44 (Rome: Biblical Institute Press, 1970), pp. 7-12.

[25] Cf. Stanton, "Origin and Purpose of Matthew's Gospel," pp. 1895-1899.

[26] Donald A. Hagner, "The *Sitz im Leben* of the Gospel of Matthew," SBLSP 24 (Atlanta, Georgia: Scholars Press, 1985), p. 243.

[27] Thompson advocates performing a linear analysis before doing a horizontal analysis, but one might then wonder how the distinct features of Matthew's gospel can be recognized without first comparing the gospels. R. Edwards also states that he rejects traditional methodologies which accumulate the data first in order to arrive at Matthew's purpose in his interpretation of the disciples. He suggests instead a reader-response approach by which the characteristics of the disciples are seen in the light of the develop-

Another recent stirring in synoptic studies has occurred in source criticism, especially with reference to Markan priority and the concommitant two- (or, four-) source theory. While this "stirring" has not shaken the hold of these theories on Matthean studies, it has caused enough reexamination that methodologies must be employed somewhat more tentatively.[28] A working model which builds its conclusions only on evidence which is compatible with the two-source theory limits the overall usefulness of its conclusions and its methodology. O. L. Cope has gone so far as to suggest that,

> As a methodological starting point, therefore, at least some of the redaction analysis of the Synoptic Gospels today should be free of any particular source theory. To require otherwise would unduly limit the process of separating tradition from redaction.[29]

Cope later clarifies that his desire is to employ a methodology which would be compatible with a variety of source theories. His desire for objectivity is commendable and will be followed in this study, but since the majority position in Matthean study is the two (or four) source theory, one cannot operate apart from the realities of current scholarship. Therefore, in order to promote the widest scholarly interaction, chapters four and five of this investigation will attempt to work within the parameters of exegetical methodologies which are generally accepted by Matthean scholars, but a more comprehensive methodology will be attempted as well. Specifically, in chapter four every occurrence of the term μαθητής will be examined in relationship to the parallels, and will employ the common terminology which assumes Matthew worked with the sources Mark and "Q";[30] yet at the same time this examination will attempt to draw conclusions which are compatible with Matthew as a self-contained entity. Matthew's distinct use of the term, both in comparison to the parallels as well in the progression of the gospel, will then lead to an understanding of his portrait of the disciples. In chapter five the same methodology will be applied to the occurrence of Simon Peter in order to compare Matthew's portrait of this named disciple with the Matthean portrait of the disciples as a group.

---

ing narrative (Edwards, "Uncertain Faith," pp. 47-52). As with Thompson, this is quite helpful for focusing on the overall theme in Matthew, but his theory appears to be unworkable without first doing a comparison with the other gospels and an exhaustive in-gospel analysis of the data. Matthean nuances would be easy to overlook without a comparison with the other gospels, and the whole picture might be given inadequate focus without first tabulating and sorting through all of the data.

[28] Cf. Stanton, "Origin and Purpose of Matthew's Gospel," pp. 1899-1903.

[29] O. Lamar Cope, *Matthew: A Scribe Trained for the Kingdom of Heaven*, CBQMS 5 (Washington, D. C.: The Catholic Biblical Association of America, 1976), p. 5.

[30] The "assumption" that Matthew used Mark and some body of tradition called "Q" is, again, merely a matter of convenience. See the introduction to chapter four for an expanded explanation.

Such are the research tools to be employed in this monograph. By means of these linguistic, sociological, and literary tools the goal of arriving at a more precise understanding of the concept of disciple in Matthew's gospel will be served. The historical background of the term, the sociological context in which Jesus made disciples, and the unique way in which the evangelist used the term, combine to give a more precise understanding of the concept of disciples in the gospel according to Matthew.

CHAPTER ONE

THE CLASSICAL AND HELLENISTIC BACKGROUND

Μαθητής (*mathētés*, "disciple, learner") only comes into prominence in the written literature of Greece in the classical period. The earliest extant occurrence of the term is found in Herodotus (4, 77; 5th century B.C.), but the casual way he uses it, and its transparent relation to the verb μανθάνειν, "to learn,"[1] suggests a common use in spoken Greek prior to its appearance in writing. The term occurs frequently in classical and Hellenistic literature, and is used consistently to denote three types of people: a learner, an adherent, and a pupil.[2] The usage varied somewhat according to the historical period, user, and context of use, and the purpose of this chapter is to clarify the usage as a background to understanding its use in the New Testament period.

I. Classical Usage

A) "Learner" (Early General Use)

Μαθητής was used in the early classical period in a general way to denote a "learner." As a "learner," μαθητής is morphologically motivated by the verb μανθάνειν, "to learn," and therefore sustains a transparent relation to the verb. This is illustrated in a passage in Plato, where one translator[3] has rendered the noun verbally, and where μαθητής parallels the verbal form μαθεῖν. Socrates makes the statement, "And this is the chief reason why it should be our main concern that each of us, neglecting all other studies, should seek after and study (μαθητὴς ἔσται) this thing [the good]—if in any way he may be able to learn of (μαθεῖν) and discover..." (*Republic* 618. C. 2).[4] The noun is transparently

---

[1] Μανθάνειν occurs as early as Herodotus (Karl H. Rengstorf, "μανθάνω," *TDNT*, IV [Grand Rapids: Eerdmans, 1967], p. 391), but only three times. Μαθητής does not occur in Homer, nor in some of the earlier writers such as Hesiod, where the subject material might have warranted its use.

[2] These designations denote distinguishable nuances of meaning in English usage, but all are appropriate for the field of meaning for μαθητής. The word "disciple" will be avoided for the present because of the technical connotations most English readers would understand by its use. "Adherent" is probably the closest formal synonym to "disciple," and will be used for the time being to give clarity to the discussion.

[3] All translations are taken from the *Loeb Classical Library* (*LCL*) unless otherwise stated.

[4] Plato, *The Republic*, Vol. II, trans. Paul Shorey, *LCL* (Cambridge, Massachusetts: Harvard University Press, 1935), p. 509: καὶ διὰ ταῦτα μάλιστα ἐπιμελητέον ὅπως ἕκαστος ἡμῶν τῶν ἄλλων μαθημάτων ἀμελήσας τούτου τοῦ μαθήματος καὶ ζητητὴς καὶ μαθητὴς ἔσται, ἐάν ποθεν οἷός τ᾽ ᾖ μαθεῖν καὶ ἐξευρεῖν.... Another translator has rendered μαθητής as a noun, but has retained the morphological relationship to μανθάνειν by translating μαθητής

associated with the verb, so that μαθητής is used generally to denote one who is a diligent student of the matter under consideration. Another example is found in Plato, *Laws*, 968. D. 4, where μαθητής is used in a context dealing with the education of wardens by the state. The noun has been rendered verbally by the translator in *Loeb*, quite likely because it parallels the verb μανθάνω: "but as regards the next point, the subjects they should learn (ἃ δεῖ μανθάνειν),—these it is neither easy to discover for oneself nor is it easy to learn from him" (ἄλλου μαθητὴν γενέσθαι).[5]

In other places the "learner" might be one studying gymnastics (including instruction in dancing and wrestling) (Plato, *Laws* 796. A. 8), music (Plato, *Laches*, 180. D; Plato, *Meno* 90. E. 6), astronomy (Plato, *Epistles*, 360. C. 4), writing (Plato, *Euthydemus*, 276. A 7), or medicine (Plato, *Republic*, 599. C. 4). The general use of μαθητής suggests a person engaged in learning from someone who already has the desired skill or knowledge, and is the use which is most transparently related to the verb μανθάνω.

B) Technical Use

Μαθητής was also used at an early stage of the classical period with a technical sense. That is, the term denoted "a direct dependence of the one under instruction upon an authority superior in knowledge, and which emphasizes the fact that this relation cannot be dissolved."[6] This technical use derived from the general, but reduced the semantical field of meaning.[7] The technical use placed more emphasis upon dependency, life-commitment, and the ongoing nature of the relationship. There were several applications of the technical use, depending on the association established, and these variations of technical reductions in the field of meaning will be designated in this paper by nomenclature which show the type of technical reduction: e.g., "non-specific technical use," "specialized technical use."[8]

"learner": "Each of us ... is to become an inquirer and learner in this study" (Plato, "The Republic," trans. Henry Davis, in *The Works of Plato*, II [London: George Bell and Sons, 1904], p. 309).

[5] μετὰ δέ τοῦτο, α δεῖ μανθάνειν, οὔτε εὑρεῖν ῥᾴδιον οὔτε εὑρηκότος ἄλλου μαθητὴν γενέσθαι. Plato, *Laws*, II, trans. R. G. Bury, *LCL* (Cambridge, Massachusetts: Harvard University Press, 1926), p. 567.

[6] Karl H. Rengstorf, "μαθητής," *TDNT*, IV, trans. and ed. by Geoffrey W. Bromiley (Grand Rapids: Eerdmans, 1967), p. 416.

[7] Cf. Moisés Silva, *Biblical Words and Their Meaning: An Introduction to Lexical Semantics*, (Grand Rapids: Zondervan, 1983), pp. 76-78, for a convenient summary of the logic behind semantic classification.

[8] Cf. ibid., pp. 82-86, 94, 151ff., for a methodology leading to the categories "technical term" and "specialized term." Rengstorf blurs the distinction between various uses of μαθητής. For example, he lists the category "The General Use," but under that category refers to "the almost technical sense of the word" (Rengstorf, "μαθητής," p. 416).

1. Adherent (non-specific technical use)

Early in the classical period μαθητής also designated an adherent and representative of a particular cultural milieu. In the earliest extant occurrence of the term[9] (Herodotus 4, 77; 5th century B.C.) a Scythian named Anacharsis is said to have been "a learner of the ways of Hellas" (τῆς Ἑλλάδος μαθητής). Notice that the translator in *Loeb* has rendered μαθητής "learner."[10] There is a close relationship to the general use here because Anacharsis had travelled through Greece and observed the practices and wisdom of the various city-states. But the context reveals that he is not just a μαθητής in a general way ("learner"). He is now an adherent and representative of the customs of Hellas. Anacharsis had been so enchanted by the Cyzicenes' celebration of the feast of the Mother of the Gods that when he went back to his homeland he performed the same ritual sacrifice. Although he was in hiding in his own country when he performed the ritual, he was observed, and was slain by his own brother and banished from memory among the Scythians "because he left his country for Hellas and followed the customs of strangers" (4, 76).[11] This use of the term reveals that he was not just a learner of Greek practices. He had now become an adherent.

Socrates speaks similarly of adherents of the Spartan culture: "All these were enthusiasts, lovers and disciples (μαθηταί) of the Spartan culture; and you can recognize that character in their wisdom by the short, memorable sayings that fell from each of them" (Plato, *Protagoras* 343. A. 6) In another place he speaks of certain men who are called μαθηταί of Marathon because they were representative of the city's cultural distinctives (Plato, *Menexenus* 240. E. 5).

This use of μαθητής signifies one who is more than a student gaining a skill or pursuing an academic course of study. He has adopted the way of life of a cultural milieu which now characterizes him, and of which he is now an adherent and representative.

2. Institutional pupil (specialized-technical use)

Rengstorf suggests that μαθητής was also used in a specialized-technical manner to refer to a student of the Sophists, and especially cites the use in Plato (e.g., *Sophist* 233. B. 6; *Gorgias* 519. C. 6). Rengstorf further suggests that the association of μαθητής with a Sophistic-type educational

---

[9] Rengstorf, "μαθητής," p. 416.
[10] Herodotus, *Books III and IV*, trans. A. D. Godley, Vol. II, *LCL* (Cambridge, Massachusetts: Harvard University Press, 1921), p. 277.
[11] ...διὰ τούτου ὅτι ἐξεδήμησέ τε ἐς τὴν Ἑλλάδα καὶ ξεινικοῖσι ἔθεσι διεχρήσατο.

process became so pronounced in the early classical period that those opposed to Sophistic practices, such as Socrates, refused to use the term.

> Socrates refused to be called a διδάσκαλος, or to let his teaching be called διδάσκειν. Similarly, μαθητής was not for him the word to describe the relation of his companions to him. He would have called the use of this word a calumny, just as he expressly rejected the phrase μαθητὴν εἶναι in personal application. The Sophists have μαθηταί, but not he.[12]

Rengstorf contends that the usage is fixed:[13] i.e., μαθητής was so closely associated with the concept of an institutional pupil of the Sophists in the minds and usage of the Greeks at the time of Socrates that it was no longer appropriate to use to describe other types of master-disciple relationships (such as Socrates') without grave danger of misassociation.

Rengstorf's interpretation of the classical usage has had a major influence on an entire generation of New Testament students, quite likely because of the stature of the *TDNT*.[14] But a close examination of representative classical and Hellenistic Greek writers[15] reveals that he has overstated the case. Μαθητής *is* used in many situations to refer to Sophistic practices, but this specialized-technical use is less uniform than Rengstorf implies. At this point Rengstorf's treatment of μαθητής displays some of the faulty linguistic (i.e., semantical) methodological characteristics of which Barr has accused *TDNT* as a whole. Specifically, Rengstorf has too readily associated a specific *concept* of master-disciple relationship with specific *terminology*, without paying close enough attention to *contextual usage*. The following survey of representative authors will show the varied use of the term by authors who were familiar with the Sophistic specialized-technical associations, but who used the term

---

[12] Rengstorf, "μαθητής," p. 418. Cf. the similar statements in his article on μανθάνω (Rengstorf, "μανθάνω," *TDNT*, IV, pp. 394-399), and his article on διδάσκαλος (Karl H. Rengstorf, "διδάσκω, διδάσκαλος," ed. Gerhard Kittel, *TDNT*, II, trans. and ed. by Geoffrey W. Bromiley [Grand Rapids: Eerdmans, 1967], p. 150).

[13] Rengstorf, "μαθητής," p. 418 n. 17.

[14] The indiscriminate use of *TDNT* has been denounced resoundingly by James Barr, *The Semantics of Biblical Language* (Oxford: Oxford University Press, 1961), pp. 206ff., but the influence of Rengstorf's imprecise linguistic analysis is still to be felt today. See the discussion in the "Introduction" above.

[15] An exhaustive examination of μαθητής in selected writers was made possible through access to the computer database, *Thesaurus Linguae Graecae*, developed and housed at the University of California, Irvine. Helpful guidance in the use of *TLG*, and in the selection of the Greek authors was given by Dr. Jay Shanor, Associate Professor of Classics, Biola University. The representative writers are Homer, Hesiod, Herodotus, Aristophanes, Isocrates, Demosthanes, Plato, Aristotle, Xenophon, Dio Chrysostom, Plutarch, Diodorus Siculus, Epictetus, Diogenes Laertius, and Iamblicus. The above were selected because they give representation to various periods and types of Greek literature, and especially because they reflect positive, negative, and relatively neutral attitudes toward Socrates, those following him, and the Sophistic tradition.

nonetheless to refer to other types of master-disciple relationships. The overriding purpose here is not to delineate the *characteristics* of the various types of master-disciple relationships, but to define carefully the *usage* of the term μαθητής.

C) Representative Writers

1. Plato of Athens (c. 427-347 B.C.)

Plato used μαθητής in different ways. His writings reveal a use which indicates his (and Socrates') opposition to the Sophistic practices, but there is also a use which is much broader, and shows that Plato considers μαθητής an appropriate word to use when the context is suitable.

Plato's writings not only reveal his own attitude toward the use of μαθητής, but they are also the main source for discovering Socrates' attitude. Rengstorf suggests that Plato was the only student of Socrates to understand and develop fully the Socratic teaching,[16] but this suggestion fails to take into account the critical issues.[17] The writings of Plato and Xenophon are the main depositories of Socratic addresses, and since there are no extant writings of Socrates in which the direct use of μαθητής is to be found, the "Socratic use" and "Socratic attitude" are actually the usage or attitude as reflected in his students. Is the use of μαθητής in Plato's writings truly Socrates', or is it Plato's read back into his master, or is it a combination of both? Is the difference between Plato and Xenophon to be attributed to relative understandings of Socrates, or to personal differences of application of the Socratic understanding? Although Rengstorf does not address this problematic issue of anachronistic reflection, it may be significant when one states whose attitude toward μαθητής is in view: Socates', Plato's, Xenophon's, or other writers'. Since in this paper the critical, anachronistic issues cannot be fully addressed, reference to the "Socratic attitude or use" means the attitude or use which is found in the writings of Plato, Xenophon, or other writers, not the direct writings of Socrates himself.

a) Opposition to the Sophists

Plato reveals a strong opposition to the Sophistic educational institution in the Socratic dialogues. This opposition is at the heart of

---

[16] Rengstorf, "διδάσκαλος," p. 150; "μανθάνω," p. 397; "μαθητής," p. 419f.

[17] Surprisingly, Rengstorf does not raise the critical issues. For a brief overview, see Albin Lesky, *A History of Greek Literature*, trans. by James Willis and Cornelis de Heer (2d. ed.; New York: Thomas Y. Crowell, 1966), pp. 494-497.

Rengstorf's observations. Plato's use of μαθητής in these contexts is basically negative, but what must be clear is that Plato was not opposed to the use of the term per se. He was in disagreement with the Sophists on epistemological and ethical issues, and the term was only a secondary concern.

Epistemological objections.

Plato differs with the Sophists on a very basic epistemological issue. The epistemological issue centers in whether or not virtue (ἀρετή) is teachable (cf. Protagoras 320. C. 1). Socrates suggests that virtue is an innate gift, and the object of education is to discover innate gifts. The older Greek thinkers had been concerned with this same issue, and the answer which Plato represents as being Socrates' had already been given in such writers as Pindar and Theognis.[18] The Sophists, on the other hand, viewed virtue as being teachable. Education became the means by which virtue was gained.

Plato's Socrates rejects the concept of "learning virtue," because learning virtue is the antithesis of the Platonic doctrines of the world of imperishable ideas, of anamnesis, and of the association of the soul with those ideas.[19] Therefore, the epistemological issue is central in the dispute with the Sophists. A formalized student of the Sophists is involved in a futile study, because virtue cannot be learned through institutionalized education. The reason why Socrates cannot advise fathers on the ways of helping their sons attain the highest good, virtue, is because he himself "has never been either a discoverer (εὑρετής) or a learner (μαθητής) of anything of the sort" (Laches 186. E. 3).

Socrates refers to the Sophistic διδάσκαλος—μαθητής relationship in a consistently derisive manner, and on the surface it does appear that he rejects the relationship. But an analysis of the epistemologically oriented occurrences reveals that Socrates is primarily critical of the belief that one can learn virtue. Because the Sophistic master-pupil relationship pursues that which is unattainable through education, the relationship (and with it the terms διδάσκαλος—μαθητής) receives secondary (or incidental?) criticism.[20]

---

[18] Henri I. Marrou, A History of Education in Antiquity, trans. George Lamb (3d. ed.; New York: Sheed and Ward, 1956), pp. 39-40, 58. Although the earlier writers were interested in some of the same issues, they did not use μαθητής.

[19] Cf. Lesky, History of Greek Literature, pp. 525ff.

[20] E.g., Theaetetus 152. C. 10; 180. C. 1; The Sophist 233. B. 6, C. 6; Symposium 197. B. 1; Euthydemus 273. A. 2; 274. E. 2; 276. A. 7, E. 7; 278. E. 2; 304. B. 1; Protagoras 315. A. 5; Gorgias 455. C. 6; 519. C. 6; Meno 89. D. 8, E. 2; 90. E. 6; 96. C. 1; Cleitophon 407. B. 6; Republic 599. C. 4.

Ethical objections.

The writings of Plato also reveal an ethical objection to the διδάσκαλος—μαθητής relationship. Protagoras the Sophist was the first to charge fees from his μαθηταί. This was this beginning of the commercial, educational institution.[21] Plato objects to this commercial practice throughout his writings. In an illustrative passage from *The Sophist* (233. B. 6.-C. 6), the "Stranger" interrogates Theaetetus about the practices of the Sophistic teachers and then homes in on the absurdity of a pupil (μαθητής) paying money to learn from Sophists who give the impression of being the wisest of all men. At best, the Sophists have only an opinion. They have focused only upon human educational processes, and hence do not have true knowledge. At worst, the Sophists are only clever manipulators who are greedy for the student's fees. The only reason the pupil attaches himself to the Sophist is that the teacher puts on the appearance of being wise in all things. The "Stranger" attacks the Sophistic practice of laying claim to wisdom, and, in a secondary way, the practice of paying money for the educational process. In another place Socrates abhors the fact that the Sophists are changing the pursuit of philosophic truth into a commercial venture: "Then can it be Hippocrates, that the sophist is really a sort of merchant or dealer in provisions on which a soul is nourished? For such is the view I take of him" (*Protagoras* 313. C. 5ff.).

Plato's ethical objection stems from the epistemological objection, and is primarily directed toward what he views as arrogant, Sophistic deception. The Sophists do not have the ability to teach virtue, yet they charge their students fees for teaching that which they do not have. As a result, when these issues arise in Plato's writings he invariably speaks negatively and derisively.[22] Plato sees that the Sophistic educational institution stands for all that was wrong with their epistemology and educational ethics.

As in the epistemological issue, the διδάσκαλος—μαθητής relationship is not the primary focus of attack from Plato. Rather, he rejects the commercialism of an educational institution which professes to teach something impossible for them to teach. On the surface he appears to attack the διδάσκαλος—μαθητής relationship, but he is actually attacking the Sophistic institutionalism which lies behind it.

---

[21] W. R. M. Lamb, "Introduction to *Protagoras*," in Plato, *Laches, Protagoras, Meno, Euthydemus*, trans. W. R. M. Lamb, *LCL* (Cambridge, Massachusetts: Harvard University Press, 1924), IV, 91. Cf. also Marrou, *History of Education*, pp. 49-50.

[22] Cf. *Euthydemus* 273. A. 2; 274. E. 2; 276. A. 7, E. 7; 278. E. 2; 304. B. 1; *Protagoras* 312. E. 5; 315. A. 5; *Gorgias* 455. C. 6; 519. C. 6; *Meno* 90. E. 6; *Republic* 599. C. 4.

b) Contextual suitability

Rengstorf is partially correct when he says that Socrates rejects the application of διδάσκαλος—μαθητής to himself and his followers. Socrates (in Plato) uses these terms negatively when discussing the Sophists and their practices. Therefore, in a Sophistic context Socrates would, of course, reject these terms being applied to himself because of the chance that Sophistic associations might be attached to himself.

On the other hand, διδάσκαλος and μαθητής are not uniquely associated with the Sophists, even in Plato's writings. Plato uses the μαθητής almost equally with Sophistic and non-Sophistic associations.[23] The term is distributed quite evenly in Plato's writings. When a work is concerned with Sophistic matters, Plato speaks of a specialized, technical μαθητής who is an institutional pupil of the Sophists. But when the work of Plato is dealing with other matters, μαθητής is used either with reference to a general learner or a technical adherent.

General usage—a "learner".

Plato uses μαθητής in several passages in a general way to speak of a διδάσκαλος—μαθητής relationship where there are no negative connotations. Μαθητής occurs only twice in the *Cratylus*, but these two are enlightening. The dialogue discusses the theory and application of etymology, and in one interaction Socrates suggests that the great knowledge of Cratylus in the matter of the theory of the origin of names should force Socrates to put himself down as a μαθητής of Cratylus:

> I think you have not only investigated such matters yourself but have been taught about them by others. So if you have any better theory to propound, put me down as one of your pupils (μαθητῶν) in the course on the correctness of names (*Cratylus* 428. B. 4).

Socrates' statement is made somewhat tongue-in-cheek, but the cynicism is directed toward the supposed expertise of Cratylus, not the educational process or the term μαθητής. Cratylus responds to Socrates, stating, "Yes, Socrates, I have, as you say, paid attention to these matters, and perhaps I might make you my pupil (μαθητήν). However, I am afraid the opposite is the case ..." (*Cratylus* 428 C. 1). These two occurrences illustrate the way in which, when the Sophists are not the issue of the writing, Plato can use μαθητής generally to speak without negative connotations of one learning from another.[24] This is especially revealing

---

[23] The chart in appendix A shows a breakdown of occurrences of μαθητής in Plato's writings.

[24] Cf. also *Euthyphron* 5. A. 4.; 5. A. 8; 5. C. 5, for an almost identical usage as that found in the *Cratylus*. There is a tongue-in-cheek statement by Socrates that he should become the μαθητής of Euthyphron, a self-proclaimed expert in divine matters.

when a passage from the *Republic* is compared with Rengstorf's pronouncement. "Each of us," Socrates remarks, "omitting other studies, is to become an inquirer and learner (μαθητὴς ἔσται) in this study...."[25] Socrates declares himself to be a μαθητής of the matters under consideration. However, this is the opposite of Rengstorf's interpretation of the "Socratic attitude": "...μαθητής was not for him [Socrates] the word to describe the relation of his companions to him. He would have called the use of this word a calumny, just as he expressly rejected the phrase μαθητὴν εἶναι in personal application."[26] The phrase cited in the *Republic* is similar to the one Rengstorf argues that Socrates rejects, and in this passage Socrates uses it to denote himself, here in a positive, general sense for diligence of commitment of study. The telling difference is that the term is not used in reference to the Sophists, and therefore is not used negatively. Although Rengstorf stresses that μαθητής was rejected by Socrates, the analysis of the use of the term in these contexts indicates that it is appropriate for use by Socrates when the Sophists are not under consideration, even to the point of Socrates referring to himself as a μαθητής.

Such is also the case in the *Laches*. The dialogue at first concerns the question of the best lessons or pursuits which will lead sons to the highest attainable excellence. Laches introduces Socrates to the other participants in the dialogue by indicating that Socrates has valuable experience in guiding young men in these pursuits. Nicias concurs with this opinion of Socrates, stating,

...quite recently he [Socrates] introduced to myself a music-teacher for my son—Damon, pupil (μαθητής) of Agathocles, who is not only the most exquisitely skilled of musicians, but in every other way as profitable a companion (ἄξιον συνδιατρίβειν) as you could wish for young men of that age (*Laches* 180. D. 1).

This illustrates the most general usage of the term: one taken into the tutelage of a master in order to learn a skill. In this context, on the one hand, μαθητής has no negative connotations. On the other hand, at a later point in the same dialogue Socrates gives a negative connotation to μαθητής when he contends that the attainment of the highest good, virtue, is not possible through education. He cannot give advice to fathers as to how they should direct their sons to learn virtue because he himself "... has never been either a discoverer (εὑρετής) or a learner (μαθητής) of

[25] Translation taken from *The Republic*, trans. Henry Davis, in *The Works of Plato*, II [London: George Bell and Sons, 1904], p. 309. The Greek is, καὶ διὰ ταῦτα μάλιστα ἐπιμελητέον ὅπως ἕκαστος ἡμῶν τῶν ἄλλων μαθημάτων ἀμελήσας τούτου τοῦ μαθήματος καὶ ζητητὴς καὶ μαθητὴς ἔσται.
[26] Rengstorf, "μαθητής, p. 150.

anything of the sort" (*Laches* 186. E. 3). These two passages from *Laches* are extremely significant because they show that the term is used negatively only when it refers to a person involved in Sophistic philosophical pursuits. The term can be used in the same work, in near proximity, with both a positive and negative sense, depending on the object of the pursuit. Socrates / Plato is concerned to show that in the realm of the pursuit of virtue one can be neither a teacher nor a pupil, because virtue is not obtainable through education. Therefore, even though μαθητής is inappropriate to use to designate one engaged in pursuing virtue, it is appropriate to use when it designates a general learner of arts and skills which are obtainable through education. The suitability of the use of the term depends on contextual connotations, especially whether or not Sophistic issues are in view, and a significant proportion of the occurrences find the term used as a general learner.[27]

Technical usage—an "adherent".

Plato also uses μαθητής with a technical sense to refer to adherents of a particular master-teacher who have an ongoing relationship and commitment to common goals, but who are not Sophistic associates. Even as Herodotus uses μαθητής to describe those who are adherents of a cultural milieu, Socrates uses the term to refer to partisans of the Spartan culture (*Protagoras* 343. A. 6) and certain men of Marathon (*Menexenus* 240. E. 5). These individuals are called μαθηταί because they are adherents and representatives of their city's cultural ethos.

Another example is a passage in the *Symposium*, where Agathon is the host at a banquet at which Socrates and several others are having a dialogue on love. Agathon, a brilliant Sophist, addresses Phaedrus:

> ...do we not know that a man who has this god [Love] for teacher turns out a brilliant success, whereas he on whom Love has laid no hold is obscure? If Apollo invented archery and medicine and divination, it was under the guidance of Desire and Love; so that he too may be deemed a disciple (μαθητής) of Love, as likewise may the Muses in music, Hephaestus in metal-work, Athene in weaving and Zeus 'in pilotage of gods and men.'[28]

Although the term is on the lips of a Sophist, the use is not directed toward a technical, Sophistic application. It is simply a discussion of

---

[27] Cf. also *Symposium* 197. B. 1; *Lysis* 211. C. 5; *Protagoras* 341. A. 4; 343. A. 6; *Menexenus* 240. E. 5; *Republic* 618. C. 2; *Laws* 659. B. 2; 770. C. 4;796. A. 8; 813. E. 5; 968. D. 4; *Epistles* 360. C. 4; *Phaedo* 99. C. 7; *Phaedrus* 275. A. 6. There is some overlapping between "General, learner" usage and "Technical, adherent" usage, but they show no, or at least very little, overlapping with Sophistic association.

[28] *Symposium* 197. B. 1.

apprentices in various trades, Apollo's trade being that of love. In the light of the fact that there are others who are taught trade skills, this μαθητής is a learner of the trade of love, but he goes beyond learning to be an adherent.[29]

c) Summary of and conclusion concerning Plato's use

The use of μαθητής in Plato's writings, even in those passages which one might say reveal the "use of Socrates," is not as uniform as Rengstorf suggests. Rengstorf implies that the Socratic attitude was uniform in its basic rejection of the term, but, in fact, just over half of the occurrences designate a learner in a general sense, or designate an adherent in a technical sense. Of the forty seven occurrences of μαθητής, at least twenty-four refer to one being a μαθητής in a positive, or at least neutral, sense. Just less than half of the occurrences have a specialized-technical, negative connotation, because in these μαθητής designates one involved in Sophistic educational practices. Importantly, these latter occurrences were confined to dialogues with the Sophists. Rengstorf's observations are correct insofar as he refers to sophistically oriented passages, but he has not accounted for the broader use by Plato / Socrates. Plato uses μαθητής in a general way to refer to those learning from a master, he uses it in a non-specific, technical way to refer to adherents of a teacher or a cultural milieu, and he uses it in a specialized, technical way to refer to the commercial, institutionalized pupils of the Sophists. At least in the writings of Plato, the conceptual meaning of μαθητής was determined by its contextual associations.

The heart of Rengstorf's discussion of Socrates' use of μαθητής is found in the supposed distinction of "inner fellowship" and "formal education." Rengstorf suggests that the character of the μαθητής — διδάσκαλος necessarily emphasizes the technical and rational element, and takes precedence over any inner fellowship which might be desired in the relationship. He further suggests that Socrates grounded the philosophy of his circle of followers in μιμεῖσθαι, so that there is a

> materially grounded fellowship which arises under a goal which is certainly directed by an individual, but towards which all who participate are equally striving. This explains the aversion of Socrates and his circle to this word, an aversion whose effects may seen throughout the history of its use on Greek soil. The desire is to have disciples, not pupils.[30]

---

[29] There is a possibility that Plato is emphasizing the "learning of love" as a typical Sophistic doctrine, but the context leans more toward a less specialized use. This is the only use of the term in the *Symposium*, and does not seem to be the special focus of attention by Plato in this work.

[30] Rengstorf, "μαθητής," pp. 417-418. Rengstorf makes a firm distinction in the headings of his discussion between the terms "disciple" (*Jünger*) *and* "*pupil*" (*Lehrling*).

There is an element of truth to Rengstorf's statement, but he has overstated the case in at least three ways. First, he implies that the issue begins with Socrates' desire for "inner fellowship." Instead, epistemology is the beginning point. Socrates began the discussion with the Sophists with the issue of learning eternal truth. Socrates declared that these truths would not be learned because they were innately given gifts. Therefore Plato's Socrates naturally avoids μαθητής because of its transparent relation to the verb μανθάνειν, "to learn." The issues of μιμεῖσθαι and "inner fellowship" followed from that epistemological beginning point. Since "learning" was the Sophists' epistemological starting point, μαθητής became a convenient term to describe their followers. Rengstorf has understressed the epistemological, and overstressed the "fellowship" issue. Second, Rengstorf has overstated Socrates' / Plato's avoidance of the term. The Sophistic debate forced him to reject μαθητής when considering the epistemological and ethical issues raised by the Sophist phenomenon, but the term was fully appropriate in other contexts. Third, Rengstorf has overstated the effects of Socrates' aversion to the term, "throughout the history of its use on Greek soil." In some ways the history of the μαθητής — διδάσκαλος relationship on Greek soil *is* affected by the transparency of the verbal relationship to "learning," but as will be seen, this did not cause an aversion to the term later on. The use of the term which stressed "learning" as the central concept became less and less frequent, until μαθητής became a term to designate certain followers who had very little to do with learning. In fact, some of the later μαθηταί relationships began to stress "inner fellowship" far more than education. These clarifications of Socrates' / Plato's use of μαθητής need to be kept in mind as the investigation of other Greek writers continues.

2. *Xenophon of Athens (c. 430-348/7 B.C.)*

Xenophon of Athens was another student of Socrates, and the second major source of tradition concerning Socrates.[31] Plato used μαθητής at least forty-seven times, while Xenophon used the term only three times.[32] Plato was a more prolific writer, but nonetheless Plato used the term with more proportional frequency.[33] Rengstorf declares that "as in Plato, so

These terms reveal his dichotomy between the "rational" and "inner fellowship" elements of a relationship. Cf. the German edition, Karl H. Rengstorf, "μαθητής," *Theologisches Wörterbuch zum Neuen Testament*, ed. Gerhard Kittel, Λ—N (Stuttgart: W. Kohlhammer), pp. 419, 421.

[31] Cf. Lesky, *History of Greek Literature*, pp. 494-496, for a discussion of the differences between the Platonic and Xenophonic pictures of Socrates.

[32] *TLG*, University of California, Irvine.

[33] Xenophon's writings are collected in seven volumes in *Loeb*, Plato's in twelve.

in Xenophon μαθητής is not used for a follower of Socrates ... Avoiding μαθητής, he shows that he has taken up, or tried to take up, the concern of Socrates."[34] Since Xenophon uses the term only three times, Rengstorf might be correct that Xenophon avoids the term, but the three occurrences indicate a broader use of the term than Rengstorf indicates.

Xenophon uses μαθητής once in *On Hunting* (1. 2. 2). It is found at the very beginning of the work and is used in a general way to refer to a "learner."

> Game and hounds are the invention of gods, of Apollo and Artemis. They bestowed it on Cheiron and honoured him therewith for his righteousness. And he, receiving it, rejoiced in the gift, and used it. And he had for pupils (μαθηταί) in [hunting game] and in other noble pursuits—Cephalus, Asclepius, Meilanion, Nestor, ... of whom each in his time was honoured by gods.

Xenophon uses the term here simply to refer to those to whom practical skills had been passed by Cheiron.

The second occurrence is in *Memorabilia* (1. 2. 27. 3). This is a most interesting passage, because Xenophon discusses certain followers of Socrates who had been accused of wrongdoing by Socrates' opponents. Xenophon defends Socrates by saying,

> For their wrongdoing, then, is Socrates to be called to account by his accuser? And does he deserve no word of praise for having controlled them in the days of their youth, when they would naturally be most reckless and licentious? Other cases, at least, are not so judged. For what teacher (διδάσκαλος) of flute, lyre, or anything else, after making his pupils (μαθητάς), is held to blame if they leave him for another master, and then turn out incompetent? What father, whose son bears a good character so long as he is with one master, but goes wrong after he has attached himself to another, throws the blame on the earlier teacher?

Μαθητής is used here in a general way to refer to an apprentice-type training in a musical skill. It is used as an illustrative parallel to the followers of Socrates, and further, διδάσκαλος is used as a parallel to Socrates. The significant point is that Xenophon would not have used μαθητής here (or διδάσκαλος) if it carried inherently negative connotations.

The third occurrence of μαθητής is also found in *Memorabilia* (1. 6. 3. 4). The Sophistic teacher Antiphon mocks the poverty of Socrates, charging that poverty can bring only unhappiness. Xenophon introduces the passage by saying, "Antiphon came to Socrates with the intention of drawing his companions (τοὺς συνουσιαστὰς αὐτοῦ) away from him, and spoke thus in their presence" (1. 6. 1. 3). Then Antiphon says,

---

[34] Rengstorf, "μαθητής," pp. 418, 419.

Now the professors (διδάσκαλοι) of other subjects try to make their pupils (μαθητάς) copy their teachers: if you too intend to make your companions (συνόντας) do that, you must consider yourself a professor (διδάσκαλος) of unhappiness.

Μαθητής is used here in a general sense to designate a "learner," but there are traces of a technical application in the reference to "imitation" (μιμητής). Antiphon alludes to διδάσκαλος — μαθητής relationships found in other disciplines (ostensibly neither Sophistic nor Socratic), where the μαθηταί copy (μιμητάς) the διδάσκαλοι, and this allusion functions as an illustrative parallel to Socrates' followers. Antiphon makes μαθητάς synonymously parallel to "companions." There is no negative connotation to the title "companion," and apparently none with the parallel μαθητής either. Neither does Socrates try to refute the title διδάσκαλος in the ensuing exchange. He addresses and refutes only the charge that unhappiness results from poverty and that his followers will also be poor and unhappy. Socrates neither makes an issue of the fact that his followers are referred to as the equivalent of μαθηταί, nor objects to being called διδάσκαλος himself.

Although Xenophon uses μαθητής only three times, these three references are significant. In the first there is a very general use of the term. In the second there is another general use, and it occurs as an illustrative parallel for Socrates' followers. In the third there is a technical use by a Sophist, but it is used as a description of an adherent of other teachers, not as a specialized term referring to the followers of the Sophists. Rengstorf correctly notes that Xenophon does not use the term to describe the followers of Socrates, but importantly, Xenophon does not associate μαθητής with the Sophists either. Μαθητής refers to a general learner and/or a technical adherent. The suggestion that Xenophon *avoided* using the term to describe Socrates' followers is based on an argument from silence. Such may be the case, but one might also argue that since Xenophon avoided using μαθητής to refer to the Sophists, he avoided the specialized-technical usage as well. Aside from these arguments, Xenophon uses the term *explicitly* in a general and nonspecialized, technical way, and what is striking is that two of the three occurrences come in Socratic contexts and that in one of those Socrates debates a Sophist. Xenophon uses μαθητής to describe a learner and an adherent of a teacher. He does not use the term (nor the corresponding διδάσκαλος) as a platform for discussing the epistemological and ethical issues which Plato's Socrates does. Although Xenophon was not at the intellectual stature of Plato, it does not necessarily mean, as Rengstorf contends, that Xenophon has failed to grasp the "distinctiveness of

Socrates"[35] with respect to the usage of this term. Rather, Xenophon's usage points to a differentiation between concept and terminology. Xenophon retains the same distinctive epistemological and ethical concept of discipleship as does Plato's Socrates, but he does not center his discussion on the term μαθητής. Instead, μαθητής in Xenophon was a general term for a learner, or at most, a non-specialized, technical term for an adherent.

3. Aristotle of Stageiros (c. 384-322 B.C.)

Although Aristotle was a voluminous writer who covered a wide spectrum of subjects, μαθητής occurs only once in all of his writings.[36] It occurs in *Metaphysics* 5. 986b. 22, where Aristotle discusses the differences between Parmenides' and Melissus' conception of the Unity. As a point of clarification he mentions Xenophanes' concept, stating, "But Xenophanes, the first exponent of the Unity (for Parmenides is said to have been his disciple [μαθητής]), gave no definite teaching, nor does he seem to have grasped either of these conceptions of unity." Aristotle's point is that, while Parmenides is a student and follower of the teachings of Xenophanes, Parmenides owed his concept of Unity not to his master, but to his own insight. Μαθητής is used here to refer to a student who follows in the line of the master but who is able to advance ideas of his own.

The overall absence of μαθητής in Aristotle's writings suggests to Rengstorf that Aristotle was influenced by Socrates' supposed rejection of the term.

> Aristotle, too, stands under the influence of the Socratic-Platonic judgment on the relation between master and disciple, for he generally avoids μαθητής when compelled to mention these relations. In the one passage in which he uses it...it serves to denote, not the relation between teacher and pupil, but the incontestable dependence of the pupil on the teacher, here within the school or trend of the Eleatics.[37]

Once again this is an argument from silence, and as such must be accepted only tentatively. But Rengstorf's last statement (μαθητής "serves to denote, not the relation between teacher and pupil, but the incontestable dependence of the pupil on the teacher") must be corrected. This statement reflects his thinking that the term μαθητής itself marked the distinction between the "relationship" of the master and

---

[35] Ibid., p. 419.

[36] H. Bonitz, *Index Aristotelicus* (2d. ed.; Graz: Akademische Druck- u. Verlagsanstalt, 1955), p. 441. Aristotle's writings are collected in twenty-five volumes in *Loeb*.

[37] Rengstorf, "μαθητής," p. 418.

pupil and the formal side of the educational process ("incontestable dependence"). His assumption is, on the one hand, that μαθητής cannot carry connotations of "relationship," and, on the other hand, that it must denote a formal relationship. But both Plato and Xenophon use the term to denote intimate relationships found between masters and μαθηταί which were not limited to a formal one among the Sophists. Aristotle might have avoided the use of μαθητής, but his avoidance of the term cannot be traced to an inherently formal meaning of the term. Μαθητής might not have been the term which Aristotle preferred to use to describe his followers, but neither was the term ἑταῖρος,[38] one which Socrates / Plato did prefer.[39] If statistical frequency is also the basic criterion applied to ἑταῖρος, then one might say that Aristotle rejected the use of ἑταῖρος also, a proposal which Rengstorf would not advance. The most that should be drawn from the usage in Aristotle is that he preferred not to use μαθητής and ἑταῖρος, and instead chose to use other terms.[40] His choice might have had to do with Sophistic associations of the term, but not inherent meaning.

4. Aristophanes of Athens (c. 446-385 B.C.)

Aristophanes is important for this study because he was a contemporary of Socrates and his students, and shared many of the same concerns about Sophistic practices, but was not a student of Socrates. Therefore, he reveals a use of μαθητής somewhat independent of the Socratic point of view.

Μαθητής occurs in the *Clouds* to denote the students of the Sophists (cf. *Clouds* 133, 142, 502). The *Clouds* is a satirical comedy which parodies the Sophistic educational institution, methodology, and philosophy. Aristophanes satirized the Sophistical system of education because he felt it was sapping the life of the old Athenian system through commercialism, utilitarianism, and rejection of traditional beliefs. The interesting and notoriously unjust twist of *Clouds* is that Aristophanes portrayed Socrates as the representative and embodiment of the Sophistic school (cf. *Clouds*, 183).[41]

Although the debate continues whether Aristophanes used Socrates as a convenient, yet unreal, transparency to attack the Sophists, or whether

---

[38] Ἑταῖρος was used only seven times in all of Aristotle's writings; Bonitz, *Index Aristotelicus*, p. 290.

[39] Ἑταῖρος is used some two hundred and six times in Plato's writing's (*TLG*).

[40] The term which Aristotle used frequently was γνώριμος (Bonitz, *Index Aristotelicus*, p. 290; γνώριμος was also used frequently by Socrates / Plato).

[41] K. J. Dover, "Comedy," in *Ancient Greek Literature*, ed. K. J. Dover (Oxford: Oxford University Press, 1980), p. 77.

he meant the comedy as a true characterization, the general consensus in classical studies today is that the satirization of Socrates was not meant maliciously.[42] Modern analyses have identified in the Socrates of *Clouds* traits that are, on the one hand, Socratic, but not Sophistic, and, on the other hand, traits that are clearly irreconcilable with the Socrates of history.[43] By using Socrates, whose physical idiosyncrasies invited comedic caricature, yet who was well-known and respected, Aristophanes' play was able to generate a light-hearted yet pointed attack on the Sophistic practices, even while it was understood that the attack was not personally directed toward Socrates.[44] Aristophanes used the comedic satirization of Socrates as a means of attacking the dangerous Sophistic system. Aristophanes could give such an unjust characterization to Socrates because the common Athenian of his day would have referred to Socrates as one of the leading Sophists. He was known as the leading philosopher who had followers around him continually, and a casual observation would detect no apparent difference between him and the Sophists.[45] The external similarity prompted the Socratic picture in the theatrical comedy *Clouds*. Only the most discerning Athenian would have known that Socrates considered taking students for payment a crime and that he despised Sophistic methodology and goals.[46]

The significant point for this study is that Aristophanes used μαθητής as the term to describe the followers of Socrates. Was his use of μαθητής part of the Socratic or non-Socratic picture? If the former, the term is used in a non-specialized, technical way and is broad enough in its connotation to include followers of both the Sophists and Socrates. If the latter, the term is used in a specialized sense and indicates a fixed usage[47] referring to the students of the Sophists. The imprecise treatment of the Socratic and Sophistic distinctives could argue either way. Aristophanes does not reveal an appreciation for some of the most basic differences between Socrates and the Sophists;[48] hence, his incorrect attribution of

---

[42] Ibid., pp. 77-78.

[43] E.g., there are ascetic practices, methods and doctrine which are clearly Socratic but not sophistic. The association of Socrates with the teaching which made the worse appear the better cause, is clearly sophistic, but adamantly not Socratic. Cf. Lesky, *History of Greek Literature*, pp. 433-434.

[44] Moses Hadas, *A History of Greek Literature* (New York: Columbia University Press, 1950), p. 106.

[45] Benjamin Bickley Rogers, "Introduction to *Clouds*," in Aristophanes, in 3 vols., vol. I, *LCL* (1924; rev. and rpt.; Cambridge, Massachusetts: Harvard University Press, 1950), 263.

[46] Lesky, *History of Greek Literature*, pp. 433-434.

[47] Rengstorf, "μαθητής," p. 418 n. 17.

[48] E.g., Socrates did not study natural science, did not charge fees, was not a Sophist, was not an advocate of a science which questioned all traditions, and did not seek new knowledge in an attempt to avoid responsibility, all of which Socrates is accused in *Clouds* (cf. Hadas, *History of Greek Literature*, p. 106).

Sophistic characteristics to Socrates possibly extends to the term μαθητής as well. On the other hand, within the play the term is used to speak of followers of both known Sophistic teachers and of Socrates, and as such could point to a common use of the term to denote students of a philosopher, without specialized Sophistic technicality.

The one other time Aristophanes uses the term may shed some light on his usage. In *Frogs* (964), μαθητής denotes the pupils of the Greek tragedians Euripides and Aeschylus. Euripides says of Aeschylus' pupils and of his own:

> Look at his pupil's (μαθητάς), look at mine:
>   and there the contrast view.
> Uncouth Megaenetus is his,
>   and rough Phormisius too;
> Great long-beard-lance-and-trumpet-men,
>   flesh-tearers with the pine:
> But natty smart Theramenes,
>   and Cleitophon are mine.

Μαθητής occurs here as a designation for a pupil of non-Sophistic masters. The μαθητής is an adherent and representative of his master. This is a technical use of μαθητής to denote one committed to his master, of whom he is a reflection, but it is not a specialized use of the term. The term is used to refer to followers of the two masters of Greek tragedy and is devoid of specialized connotation.

Aristophanes' intended use of μαθητής is difficult to assess since he used the term in only two of his works, *Clouds* and *Frogs*, and since the intended usage in *Clouds* is hidden somewhat behind the inappropriately Sophistic picture of Socrates. However, certain characteristics of Aristophanes' use of the term may be stated with some certainty. The first is that Aristophanes uses μαθητής with general-technical connotations. The use in *Frogs* is definitely not specialized. Second, μαθητής was not a fixed term at the time of Aristophanes. *Frogs* was written some eighteen years after *Clouds*, and the Sophistic influence had, if anything, become more pronounced. Yet Aristophanes can use μαθητής in *Frogs* without qualification to refer to followers of masters other than Sophists. Third, based upon the fact that Aristophanes uses the term in *Frogs* with non-fixed connotations to refer to an adherent, the usage in *Clouds* should not be identified too quickly as "a fixed, specialized usage." Taken at face value, μαθητής is merely a term used to denote followers of a philosopher, whether Socrates or the Sophists. Fourth, some of the Sophistic characteristics which are attributed to Socrates are known to have been damaging to Socrates' reputation, because in the *Apology*, twenty-five years later, Socrates blamed the play for creating prejudice against him.[49] Similarly, it is quite likely that by denouncing the terms μαθητής and διδάσκαλος (*Apology* 33a) Socrates sought to disassociate himself from an unwarranted Sophistic characterization which stemmed from the use in the *Clouds*.

These points indicate that Aristophanes' usage is similar to Xenophon's. The term refers to a student of a philosopher, but in this case it refers to the student of Socrates. It does not necessarily imply Sophistic characteristics. Aristophanes uses μαθητής to designate both the student of a philosopher and the follower of a tragedian. Therefore, a fixed usage should not be assigned to μαθητής in the writings of Aristophanes.[50]

5. Isocrates (c. 436-338 B.C.)

Isocrates is important for this study because he is a contemporary of Socrates and those who follow him, and he is in a somewhat middle ground between the Sophists and Socrates. He argues against the common forms of Sophism in *Against the Sophists* and *Antidosis*. The forms he argues against are the *Eristics*, theorists in the field of ethics, and those Sophists of the rhetorical school who taught oratory as an instrument of practical succcess.[51] In these arguments he shares some of the same ethical objections which Socrates / Plato has against the Sophists. In spite of this, Isocrates claimed to be a Sophist. He had studied under Gorgias and viewed himself as a unique Sophistic orator who sought for the highest good.[52] The claim to a partial Sophistic heritage separated him from Socrates / Plato.

Isocrates' use of μαθητής is possibly the most helpful for understanding the common use of the term in the classical period. He does not use the term in his criticism of the Sophists, although two of his major works are directed against them (*Against the Sophists and Antidosis*). He uses the term some forty-one times,[53] and reveals neither special attachment to nor antipathy toward the term. For Isocrates it is simply a term to denote either a learner, an adherent, or a pupil.

Isocrates uses μαθητής four times in his final work, the *Panathenaicus*. Each time it occurs in a general sense to refer to a "learner." It

---

[49] Ibid.; Dover, "Comedy," p. 77.
[50] Contra Rengstorf, "μαθητής," p. 418 n. 17.
[51] Hadas, *A History of Greek Literature*, pp. 170ff.
[52] K. J. Dover, "Classical Oratory," *Ancient Greek Literature*, ed. K. J. Dover (Oxford: Oxford University Press, 1980), pp. 127-128.
[53] *TLG*.

designates one who is engaged in general education from a tutor (16. 7;
28. 7; 101. 4) and in one place designates, in a positive sense, the barbarians who were noted for being μαθηταὶ καὶ διδάσκαλοι of many types
of discoveries (209. 1). Μαθητής is also used of the student of a tutor in
the epistle *To Antipator* (4. 10. 4). The one time it occurs in *To Nicoles* (13.
5) Isocrates gives a general admonishment to listen to the poets and to
be a learner (μαθητής) of the sages. The word 'sage' (σόφιστος) was not
meant in a technical sense; it merely referred to one who was learned.

Isocrates also used μαθητής to designate an adherent. The only occurrence of the term in *Panegyricus* is most interesting. Isocrates says, "And
so far has our city distanced the rest of mankind in thought and in speech
that her pupils (μαθηταί) have become the teachers (διδάσκαλοι) of the rest
of the world." This passage reveals Isocrates' driving passion:[54]

> ...a worship of Hellenism as a way of life, a saving religion of which he con-
> ceives Athens to be the central shrine and himself a prophet commissioned
> by the gods to reconcile the quarrels of the Greeks and unite them in a
> crusade against the barbarian world.[55]

Isocrates advances his argument by declaring that the name "Hellenes"
denotes not so much a "race" as an "intelligence," and indicates those
who share in the culture of Hellas (50. 5-8). This use of the term suggests
that the great teachers of Athens are adherents of the very life of the city
of Athens. A similar use is found in *Antidosis* (296. 8), where all the most
clever speakers are said to be the μαθηταί of Athens.

Isocrates uses μαθητής with the greatest frequency to refer to "pupils."
This indicates his technical use of the term. In *Against the Sophists* the term
is used to denote the pupils of those Sophists he writes against (5. 4; 6.
6; 7. 5; 10. 2; 12. 1; 17. 3). If this work were taken alone, the usage
would be quite similar to those works in which Plato attacks the Sophistic
educational institution (e. g., *Gorgias*). But the consistent use in *Antidosis*,
where the term is used the more frequently than in any of Isocrates'
works, refers in an apologetic fashion to his own μαθηταί.[56] In *Busiris* the
term is used to designate both Pythagoras as a student of a religion (28.
6), and those who were later called the μαθηταί of Pythagoras (29. 3, 7).
Busiris also has an occurrence of the term to refer to one who was
mistakenly called a μαθητής of Socrates (5. 11). This technical use of
μαθητής to designate a pupil gives a general idea of the way in which the
term was basically used to describe a pupil of some great teacher. It could

[54] Lesky, *History of Greek Literature*, pp. 589f.
[55] George Norlin, "General Introduction," to *Isocrates*, trans. George Norlin, I, *The Loeb Classical Library* (Cambridge, Massachusetts: Harvard University Press, 1929), p. x.
[56] Cf., *Antidosis* 5.5; 30.7; 31.3; 41.5; 42.4; 87.2; 92.3; 98.5; 183.2,5; 185.3; 205.4; 220.3; 222.2,7; 235.7; 243.8.

be used of the Sophists whom Isocrates despises, of himself, of a philosophical-religious figure like Pythagoras, and even of Socrates. Μαθητής was becoming a technical term to indicate a pupil in Isocrates, but not in the specialized, technical sense to indicate the Sophists which Rengstorf suggests.

Isocrates therefore displays what may be the most common use of the term. It can transparently designate a learner; it can designate an adherent of teaching or thought; or it can be used most commonly to designate a pupil of a great teacher. This varied usage by Isocrates coincides with the use found in the writers already considered, and provides a corrective to Rengstorf's overstatement of the fixed, Sophistic, specialized-technical association.[57]

6. Demosthenes (c. 384-322 B. C.)

Demosthenes provides another control to understanding the usage of μαθητής in the classical period. Demosthenes moved as an orator (in antiquity he was known as *the* orator) in the realm of the court and politics. He only uses μαθητής four times, which is proportionately an infrequent use of the term in his writings.

In *Against Lacritus* the term is used twice. The oration is centered in a lawsuit against Lacritus, who is called a μαθητής of Isocrates (35. 15. 7). There is a subtle twist to the use of the term in the oration, because the speaker plays on the general unpopularity of the Sophists as a means of discrediting Lacritus.[58] He says, "For it is precisely in these matters that he professes himself to be clever, and he asks money, and collects pupils, promising to instruct them in these very things" (35. 41. 7). The twist in the use of the term is that Isocrates rejected the very things of which Lacritus is here charged, and so would Lacritus as his μαθητής; but because the popular mind did not distinguish between the rhetorician of Isocrates' sort and that of the other types of Sophistic rhetoricians, the speaker is able to unjustly accuse Lacritus of Sophistic associations in which he did not participate.

Μαθητής occurs once in each of two disputed works,[59] *The Erotic Essay* and *Against Aristogeiton*. In *The Erotic Essay* the term is used with positive

---

[57] Rengstorf does not give any real attention to Isocrates' usage, which, if he had, might have prevented him from his overstatement.

[58] A. T. Murray, "*Introduction to Against Lacritus,*" in Demosthenes, *Private Orations XXVII-XL*, trans. A. T. Murray, IV, *The Loeb Classical Library* (Cambridge, Massachusetts: Harvard University Press, 1936), p. 277.

[59] See Lesky, *History of Greek Literature*, pp. 599ff., for a discussion of the authenticity of these works.

connotations to denote Pericles as the pupil (μαθητής) of Anaxagoras of
Clazomenae. In *Against Aristogeiton* the term is used with negative con-
notations to denote Aristogeiton the orator as the pupil (μαθητής) of
Philocrates of Eleusis.

Although Demosthenes uses the term so infrequently, it denotes both
positive and negative pupils. In this sense the usage in Demosthenes is
in line with the developing technical usage. There are negative overtones
of Sophistic usage in *Against Lacritus*, but these overtones are brought into
the usage by association with certain negative Sophistic practices.

II. HELLENISTIC USAGE

A) Characteristics

The Classical and Hellenistic (and Roman)[60] use of μαθητής contains
similarity and dissimilarity, and much like the overall literature of these
periods, exhibits features of both semantical continuity and originality.

> It is sometimes said that the later Greeks were altogether lacking in
> originality and that they merely followed along the paths which their great
> ancestors had made. It would be more correct to say that the men of the
> fifth and fourth centuries B.C. were the pioneers who constructed the main
> roads through a new country, and that the later Greeks were the settlers
> who completed their work by thoroughly surveying the whole land.[61]

This metaphor describes the use of μαθητής. The classical writers
explored different uses of μαθητής, and the Hellentistic writers settled into
areas of established usage. The Hellenistic use is similar to that found in
the classical period, but it also has unique applications by various writers.
The basic similarities lie in the general use of the term to designate a
"learner" in a course of study, and in the technical use of the term to
designate an "adherent" of an individual teacher, philosophy, or
cultural milieu. The use of μαθητής as a *terminus technicus* appears prominently in this period, but the striking feature is that it is not restricted
to any one particular teacher, philosophy, or milieu. This will be
explained in more depth as the term is analyzed in each representative

---

[60] This section is referred to as the "Hellenistic" period for convenience only.
Technically, the Hellenistic period extends from the death of Alexander in 323 B.C. to
the battle of Actium in 31 B.C. The period from 31 B.C. to A.D. 313 is technically
known as the "Roman" period (cf. F. A. Wright, *A History of Later Greek Literature: From
the Death of Alexander in 323 B.C. to the Death of Justinian in 565 A.D.* [London: Routledge
and Kegan Paul Ltd., 1932], pp. 3-6). Since this section is only background to the use
in Matthew's gospel, a more precise delineation of use in the separate "Hellenistic" and
"Roman" periods was thought to be unnecessary.

[61] Ibid., p. 2.

writer. The writers selected for analysis cover the period from just before the time of Christ (Diodorus), to the time of the apostolic church (Dio, Epictetus, and Plutarch), to the third century A.D. (Diogenes Laertius[62]). The Hellenistic use of μαθητής is significant for this study because it is relatively contemporary to that found in the New Testament.

B) Representative Writers

1. Diodorus of Sicily (c. 60-30 B.C.[63])

Diodorus of Sicily is not an important writer of the Hellenistic period, but he is relevant for this study because he lived just prior to the time of Christ and because he is a transitional figure from Hellenistic to Roman stylistic features.[64] Diodorus used μαθητής thirteen times, and the occurrences are found scattered throughout his *Bibliotheca Historica*.

Diodorus used μαθητής three times in a general way to designate "learners" of a skill. In Book Twenty-three (2. 1. 13, 26) he says,

> The Romans, for their part, advised the Carthaginians not to teach them [the Romans] to meddle with maritime affairs, since the Romans, so they asserted, were pupils (μαθητάς) who always outstripped their masters (διδασκάλων) ... So now, should the Carthaginians compel them to learn naval warfare, they would soon see that the pupils (μαθητάς) had become superior to their teachers (διδασκάλων).

This is a general educational reference of the Romans learning a skill from the master teachers of sailing, the Carthaginians. A slightly different general usage is found in Book Sixteen (2. 3. 4), where the μαθητής is a pupil of a tutor.

> They in turn entrusted the lad to the father of Epameinondas and directed him both to keep careful watch over his ward and to superintend his upbringing and education. Since Epameinondas had as his instructor a phi-

---

[62] Diogenes Laertius was chosen, not for background to New Testament usage, but for his use of μαθητής in his biographical accounts of the major Greek figures.

[63] These are not the dates for his life, but the only firm dates known of his career. He visited Egypt somewhere around 60-57 B.C., where he began the process of gathering materials for his history, and the latest contemporary event mentioned by him in his *History* is the removal of of the citizens of Tauromenium in Sicily by Ceasar in c. 30 B.C. (cf., C. H. Oldfather, "Introduction," *Diodorus of Sicily*, trans. C. H. Oldfather, in Ten [sic. Twelve] Volumes, I, *The Loeb Classical Library* [Cambridge, Massachusetts: Harvard University Press, 1933], pp. viii-xx).

[64] Cf. Lesky, *History of Greek Literature*, pp. 778-779; Wright, *History of Later Greek Literature*, pp. 173-175; Hadas, *History of Greek Literature*, pp. 231-232. Lesky lists Diodorus under the Hellenistic period, while Wright and Hadas list him under the Roman.

losopher of the Pythagorean school, Philip, who was reared along with him, acquired a wide acquaintance with the Pythagorean philosophy. Inasmuch as both students (μαθητῶν) showed natural ability and diligence they proved to be superior in deeds of valour.

This is a general reference to students of a master teacher, here in a private tutorial sense. This usage by Diodorus shows that μαθητής still maintains its transparent relation to μανθάνω.

Diodorus also used μαθητής in a technical way to designate an adherent of a master teacher or teaching. Euripides is the μαθητής of Anaxagoras, a natural philosopher (1. 7. 7. 3; 1. 38. 4. 4.). Linus, admired for his skill in poetry and singing, had several μαθηταί, who were always characterized by the traits of their master (3. 67. 2. 2; 3. 67. 4. 1). Zaleucus was known for his noble birth as a Locrian of Italy, but was admired because he was a pupil (μαθητής) of the philosopher Pythagoras (12. 20. 1. 3). Orpheus is said to have become the μαθητής of the wizards known as the Idaean Dactyli, and was subsequently the first to introduce their rites and mysteries to the Greeks (5. 64. 4. 9). Diodorus mentions the μαθηταί of the Sophist Gorgias and says, "He was the first man to devise rules of rhetoric and so far excelled all other men in the instruction offered by the sophists that he received from his pupils (μαθητῶν) a fee of one hundred minas" (12. 53. 3. 1). Diodorus also refers to the μαθηταί of Isocrates on three different occasions (4. 1. 3. 2; 12. 1. 5. 4; 15. 76. 4. 3). This use refers to the student of a master teacher. In one place the μαθητής is simply identified by his attachment to Isocrates: "Ephorus of Cymê, ... a pupil (μαθητής) of Isocrates, when he undertook to write his universal history ..." (4. 1. 3. 2). In another place, Diodorus, speaking of the advancement of education, philosophy, and oratory, states, "For the philosophers were Socrates and Plato and Aristotle, and the orators were Pericles and Isocrates and his pupils (μαθηταί)" (12. 1. 5. 4). A similar usage is found in another place, where Diodorus says, "In this period there were men memorable for their culture, Isocrates the orator and those who became his pupils (μαθηταί), Aristotle the philosopher, and besides these Anaximenes of Lampsacus, Plato of Athens, the last of the Pythagorean philosophers, and Xenophon who composed his histories in extreme old age" (15. 76. 4. 3). The μαθηταί of Isocrates are students of a master teacher, and no specialized connotation is implied in the use of the term.[65]

---

[65] It is doubtful that any significance should be attributed to the mention of μαθηταί of Isocrates but not those of Socrates, Plato, Aristotle, Anaximenes, Xenophon, or Pericles. If there is is any significance at all, rather than finding it in a specialized use of μαθητής, it more likely because Isocrates had less personal genius than the others, and was known essentially for his abilities as a teacher of rhetoric and the permanent impact he had on educational models. Cf. Marrou, *History of Education*, pp. 79-91, 196.

Diodorus uses μαθητής in a general way to refer to "learners" and in a non-specialized way to refer to adherents of a natural philosopher, musician, philosopher, sophistical teacher, and rhetorician. This latter use approaches technical term status, because the emphasis is less upon "learning" than upon the extra-linguistic "relationship." Μαθητής here refers to a relationship between a master and his follower, and the type of relationship is determined only by the individuals involved, not the term itself.

2. Dio Chrysostom [Dion of Prusa in Bithynia] (c. A.D. 40-120)

Dio Chrysostom belongs to the so-called Second Sophistic period.[66] His rejection of Sophistic vanities and the adoption of the austere life of a militant philosopher at about the age of fifty-two has been described as a "conversion."[67] This conversion seems to play a significant role in his use of the term μαθητής, because negative connotations are attached to the term in those contexts where he considers the Sophists. On the other hand, there are no negative connotations attached to the term when other teachers are considered. In this way his use of μαθητής is similar to that of Plato, yet his objection to the Sophistic μαθηταί focuses almost exclusively on the ethical issue, not the epistemological.

Dio Chrysostom uses μαθητής in a general way to refer to a "learner." There are only two occurrences of the term in the discourse On Slavery and Freedom, and both refer to students, either of the schoolmaster, the gymnastics instructor or "other teachers."

> Speaker A. And yet, so far as obeying and being thrashed are concerned, you can go on and assert that the boys who take lessons of schoolmasters are likewise their servants and that the gymnastic trainers are slavemasters of their pupils (μαθητῶν), or those who teach anything else; for they give orders to their pupils[68] and trounce them when they are disobedient."
>
> Speaker B. "Indeed that's true," replied the other, "but it is not permissible for the gymnastic instructors or for the other teachers to imprison their pupils (μαθητάς) or to sell them or to cast them into the mill, but to slavemasters all these things are allowed" (65. 19. 3, 6).

---

[66] This appellation harks back to the old educational controversy between Plato and Isocrates. Plato contended for the prerogative of philosophy, whereas Isocrates contended for rhetoric. Rhetoric dominated advanced education and determined the characteristics of literature during the first two centuries of the Roman period. Cf. Lesky, History of Greek Literature, p. 829; G. W. Bowersock, Greek Sophists in the Roman Empire (Oxford: Clarendon, 1969); Wright, History of Later Greek Literature, pp. 224ff.

[67] Marrou, History of Education, p. 206.

[68] This is only a reference by way of the dative pronoun αὐτοῖς, not an actual occurrence of μαθητής or any other term for pupil.

This shows a broad use of the term to designate a student involved in educational and physical training. Here the term is semantically associated with μανθάνειν.

Dio also uses the term technically to refer to adherents. In the discourse *A Refusal of the Office of Archon Delivered Before the Council*, the term is used twice; in one place to refer to the μαθητής of Pythagoras (32. 5. 7) and in the other the μαθητής of Anaxagoras (32. 6. 5). In another place Hesiod is said to have been able to compose and chant his poems because "he held converse with the Muses and had become a pupil (μαθητής) of those very beings" (60, 61. 1. 4). Hesiod is a student and imitator of the Muses; he is an adherent of their art. On at least three occasions Dio refers to mortal kings as the μαθηταί of Zeus. In the first discourse on *Kingship* Dio uses the term to designate mortal kings who are "Zeus-nurtured" and "like Zeus in counsel." "In fact, it stands to reason that practically all the kings among Greeks or barbarians who have proved themselves not unworthy of this title [king] have been disciples (μαθητάς) and emulators of this god" (1. 38. 6). Likewise, in the fourth discourse on *Kingship*, it is asserted that since Homer called Minos the consort (ὀαριστήν) of Zeus, he was the associate (ὁμιλητήν) of Zeus. Conversing with Alexander the Great, Diogenes declares, "Well then, he [Homer] says that he was an associate (ὁμιλητήν) of Zeus, which could virtually be calling him his disciple (μαθητήν)" (4. 40. 3). Here Diogenes goes out of his way to equate μαθητής with other positive terms. In the discourse *On Homer*, Dio says

> Whenever, for instance, he [Homer] praises any king, he calls him 'the peer of Zeus in wisdom'; and all the good kings are 'Zeus-nurtured'; and Minos, who has the highest reputation among the Greeks for justice, he says is both the associate (ὁμιλητήν) and pupil (μαθητήν) of Zeus, his idea being that Minos was the first and greatest king of all, and the only one who himself understood and handed down the art of kingship, and also that good kings should shape their course with an eye to Minos, patterning their own conduct after a god, so far as humanly possible.

This latter use is most interesting, because here the concept of the μαθητής is almost defined in the last phrases, and, along with the prior two, is extremely positive when used in the realm of kingly art and wisdom. This usage is instructive for the way in which the relationship has moved away from "learning." The relationship is defined by the concept of imitation of conduct. This indicates that μαθητής does not necessarily sustain an immediate semantic association with μανθάνω, and can now be used as a technical term for a follower of a master.

Dio also uses μαθητής in two separate ways which at first seem contradictory. In the first, the term occurs eight times to designate the stu-

dent of the Sophists.[69] In each of these μαθητής designates the student of
the Sophists, and there is a negative connotation attached to the use of
the term. For example, he says, "one could hear crowds of wretched
sophists around Poseidon's temple shouting and reviling one another,
and their disciples (μαθητῶν), as they were called, fighting with one
another, many writers reading aloud their stupid words" (On Virtue 9. 3).
In another place (On Man's First Conception of God 5. 5) he discusses
various types of teachers, and ends by mentioning the Sophists and their
μαθηταί: "finally, like gorgeous peacocks, sophists in large numbers, men
who are lifted aloft as on wings by their fame and discples (μαθηταῖς)...."
He then contrasts himself to the Sophists by describing himself as "a man
who knows nothing and makes no claim to knowing." This last phrase
harks back to the epistemological issue found in the writings of Plato.
Another passage accentuates Dio's epistemological orientation:

> For I do not take disciples (μαθητάς), since I know there is nothing I should
> be able to teach them, seeing that I know nothing myself; but to lie and
> deceive by my promises, I have not the courage for that. But if I associated
> myself with a professional sophist, I should help him greatly by gathering
> a great crowd to him and then allowing him to dispose of the catch as he
> wished (On Man's First Conception of God 13. 6).

Dio's statement here sounds similar to Plato's / Socrates' claim to have
no knowledge, and similar also to the avoidance of the audacity to claim
the right to teach other disciples. At first glance Dio appears to have the
same negative attitude as Plato / Socrates toward the epistemological and
ethical practices of the arrogant Sophists who are gathering disciples, but
on closer examination, Dio's emphasis differs. His epistemological objection is based on an asceticism which is closer to the Stoic's philosophy
than to Plato's.[70] This is illustrated in a passage in On Man's First Conception of God (15. 3).

> But notwithstanding, I declare to you that, great as is your number [of
> sophists], you have been eager to hear a man who is neither handsome in
> appearance nor strong, and in age is already past his prime, one who has
> no disciple (μαθητήν), who professes, I may almost say, no art or special
> knowledge either of the nobler or of the meaner sort, no ability either as
> a prophet or a sophist, nay, not even as an orator or as a flatterer, one who
> is not even a clever writer, who does not even have a craft deserving of
> praise or of interest, but who simply—wears his hair long!

---

[69] On Kingship 14. 2; On Virtue 9. 3; On Man's First Conception of God 5. 5; 13. 6; 15.
3; Discourse Delivered in Celaenae in Phrygia 10. 1; On Reputation 12. 5; On Envy 27. 3.
[70] Cf. Lesky, History of Greek Literature, pp. 834-835.

In another place he says,

> Nay, whenever fame lays hold upon a man and that sort of talk starts to
> smoulder, he should tear off his garments and leap forth naked upon the
> public highways, proving to all the world that he is no better than any other
> man. And if someone follows at his heels claiming to be his pupil (μαθητής),
> he must try to drive him away, striking him with his fists and pelting him
> with clods of earth and stones, knowing that the fellow is either fool or
> knave (*Discourse Delivered in Celaenae in Phrygia* 10. 1).

Dio rejects the practice of gathering μαθηταί, but it is based upon his
rejection of the ethical practices of the Sophists and upon his own ascetic
humility.

But Dio also uses μαθητής in a different way, which appears to con-
tradict this attitude. In his 55th discourse, *On Homer and Socrates*, Dio uses
the term eight times (1. 2; 3. 3, 8 [2x]; 4. 5 [2x]; 5. 1, 6), and in each
his intent is to show that Socrates is the μαθητής of Homer. The
interlocutor asks who was Socrates' teacher (διδάσκαλος) in wisdom, and
Dio says, "Socrates is in truth a pupil (μαθητής) of Homer, and not of
Archelaüs, as some say" (3. 3). The interlocutor objects that Socrates
was too far removed in time from Homer to be his μαθητής, and Dio
answers by showing that one who lived in Homer's day, but who never
heard the poetry of Homer, and who was not familiar with the thought
of Homer, certainly was not the pupil of Homer. Dio proceeds, "Then
it is not absurd that the man who neither met nor saw Homer and yet
understood his poetry and became familiar with all his thought should be
called a pupil (μαθητήν) of Homer" (4. 5). Dio then suggests that the very
reason Socrates is the μαθητής of Homer is because he is his "zealous
follower" (ζηλωτής). The dialogue continues as Dio says,

> Then, if a follower (ζηλωτής), he would also be a pupil (μαθητής). For
> whoever really follows any one surely knows what that person was like, and
> by imitating his acts and words he tries as best he can to make himself like
> him. But that is precisely, it seems, what the pupil (μαθητής) does—by
> imitating his teacher and paying heed to him he tries to acquire his art. On
> the other hand, seeing people and associating with them has nothing to do
> with the process of learning. For instance, many persons not only see pipers
> but associate with and hear them every day, and yet they could not even
> blow on the pipes unless they associate with the pipers for professional ends
> and pay strict heed. However, if you shrink from calling Socrates a pupil
> (μαθητής) of Homer, but would prefer to call him just a follower (ζηλωτής),
> it will make no difference to me (4. 5 - 5. 6).

Several observations may be made about Dio's use of μαθητής in the
above passage: 1) The term is used with reference to Socrates, even
though Dio knew the negative aspects of the Sophists and the way in
which μαθητής was the term used to describe their followers. It functions

as a technical term to designate a true follower instead of being restricted to Sophistic usage. 2) One can be the μαθητής of a teacher even though the teacher has long been dead, and even though they never met nor had any specific input between them. 3) The reason why one could be the μαθητής of one long dead is because he is a *zealous follower* (ζηλωτής, 4. 6) of the teacher, not just an academic student. Being a μαθητής is not just hearing, giving attention to, and associating with, a master. 4) "Imitation" of the acts and words of the master, as the student attempts to make himself like the master and acquire his art, is at the heart of the relationship. 5) Dio sees no problem with Homer being the διδάσκαλος of Socrates and having Socrates learn from him. Even as Socrates was free to call himself a μαθητής in Plato's writings when there was no possibility of being mistaken for a Sophist, so Dio is free to call Socrates a disciple of Homer, and to mean it in a very positive way.

Dio uses μαθητής in two basic ways. He uses it to refer to a "learner," and he also uses it as a technical term for an intimate relationship involving imitation, learning, and zealous following of the master. When the master is a Sophist negative connotations surround the relationship, but when the master is one such as Homer, positive connotations surround the relationship.

3. Epictetus (c. A.D. 50-130)

Epictetus was a Stoic philosopher who reflects his philosophical outlook in his use of the term. He used μαθητής only twice. In the context of a philosophical treatise on learning for oneself, and not just letting the opinions of others dictate one's thoughts, Epictetus says, "Will you not, then, let other men alone, and become your own pupil (μαθητής) and your own teacher (διδάσκαλος)?" (*Arrian's Discourses of Epictetus* 4. 6. 11. 2). This is a very general use of the term in a Stoic discussion of education. In another place, as he discusses the highest goals of man, he refers to Socrates, and asks, "What is the function of a good and excellent man? To have many pupils (μαθητάς)? Not at all. Those who have set their hearts on it shall see to that" (*Arrian's Discourses of Epictetus* 4. 8. 24. 1) Epictetus here rejects an emphasis on educational institutionalism in favor of independency as a Stoic. This does not negate the general sense above, but rather makes a distinction between an institutional and general use of the term.

Epictetus recognized the general and institutional usage of μαθητής, but rejected it and chose another word, ἀνδράποδον ("slaves"), to designate his followers.[71] This most likely has to do with the the fact that

---

[71] M. L. Clarke, *Higher Education in the Ancient World* (Albuquerque: University of New Mexico Press, 1971), p. 90. The *TLG* confirms Clarke's statement, in that ἀνδράποδον is used some twenty-four times to designate the followers of Epictetus.

μαθητής had now become a technical term to refer to intimate followers of a master, and for the Stoic this would not be desirable. The Stoic desired to be in control, hence the term ἀνδράποδον would describe a subservience of his followers which would render the master in control. What is important for this study is that Epictetus confirms the status of *terminus technicus* for μαθητής at this time. Μαθητής refers to the intimate follower of a master, and the type of relationship is determined by the type of master.

4. Plutarch (c. A.D. 46-120)

Plutarch's use of μαθητής clearly indicates that it has become a *terminus technicus* in this period. Plutarch uses μαθητής forty-three times[72] five of which may be classified as a general use, nine of which may be classified as designating a general-technical adherence, and twenty-eight of which may be classified as designating a technical adherence.

Plutarch used μαθητής to refer to a general learner on at least five occasions. It was used for one engaged in learning the skill of flute-playing (*Demetrius and Antony, Lives* 1. 6. 2), one who was engaged in general education (*The Oracles at Delphi No Longer Given in Verse* 406. F. 4), younger statesmen who follow the example of the older statesmen (*Whether an Old Man Should Engage in Public Affairs* 790. D. 6), the way in which men are followers of the animal world in various technical matters (*Whether Land or Sea Animals are Cleverer* 974. A. 8), and the way in which physicians, musicians and singers learn their trade (*On Stoic Self-Contradictions* 1037. E. 2). This usage reveals that the term still maintained an association with the verb μανθάνω.

Plutarch also used μαθητής in a semi-technical way to refer to general adherence to military tactics (*Sertorius and Eumenes* 18. 8. 1), a good life-model (*Sayings of Spartans* 208. B. 2), teachers with loving affection (*On Moral Virtue* 448. E. 7), the Muses' teaching (*A Letter of Condolence to Apollonius* 105. D. 7; *On Brotherly Love* 480. E. 11), justice (*On the Delays of the Divine Vengeance* 550. A. 12), Zeus (*Demetrius and Anthony, Lives* 42. 10. 1), and the gods in general (*That a Philosopher Ought to Converse Especially with Men in Power* 776. E. 11).

The majority of occurrences of μαθητής in Plutarch's writings are simply references to followers of great masters. There is a diverse range of various types of great masters: e.g., Zeno,[73] Theophrastus,[74]

---

[72] *TLG*, University of California, Irvine.

[73] *Agis and Cleomenes* 23. 3. 2; *How a man may become aware of his progress in virtue* 78. E. 2; *On Moral Virtue* 443. A. 8; *On Stoic Self-Contradictions* 1034. F. 1.

[74] *How a man may become aware of his progress in virtue* 78. E. 2; *On Praising Oneself Inoffensively* 545. F. 6.

Xenocrates,[75] Socrates, Plato, and Alexander,[76] Isocrates,[77] and
Epicurus.[78] This type of usage can most readily be classified as a
technical usage referring to the follower of a great master.

Although Plutarch uses μαθητής quite frequently, his usage is easily
classified because he is so regular. He uses the term to refer to either a
general learner, a general-technical adherent of a principle of teaching,
or a committed follower / student of a great master.

5. Diogenes Laertius (c. 3rd century A.D.)

Diogenes Laertius uses μαθητής more that any of the writers surveyed
(eighty-four times), yet his use is by far the easiest to categorize. Without
exception he uses μαθητής as a technical term to refer to an adherent of
a teacher, school, or great master. His consistent usage most likely has
to do with his subject material (his *Lives* tend to merely recount the story
of great figures of the past), but it also shows a progression in the use of
the term. By the third century A.D. μαθητής is used for a follower of a
master, whether it is Socrates (2. 102. 14; 6. 2. 6) or Plato (4. 2. 1; 5.
1. 5), or Aristotle (3. 109. 9; 5. 2. 8; 5. 3. 3), or a Sophist (4. 2. 4; 9.
54. 7; 9. 56. 10), or Stoic like Zeno (6. 105. 13; 7. 36. 1) or Pythagorians
(8. 3. 9; 8. 10. 7; 8. 11. 2), or Epicurus (10. 2. 2;10. 6. 10; 10. 22. 11).
In the writings of Diogenes Laertius μαθητής has become a fixed *terminus
technicus* to designate a committed follower of a great master.

III. Conclusion Concerning the Classical and Hellenistic Usage

This survey of the use of the term μαθητής in in the classical and
Hellenistic Greek literature reveals a historical progression. In the
earliest written use (the early classical period) the term was used in three
ways: it was used with a general sense, in morphological relation to
μανθάνειν, to refer to a "learner;" it was also used quite early with a
technical sense to refer to an "adherent" of a great teacher, teaching, or
master; and it was also used somewhat more restrictedly by the Sophists
to refer to the "institutional pupil" of the Sophists. Socrates / Plato (and
those opposed to the Sophists) tended to avoid using the term to designate

---

[75] *Sayings of Kings and Commanders* 192. A. 9.
[76] *On the Fortune or the Virtue of Alexander* 328. B. 10.
[77] *Lives of the Ten Orators* 837. B. 7.
[78] *That Epicurus Actually Makes a Pleasant Life Impossible* 1100. A. 6; *Reply to Colotes in Defence of the Other Philosophers* 1108. E. 6).

his followers in order to avoid Sophistic misassociations, but he used the term freely to refer to "learners" and "adherents" where there was no danger of misunderstanding.

In the late Hellenistic period μαθητής continued to be used with general connotations of a "learner" and "adherent," but it was being used more regularly to refer to an "adherent." The type of adherency was determined by the master, but it ranged from being the pupil of a philosopher, to being the follower of a great thinker and master of the past, to being the devotee of a religious figure. By the time of the third century A.D. the term was used by one prolific writer to refer exclusively to an adherent. Μαθητής became a *terminus technicus* to refer to an adherent.

The progression to "adherent" in Hellenism at the time of Christ and the early church made μαθητής a convenient term to designate the followers of Jesus, because the emphasis in the common use of the term was not upon "learning," or upon being a pupil, but upon adherence to a great master. Hence a "disciple" of Jesus, designated by the Greek term μαθητής, was one who adhered to his master, and the type of adherence was determined by the master himself. The type of adherence will be considered in the next chapters.

CHAPTER TWO

THE OLD TESTAMENT BACKGROUND

I. Introduction

One of the striking features of going to the Old Testament for help in understanding the background of μαθητής is the relative absence of discipleship terminology. Karl H. Rengstorf, on the basis of his observation that there is an absence of "disciple" *terminology* in the Old Testament, concludes that there is a corresponding absence of the *concept* of discipleship as well:

> If the term is missing, so, too, is that which it serves to denote. Apart from the formal relation of teacher and pupil, the OT, unlike the classical Greek world and Hellenism, has no master-disciple relation. Whether among the prophets or the scribes we seek in vain for anything corresponding to it.[1]

Specifically, Rengstorf argues that since the *terms* which later specify master-disciple relationships in Judaism are absent in the Old Testament (i.e., *talmîdh* and *limmûdh*), the *concept* of discipleship is absent as well. His several proposals to account for the absence of disciple terminology and concept converge in his understanding of Israel as the covenantal community.

> The self-awareness of the OT community is thus controlled by the fact of its divine election, and on this basis it is quite impossible for it to use a noun formed from *lāmadh* to denote the individual who gives himself specially to *lāmadh*, and thereby to differentiate him from the other members of the chosen people.[2]

Rengstorf argues that, since all of Israel is elect, no distinction can be made between individuals who "learn" more of God than others within the covenantal community. In addition, he contends that since the "ideal" of discipleship in the Old Testament is that between Israel and Yahweh, to be the disciple of any other master would preempt the supreme place of Yahweh.[3]

Although his conclusions are followed by many popular as well as scholarly works on the Old Testament background of disciple,[4] Rengstorf

---

[1] Karl H. Rengstorf, "μαθητής," *TDNT*, IV, p. 427.
[2] Ibid., p. 427.
[3] Ibid., pp. 427-431.
[4] E.g., Ernst Jenni, "*lmd*," *THAT*, II, ed. Ernst Jenni and Claus Westermann (München: Chr. Kaiser, 1971), col. 875; Dietrich Müller, "μαθητής," *NIDNTT*, I, p. 485; Andre Feuillet, "Disciple," *Dictionary of Biblical Theology*, ed., Xavier Leon-Dufour (2d. ed.; New York: Seabury, 1973), p. 125.

appears to overstate his case.[5] In the first place he overlooks the adjectival form *limmûdh* which is derived from *lâmadh*. Even as he overstates the absence of terminology, he overlooks that evidence which is to be found. In the second place, because he inadequately defines the relationship between the terminology and concept of discipleship, he inordinately overstates the absence of discipleship. Although he draws his conclusions about the classical and Hellenistic concept from only one particular usage of the term μαθητής (the Sophists), here he draws his conclusions about the Old Testament concept from the absence of one particular term, *talmîdh*. Even though traditional Jewish "disciple" terminology is used only marginally, recent educational[6] and sociological[7] studies have suggested forms of master-disciple relations in existence in the Old Testament. Therefore, the study of the Old Testament background must focus first on the relevent *terminology*, but then the focus must shift to other relevant evidence for the *concept* of disciples.

Since this study is only background to the more central study of the use of the term μαθητής in the New Testament, certain limitations must be placed on this chapter. The terms examined in this section have been intentionally limited to *talmîdh* and *limmûdh*. The intention is to explore those terms which are synonymous to the Greek term μαθητής in order to find Old Testament precedents (or lack thereof) for the use of μαθητής in the New Testament. The major reason for focusing on *talmîdh* and *limmûdh* is because these terms were the closest Hebrew / Aramaic equivalents in Jewish literature to μαθητής.[8] The purpose here is not to explore all of the tangent terms. For example, the tangent nouns from the verb *shᵉlach*, "to send," which is the equivalent of the Greek term ἀποστέλλω, will not be considered because "apostle" is not a term central to the lexical history of μαθητής. Since the purpose is not to explore all the tangent associations, only those terms which can be considered equivalents of μαθητής will be examined.

The methodology used here for ascertaining the existence of the concept of master-disciple relations will emphasize a balance of breadth and depth. On the positive side, one purpose is to search for the *extent* of the occurrence of master-disciple relations, but the true extent can be delineated only through a relatively in-depth analysis. On the negative

---

[5] Robert Meye is influenced by Rengstorf's study, but he advocates caution because of possible overstatement by Rengstorf; Robert P. Meye, *Jesus and the Twelve: Discipleship and Revelation in Mark's Gospel* (Grand Rapids: Eerdmans, 1968), pp. 94-95.

[6] E.g., Wallace A. Alcorn, "Biblical Concept of Discipleship as Education for Ministry," (unpublished Ph.D. dissertation, New York University, 1974).

[7] E.g., Robert R. Wilson, *Prophecy and Society in Ancient Israel* (Philadelphia: Fortress, 1980).

[8] Cf. Chapter Three, III. H., below, "The Rabbinic Literature."

side, a degree of extent and depth must be sacrificed in order to handle adequately the phenomena. For example, recent studies of *individual relations* have proven valuable for ascertaining discipleship relations,[9] but because of necessary limitations this chapter must forego primary analysis of individual relations[10] so that certain *group relations* can be examined with greater depth. These group relations have received significant attention lately because they appear to suggest extensive master-disciple relationships within the group. Recent studies of these groups suggest that the relationships found within the group are indicative of corresponding relationships throughout Israel. Further, these groups provide analogies to the type of master-disciple relationships which later appear in Israel in the intertestamental literature, the New Testament, and the Rabbinical literature. The groups selected for this study are the prophets, the wise men, and the scribes. The purpose is to analyze broad characteristics within these groups which can help either affirm or deny the existence of master-disciple relationships in the Old Testament.

II. The Terms for Disciple in the Old Testament

A) *Talmîdh*

Talmîdh appears to be the Hebrew equivalent of μαθητής. Just as μαθητής ("learner," "disciple") derived from the verb for "learn" (μανθάνω), so *talmîdh* derived from the Hebrew verb for "learn" (*lâmadh*), literally meaning "taught one".[11] *Talmîdh* is the equivalent of μαθητής in later Rabbinical Hebrew, although it normally designates a "beginning scholar" in Rabbinical use.[12]

[9] E.g., M. Hengel starts with the relationship between Elijah and Elisha for understanding the Old Testament background of Jesus and his disciples (Martin Hengel, *The Charismatic Leader and His Followers*, trans. James Greig [1968; New York: Crossroad, 1981], pp. 16 ff.); cf. also Robert Arnold Hausman, "The Function of Elijah as a Model in Luke-Acts," (unpublished Ph.D. dissertation, University of Chicago, 1975), p. 98, who suggests that "Elijah and Elisha together stand out in the Old Testament as the primary model of the true master-disciple relationship."

[10] While primary analysis cannot be given to these individual relationships, limited analysis will be given to the relationships between Elijah-Elisha and between Jeremiah-Baruch in the analysis of the prophetic and scribals groups below.

[11] Jenni, "*lmd*," col. 872; Francis Brown, S. R. Driver, and Charles A. Briggs, *A Hebrew and English Lexicon of the Old Testament* (ET; Oxford: Clarendon, 1974), p. 541. This derivation is also true for the Aramaic term *talmîdhaʾ*; cf. Marcus Jastrow, ed., *A Dictionary of the Targumim, the Talmud Babli and Yerushalmi, and the Midrashic Literature* (New York: Pardes, 1950), II, 1673.

[12] M. Aberbach, "The Relations Between Master and Disciple in the Talmudic Age," *Essays Presented to Chief Rabbi Israel Brodie on the Occasion of His Seventieth Birthday*, ed. H. J. Zimmels, J. Rabbinowitz, and I. Finestein, Vol. I, Jews' College Publications New Series, No. 3 (London: Soncino, 1967), pp. 1-24.

Talmîdh is used only once in the Hebrew Old Testament. Within a classification of musicians in I Chron 25, the noun is used to denote a pupil in contrast to a teacher (*mēbhîn*), or a novice in contrast to a master: "They cast lots for relays of service, for the younger as for the older, for the master as for the pupil (*talmîdh*)" (I Chron 25:8).[13] Some have understood this to mean that a formal school existed in Jerusalem for the training of temple musicians.[14] The existence of a school is a possibility, but here the text merely states that the musicians, whether small or great, or whether (chiastically) an accomplished musician or one learning, all cast lots for their duties. R. N. Whybray states that the text

> . . . implies no more than the obvious fact that there must have been musical instruction in order to preserve a continuity of skilled musicians; but such instruction may well have been private and comparable to the normal instruction in the hereditary craft of the family given by fathers to their sons.[15]

Talmîdh in I Chron 25:8 is best understood in the most basic sense of the term: one engaged in the learning process, or an apprentice learning a trade.

B) *Limmûdh*

The adjective *limmûdh*, "taught," is also derived from the verb *lāmadh*, but as a passive participle. The term occurs six times in the Old Testament, always in the prophets (Isa 8:16; 50:4 [2x]; 54:13; Jer 2:24; 13:23). *Limmûdh* was rendered as a substantive, "taught one," but it did not become a common term for a "disciple" in Judaism as did the related noun *talmîdh*. In Jeremiah the adjective has the meaning of "accustomed to" something,[16] while in Isaiah it means "taught" or "instructed" (8:16; 50:4; 54:13).[17] The occurrences in Isaiah have the most significance for this study, especially since lexicographers have

---

[13] The translation of the verse and options for *talmîdh* are given by Jacob M. Myers, *I Chronicles, AB*, vol. 12 (1965; 2d. ed.; Garden City, N. Y.: Doubleday, 1974), p. 170.

[14] C. F. Keil renders *talmîdh* "scholar" and tends to imply a formal school setting (this is also the rendering of the AV). Quite possibly this was assumed from the later Rabbinic usage (cf. C. F. Keil and F. Delitzsch, *The First Book of Chronicles*, trans. Andrew Harper, Commentary on the Old Testament [n.d.; rpt.; Grand Rapids: Eerdmans, 1975], pp. 272-273).

[15] R. N. Whybray, *The Intellectual Tradition in the Old Testament*, BZAW 135, ed. Georg Fohrer (Berlin: Walter de Gruyter, 1974), p. 37.

[16] E.g., Jer 2:24: a wild donkey accustomed to the wilderness; Jer 13:23: a person accustomed to doing evil.

[17] Jenni, "*lmd*," col. 872, 875; Brown, Driver, Briggs, *Lexicon*, p. 541; Walter C. Kaiser, "*lāmadh*," *TWOT*, ed. R. Laird Harris, Gleason L. Archer, Jr., and Bruce K. Waltke (Chicago: Moody, 1980), I, 480.

given it the force of "taught, as disciples,"[18] or "disciple, follower."[19] The AV and RSV render the use in 8:16 "disciples," the NASB renders the use in 50:4 "disciples," and the NASB also gives that translation as an alternate in 54:13. The issue here is the identity of these "taught ones," or "disciples," and whether the occurrence of the term in these passages in Isaiah gives evidence of a master-disciple relationship in the Old Testament.

1. Isaiah 8:16

In the middle of a prophecy concerning the downfall of Damascus and Samaria (Isa 8:4) at the hand of Assyria comes a warning to both houses of Israel (Isa 8:14). Then comes a passage in which *limmûdh* occurs. *Limmûdh* refers to those who are to be the recipients of the binding and sealing of the divine revelation: "Bind up the testimony, seal the law among my disciples (*belimmudhâi*)." The basic question is whether the verse should be taken as a continuation of the preceding statements from God, and hence a command from God to Isaiah, or whether v. 16 should be taken as a prayer from Isaiah to God and connects with the following statements of Isaiah. In the former case the *limmûdhîm* would be *God's* disciples, but in the latter they are *Isaiah's* disciples. In either case it is appropiate to call these *limmûdhîm* (the adjective functions as a noun) "disciples," in that they are gathered around an individual (either God or Isaiah) for instruction, and that individual refers to them as "my" disciples, implying an on-going relationship.

While some commentators interpret the *limmûdhîm* as the disciples of God because there is no grammatical adversative beginning v. 16 to signal a new subject,[20] the majority interpret this as a prayer or statement of resolve by Isaiah, asking God to seal up among his (Isaiah's) *limmûdhîm* the preceding words from God, as well as all of God's teaching.[21] The structure of the passage supports the latter view more readily since

---

[18] Brown, Driver, Briggs, *Lexicon*, p. 541.

[19] Ludwig Koehler and Walter Baumgartner, eds., *Lexicon in Veteris Testamenti Libros*, I (Leiden: E. J. Brill, 1951), p. 483.

[20] E.g., Derek Kidner, "Isaiah," *The New Bible Commentary: Revised*, ed. D. Guthrie and J. A. Motyer (1953; 3d ed.; Grand Rapids: Eerdmans, 1970), p. 597; Edward J. Young, *The Book of Isaiah* (1965; 2d ed.; Grand Rapids: Eerdmans, 1972), I, 314.

[21] E.g., Gerhard von Rad, *The Message of the Prophets*, trans. D. M. G. Stalker (New York: Harper and Row, 1962), pp. 22-23; "statement of resolve" is cautiously offered by Emil G. Kraeling, *Commentary on the Prophets, Vol. I: Isaiah, Jeremiah, Ezekiel* (Camden, N. J.: Thomas Nelson and Sons, 1956), p. 72. O. Kaiser suggests that these *limmûdhîm* were possibly temple personnel, or prophets in training (Otto Kaiser, Isaiah 1-12: A Commentary, The Old Testament Library, ed. Peter Ackroyd, James Barr, John Bright and G. Ernest Wright [Philadelphia: Westminster, 1972], p. 120).

the simple *waw* beginning v. 17 ties vv. 16 and 17 together quite naturally; the prophet speaking in the first person in v. 17 is syntactically the
same person speaking in v. 16. That the prophet is uttering a prayer for
the Lord's words to be bound up among his (Isaiah's) *limmûdhîm* is further suggested by v. 18, because the "children" given to the prophet by
the Lord are a poetically-parallel reference to the *limmûdhîm*, and v. 18
gives a purpose for the "binding": they and Isaiah would be for signs
and wonders in Israel. Despite the difficulties of the passage,[22] the *limmûdhîm* in v. 16 are most easily understood to be Isaiah's.

Rengstorf acknowledges that the *limmûdhîm* in v. 16 most naturally
appear to be Isaiah's, but he still hesitates to call them a fellowship of
"disciples." He prefers to call them "the new community gathered
around the prophet."[23] Rengstorf most likely hesitates because he
assumes that the terminology of discipleship necessitates a human
organization which would contest the divine revelation through its own
tradition and teaching, and because discipleship relationships would be
the antithesis of the Yahweh-centered community.

Although the type of organization Rengstorf fears *can* be reflected in
discipleship terminology, it certainly is not necessitated, and assumes a
use of discipleship terminology which is more restricted than is the actual
case. To be gathered around a prophet as a disciple does not necessarily
obviate primary discipleship to Yahweh. No serious heir of Abraham,
Isaac, and Jacob thought of supplanting the central place of Yahweh with
any other teacher, but human instruments had always been crucial in
fostering the Yahweh-Israel relationship. While human instruments
worked to promote *primary* discipleship to Yahweh, there is no compelling
reason to deny *secondary* discipleship to the human instrument as one of
the means for obtaining a greater intimacy with, and understanding of,
Yahweh. Even though he sees these *limmûdhîm* as God's disciples, E. J.
Young offers the possibility of primary and secondary discipleship for the
limmûdhîm in Isa 8:16 when he says:

> They [God's *limmûdhîm*] were taught of Him, however, by means of the
> instruction of the law and of the prophets, and here particularly by means
> of the teaching of Isaiah. In this derivative or secondary sense, then, they
> may also be denominated the disciples of Isaiah. In their hearts he would
> seal the teaching by means of faithfully proclaiming it to them and explain-
> ing it.[24]

---

[22] These difficulties basically center on the identity of the speaker in the three verses,
16-18. What complicates the issue is that Heb 2:13 refers to Isa 8:18 as a Messianic statement. See Young, *Isaiah*, I, 314-316 for a discussion of the various interpretations.
[23] Rengstorf, "μαθητής," p. 430.
[24] Young, *Isaiah*, I, 314.

Rengstorf's hesitations therefore are unnecessary. The *limmûdhîm* can be disciples of both Isaiah and Yahweh at the same time. The *function* and *kind* of discipleship are different, as will be delineated later, but both relationships can be designated discipleship nonetheless.

2. Isaiah 50:4

Two occurrences of *limmûdh* are found in Isa 50:4:

> The Lord Yahweh has given me the tongue of disciples (*limmûdhîm*),
> That I may know how to answer the weary;
> With a word he awakens in the morning,
> In the morning he awakens my ear to listen as disciples do (*limmûdhîm*).[25]

The servant[26] who speaks emphasizes that the relation sustained between himself and the Lord is as a disciple to a master. In doing so, he stresses that the words he speaks are not his own but are divinely given by the Lord God. The meaning of the passage is that the Lord God has equipped him to speak and to hear, as do "the taught ones."

Now the question arises, is there a *specific group* identified as the "taught ones," or is *limmûdhîm* simply a *characteristic*? That is, is the servant enabled to speak and hear as do a group of *limmûdhîm* with whom the readers are familiar, or is he enabled to speak and hear as would a truly taught person? J. L. McKenzie sees in the terminology of the passage an allusion to a school of disciples: the "tongue" of the disciple faithfully repeats what it has learned and the "ear" of the disciple docilely receives every word of the teacher. McKenzie says that *limmûdh* should be rendered, "disciple," in this case, and that "its use suggests the existence of a school of disciples which became a tradition, a tradition of which the authors of Second Isaiah and Third Isaiah knew themselves to be continuators."[27] This view assumes that there was an organized circle of disciple-prophets in Israel and that this school passed on the basic content of the prophecy. It further assumes an organizational model similar to that found later in Israel, and assumes that it is the precursor of those later Jewish schools. *Limmûdh* means " the student who commits the words of the teacher to memory."[28] Although the term is rare, as are allusions to a circle of disciples, the way in which the servant alludes to

---

[25] Translation by John L. McKenzie, *Second Isaiah, AB*, vol. 20 (Garden City, New York: Doubleday, 1968), p. 115.

[26] The person speaking has been identified as either Isaiah (cf. R. N. Whybray, *Isaiah 40-66, NCB* [London: Marshall, Morgan & Scott, 1975], pp. 150-153), or the Servant of the Lord (cf. McKenzie, *Second Isaiah*, pp. 116-117). While this is an important topic for Isaianic studies, the resolution of the problem does not significantly affect the present discussion.

[27] McKenzie, *Second Isaiah*, pp. 116-117.

[28] Ibid., p. 116, note on v. 4.

these "taught ones" seems to point to the existence of a category of persons with whom the readers were familiar.

R. N. Whybray suggests that the author was thinking of the general category of disciples of the prophets, and the idealized *relationship* of the disciple to the master was held up as an illustrative example for the servant.[29] He suggests that the author records this as an illustrative example which draws upon the acquaintance of the readers with the general category of persons known as "learners," and that the *characteristics* of the "learners" are used as illustrative material.

Whybray contends that the servant does not point to a specific "institution" of prophet-disciples in Jerusalem with which all his readers were familiar, whereas McKenzie suggests that a school of disciples were in existence and that the readers were to draw upon their acquaintance with that school in order to understand the metaphors. The use of *limmûdhîm* presupposes some kind of educational process, but whether the term should be rendered substantively or adjectivally is difficult to decide. Since *limmûdh* was not a common term either in Isaiah or in any of the biblical writings, and since it most likely designates a group gathered around Isaiah in 8:16, the implication is that this term suggested a recognizable group to the readers. The most that should be concluded is that there was a recognizable category of persons in Israel known as "taught ones" who were known to have facility in speaking and attentive listening. The *limmûdhîm* in 8:16 and 50:4 were a group gathered around a master in such a way that they were referred to by an intimate possessive ("my disciples," Isa 8:16) and that their relationship was characterized by some kind of educational process which accentuated speaking and listening (Isa 50:4).

3. Isaiah 54:13

The prophecy in Isa 54:13 notes that the sons of Zion will be directly instructed by the Lord: "All your sons are instructed by Yahweh (*limmûdhê YHWH*), and great is the prosperity of your sons."[30] The context does not indicate the content of the teaching, but to say "God-taught" is not much different than to say "disciple of God," especially when the two prior uses of *limmûdh* in Isaiah are kept in mind. The prophetic picture of sons of Zion being characterized as "God-taught" is the same as saying that they are God's disciples.[31]

---

[29] Whybray, *Intellectual Tradition*, p. 37.
[30] Translation by McKenzie, *Second Isaiah*, p. 138.
[31] The RSV and NASB give "disciples" as a possible translation in their respective margins.

Rengstorf strongly emphasizes that this relationship is the ideal in Israel. All of Israel is ideally to be in an intimate discipleship relation with Yahweh, by whom they are taught directly (cf. Jer 31:34). Rengstorf declares that this ideal excludes other master-disciple relationships.[32] But the prior uses of *limmûdh* in Isaiah indicate that there was evidence of such relationships among the prophets. In addition, the single use of *talmîdh* (1 Chron 25:8) in the Old Testament also designates some type of disciple or apprentice relationship. Therefore, even though "disciple" terminology is rare in the Old Testament, the use of *talmîdh* and *limmûdh* suggests at least some evidence of master-disciple relationships in Israel.

III. The Concept of Master-Disciple Relations in the Old Testament

A) Statement of Problem

1. The concept of discipleship in the Old Testament

Rengstorf hesitates to see any concept of a master-disciple relationship in the Old Testament partly because he perceives an absence of discipleship terminology, partly because he understands discipleship as falling into an either/or dichotomy (it is either a discipleship of the Sophistic and Rabbinic models, or discipleship of Israel to Yahweh), and partly because he thinks that discipleship to a person necessarily preempts the place of the covenant relationship between God and Israel. Once again Rengstorf has fallen prey to the faulty linguistic presupposition to which Barr calls attention: *concept history* is not necessarily equivalent to the *history of terminology*. As was demonstrated in the previous chapter, the concept of discipleship in the Greek world was not primarily determined by the terminology, but by the contextual purpose of the author. Likewise, in the Old Testament world the concept of discipleship derives from the perceived needs and purposes of the people involved, not from the terminology. Simply because certain terms are similar in meaning to those found in the Greek world does not mean that the same types of discipleship will occur. Evidences of the concept may be aided by an analysis of the terminlogy, but other criteria must be examined as well. The relative absence of disciple terminology in the Old Testament should not be taken as a lack of the concept, and the type of concept needs to be delineated by the use of the terms in context as well as other evidences.

---

[32] Rengstorf, "μαθητής," pp. 430-431.

Rengstorf's hesitations are unnecessary. In the first place, although there is a significant lack of discipleship terminology, it is not entirely absent. The use of *talmîdh* and *limmûdh* indicates some kind of learning and training and personal relationship in Israel from a master to a pupil / disciple. Also, the comparative lack of terminology should not be the primary reason for suggesting a corresponding lack of the concept being found. This is exemplified in the New Testament, because few would want to exclude the concept from the life of the church represented in the New Testament epistles, yet the term μαθητής does not occur outside the Gospels and Acts. In the second place, discipleship should not, and indeed cannot, be limited to the either/or dichotomy of the Sophistic and Rabbinic models, or the "Israel to Yahweh" model. Several types of discipleship relationships occurred in ancient Greece, and even in later Israel, which followed a model determined by the master and the goals of the relationship, not by conformity to preestablished terminology or previous master-disciple models. Further, even though discipleship in the early church did not follow the Sophistic or Rabbinic model, and even though the term μαθητής was not used in the epistles to the churches, a form of discipleship was in evidence nonetheless (especially centered on μιμεῖσθαι). Therefore, a working model for this chapter suggests that even though the terms for disciple are not found in abundance in the Old Testament, various relationships in Israel were true "discipleship" relations since they share universal characteristics of discipleship relations (e.g., learning, commitment to one person or teaching, personal life involvement).

Since the terms for "disciple" give some indication of discipleship relations, other means may help give further evidence of the concept. One such possible means is the recent employment of sociological tools as an aid to understanding the Biblical cultural milieu. Even though this type of study is in the beginning stages in the Old Testament (and in the New Testament), it provides another means of delineating whether or not master-disciple relations were in evidence. The rest of this chapter therefore, will be devoted to a brief sociological-exegetical analysis of various relationships within Israel.

2. Group discipleship relations

The issues to be addressed in this section are raised by the following questions: Do the various groups found in the Old Testament participate in a discipleship organization, can they actually be called "disciples," and what is the function of these groups in the Old Testament?

---

[33] Sigmund Mowinckel, *Psalmenstudien*, I-VI (1921-1924).

The appearance of prophetic groups, scribes, and the entire wisdom corpus provokes immediate images of schools, a formal educational process, and a continuing institution in Israel perpetuating scribal and literary arts. Are these accurate images? Can they be referred to as groups of disciples? Two other groups, the priestly order and the judges, present interesting possibilities as well, but space and time limitations prevent examination here. In the priestly order there is a fixed hereditary order, but what is the exact nature of the way in which future generations are prepared for service? Can their preparation be called a type of discipleship? This may broaden the parameters inordinately so that discipleship is only another word for "education," but such preparation might present a possibility nonetheless. In addition, what of the relationship of the prophets to the priests and the so-called temple cult? This is an entire area of study which was introduced by S. Mowinckel's third volume of his *Psalmenstudien*, entitled *Kultusprophetie und prophetische Psalmen*.[33] This issue will be touched upon in this chapter, but it is far too involved for an exhausive treatment here. In another direction, the judges bear many similarities to the prophets, and, in fact, some have suggested that the prophets find their origin in the judges,[34] but the judges will have to remain a future project. The major groups remain the scribes, the wise men, and the prophets, and it is to the latter that attention will now be given.

B) The Prophets

1. The prophets associated with Saul and Samuel

The first evidence of a group of prophets in the Old Testament is found during the days of Samuel. In 1 Sam 10:5-10 a "group" or "band" (*chebhel*) of prophets encounters Saul as was prophecied by Samuel. In contrast to *cheber* ("gang," Hos 6:9), *chebhel*, most likely signifies an organized band of prophets.[35] Another group appears in 1 Sam 19:20-24, a "company" or "band" (*lahᵃqath*) of prophets over whom Samuel was presiding. The range of opinions concerning the nature of these prophetic groups around Samuel is quite broad, ranging from seeing them as ecstatic, communal societies,[36] to seeing them as sedate schools for

---

[34] E.g., V. Eppstein, "Was Saul Also Among the Prophets?," *ZAW* 81 (1969), 287-304, who refers to the genuine Israelite prophet as a "judge-prophet" (pp. 290ff.).

[35] H. J. Fabry, "*chbhl*," *TDOT*, IV, eds. G. J. Botterweck and H. Ringgren, trans. D. E. Green (1975-1977; Grand Rapids: Eerdmans, 1980), p. 178.

[36] Johannes Lindblom, *Prophecy in Ancient Israel* (Oxford: Blackwell, 1962), pp. 69-70.

aspiring prophets.[37] In spite of the meager information about these groups, many have conjectured (often far beyond the actual data) as to their origin, their relation to each other, their relation to Samuel,and their function and purpose.

As to the origin of these prophetic groups around Samuel, no clue is given in Scripture. While the prophetic ministry in Israel was quite ancient, it was not a widespread phenomenon and it was associated with specific individuals.[38] Groups of prophets are found for the first time around Samuel. Since Samuel seems to be the transition point from the judges to the prophets (cf. 1 Sam 7:6; 15:7 with 1 Sam 3:20) some have suggested that he gathered these prophets together and became their leader in an attempt to preserve the amphictyonic supervision which the prophetic office enjoyed.[39] This would account for the origin of these prophets and explain their relation to Samuel, but the lack of evidence for the theory has rendered it a serious blow.[40] The most that can be said of the origin of these groups is that they seem to have arisen at a time when the whole prophetic ministry was on the ascendency.

The relation of the two groups of prophets around Samuel is a puzzling issue. Even though the descriptive nouns differ which are used to denote the groups (*chebhel* and *lah^aqath*), and the forms of the root for "prophet" differ (one is hithpael and the other niphal) their identity as *n^ebhi^'im* is never questioned.[41] The differences evident in the groups may be incidental, or it may be that the period of approximately thirty-five years which transpired between accounts reflect a change of emphasis within the group.[42] Some suggest that the two nouns specify two different groups; one had passed from the scene and another had arisen. But the

---

[37] Hobart E. Freeman, *An Introduction to the Old Testament Prophets* (Chicago: Moody, 1968), pp. 33-34.

[38] Robert R. Wilson, *Prophecy and Society in Ancient Israel* (Philadelphia: Fortress, 1980), pp. 300-301.

[39] For this basic position see, William F. Albright, "Samuel and the Beginnings of the Prophetic Movement," The Goldenson Lecture of 1961, in *Interpreting the Prophetic Tradition: The Goldenson Lectures 1955-1966,* The Library of Biblical Studies, ed. H. O. Orlinsky (New York: Hebrew Union College, 1969), pp. 157ff.

[40] For discussion and criticism of this position see R. E. Clements, *Prophecy and Tradition* (Atlanta: John Knox, 1975), pp. 9-14, 22-23.

[41] Gerhard Friedrich, "προφήτης," *TDNT*, VI, trans. and ed. Geoffrey W. Bromiley (Grand Rapids: Eerdmans, 1968), pp. 799-800.

[42] J. Porter suggests that the change in form from hithpael to niphal reflects a change of prophetic activity from "expression by ecstasy" to "expression by intelligible speech" (J. R. Porter, "The Origins of Prophecy in Israel," in *Israel's Prophetic Tradition: Essays in Honour of Peter R. Ackroyd*, ed. R. Coggins, A. Phillips, and M. Knibb [Cambridge: Cambridge University Press, 1982], pp. 23-24). But this cannot apply, because both forms occur at once in 1 Sam 19:20-21.

fact that Samuel is connected with both incidents gives at least some support for seeing them as basically the same group.[43]

The relationship of Samuel to these groups is another problematic
issue, but the phrase ʿômèdh niṭṣàbh (1Sam 19:20) indicates that he was
standing in a position of authority over them.[44] This phrase has been
traditionally interpreted to mean that this was an actual school for the
prophets and that Samuel, as the leading prophetic figure, was a sort of
mentor in the prophetic ministry. Some go so far as to try to determine
the structure of the school, the teaching emphasis, and the location in a
school building, but usually these arguments are based on the term
nàwôth,[45] which occurs throughout 1 Sam 19:18-20:1, but only here in the
Old Testament. The term nàwôth has been subjected to serious examination in recent years, and the evidence leans, not toward it referring to an
actual structured school, but toward seeing it as a term for a ''camp
area.'' The meaning of the term has been clarified by comparison to the
''Akkadian nawum, 'pasturage, steppe,' which at Mari refers to the
encampments of West Semitic nomadic or seminomadic tribes.''[46] This
gives some evidence then that this prophetic group lived in shepherd
camps pitched outside the city. The scene suggests a group of prophets
engaged in some sort of mutual prophetic ministry, and Samuel exercising authority over the group while they prophesied. Although this is not
a school of prophets as such, i.e., they do not appear to be in training,
they are gathered around a respected master prophet who exercises
authority over them. This may be termed a mentor role over the other
prophets, but these points of clarification need to be remembered.

Samuel's authority over the group may contribute to an understanding
of the purpose and function of the group. Samuel did not inherit his prophetic office, but rather was called by God to perform a prophetic
ministry at a crucial point in the life of the nation. Although he appears
to be the leading prophetic figure, this does not exclude the concurrent
ministry of other prophets; God raised up other prophets to minister at
this same crisis period. These groups (or one group) were prophets in
their own right, also called by God to a prophetic ministry. Samuel is

---

[43] This is in distinction from Macrae, who says that they are different groups; cf. A.
A. Macrae, ''Prophets and Prophecy,'' *The Zondervan Pictorial Encyclopedia of the Bible*, ed.
Merrill C. Tenney, 5 vols. (Grand Rapids: Zondervan, 1975), IV, 298.

[44] P. Kyle McCarter, Jr., *I Samuel, AB*, vol. 8 (Garden City, N. Y.: Doubleday, 1980),
p. 329.

[45] E. g., C. F. Keil and F. Delitzsch, *Biblical Commentary on the Books of Samuel*, trans.
James Martin, *Commentary on the Old Testament in Ten Volumes*, (n.d.; rpt.; Grand Rapids:
Eerdmans, 1975), II, 199-206; Leon Wood, *The Prophets of Israel*, (Grand Rapids: Baker,
1979), pp. 164-166; Freeman, *Prophets*, pp. 28-34.

[46] McCarter, *1 Samuel*, pp. 328-329.

aware of their activities and exercises authority over them, but whether it is an authority of position, or an organizational authority which was exercised in a group (worship?) setting, cannot be determined with certainty. They are nowhere described as pupils, or students, or apprentices, or servants, or any such terminology which would imply a training role. Rather, they are simply designated a "group" or "band" of prophets. There is nothing in the terminology or context to assume that they are becoming prophets, or that they are followers of prophets; they are simply designated as a group of prophets. The characteristics which are often distinguished as "school" features would be explained better by seeing this as a "fellowship" of prophets who are associated together as one body. The significance of this distinction is that if the relationship between Samuel and the group of prophets is to be called "discipleship," it must be clear that it is not a training type discipleship. It is best to clarify that these groups of prophets were raised up by God to meet the needs of the nation for prophetic activity even as was Samuel. They are full prophets engaged in a prophetic fellowship rather than students who were following a prophet or learning from one. If this understanding of the equal status of the concept of the prophets is kept in mind, then this group of prophets might be called *guilds* as Rengstorf suggests,[47] but the authority factor of Samuel over them indicates a mentor who gives guidance to the less authoritative. Such a relationship can certainly be denoted "discipleship."

2. The sons of the prophets

The next group associated with prophets are called the "sons of the prophets" ($b^e n\hat{e}$ $hann^e b\hat{i}\,{}^\gamma\hat{\imath}m$). This description is found only in the books of 1 and 2 Kings (1 Kings 20:35; 2 Kings 2:3, 5, 7, 15; 4:1, 38; 5:22; 6:1; 9:1), and there only with reference to the Northern Kingdom. It is identified particularly with the prophetic activities of Elisha. The expression "$b\dot{e}n$..." or "$b^e n\hat{e}$..." is a common Semitic expression to refer to membership in certain social and professional groups, as well as to classify men individually in different groups according to ethical and moral standards.[48] The expression "sons of the prophets" falls into the category of the "professional group."[49]

---

[47] Rengstorf, "μαθητής," p. 428. The use of term "guilds" is appropriate, but Rengstorf confuses the issue by not distinguishing between the "bands" and the "sons" of the prophets.

[48] H. Haag, "$b\dot{e}n$," *TDOT*, II, ed. G. Johannes Botterweck and Helmer Ringgren, trans. John T. Willis (1972; rev. ed.; Grand Rapids: Eerdmans, 1977), pp. 152-153.

[49] Ibid., p. 152.

In the same way that the "bands of prophets" appeared only during a relatively short period in the lifetime of Samuel, the "sons of the prophets" appeared about two hundred years later only during the lifetimes of Elijah and Elisha. Many scholars make no clear distinction between the "'bands" and the "sons" of the prophets,[50] but such a distinction appears to be necessary. In the first place the titles are different and there is a time lapse of about two hundred years intervening with no recorded connection. Secondly, the prophetic group(s) in the days of Samuel were a relatively small group manifesting restricted, ecstatic, prophetic activities and were restricted to a compact geographical area, while the phrase "sons of the prophets" appears to be a "technical expression for the followers of Elisha, under whom a prophetic movement was organized on a national basis...to resist the religious policy of the Omrides and Jezebel in particular."[51] Similarities found between the prophets around Samuel and those in the time of Elisha no doubt appear because both groups are connected with prophetic activity, but these similarities should not be pressed too far. A theme necessary to apply again is that the prophetic activity occurs in response to the call of God during a crisis of Israel's history. Therefore, once the activities of the prophets of Samuel's day were carried out, the prophets passed from the scene until the next major period of prophetic activity, which was with Elijah, Elisha, and the "sons of the prophets." There is no recorded historical continuity between these two groups;[52] therefore it is best not to draw lines of continuity which can only be argued from silence. The most that can be said is that the "bands of prophets" were the most primitive form of a *guild* of prophets in Israel, and it is possible that this became a professional guild as time unfolded. This possibly suggests that the professional class may have been at odds with the prophet God caused to arise for a special time, *if* the professional guild had become so rigidly institutionalized that it was insensitive to the voice of Yahweh. Sensitivity to the voice of Yahweh was a hallmark of the prophet.[53]

---

[50] E.g., Rengstorf, "μαθητής," p. 428; cf. also Lindblom, *Prophecy in Ancient Israel*, pp. 69-70, Klaus Koch, *The Prophets: Volume I, The Assyrian Period*, trans. M. Kohl (Philadelphia: Fortress, 1983), pp. 24-25.

[51] Porter, "Origins of Prophecy," p. 19; cf. also Wilson, *Prophecy and Society*, p. 141.

[52] Although the books of Samuel and Kings do mention individual prophets operating throughout the intervening centuries.

[53] Freeman (*Prophets*, p. 31) argues to the contrary, that the large number of prophets in the time of Elijah and Elisha, plus their more rigid organization, is "strong evidence for the uninterrupted continuance of those schools from the time of Samuel." If there was an uninterrupted continuation of the prophets, and if it became a professional guild in Israel, this would be some support for the existence of the so-called 'cultic prophets,' to whom modern scholarship has given so much attention in recent years.

The characteristics of the "sons of the prophets" are more fully revealed than were those of the "bands" of prophets. They appear to have a more rigidly organized structure, with communal practices, the capability of coordinated social action and some kind of a hierarchical structure.[54] The important question here is, once again, could these "sons of the prophets" be considered "disciples"? This question may be answered by delineating their function and purpose.

E. J. Young suggests that the sons of the prophets were "assistants" to the great prophets Elijah and Elisha "in making known the will of God at this particular time to the nation."[55] He especially emphasizes the term "son" as signifying a close and intimate relationship, best described by the concept "discipleship."[56] He stresses that this form of relationship was apparently not present in the groups of prophets around Samuel, but, with the public and royal opposition which existed in the days of Elijah and Elisha, the prophets and sons of the prophets were forced together in carrying out their prophetic activity. The reason they are called "sons" is because they are dependent on the great prophets as their spiritual fathers.[57] Josephus also interprets the relationship between Elisha and the "sons of the prophets" as a discipleship relation, because, when he comments on the passage where Elisha sits in his own house with the "elders" in front of him, he refers to them as "disciples" (μαθηταί; *Antiquities* 9:68). When Elisha sends one of the "sons of the prophets" on a holy errand, Josephus calls the individual a "disciple" (μαθητής, *Antiquities* 9:106). The latter passage is directly applicable since in the Hebrew text the "one sent" is one of the "sons of the prophets" (cf. 2 Kings 9:1), but the former passage is more likely a misinterpretation of the text by Josephus, since the ones he calls μαθηταί are actually "the elders" (*hazqēnîm*, cf. 2 Kings 6:32, unless he has interpolated the "sons of the prophets" of 4:38 into a wrong context). Hengel agrees with this interpretation, because he refers to the sons of the prophets sitting before Elisha in 2 Kings 4:38 as "disciples" in a teacher-pupil relationship.[58]

R. Wilson would also agree with much of Young's suggestion, but he describes the relationship from a sociological perspective. He also suggests that these prophets began outside the favor of the leadership of the nation. Once they had moved out of favor they became peripheral individuals, forced out of the leading institutions. Wilson then goes on to say that,

[54] Wilson, *Prophecy and Society*, pp. 202-203.
[55] E. J. Young, *My Servants the Prophets* (Grand Rapids: Eerdmans, 1955), p. 94.
[56] Ibid., p. 93.
[57] Ibid., pp. 92-94.
[58] Hengel, *Charismatic Leader*, pp. 17-18.

After having prophetic experiences, these individuals joined the group, which was under the leadership of Elisha. In the group they found mutual support and were encouraged to use prophecy to bring about changes in the social order. In addition to supporting its regular members, the group also functioned as Elisha's support group and may well have been responsible for preserving and elaborating the legends about him.[59]

The striking feature of Wilson's suggestion is that the group functions as a "support group." The group supports one another and the leader Elisha, and the leader in turn supports the group through his leadership. Could it be, perhaps, that some of the relationship shared between Elijah and Elisha acted as a model for the sons of the prophets? In this direction L. Goppelt makes reference to the call of Elisha and says, "Such a call did not lead to the establishment of a school, but rather to a fundamentally new form of fellowship."[60] Goppelt does not develop his intriguing statement to say so, but the implication is that instead of establishing a school for prophets, Elisha patterned his relationship with the "sons of the prophets" on the relationship which transpired between himself and Elijah. The relationship functioned as a new model for discipleship: fellowship as a basis for carrying out the prophetic activity.

The above suggestions potentially explain the functions of the sons of the prophets, but some clarification is in order. First, Young's emphasis, that the term "sons" describes an intimate relationship, is appealing, but it does not fit the Old Testament data. The term could hold that connotation, and in the appropriate context it does, but it normally has a broader meaning: it signifies more of a professional guild.[61] In addition, the title ʾābh, "Father," is never used by the sons of the prophets to refer to Elisha.[62] Elisha called out to Elijah as ʾābh, and this would more securely establish the intimate relationship of that pair in discipleship, but not the sons of the prophets. Interestingly, a targum on 2 Kings 2:12 changes Elisha's cry to Elijah from "my father" to "my rabbi."[63] Second, the sons of the prophets were already in existence as a group prior to Elisha beginning his own separate prophetic ministry (cf. 1 Kings 20:35), and appear to have been so for some period of time. Hence, they were not rejected individuals joining his company, but rather as a group they

---

[59] Wilson, *Prophecy and Society*, p. 202.

[60] Leonhard Goppelt, *Theology of the New Testament*, Vol. 1, trans. J. A. Alsup, ed. J. Roloff (Grand Rapids: Eerdmans, 1981), p. 209, and n. 6.

[61] Haag, "*bēn*," pp. 152-153.

[62] Cf. Porter, "Origins of Prophecy," pp. 19-20, who also uses this datum to indicate the discontinuity between the prophets in Samuel's day and those in Elisha's.

[63] Cited in J. T. Forestell, *Targumic Traditions and the New Testament: An Annotated Bibliography with a New Testament Index*, Society of Biblical Literature: Aramaic Studies No. 4 (Chico, California: Scholar's Press, 1979), p. 78, note on Mt 23:8-10.

came into contact with Elisha in the course of his activities. H. L. Ellison suggests that during the course of Elisha's separate prophetic ministry certain sons of the prophets were sympathetic to God's work through him and came to join forces with him.[64] Along with this, at the departure of Elijah the sons of the prophets spoke of "*your* master" being taken away "from over *you* today" when they questioned Elisha about the departure (2 Kings 2:3).[65] Elijah is not *their* master, and he is not over *them*. The sons of the prophets had as yet not joined forces with Elisha, but they were already known to each other. Apparently they were already functioning as prophets and later would be associated with Elisha. Third, once they were in some kind of joint prophetic endeavor the sons showed great respect for Elisha by "sitting before" him (2 Kings 4:38) and obeying his directives (2 Kings 6:1; 9:1), but they still retained a sense of independence because they continued to carry on their own prophetic ministry. They were not in a trainee status, but were functioning prophets who respected Elisha as a prophet worthy of respect.

With these qualifications in mind, the suggestions by Young and Wilson are helpful for understanding the function of the sons of the prophets. The sons of the prophets were already performing a prophetic ministry when Elisha undertook his own ministry, but it appears that they soon recognized the powerful way that Yahweh was using him and they joined forces with him. They submitted themselves to his leadership authority and followed his lead while they continued to perform their own prophetic activity. The company which resulted was centered around mutual encouragement and support in carrying out prophetic activities. Even as Elisha had been raised up for a specific ministry during a crisis period in the history of the nation and passed from the scene without leaving a prophetic institution once that ministry was performed, so too the sons of the prophets were raised up for that crisis ministry and once that was fulfilled they left without a trace.

The relationship between Samuel and the bands of prophets appears to be quite similar to that of Elisha and the sons of the prophets. There is a degree of authority of Elisha over these prophets, and they appear to follow his leadership, but at the same time they are not prophets-in-training. When they join forces with Elisha they are already a group. With these qualifications in mind the relationship may be designated a form of discipleship, but caution is suggestion. One must not imply that discipleship means that these "sons" were in training to become pro-

[64] H. L. Ellison, *The Prophets of Israel: From Ahijah to Hosea* (Grand Rapids: Eerdmans, 1969), pp. 37-38.
[65] Italics mine.

phets. It appears that some of them had been prophets for quite some time; they were far from novices. Yet as they submitted themselves to the leadership of the man of God, they were led more intimately into the will of God in the expression of their own prophetic ministry.

C) The Scribes

The existence of scribes (*sōph^erîm*) in the Old Testament offers another significant focal point for testing Rengstorf's thesis that Old Testament Israelite society did not have master-disciple relationships. This section will examine the biblical data concerning the scribes, which may be divided into two periods for convenience and emphasis: the pre-exilic scribes and the post-exilic scribes.

1. Pre-exilic scribes

The term *sōphèr* was used to designate a variety of individuals in pre-exilic Israel. *Sōphèr* was used to refer to families who were members of a craft engaged in preserving the art of writing.[66] 1 Chron 2:55 speaks of certain families of the Kenites dwelling at Jabez who were referred to as *sōph^erîm*, and may indicate that the earliest scribal guilds were found in family units,[67] where the art of writing was passed on from father to son. It is possible that these families instructed suitable priests and Levites, who in turn instructed the people in the law and made legal rulings based upon the law and the legal tradition.[68]

The term was also used to denote individuals who were considered skillful and dexterious writers. Baruch, the amanuensis of Jeremiah, was a *sōphèr* (Jer 36:32), and in Jer 8:8 the *sōphèr* is mentioned in conjunction with the instrument which most characterized him: the pen. The metaphor in Ps 45:2[1] refers to the psalmist's tongue as the pen of a "dexterious writer" (*sōphèr māhîr*). This is the most common sense of the term *sōphèr*, one who is especially skilled at writing, a secretary.[69]

---

[66] Norman Hillyer, "*sōphèr*, Scribe," *NIDNTT*, III, trans. and ed. Colin Brown (Grand Rapids: Zondervan, 1978), p. 478.

[67] Ibid.; Jacob M. Myers, *1 Chronicles*, *AB*, vol. 12 (1965; 2d. ed.; Garden City, New York: Doubleday and Company, 1974), p. 16.

[68] Martin Hengel, *Judaism and Hellenism: Studies in their Encounter in Palestine during the Early Hellenistic Period*, 2 vols., trans. John Bowden, WUNT 10 (2d. ed.; Philadelphia: Fortress, 1974), p. 78. Hengel (*Judaism and Hellenism*, II, p. 53 n. 159) and Myers, (*1 Chronicles*, p. 16) both note that the 1 Chron. 2:55 passage is disputed, but they nonetheless propose the above interpretation.

[69] McKane, *Prophets and Wise Men*, pp. 33-34.

Sōphēr was also the term used to designate Levitical scribes during the monarchy who were involved in various aspects of temple organization: e.g., recording priestly assignments (1 Chron 24:6) and keeping fiscal records for temple repairs (2 Kings 12:10; 2 Chron 34:13). Deut 17:18 implies that the furnishing of written copies of the law was to be the responsibility of the Levitical priests.[70] This close association of the scribes and the priests is illustrated in Samuel, who, as a Levitical priest (1 Chron 6: 26, 33) also acted as a scribe by writing the ordinances of the kingdom and placing them before the Lord.[71] W. Eichrodt suggests that by the time of Josiah (2 Chron 34:13) the 'scribal office' was a privilege of the Levites.[72]

In close proximity to the verb *sāphar*, "to count", *sōphēr* was also used of an enumerator or muster-officer in the military.[73] R. Boling indicates a possible connection with the Akkadian verb *saparu*, "to rule,"[74] and in this sense *sōphēr* came to denote a high ranking military leader of Israel, somewhat analogous to a present day Secretary of State of War[75] (Judg 5:14; 2 Kings 25:19 par. Jer 52:25).

The term *sōphēr* was also used of a variety of government officials in Israel. Jonathan, David's uncle, was "a counselor, a man of understanding, and a scribe (*sōphēr*)" (1 Chron 27:32), indicating that he was one of "a professional class whose members are distinguished by their mental habits and who serve in high places in the government and administration."[76] Even more technically, *sōphēr* also, according to W. McKane, designated a political official of the highest rank in the the royal government of Israel. The associations with 'skilled in writing' are still to be recognized in the term, but only in a most basic sense. This *sōphēr* had to master those skills at the beginning of his training, but he advanced beyond them to a high level governing and administrative office within the royal administration.[77] In the official listings of the

---

[70] Cf., Hillyer, "*sōphēr*," p. 478; Walther Eichrodt, *Theology of the Old Testament*, 2 vols., trans. J. A. Baker, *The Old Testament Library* (6th German ed.; Philadelphia: Westminster, 1961), I, 417 and n. 2.

[71] Cf. Eichrodt, *Theology of the Old Testament*, I, 417. During the reign of Jehoshaphat the Levites accompanied the priests throughout the land of Judah with the law of the Lord and taught the people (2 Chron 17: 8-9), accompanied the priests to judge the people in Jerusalem (2 Chron 19:8, 11), and also accompanied the priests while they were "guardians" of the king (2 Chron 23:7-8).

[72] Hengel, *Judaism and Hellenism*, I, 78.

[73] Brown, Driver, Briggs, *Lexicon*, pp. 707-708.

[74] Robert G. Boling, *Judges*, AB, vol. 6A (Garden City, New York: Doubleday and Company, 1975), p. 112.

[75] McKane, *Prophets and Wise Men*, pp. 22-23.

[76] Ibid., p. 18.

[77] See the extended discussion by McKane (ibid., pp. 23-47).

THE OLD TESTAMENT BACKGROUND

leading members of David and Solomon's ecclesiastical, civil, and military cabinets (2 Sam 8:16-18; 20:23-25; 1 Kings 4:1-6), the *sōphēr* is one of the highest political figures, and as such is a "Secretary," analogous to a present day "Secretary of State" or the equivalent.[78] If the cabinet listings are in order, at the time of David the king's scribe ranked below the military commander, recorder, and the high priest, but above the palace priests; by Josiah's reign the scribe preceded the recorder as well as the governor of the city (1 Kings 22:3-13; 2 Chron 34:8-21).[79]

2. Post-exilic scribes

What has been referred to as the "great period of the *sōphᵉrîm*" began with Ezra on the return of the people of Israel from exile.[80] The book of Ezra marks a turning point in the history of the *sōphᵉrîm*.[81] The pre-exilic sense of 'scribe' as a title for a royal official is attributed to Ezra in the official decree in Ezra 7:12-26: "Ezra the priest, the scribe of the law of the God of heaven." But alongside this earlier use are found the statements that Ezra was "a scribe skilled (*sōphēr māhîr*) in the law of Moses, which the Lord God of Israel had given" (Ezra 7:6), and "Ezra the priest, the scribe (*sōphēr*), learned in the words of the commandments of the Lord and His statutes to Israel" (Ezra 7:11).

> With Ezra the picture of a scribe takes on more and more the features of a scholar and an expert in the sacred law. In his case it is emphasized by the word skilled, ... —suggesting a quickness of grasp and ease of movement amid this complex material which was the fruit of the devoted study described in [Ezra 7] verse 10.[82]

The reason for this transition in scribal practice is usually attributed to an increasingly centralized place of the law among the exiled people of Israel where the cultic practices were severely limited.[83] The scribe, who

---

[78] Ibid., pp. 17-21.

[79] Hillyer, "*sōphēr*," p. 478. In the listings of Solomon's officials the *sōphᵉrîm* are listed second under the priest (1 Ki 4:1-6).

[80] Hengel, *Judaism and Hellenism*, I, 79.

[81] Joachim Jeremias, "γραμματεύς," *TDNT*, I (Grand Rapids: Eerdmans, 1964), p. 740 and n. 5.

[82] Derek Kidner, *Ezra and Nehemiah: An Introduction and Commentary*, *TOTC* (Downers Grove, Illinois: InterVarsity, 1979), p. 62. McKane (*Prophets and Wise Men*, pp. 34-36) also suggests that the phrase *sōphēr māhîr* properly meant "dexterous writer" in pre-exilic usage as was noted above, but with Ezra the meaning indicates a technical association with the Torah, and therefore should be rendered "skillful scholar."

[83] Cf., Eichrodt, *Theology of the Old Testament*, I, 401-402; II, 250-251; Jacob M. Myers, *Ezra-Nehemiah*, AB, vol. 14 (Garden City, New York: Doubleday and Company, 1965), pp. lviii-lix.

was recognized as having an important official position in pre-exilic Israel, became the spokesman for warning and exhorting the people in post-exilic Israel.[84] Ezra, as priest and scribe, symbolizes the close connection between the priesthood and the scribe,[85] and with the failure of the priests to teach the law (Mal 2:6-9), he is representative of the scribes who took a central place in the life of the nation through their teaching of Torah.[86]

One major difficulty with tracing the training of scribes in this period is that, besides Ezra, the only other scribe mentioned is Zadok (Neh 13:13), who was listed with the priest and the Levites as being given charge over the temple storehouses after the second return of Nehemiah to Jerusalem. Nothing more is said of his role, nor of his lineage,[87] so it is impossible to speak with certainty as to whether he was a scribe in the pre-exilic sense, or in the sense which Ezra exemplified. Therefore, information concerning the post-exilic scribes is essentially limited to Ezra.

3. The existence of scribal schools as a possible source for master-disciple relationships

A striking feature in the study of Old Testament education is the absence of explicit references to schools. Rengstorf noted this absence, and linked with the perceived omission of references to "disciples," became the basis for declaring an absence of master-disciple relationships in the Old Testament. Several recent studies have acknowledged this lack of explicit reference, but have pointed to 'allusions' or 'implicit references' to schools.[88] F. Golka has criticized some of these studies which, he says, since the work of A. Klostermann in 1908 ("Schulwesen im alten Israel"), have issued in a deceptive "*Konsens der Wissenschaft*" which assumes as an established fact the reconstruction of schools in ancient Israel, even though the biblical data is absent.[89] The entire issue

---

[84] Eichrodt, *Theology of the Old Testament*, I, 402; Myers, *Ezra-Nehemiah*, pp. lviii-lix.

[85] Hillyer, "*sôphér*," p. 479.

[86] Kidner, *Ezra and Nehemiah*, p. 26.

[87] The name Zadok is mentioned four times in Nehemiah, with at least two individuals involved: 3:4, Zadok, the son of Baana; 3:29, Zadok, the son of Immer; 10:21, a person named Zadok sealed the covenant; 13:13, Zadok the scribe. The relationship of the latter two to the former cannot be determined, although one or the other may be the same.

[88] E.g., Hans-Jürgen Hermisson, *Studien zur israelitischen Spruchweisheit*, WMANT 28 (Neukirchen-Vluyn: Neukirchener, 1968), p. 192; André Lemaire, *Les écoles et la formation de la Bible dans l'ancien Israël* (Fribourg / Göttingen: Universitaires / Vandenhoeck & Ruprecht, 1981), esp. pp. 34-41; Bernhard Lang, *Die weisheitliche Lehrrede: Eine Untersuchung von Sprüche 1-7*, Stuttgarter Bibelstudien 54 (Stuttgart: Kath. Bibelwerk; 1972), esp. pp. 36-46.

[89] F. Golka, "Die israelitische Weisheitsschule oder 'Des Kaisers neue Kleider'," pp. 257-258.

of schools and education in ancient Israel cannot be undertaken here, but the question of the existence of schools for scribes and wise men is relevant to the discussion of master-disciple relationships. Therefore, the present section will look at the "school" as a possible explanation for the existence of those referred to in the Old Testament as "the scribe". Later in this chapter a discussion of the "school" as a possible explanation for the existence of those referred to in the Old Testament as "wise men" will be undertaken. In the conclusion a comparison of the results of both sections will be given in an attempt to clarify the relationship between "the wise man" and "the scribe".

The discussion of "schools" as a possible source of scribal training begins with the attempt to account for the professional skills of the scribes. The *sôphêr* in pre-exilic times was an individual skilled in a fairly broad range of activities, but skill in writing, counting, and organization was basic to each. The post-exilic picture of Ezra as a *sôphêr* indicates a person skilled in an even broader range of activities. This skill is accounted for in various ways.

a) Family scribes

A point for which Golka contends,[90] and which others have recently stressed,[91] is that the Israelite family played a key role in the education of their young in almost all areas, ranging from common familial affairs to military training to religious education.[92] "One institution, the family, has remained a vital educational influence in Israel from biblical times to the present. The family educated the whole man, only delegating some of its responsibilities in periods of technical specialization."[93] Families educated their sons in occupational trades and these eventually developed into professional guilds which encompassed the extended family / clan. Even entire villages were noted for their specialization in a single trade (1 Chron 4:21-23).[94] Families of the Kenites appear to be among the first scribal guilds (1 Chron 2:55), and it is likely that the position of "the king's scribe" (2 Sam 8:17; 1 Chron 18:16; 1 Kings 4:3; cf. Ezra 2:55 and Neh 7:57) was passed along kinship lines. The family of Shaphan is a striking example in that they dominated the bureaucracy

---

[90] Ibid., pp. 263ff.

[91] E.g., Gerstenberger, "Covenant and Commandment," pp. 47-49; J. L. Crenshaw, "Prolegomenon," pp. 20-22; Murphy, "Wisdom—Theses and Hypotheses," p. 39.

[92] A. Demsky, "Education (Jewish) In the Biblical Period," *Encyclopedia Judaica* (Jerusalem, 1971), VI, col. 383-388.

[93] Ibid., col. 387.

[94] Cf. Roland de Vaux, *Ancient Israel: Its Life and Institutions*, trans. John McHugh (New York: McGraw-Hill, 1961), pp. 49-50.

and held the position of king's scribe from the time of Josiah until the Exile (2 Kings 22:3; Jer 36:11, 12, 20 21; 40:9).[95]

Scribes such as Baruch could have been trained by these families or the scribal profession could have been his own family profession. Baruch's brother, Seriah,[96] was a governmental official (*śar meṅûchȧh*) whose responsibilities allowed him to read aloud before the people the words of prophecy which Jeremiah gave to him (cf. Jer 51:59-64). It appears that both brothers were trained in the scribal practices of reading and writing.[97]

The hereditary nature of professions within the tribes of Israel indicates that the scribal art was basically passed on within families. Within the family the skill of writing was passed on from father to son, implying a teaching process. One of the distinctive features in the history of education in Israel, which set it apart from traditional scribal cultures of Egypt, Mesopotamia, and second-millenium Canaan, was the development of alphabetic writing. Israel's relatively simple alphabet made it much easier to learn to read and write, and therefore, "to be literate was no longer the identifying and exclusive characteristic of a class of professional scribes and priests, versed in the abstruse cuneiform and hieroglyphic scripts."[98] General education in reading and basic writing could therefore be passed on from father to son in almost any family. A. Cundall sees this illustrated in Judg 8:14, where a youth (*naʿar*) had the ability to write out the names of all the princes and elders of his home city, and Gideon, or someone of his army, was able to read them.[99]

But aside from basic literacy skills, the scribal family supplied the local scribe who was trained in the more technical scribal arts of epistolary and administrative formulae, such as mastering the forms of deeds of sale (Jer 32:10-14), marriage contracts (Tob. 7:13), bills of divorce (Deut 24:1-3; Isa 50:1; Jer 3:8), court pleas (an ostracon from *Mezad Hashavyahu*; Job 31:35), and the standard tax form of the monarchy (Samaria Ostraca; inscribed jar handles from Gibeon).[100] As the family groupings

---

[95] Demsky, "Education in the Biblical Period," col. 392.
[96] Both are described as *ben nêrîyȧh ben machsêyȧh*: Baruch in Jer. 36:4 and Seriah in Jer. 51:59.
[97] The scribal training of Seriah would be especially apparent if *śar meṅûchȧh* signifies a "quartermaster," as in the RSV, NEB, and NASB.
[98] Demsky, "Education in the Biblical Period," col. 391-2.
[99] Arthur E. Cundall, "Judges: An Introduction and Commentary," in *Judges, Ruth*, by Arthur E. Cundall, Leon Morris, *TOTC* (Downers Grove / London: Inter-Varsity, 1968), p. 118. Demsky ("Education in the Biblical Period," col. 392) speculates that perhaps the youth was a local scribe.
[100] Demsky, "Education in the Biblical Period", col. 392-393.

broadened into a guild of scribes, it is possible that groups of children were trained together by specialists within the guild. But in the above listing, nothing demands a "school" for aspiring scribes which could not be learned from one's own father.

b) Levitical scribes

Family training also seems to be the case with reference to training Levitical scribes. The most natural explanation of scribal training within the Levitical tribe would be from father to son, in much the same way as other priestly skills were learned and passed on. The Levitical scribe was skilled in epistolary and administrative formulae which were pertinent to his responsibilities within the temple; e. g., recording priestly assignments (1 Chron 24:6), keeping fiscal records for temple repairs (2 Kings 12:10; 2 Chron 34:13), and furnishing written copies of the law (Deut 17:18). The basics of these responsibilities could easily be learned within the family circle as the child stayed by the father's side throughout the day. More in-depth knowledge of scribal skills would be learned through experience and association with the other Levitical scribes as the apprentice began carrying out his trade.

The possibility of a person entering into a trade other than his family's is said to be illustrated in the the training of Samuel by Eli. Here Eli trained Samuel for priestly ministrations, and this has been suggested as an illustration of a priestly school into which parents enrolled their children (1 Sam 1-3). This is a possibility, but it is the exception rather than the rule,[101] and there is no explicit evidence of a school. Rather, the intimacy of Eli and Samuel is stressed, so that Samuel is the positive example of a son in antithesis to the negative example of Eli's own sons. The father-son example of training is a strong element in the story,[102] and tends to support the example of father-son training rather than school training. The most that this story might indicate is the possibility of one family arranging for a son to be trained in a profession outside of his own family profession, but even this training appears to be done within the context of father-son type education.

c) Royal scribes

The *sôphèr*, who was engaged in governmental, administrative tasks, or the one who was a military ruler, offers the most possibility for a

---

[101] The main emphasis is upon the exceptional nature of the incident, especially in the miraculous birth, the Nazaritic presentation, and the unique office of prophet to which Samuel was called in the vision; cf., McCarter, *1 Samuel*, pp. 60-101.

[102] Ibid.

specialized school for professional *sōphᵉrîm*. In these schools, which are usually suggested as being attached to the royal court,[103] students were trained in the art of writing and reading, but also in the advanced arts of national and international statesmanship or military tactics, respectively.[104] Relying upon examples from royal courts in Mesopotamia, Egypt, and Levant, some scholars have suggested that these court schools trained potential scribes to be the equivalent of "secretary of state" (2 Sam 8:16), royal advisers (1 Chron 27:32), experts in international law and treaty formulae (2 Chron 20:35-37), trade agreements (Ezek 27), and military expertise (Jer 36:10).[105]

Even here the comparison of the listings from the time of David to the time of Solomon reveals that the hereditary factor was an important ingredient in obtaining the highest level administrative, as well as priestly, positions. Elihoreph and Ahijah, the sons of Seraiah (Shisha)[106] inherited the scribal office, which was a high level governmental office, even as Azariah, son of Zadok, inherited the priestly office (cf. 2 Sam 8:17 and 1 Kings 4:2-3). The family of Shaphan is a striking example in that they dominated the bureaucracy and held the position of king's scribe from the time of Josiah until the Exile (2 Kings 22:3; Jer 36:11, 12, 20 21; 40:9).[107]

These examples offer evidence that family ties played a significant role in obtaining the office of scribe, and they may also have accounted for the training of the inherited office. As long as the scribal office was being passed through the family the most likely place for education to occur was in the family itself. One difficulty comes in trying to account for the family background of all the scribes. Very seldom is information given for the profession of the scribe's father, but what evidence there is usually points to an inherited office. This is in line with the inherited guild status of the local and Levitical scribes, and also reflects the normal practice of the family carrying on the trade whatever the profession. Because of this, it is best to suggest that the normal case for the royal scribe was to inherit his office, and the bulk of his training would be through the teaching of his family. Another difficulty comes in trying to account for all specializa-

---

[103] Lemaire, "Sagesse et écoles," pp. 275-281; McKane, *Prophets and Wise Men*, pp. 36-40.

[104] See especially McKane, *Prophets and Wise Men*, pp. 23-47.

[105] Lemaire, "Sagesse et écoles," pp. 275ff.; J. P. J. Olivier, "Schools and Wisdom Literature," *JNSL* IV (1975), 49-60.

[106] McKane (*Prophets and Wise Men*, pp. 18, 27 n. 4), suggests that there is a textual variant here, and that Seraiah is the same person as Shisha; cf. also James A. Montgomery, *A Critical and Exegetical Commentary on the Books of Kings*, ed. Henry S. Gehman, *ICC* (Edinburgh: T. & T. Clark, 1951), p. 118.

[107] Demsky, "Education in the Biblical Period," col. 392.

tion within the educational model from father to son, or within an extended family guild. The ''bulk'' of scribal training could come from such training, but as greater complexity within the profession was encountered beyond the skill of the family, specialists would be required to carry on the training.

The training of royalty may offer some insight into the educational process within the court. The young prince's first teacher was his mother (cf. 1 Kings 1-2; Prov 31:1-9), and she continued a strong influence throughout his lifetime.[108] In addition, the prince was strongly influenced by his father the king, who supervised the transfer of responsibilities (2 Kings 15:5; 2 Chron 21:2-3), and had his son serve in various capacities in a royal apprenticeship (2 Kings 15:5).[109] In addition to this family training, from the time of the Davidic monarchy there is some evidence of formal instruction for the king's sons by private tutors, both within the court (1 Chron 27:32),[110] and to whom sons were sent outside the court for specialized training (2 Kings 10:1ff.).[111] These examples might show the existence of schools within the court, but more likely point to a privilged status for sons of the king, who could afford the luxury, and who had such time demands on him that he needed to delegate some of the responsiblity for training his sons to others.

The primary training of the scribe in the royal court is explained most naturally through the teaching of his father. This includes both the most fundamental skills of writing and reading as well as the skills associated with a scribe of the royal court. There is no mention of teachers or tutors or schools for the scribal candidate, as was implied for the sons of the king. This does not rule out the possibility of a professional scribal school, but at this point the evidence for such a school is conjectural, whereas the hereditary factor offers at least inferential evidence for positing the training of scribes in pre-exilic Israel in the family structure, with specialized training occurring in the scribal guild.

d) Scribes of the Law

In his training as a priest in exile, Ezra (on the basis of the information available) must have been subject to concurrent training in literary as

---

[108] Ibid., col. 389.

[109] Demsky (ibid., col. 390-391) notes that several personal seals with the inscription *ben hammeledh* have been found in excavations around Palestine, and they point to their use by princes in minor administrative postitions in the royal government.

[110] Myers (*2 Chronicles*, pp. 185-186), understands the prepositional phrase (''with the king's sons'') to indicate that Jehiel (and Jonathan?, David's uncle), was in charge of the king's sons; i.e., in charge of their education and upbringing.

[111] Demsky, ''Education in the Biblical Period,'' col. 390.

well as statesmanship arts, because he acted not only as a priest, but also as a teacher of the law (Neh 8:1ff.) and as a politically influential figure (Ezra 7:1ff., 11ff., 25f.). With Ezra there seems to occur a centralization of activities which prior to him were performed by separate individuals. The efforts, of what would have been three different offices prior to the exile (priest, teacher, political leader), became focused in one individual during and after the exile: Ezra the priest-scribe-official leader. In addition, the destruction of the temple and the power of the royal court left such a void that educational efforts became centralized in the law, rather than being able to be diversified in the training for cultic ministrations or service in the kingdom. Idealized education in Israel now became centralized in one basic pursuit, the study of Torah, and Ezra was the individual who exemplified that centralization. Further, since the scribal office had been, in part, associated with the Levitical priesthood, and since the teaching of the law to the people was the responsibility of the priests (2 Chron 15:3) and the Levites (2 Chron 17:7-9), Ezra was a natural candidate for blending the responsibilities of the priest and the scribe in a lifelong study and teaching of Torah.

While there are indications of more focused educational processes, no explicit information regarding the education of Ezra occurs. Ezra's ancestors are known to have been priests, and therefore he would have received training as a priest, but, as noted above, when the temple was destroyed, the focus in the exile came to be upon Torah. Ezra therefore became an expert in scribal arts. The additional element which sets the tone for all future scribal training after him is concentration on the study, interpretation, and teaching of Torah. This was not only important in the religious realm, but was also important in the civil. By Persian royal decree the law of Moses was made civilly binding on all "beyond the River" (west of the Euphrates) (Ezra 7:25), and therefore the expert in the law held binding religious, as well as civil, authority.

This marks the "watershed for the later development of the understanding of 'scribe'."[112] While Ezra marks a distinct advance in the operation of the scribe, during the time of the intertestamental period the scribe carried the study of Torah to new extremes. The next extant literature making reference to the Jewish scribe is the writing of ben Sirach, where there is an "ode to the perfect scribe" (Sir. 38:24—39:11) idealizing the scribe as "one schooled in the law and religious wisdom, understanding the implications of both the written law and oral traditions."[113] In Sirach also occurs the first reference in Jewish literature to

---

[112] Anson. F. Rainey, "Scribe, Scribes," *The Zondervan Pictorial Encyclopedia of the Bible*, ed. M. C. Tenney, 5 vol. (Grand Rapids: Zondervan, 1975), V, 300.
[113] Ibid., p. 301.

an actual school, which was referred to as *bêth midhrash* (Sir. 51:23). Most scholars conclude that with the focusing of the national life of Israel upon the Torah came a corresponding focusing of authority in the scribe. This tended to an increased institutionalism of the scribal profession, and reciprocally, an increased institutionalism within Israelite religious life. This has been referred to as the difference between Israelite religion and Judaism. The movement to scribal schools was the beginning of Judaism, where the prophetic voice from God was eclipsed by the scribal scholar who found evidence for his new teaching in the old Scripture.[114] The increased institutionalism of the scribal profession brought with it an established school order, and the Talmud looks back to this period of time for the beginnings of the Great Assembly, where the ideal for Israel is supposedly first stated as: "Be patient in [the administration of] justice, rear many disciples (*talmidhîm*) and make a fence round the Torah" (Aboth 1:1). The dating of this Great Assembly is uncertain, but it reflects a far more advanced concept of education than is to be found in the biblical period.

4. Conclusion: Indications of master-disciple relationships among the scribes

The Old Testament does not yield any explicit statement of scribal schools. The family offers the most likely possibility for reconstructing the education of scribes, both because of the the family guild structure in the nation and because of the lines of inheritance found in instances of actual scribal offices. This type of education involves teaching from one generation to another. Some would not refer this type of education as a formal master-disciple relationship as might occur within a school, but even here the father is the master and the son the disciple of the trade. In this sense one might speak of professional discipleship within families.

The families and clans of scribes appear to constitute a class of scribes within Israel. One might refer to the class of scribes as a "fellowship of professionals." This designation allows for a sharing of expertise and understanding of traditional materials, but not in such an institutional way as would be implied by the use of the designation "school." The training of potential scribes would occur within the family, but once a youth had been trained he was considered among the class of scribes. The older, outstanding scribes would provide guidance for the others, and this certainly could be considered as a type of master-disciple relation-

---

[114] Bernhard Lang, *Monotheism and the Prophetic Minority: An Essay in Biblical History and Sociology*, The Social World of Biblical Antiquity Series, No. 1 (Sheffield: Almond, 1983), pp. 128ff.

ship. This fellowship of scribes would provide a pool from which outstanding scribes could be selected for special service in the royal court, and which would provide a vehicle for the continuity and uniformity of scribal practice. The outstanding scribes would be the ones who gave guidance to scribal activites, both within the court (in an primary way) and throughout the nation (in a secondary way). This proposal accounts for some of the evidence which leads to the suggestion of a school by allowing for an ongoing body of scibes in the pre-exilic period, but avoids advocating a formal school for which there is no explicit evidence. This proposal also satisfies the fairly strong evidence for scribal training within the family context, yet also leaves room for advanced training to meet the demands of developing complexities within the national court.

Because of the developments found in the status of the scribe, beginning with Ezra, one might be tempted to say he was the product of formal school training. It is possible that the scribal school originated in the Exile, and in turn Ezra was the first of the products of that school, but this possiblity is more of an anachronistic statement in light of the way the scribe was trained in later Judaism. Instead, Ezra, as a unique scribe, appears to be a product of the necessities of the times, as well as his own charismatic genius.[115] Indeed, the rabbinical literature looks back to Ezra as some kind of beginning point for the rabbinical heritage.

There appears to be some kind of continuity behind the development of the scribal class in Israel, although the specifics are somewhat lost in the mists of time. While there is no obvious dependence on any Old Testament model of master-disciple relationship within the scribes, there does appear to be a sociological development: from scribal families, to a fellowship of scribes within the nation, to the sophistication of the court, to the Torah-centered activities of Ezra, to later rabbinic thinking. Such a development implies various master-disciple relationships.

D) The "Wise Men"

Wisdom literature and wisdom influence in the Old Testament provide another convenient focal point for testing Rengstorf's thesis, because both have been subjected to intense, scholarly examination in recent decades, and one major issue has been to reconstruct the sociological phenomena in Israel which gave rise to "wisdom." As a result of these studies, A. Lemaire notes that among wisdom scholars there is now *"un certain consensus en faveur de l'existence d'écoles à l'époque*

---

[115] Ibid., pp. 152-156.

royale israelite",[116] with the attendant implication that masters and disciples made up those "schools." This "consensus" is obviously the antithesis to Rengstorf's thesis, and must be carefully scrutinized to see if it contributes to the evidence for the existence of master-disciple relationships in the Old Testament.

1. Recent studies of the sociological background of Old Testament wisdom

The modern study of Old Testament wisdom dates from the 1920's with the "discovery" of literary relationships between an ancient Egyptian text, the "Wisdom of Amenemope," and the biblical text of Proverbs 22:17-23:11.[117] This modern study has developed at least three different theories concerning the sociological background of Old Testament wisdom.

a) Wisdom as a product of schools

Early comparisons of the "Wisdom of Amenemope" to Old Testament wisdom suggested sociological parallels between the Egyptian royal court and the Israelite royal court. G. von Rad suggests that the Joseph narrative in Genesis was a reflection of the time of David and Solomon, a time when there was a kind of "enlightenment" occurring in Israel, when the spiritual and rational powers in man were being explored in new dimensions.[118] This "enlightenment" occurred especially in the "anthropological" dimension, where there was "concentration upon the phenomenon of man in the broadest sense, his potentialities and his limitations, his psychological complexity and profundity."[119] Von Rad suggests further that the "enlightenment" caused the recognition that the human factor can and must be developed and educated, and the underlying purpose of the earliest wisdom literature was to bring this about. For von Rad, this points definitely to a school origin for the wisdom literature, and he states emphatically that "none would dispute

---

[116] André Lemaire, "Sagesse et écoles," *VT* XXXIV, 3 (1984), 273. Lemaire's purpose in this article is to discuss recent challenges to the "consensus;" in particular, Friedemann W. Golka, "Die Israelitische Weitheitsschule oder 'Des Kaisers neue Kleider'," *VT* XXXIII, 3 (1983), 257-270.

[117] Cf. Gerhard von Rad, *Wisdom in Israel* (n.d.; ET 1972; Nashville: Abingdon, 1984), p. 9 and n. 5, who describes this "discovery" as having a "revolutionary" effect on the course of wisdom studies.

[118] Gerhard von Rad, "The Joseph Narrative and Ancient Wisdom," *Studies in Ancient Israelite Wisdom*, ed. James L. Crenshaw (New York: KTAV, 1976), pp. 439-440. This article was originally published in 1953 under the title "Josephsgeschichte und ältere Chokma."

[119] Ibid., p. 440.

the fact that this early wisdom literature belongs within the context of the royal court, and that its principal aim was to build up a competent body of future administrators.''[120]

This early attempt at delineating the sociological setting of Old Testament wisdom suggests that a school was associated with the court which set as its ideal the education of young men into nobility of character. 'Nobility of character' worked outwards from the priestly cult and the divine revelation, and was best described as ''godly fear'' (Prov 1:7;15:13; Gen 42:18).[121] The 'wisdom schools' therefore reflected the interests of the ruling class and were designed to perpetuate a professional body of advisers to the rulers. 'Wisdom' for von Rad is ''school wisdom'' within the royal court of Israel.[122]

''School wisdom'' as the sociological background of Old Testament wisdom is the simplest expression of what was referred to above as the ''consensus'' opinion among wisdom scholars.[123] Such a school, associated with a professional class within the royal court, implies a formal master-disciple relationship. The goal of the relationship was to instruct the disciple in the ways of wisdom: specifically, an arduous education in the arts of literature, statesmanship, administration, and policymaking.[124] Formal education is therefore the heart of this professional school, and implies a formal, institutional, master-disciple relationship.

b) Wisdom as an oral Israelite tradition

A different theory concerning the origin of wisdom suggests that wisdom was a developing oral tradition within Israel which permeated all aspects of life and crossed all boundaries of professions and classes of people within the nation.[125] The root of this suggestion is an understanding

---

[120] Ibid., pp. 440-441.

[121] Ibid., p. 442.

[122] In his most recent book on this subject (1972), von Rad acknowledges other explanations for the origin of wisdom (e.g., ancient oral wisdom), but suggests that the collections of Proverbs [and recorded wisdom in general] as we have them are best explained as ''school wisdom'' (*Wisdom in Israel*, pp. 11-12, and n. 9).

[123] Recent adherents tend to assume this position is the accepted position, and give only passing attention to alternate explanations for the origin of Old Testament wisdom; e.g., William McKane, *Prophets and Wise Men*, SBT 44 (Naperville, Ill.: Alec R. Allenson, 1965); Hans-Jürgen Hermisson, *Studien zur israelitischen Spruchweisheit*, WMANT 28 (Neukirchen-Vluyn: Neukirchener Verlag, 1968); G. E. Bryce, *A Legacy of Wisdom: The Egyptian Contribution to the Wisdom of Israel* (Lewisburg: Bucknell University Press, 1979).

[124] Cf. McKane, *Prophets and Wise Men*, pp. 23-47.

[125] An early proposal in this direction is found in Johannes Lindblom, ''Wisdom in the Old Testament Prophets,'' *Wisdom in Israel and in the Ancient Near East: Presented to Professor Harold Henry Rowley*, ed. M. Noth and D. Winton Thomas, VTSup, Vol. III (Leiden: E. J. Brill, 1955), p. 201.

of wisdom which does not see it limited to 'courtly' matters, but pertaining to all of life. Wisdom was a common Israelite orientation to life which was disseminated throughout the nation by means of the family / clan structure. This view contends that domestic education was the unifying feature of the family and eventually developed into the traditions found in the wisdom literature.[126]

Through form-critical analyses of wisdom admonitions and prohibitions within the Old Testament laws, E. Gerstenberger concludes that wisdom is early material associated with the primitive structures of society, where sapiential instruction is the responsibility of the head of the family or tribe, and the goal is the preservation of the *Sippenethos*.[127] He states, "Not priests or prophets but fathers, tribal heads, wise men, and secondarily court officials. . . are the earliest guardians of the precepts. Basically, it is the father who addresses his son directly, counseling him for his life."[128] H. Wolff has applied this principle to several prophetic books,[129] and notes that this wisdom was also administered by the elders in the judicial process which occurred in the gates of the country towns and was also transmitted by the elders in the instruction of the youth.[130] Folk wisdom is a "common-sense" approach to judicial decisions, learned in part within the context of the cultural milieu and growth-in-life experiences.[131]

A slightly different approach is suggested by S. Terrien and J. Lindblom. Terrien suggests that Amos received a wisdom outlook from the seminomads who lived in the south and the southeast of the Dead Sea, and that particular wisdom outlook became a part of the common oral tradition within Israel, as well as a phenomenon in which a special group of leaders specialized[132]. Lindblom speaks of a class of "the wise" who

---

[126] J. P. Audet, "Origines comparées de la double tradition de la loi et de la sagesse dans le Proche-Orient ancien," International Congress of Orientalists, Vol. I (Moscow, 1960), pp. 352-357.

[127] Erhard Gerstenberger, *Wesen und Herkunft des 'apodiktischen Rechts'*, WMANT 20 (Neukirchen-Vluyn: Neukirchener, 1965).

[128] Erhard Gerstenberger, "Covenant and Commandment," *JBL* 84 (1965), 51. Cf. also Erhard Gerstenberger, "The Woe-Oracles of the Prophets," *JBL* 81 (1962), 249-263.

[129] E.g., Hans Walter Wolff, *Amos the Prophet: The Man and his Background*, trans., F. McCurley (1964; Philadelphia: Fortress, 1973); Hans Walter Wolff, "Micah the Moreshite—The Prophet and His Background," *Israelite Wisdom: Theological and Literary Essays in Honor of Samuel Terrien*, ed. J. Gammie, W. Brueggemann, W. L. Humphreys, J. Ward (Missoula, Montana: Scholars Press, 1978), pp. 77-84.

[130] Wolff, "Micah," pp. 82-83.

[131] See James L. Crenshaw, "Prolegomenon," *Studies in Ancient Israelite Wisdom*, ed. James L. Crenshaw (New York: KTAV, 1976), pp. 20-22, for his related statements on the "class ethic" of wisdom.

[132] Samuel Terrien, "Amos and Wisdom," *Studies in Ancient Israelite Wisdom*, ed. James L. Crenshaw ([1962]; rpt.; New York: KTAV, 1976), pp. [109, 114-115]; 449, 454-455.

gave diversified oral teaching to the people, but, who, in particular, gave teaching to groups of disciples whom they gathered around them.[133] In addition to understanding wisdom being orally transmitted by the family / clan structures, Terrien and Lindblom both suggest that a group of "wise men" were specialized in oral wisdom and that they were an additional means by which wisdom was disseminated to the people, to the leaders of the people, and to future generations of wisdom specialists.

These theories of oral "folk-wisdom" suggest three different locations for the transmission of wisdom, none of which necessarily excludes the others, and two of which suggest master-disciple relations. The first location is in the family / clan. Here wisdom is transmitted in the normal course of rearing children within the context of the home and the local cultural milieu. This is the most basic sense of 'folk-wisdom' or 'clan-wisdom' (*Sippenweisheit*).[134] No formal master-disciple relationship is implied. The second location for the transmission of oral wisdom is the training of leaders. Oral family-wisdom provided a common-sense foundation for social interaction, but when binding decisions were required, a normative wisdom was needed. For example, young men in training to be elders in the local townships had "family wisdom" as a part of their family training background, but it needed to be "normalized" when it met the larger community so that decisions on judicial matters could be regulated. The older elders showed the young men how family wisdom needed to be applied in rendering decisions. Such training could be described as a master-disciple relationship. This relationship is less formal than the model suggested above for education in the sophisticated ways of the court, but it is a form of a master-disciple relationship in that the regulatory wisdom is passed on to succeeding generations of elders. The third location suggested for the transmission of wisdom is in a group of "wise men." The "wise men" were specialized in oral wisdom and they were an additional means by which the wisdom was disseminated to the people, to the leaders of the people, and to future generations of wisdom specialists. Such specialization implies a master-disciple relationship for both acquiring and passing on the specialty.

c) Wisdom as an approach to reality

R. Murphy attempted to combine the preceding views by suggesting that wisdom was "an approach to reality which was shared by all Israelites in varying degrees."[135] Murphy thinks that it is reasonable to

[133] Lindblom, "Wisdom in the Old Testament Prophets," pp. 203-204.

[134] Gerstenberger, *Wesen und Herkunft*; Wolff, *Amos*, pp. 88-89.

[135] Roland E. Murphy, "Wisdom—Theses and Hypotheses," *Israelite Wisdom: Theological and Literary Essays in Honor of Samuel Terrien*, ed. J. Gammie, W. Brueggemann, W. L. Humphreys, J. Ward (Missoula, Montana: Scholars Press, 1978), p. 39.

see wise men actively at work at the Jerusalem court,[136] but instead of understanding royal wisdom to be a product of the court school, he suggests that it was the reflection of the wisdom tradition which had been developing in Israel:

> The wisdom cultivated by Solomon and the men of Hezekiah must necessarily reflect the ethos of the people for whom it was destined. It is reasonable therefore to correlate the court activity with the experiential wisdom of the people. This would imply a recognition of the impulse given to a literary cultivation of wisdom in the court. Wisdom is well on its way to becoming a literature, thus gaining a certain prestige that will preserve it.[137]

In this view the wisdom which was in existence among the people does not necessitate formal education to promote its advancement in the national life because it is disseminated through the family and/or clan social structure. The existence of this wisdom in the royal court is somewhat more complex. On the one hand, the royal court was embedded in the cultural milieu of the people and the members of the court would therefore be participants in common folk wisdom. The members of the royal court who were involved in the writing of wisdom literature would be stating the common wisdom attitudes of the people, and for this they would not have to undergo any specific education; they would have learned this wisdom attitude through their own cultural contextualization. On the other hand, Murphy contends that wisdom author / teachers were experts in this specific mode of thinking. They were members of a professional class of sages referred to as "wise men," and the implication is that, based upon the probability of the existence of schools in Jerusalem, they became experts through an educational process.[138] This process would include masters and disciples.

d) Summary

These three views represent the basic prevailing attitudes toward the sociological background of wisdom in the Old Testament. Each suggests the existence of master-disciple relationships, although in different

---

[136] Ibid., p. 37.

[137] Murphy, "Wisdom—Theses and Hypotheses," p. 37. The advance in Murphy's thinking is clearly seen in a recent work (Roland E. Murphy, *Wisdom Literature: Job, Proverbs, Ruth, Canticles, Ecclesiastes, and Esther, The Forms of the Old Testament Literature*, Vol. XIII [Grand Rapids: Eerdmans, 1981], pp. 7-8). Here Murphy compares his thinking about the two-fold origin of wisdom, in both the family and school, to his earlier attempt at analyzing wisdom scholarship (Roland E. Murphy, "Assumptions and Problems in Old Testament Wisdom Research," *CBQ* 29 [1967], 101-112).

[138] Murphy, "Wisdom—Theses and Hypotheses," pp. 37-40.

forms. The first view stresses formal master-disciple relationships within the court schools of wisdom. The second view stresses the origin of wisdom in the family / clan setting, but as family wisdom moved into the larger community it became normalized through leadership training and the training of wisdom experts. Although less formal than the court wisdom schools suggested by the first view, master-disciple relationships were part of the training of leaders and the development of wisdom experts. The final view combines features of both the preceding views. It suggets that the origin of wisdom is in the family / clan structure, but as wisdom was developed and specialized a school arose at the court for wisdom specialists. Therefore each view stresses a type of master-disciple relationship involved with the transmission and development of wisdom in Israel.

The question of the existence of master-disciple relationships in the wisdom tradition would be assured if the existence of wisdom schools and a professional class of wise men could be established, because if either is established as an *institution* within the nation the existence of masters and disciples is a more likely possibility. The evidence for the existence of wisdom schools and a professional class of wise men will now be given brief consideration.

2. Evidence for a class of "wise men"

One of the key features for contending that there were wisdom schools attached to the royal court is the suggestion that there was a class of wise men operating within the court, and a school was needed for the training and perpetuation of the class. Several lines of evidence for the existence of a professional class of wise men associated with the royal court have been proposed in recent years: e.g., 1) the biblical references to "wise men," and especially the attacks upon the wise men in the prophetic writings; 2) the biblical references to Solomon's wisdom (1 Kings 4,10) and the activity of the men of Hezekiah (Prov 25:1); 3) analogy with Egypt and Mesopotamia; 4) training of a responsible courtier could be seen as part of the wisdom ideal; 5) the probability or likelihood that a royal court would need the particular talents which the wise men possessed.[139] The strength of these lines of evidence has been subject to examination from many different points of view in the past several years, and will be summarized here.

---

[139] Cf., James L. Crenshaw, *Old Testament Wisdom: An Introduction* (Atlanta: John Knox, 1981), pp. 28-31; Murphy, "Wisdom—Theses and Hypothesis," p. 37.

References to "the wise one" (*chàkhàm*) are found scattered throughout the biblical record. There are references to wise women(Judg 5:29; 2 Sam 14:2-20) as well as men (1 Kings 2:9; Isa 19:11,12), and there are references to individuals such as Ahithophel who was a counselor to David and Absalom: "and the advice (*waʿatsath*) of Ahithophel which he gave in those days was as if one should ask concerning the word of God" (2 Sam 16:23). This latter has been used as an illustrative example of the function of wise men in the royal court.[140] The wise counselor used common human dexterity which stemmed from the cultural milieu and personal prowess, but it was also assumed that his wisdom found its origin in God.[141]

Although there are clear references to men and women who were wise, the data is not as clear in support of a class of wise men as some propose. For example, although G. von Rad believes that wisdom teachers were a vocational group, he confesses that the "expected clarity" in the biblical text simply is not there. Instead, the adjective *chàkhàm* describes people who were competent, skilled, able to succeed in accomplishing their desired goals. Indeed, this competency was not attached to any particular set of ethical values, because it could be used in shady dealings as well as positive endeavors. When the adjective was used as a noun in the Solomonic book of Proverbs the majority of times it did not refer to a wise man as representative of a position, but rather as a wise man who was contrasted, as a type, with the fool.[142]

The semantical study of R. N. Whybray[143] has cast "considerable doubt"[144] over the traditional picture of a professional class of wise men in the royal epoch. Whybray's study attempts to show that *chàkhàm* was not a technical term for members of a professional class, but rather referred to an "intellectual tradition" in which men of intellectual prowess from a variety of circles within Israel participated.[145] He analyzes every text in which there is a reference to "wise men" and concludes that

---

[140] Cf. McKane, *Prophets and Wise Men*, pp. 13, 55ff. *Chàkhàm* is not used with reference to Ahithophel, but *ʿtsh* belongs to the semantic field of wisdom; cf., e.g., R. B. Y. Scott, *The Way of Wisdom* (New York: Macmillan, 1971), pp. 121*f.*

[141] Georg Fohrer, "σοφία," *TDNT*, VII (Grand Rapids: Eerdmans, 1971), pp. 487-494. Cf. also H.-P. Müller, "*chàkhàm*," IV, *TDOT*, trans. David E. Green (Grand Rapids: Eerdmans, 1980), pp. 379-384.

[142] Von Rad, *Wisdom in Israel*, p. 20.

[143] R. N. Whybray, *The Intellectual Tradition in the Old Testament*, BZAW 135 (Berlin: Walter de Gruyter, 1974).

[144] R. A. F. MacKenzie, "Review of R. N. Whybray, *The Intellectual Tradition in the Old Testament*," *Bib* 56 (1975), p. 267.

[145] Whybray, *Intellectual Tradition*, p. 55. Whybray prefers the phrase "intellectual tradition" to "wisdom," because he says that "wisdom" is too laden with interpretive overtones of various scholars.

the intention was to designate an individual of great knowledge, especially knowledge of the wisdom [intellectual] tradition of Israel.

This is a serious departure from the common scholarly conception of wise men. Not all scholars have been convinced, but Whybray's study demonstates the need for caution in reading too much into the title 'wise one.' W. McKane suggests that Whybray has gone too far in severing all thoughts of a professional class from *chàkhàm* (especially in Jer 8:8-9; 18:18; and Prov 22:17),[146] but he makes an important concession when he says,

> It is not a matter of importance to me to establish that *chàkhàmîm* is a technical term for members of a learned class. What I do, however, say is that in the passages where Isaiah and Jeremiah are clearly encountering politicians, there is no doubt that the *chàkhàmîm* of whom they speak are *śarim* and are exponents of political wisdom. In so far as they are *sòpherîm* or *śarim* they are members of a professional class who were close to the centre of power and exercised a decisive influence on the political destiny of Judah.[147]

This is important because if the possibility is granted that *chàkhàm* is not a technical term for members of a wisdom *class*, essentially what is left is a term which functions in a general way to designate men of a wisdom *perspective*. This may be important as this study unfolds, because it offers the possibility of reducing the number of unknowns. That is, if *chàkhàm* is not a technical term for a separate class, it could specify the perspective of persons of any professional class (e.g., *sòpherîm?*) who were so characterized by the influence of wisdom that they were considered "wise men." The three biblical passages mentioned by McKane help clarify the Old Testament usage of *chàkhàm*; (Jer 8:8-9; 18:18; and Prov 22:17).

a) Jeremiah 8:8-9

Jer 8:8-9 comes in the middle of a derisive account of Israel's apostasy and forthcoming judgment. The leadership of the nation receives a special focus of condemnation in 8:1, and then in verses 8-9 the reason for their condemnation is made clear.[148] The leadership of Jerusalem is condemned by Jeremiah in a cynical way by referring to them as the

[146] William McKane, "Review of R. N. Whybray, *The Intellectual Tradition in the Old Testament*," *J Sem St* 20 (1975), 243-248, esp. 244-245.

[147] Ibid., pp. 243-244.

[148] J. A. Thompson offers the possibility that although vv. 8-9 are linked in thought with 8:4-7, "it may have been originally a separate piece addressed to the spiritual leaders of the nation" (*The Book of Jeremiah, NICOT*, ed. R. K. Harrison [Grand Rapids: Eerdmans, 1980], p. 299).

"wise" in the first part of v. 8. Although the leaders of the nation think that they are "wise" because they possess the law, they actually reject the "word" of the Lord because they reject the message of Yahweh through the law and the preaching of the prophets (viz., Jeremiah). They are put to shame, and one result is the recognition that their supposed wisdom is of no use (v. 9). The scribes are given in parallelism in v. 8b as an explanation of how the wise falsely exalt their possession of the law: the scribes "deceive" through their use of the pen. J. Bright notes that "the delusion, or falsehood, which the scribes have created seems to be not so much the law itself, as the resultant conceit that possession of the law gives all necessary wisdom."[149]

This is a difficult passage, but the *chakhāmîm* appear to be a general designation for the leadership in Israel, and the *sōphᵉrîm* are given as a representative example. The leadership of the nation consider themselves "wise" because they have the law; this is the basic point of the condemnatory statement of the prophet. The "scribes" are an example of how one group with leadership responsibility in the nation have distorted their responsibility. They have some kind of teaching function in addition to transcribing, because they use their "deceiving pen" (*ᶜēṭ sheqer*) to turn the law of God "into a falsehood (*lasheqer*)".[150] This helps clarify the relationship between the two groups: "the wise" is a general designation for the leadership, and "the scribes" are a representative example of how that leadership have exalted themselves and perverted their responsibilities toward the law. Therefore, the wise are a category of all those who oppose the "word of the Lord" from the prophet because they pride themselves for having the "law of the Lord," and the scribes are a specific category of those who contribute to that kind of human wisdom. While this is the first specific indication of an official category of scribes in Israel, it only views "the wise" as a characteristic of the leaders who wrongly exalt themselves for having the law of the Lord.[151]

b) Jeremiah 18:18

Jer 18:18 seems to be a specific reference to three sources of religious / social authority in Judah; the "wise man" (*chākhām*) is as distinct as the "priest" (*kōhēn*) or the prophet (*nābhîʾ*). The "wise man" is linked with

---

[149] John Bright, *Jeremiah*, AB, vol. 21 (2d. ed.; Garden City, New York: Doubleday and Co., 1965), pp. 63-64.

[150] Thompson, Jeremiah, p. 300.

[151] Ibid., pp. 299-300; Bright, *Jeremiah*, pp. 63-65; R. K. Harrison, "Jeremiah," in *Jeremiah and Lamentations: An Introduction and Commentary, TOTC* (Downers Grove, Illinois: Inter-Varsity Press, 1973), p. 89.

counsel (*ʿētsàh*), the "priest" with law or instruction (*tôràh*), and the "prophet" with the word (*dhàbhàr*). Jeremiah's prophetic utterances had aroused such indignation in the influential circles of Judah that a conspiracy was plotted against him. The people and leadership of Judah do not fear going against the prophet because of their false confidence in the sources of authority (priest, wise man, prophet) which are now aligned against Jeremiah.[152]

The important point for the discussion here is that the "wise man" (*chàkhàm*) appears to specify a recognizable person who is identified with counsel (*ʿētsàh*) and who is in a significant position of authority.[153] Ezek 7:26 gives an interesting parallel because three persons of authority are once again mentioned, but there they are the prophet, the priest and the elders: "Men will go seeking a vision from a prophet; there will be no more guidance from a priest, no counsel from elders" (NEB). *ʿētsàh* is there attributed to the elders, not to the wise man. While "counsel" was supremely a characteristic of Yahweh (Ps 33:10f.; Isa 46:9-11), and was a characteristic of the godly man (Ps 32:8; 73:24), it was also needed in the royal court for the conduct of the state in difficult circumstances. Ahithophel, for example, was noted to be one who gave counsel (*ʿētsàh*) in the royal court, and this was "as if one should ask concerning the word of the Lord" (2 Sam 16:23). Therefore, Jer 18:18 points to the wise man as a recognizable person in a position of wise counsel in the nation, but Ezek 7:26 gives the same function (*ʿētsàh*) to the elders. Ezek 22:26-28 contains a similar triad, but there "nobles" (*śar*) occurs with priests (v. 26) and prophets (v. 28). An earlier triad found in Micah 3:11 speaks of the "rulers" (*rōʾsh*) the priests and the prophets. These triads make it appear likely that "wise man" (*chàkhàm*), "elder" (*zàqēn*), "nobles" (*śar*), and "ruler" (*rōʾsh*) are characteristic titles of one body of officers who give advice and direction to the court. M. Greenberg suggests that the leaders of the realm were three classes of individuals: the priests, the prophets, and officers, the latter referred to by various titles in different triads.[154] This group of "officers" should not be thought of as a homogenous group, but rather appears to be a body of individuals who perform different types of functions of leadership.

Therefore, *chàkhàm* in Jer 18:18 indicates a class of leaders in Israel, but not a separate body of "wise men" in distinction from elders, rulers,

---

[152] Harrison, "Jeremiah," p. 110.

[153] Lindblom, "Wisdom in the Old Testament Prophets," pp. 194-195; Bright, *Jeremiah*, p. 124.

[154] Moshe Greenberg, *Ezekiel 1-20, AB*, vol. 22 (Garden City, New York: Doubleday, 1983), p. 156. Cf. also G. A. Cooke, *A Critical and Exegetical Commentary on the Book of Ezekiel, ICC* (Edinburgh: T. & T. Clark, 1936), p. 244.

and nobles. Rather, as counselors of the court they availed themselves of "wisdom" as a means for giving advice to the court. *Chàkhàm* describes their function, but they also perform other functions which allow them to be called "elders," "rulers," or "nobles."

c) Proverbs 22:17

Prov 22:17 begins as a heading for Prov 22:17-24:22: "Precepts of the Sages," or more generally, "Words of the Wise Men" (*chakhàmîm*).[155] The larger section is often said to be related to the thirty precepts of the Egyptian *Instruction of Amen-en-ope*, and more recently, parallels have been found to the oriental *Sayings of Ahikar*. The relationship between Proverbs and other near eastern wisdom is still debated, but a broadly recognized conclusion is that the wisdom of Proverbs partakes of the cultural and literary milieu of the near east, and shows acquaintance with wisdom literature of other nations in existence at the time of its composition, but has a uniqely Israelite orientation to wisdom.[156] The *chakhàmîm* in Prov 22:17 appear to be those who are connected with the royal court in Israel and who compile wisdom sayings which reflect the best of the wisdom influence in Israel.[157] Although *chàkhàm* is used in antithesis to the fool in Proverbs to denote the person who listens to counsel (e.g. 12:15), the wise men of 22:17, and the men of Hezekiah in Prov 25:1 who transcribed the proverbs of Solomon, indicate a group of men who are specialists in wisdom. This does not imply that wisdom originated with these specialists at the court, but rather that these specialists were committed to preserving the wisdom which was a part of the Israelite ethos, and therefore reduced it to writing. Their specialty in wisdom allowed them to employ it in the court, as well as to write in such a way that it reflected and was applicable to the broader Israelite ethos.[158] This reflects a group of specialists in wisdom in Israel, connected with the royal court, who were firmly rooted in the wisdom of Israelite culture.

d) Summary

On the one hand, when "wisdom" was exalted to the exclusion of hearing the prophetic word of the Lord, the individuals employing it are

---

[155] R. B. Y. Scott, *Proverbs and Ecclesiastes, AB*, vol. 18 (2d ed.; Garden City, New York, 1965), p. 135.

[156] Cf. Brevard S. Childs, *Introduction to the Old Testament as Scripture*, (Philadelphia: Fortress, 1979), pp. 547-558; R. K. Harrison, *Introduction to the Old Testament* (Grand Rapids: Eerdmans, 1969), pp. 1013-1018; Scott, *Proverbs*, pp. xviiif., xxxiiff.

[157] Childs, *Introduction to the Old Testament as Scripture*, pp. 551ff.

[158] Von Rad, *Wisdom in Israel*, p. 17.

in opposition to the prophet, and are referred to in a cynical sense as "wise men" who have rejected the word of the Lord. On the other hand, when "wisdom" was used as a means for furthering the will of Yahweh, the individuals employing it are referred to in a commendatory sense as "wise men" who have advanced the word of the Lord. The term appears to have both a broad and narrower meaning, depending upon the context. The most that should be advanced from the discussion by modern scholars and the brief look at the three most crucial occurrences of the term *chākhām* is that the "wise men" were leaders of Israel who availed themselves of wisdom as a medium of revelation, but who could use it either positively or negatively. There appears to be enough evidence to suggest that there were individuals who specialized in wisdom, but who had a broader orientation than wisdom. They appear to be associated with a class of officials in Israel who are advisers to the court. The general title "wise men" could denote the group as a whole (Jer 18:18), but on the other hand the group also performed other functions which characterized them ("elders," Ezek 7:26; "nobles," Ezek 22: 27; "rulers," Micah 3:11). The specialists in wisdom also were responsible in some way for recording the wisdom tradition which reflected the ethos of Israel (Prov 22:17, 25:1).

3. Evidence for a wisdom school

Rengstorf's central argument for the lack of master-disciple relationships in the Old Testament is that explicit "disciple" and "school" terminology is lacking in the biblical text.[159] F. Golka has recently focused on the same lack of data and argues against the school reconstructions of G. von Rad, H.-J. Hermisson, and A. Lemaire. For Golka, the arguments for the existence of schools are mostly arguments from silence.[160] A. Lemaire has attempted to answer the criticisms of Golka by acknowledging the lack of explicit references and instead focuses on the "biblical allusions." He cites several passages[161] which he says are insufficient by themselves to prove the existence of schools, but which are best explained if one admits the likelihood of wisdom schools in the royal epoch.[162] This appears to be begging the question. Some of these passages *may* make passing allusion to schools of disciples in general (Isa

---

[159] Rengstorf, "μαθητής," pp. 426-431.
[160] Golka, "Die Israelitische Weisheitsschule," pp. 257ff.
[161] 1 Sam 1-3; 2 Sam 12:24-25 [sic?]; 1 Kings 12:8-10; 2 Kings 6:1ff.; 10:1, 5, 6; 12:3; 1 Chron 27:32; 2 Chron 27:7-9; Prov 12:17-21; Isa 8:16; 28:9-13; 50:4. Lemaire, "Sagesse et ecoles," p. 274 and n. 14.
[162] Ibid., pp. 274-275.

8:16; 28:9-13; 50:4), but not in a wisdom setting. The other references are to groups of elders or priests within the temple or royal court setting. Only by the assumption that these groups were trained in a wisdom perspective in preparation for their courtly and priestly activities can these groups be seen as alluding to a wisdom school setting.[163]

The existence of wisdom schools in Israel has been a fairly well accepted assumption in scholarly studies for quite some time. The arguments for assuming the existence of wisdom schools have been summarized as follows:[164]

(1) Since the existence of scribal schools in Mesopotamia, Egypt, and Levant has been proven beyond doubt, an Israelite wisdom school would not be an isolated phenomenon.

(2) The need for educated officials in the administration of the developing royal administration created the need for a scribal school.

(3) The class of 'wise men' referred to in Scripture indicates a school at which they were trained in the art and literature of wisdom.

(4) The probability or likelihood that a royal court would need the particular talents which the wise men possessed indicates a class of wise men.

(5) The wisdom literature as a literary body and genre indicates that there were wise men who either formulated it as a creative product of a school, or formulated it as a teaching tool for a school.

The assumption of the existence of wisdom schools has recently been challenged, and in this section the existence of these schools will be examined in the light of the conclusions reached in the previous sections on scribes, scribal schools, and wise men. The following analysis of the above assumptions will be given special consideration: a. The evidence for a wisdom school relies quite heavily on the evidence for scribal schools; b. The evidence for wisdom schools assumes that the biblical references to wise men refers to a professional class of wise men.

---

[163] With respect to this assumption see the pessimistic statements of W. Lee Humphreys, "The Motif of the Wise Courtier in the Book of Proverbs," *Israelite Wisdom: Theological and Literary Essays in Honor of Samuel Terrien*, ed. J. Gammie, W. Brueggemann, W. L. Humphreys, J. Ward (Missoula, Montana: Scholars Press, 1978), pp. 177-178.

[164] Lemaire, "Sagesse et ecoles," pp. 274-281; Tryggve D. Mettinger, *Solomonic State Officials: A Study of the Civil Government Officials of the Israelite Monarchy*, ConBOTS 5 (Lund: Gleerup, 1971), pp. 143ff.; Olivier, "Schools and Wisdom Literature," pp. 58-59; R. Murphy, "Wisdom—Theses and Hypothoses," p. 37; R. Murphy, *Wisdom Literature: Job, Proverbs, Ruth, Canticles, Ecclesiastes, and Esther, The Forms of the Old Testament Literature*, Vol. XIII (Grand Rapids: Eerdmans, 1981), pp. 7-8; James L. Crenshaw, *Old Testament Wisdom: An Introduction* (Atlanta: John Knox, 1981), pp. 28-31. Mettinger and Olivier have based their summaries on the work of Hermisson, *Studien zur israelitischen Spruchweisheit*.

a) The evidence for a wisdom school relies quite heavily on the evidence for scribal schools.

The evidence for a wisdom school in Israel is based on the evidence for scribal schools. For example, arguments (1) and (2) above make a tacit identification of a wisdom school and a scribal school. Is this a valid identification? One may postulate the existence of a *scribal school* in Israel based on the evidence of scribal schools in the surrounding cultures and the need for advanced scribes as administrative officials in the royal court, but this is not evidence directed at the existence of a *wisdom school*, unless, and this is significant, one also makes an identification of the wise man and the scribe. The only independent evidence cited for a wisdom school, as distinct from evidence for a scribal school, is the existence of wisdom literature [argument (5) above]. All the other evidence supports the existence of a scribal school. Even the wisdom literature does not necessitate a *wisdom* school setting to account for its existence, but could just as easily be accounted for in a *scribal* school,[165] or in the fellowship of wise men found within the court. There is such limited evidence for advanced schools in Israel that it may be stretching the data to posit the existence of two schools. Because of this limited evidence, a minimizing approach is advocated by some, where the scribal school is advanced as the source of both technical scribal activities and wisdom activities. Such a school would be directed to the training of scribes, but wisdom would be part of the curriculum or would be a specialty of certain students.[166] The advantage of this approach is that it accounts for the existence of both scribes and wise men from the same set of data, and builds on the close relationship between functions of the scribe as a high-ranking official in the court and the wise man as an officer and counselor in the court. This reduces the number of unknowns by making the wise man and the scribe almost identical.

b) The evidence for wisdom schools assumes that the biblical references to wise men refer to a professional class of wise men.

The assumption of the existence of wisdom schools relies quite heavily on the biblical references to *chàkhàm* being a professional class of wise men who have special responsibilities at the royal court, with the attendant implication that such a class would require a wisdom school for their

---

[165] Cf., R. Murphy, *Wisdom Literature: Job, Proverbs, Ruth, Canticles, Ecclesiastes, and Esther, The Forms of the Old Testament Literature*, Vol. XIII (Grand Rapids: Eerdmans, 1981), pp. 7-8. Murphy contends for a school as part of the origin of the wisdom literature, but he consistently discusses this as a scribal school.

[166] Ibid.

training [arguments (3) and (4) above]. The work of Whybray has cast considerable doubt over this thesis,[167] but has not provided a satisfactory alternative to account for all the biblical references. His suggestion that the wise men were those of any professional class who were participants in training in the wisdom ("intellectual") tradition is plausible in that it accounts for much of the data, but passages such as Jer 8:8-9 and 18:18 seem to point to a more recognizable person or class of persons.[168]

W. McKane, in his study of the "wise," has attempted to show a relationship between the *sôpherîm* and *chakhàmîm* by proposing that anyone who held a responsible position in Israel was a wise man.[169] He suggests that the scribes and wise men were essentially synonymous as a class of officials in the royal court, especially when the diatribes of the prophets Isaiah and Jeremiah (viz. Jer. 8:8-9 and 18:18) are taken into account.[170] Drawing on the scribes as a class of literary experts, von Rad suggests that there were scribes in the various classes in Israel, all with their own schools.[171] McKane is representative of a minimizing approach at this point, because he tries to account for the existence of both the scribes and wise men as professional classes by equating them; i.e., he takes seriously the references to both groups as professional classes, but he indicates that they are essentially identical. The scribes were influenced by the wisdom tradition which was disseminated orally throughout the nation, both in a positive and negative fashion. When it was an outgrowth of wise reflection on the world and was in line with Yahweh's purposes as reflected in the cult, the royal administration, and the prophets, the scribe was considered wise in a positive sense. But when wisdom's humanistic orientation exalted itself against the word of the Lord, especially as revealed through the prophet, the scribe was considered wise in a negative or cynical sense.

The implication of the minimizing approach is that the scribes constituted the professional class of advisers within the nation, especially the royal court in the monarchy, and one major aspect of the training for their office would have been the study and incorporation of the wisdom tradition. These scribes would have been the major experts in the wisdom tradition and would therefore be the most likely candidates to be called

---

[167] Whybray, *Intellectual Tradition*, passim.

[168] Cf. The review of Whybray by R. A. F. MacKenzie, *Bib* 56 (1975), 266-267, and the discussion of these passages above.

[169] McKane, *Wise Men and Prophets*, pp. 40-41.

[170] Ibid, pp. 44-47.

[171] G. von Rad, *Wisdom in Israel*, pp. 17-18. For a discussion of wisdom in relation to the temple cult see Leo G. Perdue, *Wisdom and Cult: A Critical Analysis of the Views of Cult in the Wisdom Literatures of Israel and the Ancient Near East*, SBLDS 30 (Missoula, Montana: Scholars, 1977).

"wise men." Depending on their use of this wisdom tradition, they would have been seen as either positive or negative wise men. This view is supported by the earlier observation that the expression "the wise men" can function in a general way to designate men of a certain wisdom perspective. The members of the professional class of scribes availed themselves of the wisdom tradition and were so characterized by wisdom's influence that they were given the appellative "the wise." This view stresses the very natural implication that scribes who were governmental counselors would be the ones who would be closest to the exercise of wisdom.[172]

The evidence for wise men as a separate class is somewhat less than that for the scribes, and is a significant point both for arguing against a wisdom school and for arguing in favor of identifying the wise men as scribal experts in the wisdom tradition. In addition, the fact that in the intertestamental period *chakhàmîm* were a specialized class of biblical interpreters who came from among the more generalized professional *sòphᵉrîm*[173] may show a beginning tendency toward that direction even in the Old Testament period.

c) Summary and observations

The minimizing approaches are indicative of theories which attempt to reduce the number of unknowns by staying within the actual evidence. This is the basic strength of these views, and for that reason are attractive. On the other hand, the desire to reduce those unknowns may inadvertently overlook some of the data. One such example is the attempt to account for the wisdom tradition and the wise men by making them almost identical with scribes who have a strong wisdom outlook. While this is a very attractive suggestion, and may even be the best of the current options, it forces too many wisdom references into a scribal mold. The wisdom motif throughout the Old Testament indicates that it was a nation-wide phenomenon, and the wise men are not always easily identifiable with the scribes. Something was out there of an institutional kind behind the clearly recognizable body of wisdom writings, with its own language and ideology, and disservice may be done to the wisdom tradition by identifying it too closely with the scribal tradition. Perhaps the minimizing approach can be used in part if allowance is made for some kind of independent wisdom development.

---

[172] Cf. McKane, *Wise Men and Prophets*, pp. 36-47.
[173] Ephraim E. Urbach, *The Sages: Their Concepts and Beliefs*, trans. Israel Abrahams, 2 vols. (Jerusalem: Magnes Press, 1979), I, 564-576.

Serious effort has been made recently to find the location of wisdom training. Training within the father-son relationship and clan guild offers a possibility for accounting for the wisdom tradition, but the transmission of wisdom has also been noted in the training of elders and other leaders of the nation. The provenance of wisdom in the life of ancient Israel is still a puzzling feature, with no lack for theories. Even as the reality of a wisdom tradition in the Old Testament becomes more assured, the location of its origin and transmission in one area becomes less assured. B. Childs goes so far as to suggest that "in spite of many illuminating suggestions, no one setting has emerged as offering an exclusive *Sitz im Leben*, nor is one likely."[174] He suggests that the wisest course may be to list the various sources for the wisdom tradition without allowing any one the dominant place.

The tenuous nature of the evidence for schools as a training grounds has been noted recently,[175] and together with the minimizing suggestions which associate the wisdom tradition to some degree with scribal training, indicates that the existence of a wisdom *school* is a precarious theory.[176] On the other hand, studies in the provenance of wisdom suggest a diverse origin and transmission, ranging from the family to more formal settings as greater specialization was needed.

IV. Summary and Conclusion to the Evidence for Master-Disciple Relationships in the Old Testament

Evidence for the existence of master-disciple relationships in the Old Testament is found in a limited way in the terms *talmîdh* and *limmûdh*. The single occurrence of *talmîdh* in the Old Testament indicates a student or apprentice in musical instruction (1 Chron 25:8). *Talmîdh* here indicates a master-disciple relationship which centers on instruction in a skill, and therefore is a morphological transparency for the verb *lāmadh*. *Limmûdh* is also morphologically related to *lāmadh*. The *limmûdhîm* in Isa 8:16 and 50:14 were a group gathered around a master in such a way that they were referred to by a possessive ("my disciples," Isa 8:16) and their

---

[174] Childs, *Introduction to the Old Testament as Scripture*, p. 549.

[175] Cf. J. Crenshaw's rather strong critique of the most recent discussion of the evidence for schools in Israel, where the offered conjectures are referred to as "flights of imagination;" James L. Crenshaw, "Review of *Les écoles et la formation de la Bible dans l'ancien Israël*, by André Lemaire," *JBL* 103 (December, 1984), 630-632.

[176] Crenshaw's (ibid., p. 631) basic criticism of Lemaire's thesis is that he has overlooked the family background of education in Israel: "Lemaire's hypothesis is plausible, but has not been demonstrated. The inscriptional evidence is inconclusive, and the imaginative syntheses of biblical material fails to appreciate the fact that the family had primary responsibility for education in Israel."

relationship was characterized by some kind of educational process which accentuated speaking and listening (Isa 50:4). The same term was also used to specify the "disciples" of Yahweh (Isa 54:13), which indicates that *limmûdhîm* could be disciples of both Yahweh and a human master. Although the occurrences of the these terms are scarce, they indicate that established master-disciple relationships are at least to be found among the musicians and writing prophets. The casual way in which the terms are used indicate an even broader usage behind these examples.

The prophets also demonstrate master-disciple relationships. Groups of prophets were found around Samuel, and he appears to exercise some kind of "mentor" authority over them. The relationship does not speak of a school setting, but rather of a "fellowship" of prophets who look to Samuel as an authority. A similar type relationship is found with the "sons of the prophets" and Elisha. Elisha exercised leadership authority over these prophets, but again it is not in a school setting. The sons of the prophets were not prophets in training, but were rather gathered around Elisha for guidance in performing their own prophetic activities. This is not a master-disciple relationship of the school, but is a master-disciple relationship in mutual commitment to service of Yahweh.

The scribes also demonstrate characteristics of master-disciple relationships. Based on the nature of their profession, the scribes would naturally be involved in apprentice-type training in the rudimentary skills of their trade: e.g., reading, writing, transcribing. Other skills are also associated with the Old Testament scribes, such as political responsibilites as advisers in the royal court. After the exile Ezra's responsibilites as scribe centered on teaching the law, but such a responsibility was also in evidence prior to the exile (cf. Jer 8:8-9). Much of the training for these various scribal responsibilites appears to have occurred within the family and clan, which would speak of master-disciple training in these skills being from father to son. But as advanced training and specialization was needed, the most likely place for this to occur would have been within the scribal guild. Such a guild might be described as a "fellowship of professionals." This might speak of a school for scribes, possibly located at the court, but evidence for such a school is lacking. Some kind of master-disciple relationship is required to account for the continuity of the scribal arts in Israel. While there is no obvious dependence on any Old Testament model of master-disciple relationship within the scribes, there does appear to be a sociological development from scribal families to a fellowship of scribes within the nation, to the sophistication of the court, to the Torah-centered activities of Ezra, to later rabbinic thinking. Such a development implies master-disciple relationships.

J. Crenshaw elucidates the diverse nature of "wisdom" in a three-fold manner: wisdom is a world outlook, a teaching position, and a folk tradition.[177] Understood from this point of view, "wisdom" requires master-disciple relationships for its acquisition and use, but the types of relationship vary in form and function. Master-disciple relationships behind the perpetuation and dissemination of the wisdom tradition would be found in informal father-son relationships, in training of elders for making judicial decisions in the city gate, in the wisdom orientation of advisers in the court, and within certain groups who specialized in wisdom and were involved with the recording of wisdom sayings. Those specializing in wisdom (e.g., elders and court advisers) would help regulate and fine-tune the wisdom which was originally disseminated throughout the cultural milieu by means of family / clan education and contextualization. A wisdom school is often suggested for this nation-wide wisdom specialty, and evidence of wisdom emphasis at the royal court gives some weight to this suggestion. But the absence of "school" evidence suggests that greater potential for finding master-disciple is to be found in the family / clan, elder / leader training, and "wise men" who were specialists in the wisdom tradition.

In spite of the relative absence of disciple terminology and explicit teaching on discipleship, the nature of the prophetic ministry, the writing prophets, the scribes, and the wisdom tradition speak strongly of the existence of master-disciple relationships in Israel. These types of relationship are quite different from the formal, institutionalized model Rengstorf fears would preempt the place of discipleship to Yahweh. Indeed, when these master-disciple relationships are viewed in the manner suggested here, they are recognized to be part of various means of communicating to Israel the revelation of Yahweh, and as such, promote a greater depth of discipleship to Yahweh within the national life.

---

[177] Crenshaw, *Old Testament Wisdom*, pp. 17-25.

CHAPTER THREE

THE INTERTESTAMENTAL BACKGROUND

I. Introduction

This chapter will undertake an examination of the term μαθητής and the equivalent Hebrew / Aramaic semantical field as found in the extant Jewish literature outside the Old Testament and up to the compilation of the Rabbinical literature. The purpose is to arrive at an understanding of these terms as they were used prior to, and at, the time of Jesus and the gospel writers. Jesus' ministry of gathering disciples and sending them out to make other disciples occurred in the midst of a Jewish milieu, and a more complete understanding of his ministry is aided by seeing it in light of other Jewish disciples of his day. One author has suggested that

> The importance of a correct understanding of first-century Judaism for understanding the Gospels cannot be overemphasized. Neither the nature of Jesus' mission nor the sense of His teaching can be grasped apart from an adequate knowledge of the religious life of His day.[1]

This study is devoted primarily to the primary sources, which means examining the related terms for *disciple* in the Septuagint, Apocrypha, Pseudepigrapha, Qumran literature, Philo, the Gospels, Josephus and the Rabbinic literature. The major objective will be to try to arrive at an understanding of how the terms for disciple were used at the time of Jesus. This understanding of the Jewish use contemporary to the gospels will then be compared against the use of μαθητής in Matthew's gospel in order to arrive at a more complete understanding of Matthew's concept of the disciples.

II. Major Greek and Hebrew / Aramaic Terms for "Disciple"

The central purpose of this section is to trace the use of μαθητής in the Jewish literature outside of the OT, but there were equivalent terms in use in Hebrew / Aramaic which form a semantical field important for this study.[2]

---

[1] Donald A. Hagner, *The Jewish Reclamation of Jesus: An Analysis and Critique of Modern Jewish Study of Jesus* (Grand Rapids: Zondervan, 1984), p. 171.

[2] Moisés Silva (*Biblical Words and Their Meaning: An Introduction to Lexical Semantics* [Grand Rapids, Michigan: Zondervan, 1983]), prefers "lexical field," but notes that they are equivalent expressions: "a defined area of meaning occupied by related words" (p. 192, under "field, lexical"; cf. also his chapter on "Determining Meaning," pp. 137ff, but esp. pp. 159-169).

A) Μαθητής

Μαθητής was the predominant term in classical and Hellenistic Greek for one engaged in a learning process, owing to its transparent relation to the verb μανθάνειν, "to learn." Whether the learning was a general apprenticeship, or technical adherence to a cultural milieu or master-teacher, or specialized, technical study in the school of a philosopher, or technical adherence to a religion / religious figure, the term used was μαθητής.[3] The usage of the gospel writers reflects this Greek heritage. Μαθητής is the normal term used to denote the followers of Jesus, used no less than two hundred sixty-two times in the Gospels and Acts,[4] and is the key term for New Testament studies of discipleship. The use of this term by Jewish authors writing in Greek, and Greek translations of Hebrew / Aramaic works, is significant for comparative studies (e.g. the LXX, much of the Apocrypha and Pseudepigrapha, Philo and Josephus).

B) Talmîdh

Just as the Greek term μαθητής ("learner" / "disciple") derived from the verb for "learn" (μανθάνω), the Hebrew term talmîdh ("learner" / "disciple") derived from the verb for "learn" (lâmadh).[5] The term talmîdh is found only once in the Old Testament (I Chron 25:8),[6] but by Talmudic times it became a specialized-technical term denoting a student of Torah studying under a teacher / rabbi.[7] An advanced level of the disciple / student in the Talmud is the talmîdh châkhâm, "the disciple of the wise." This disciple had advanced to the point where he was considered the intellectual equal of his teacher, could even render halakhic

---

[3] Cf. above, Chapter Two, on the classical and Hellenistic background of μαθητής; for a general discussion of the term, cf. also KarL H. Rengstorf, "Μαθητής," Theological Dictionary of the New Testament, tr. and ed. Geoffrey W. Bromiley (Grand Rapids: Eerdmans, 1967), IV, pp. 416-426; Dietrich Müller, "Disciple—Μαθητής," tr. and ed. Colin Brown, The New International Dictionary of New Testament Theology, (Grand Rapids: Zondervan, 1975), I, pp. 483-484.

[4] Robert Morgenthaler, Statistik des Neutestamentlichen Wortschatzes (Frankfurt Am Main: Gotthelf-Verlag Zürich, 1958), p. 118.

[5] Ernst Jenni, "lmdh," THAT, vol. II, col. 875. This derivation is also true of the related Aramaic term talmîdhaʾ; cf. Marcus Jastrow, ed., A Dictionary of the Targumim, the Talmud Babli and Yerushalmi, and the Midrashic Literature (New York: Pardes, 1950), II, p. 1673.

[6] Jenni, "lmd," col. 875; Francis Brown, S. R. Driver, and Charles A. Briggs, A Hebrew and English Lexicon of the Old Testament (E.T.; Oxford: Clarendon, 1974), p. 541; cf. Chapter Three above for a discussion of the occurrence of this term in the Old Testament.

[7] Cf. Jastrow, Dictionary, p. 1673, and Rengstorf, "μαθητής," pp. 431 ff., for examples.

decisions, but was not yet ordained as a fully qualified rabbi.[8] The term *talmîdh* appears to be the most common equivalent in Hebrew (or *talmîdhà'* in Aramaic) for the Greek term μαθητής in Jesus' time.

C) *Limmûdh*

The adjective *limmûdh*, "taught,"is often rendered substantively to refer to disciples or pupils of a prophet[9] (or "school" by some[10]). This term is also derived from the verb *lâmadh*, but it did not become a common term for a disciple in Judaism as did the related noun *talmîdh*.

D) *Sh^ewalyà'*[11]

This Aramaic noun was the term used to denote an "apprentice," or at times a "servant." The difference between *talmîdh* and *sh^ewalyà'* in Rabbinical literature is that *talmîdh* is used exclusively in the sense of one who has given himself to be a learner of Torah, whereas *sh^ewalyà'* stands for one engaged in the learning of a trade.[12] T. W. Manson suggests that Jesus chose *sh^ewalyà'* to describe his followers, instead of the more common word *talmîdh*. In doing so Jesus was consciously opposing the whole scribal system. He was showing by this choice of terminology that he was not advocating discipleship as a theoretical life of scholarship, but as a practical task for laborers in God's vineyard or harvest field.

> ...Jesus was their Master not so much as a teacher of right doctrine, but rather as a master-craftsman whom they were to follow and imitate. Discipleship was not matriculation in a Rabbinical College, but apprenticeship to the work of the Kingdom.[13]

---

[8] M. Aberbach, "The Relations Between Master and Disciple in the Talmudic Age," *Essays Presented to Chief Rabbi Israel Brodie on the Occasion of his Seventieth Birthday*, ed. H. J. Zimmels, J. Rabbinowitz, and I. Finestein; Jews' College Series, No. 3 (London: Soncino, 1967), I, 11; Rengstorf, "μαθητής," pp. 431ff.; cf. for examples, Hermann L. Strack and Paul Billerbeck, *Das Evangelium nach Matthäus erläutert aus Talmud und Midrasch, Kommentar zum Neuen Testament aus Talmud und Midrasch*, (München: C. H. Beck'sche, 1922-1928), I, 496-497.

[9] Jenni, "*lmdh*," col. 876; Brown, Driver, Briggs, *Lexicon*, p. 541; Walter C. Kaiser, "*lâmadh*," *TWOT*, ed. R. Laird Harris, Gleason L. Archer, Jr., and Bruce K. Waltke (Chicago: Moody, 1980), I, 480.

[10] Cf. the discussion on *limmûdh* in the Old Testament, Chapter Three above.

[11] This is the way it is written and pointed in Jastrow, *Dictionary*, p. 1534, and in Rengstorf, "μαθητής," p. 431, n. 126, who cites J. Levy *Wörterbuch über die Talmudim und Midraschim*, IV, p. 519b. T. W. Manson, in a note on the term "disciple" (*The Teaching of Jesus: Studies of its Form and Content* [2nd ed., Cambridge: Cambridge University Press, 1935], p. 238 n. 2), cites Dalman (G. H. Dalman, *Aramäisch-neuhebräisches Handwörterbuch zu Targum, Talmud und Midrasch* [1938], p. 417a) as saying this Aramaic noun is pointed *sh^ewilyà'*.

[12] Rengstorf, "μαθητής," p. 431.

[13] Manson, *Teaching*, pp. 239-240.

Manson implies that by the time of Jesus the term *talmîdh* had become a fixed designation for a rabbinical student. This is a major assumption which requires examination. At this point Manson's contention will be recognized as a possibility, but a conclusion as to Jesus' use of terms will be held in abeyance until all of the data have been examined.

The major terms for this study are μαθητής in Greek and *talmîdh* in Hebrew; *sh^ewalyâ^ʾ* may also have significance. These terms will now be examined in the Jewish literature outside of the OT to ascertain their usage.

III. Analysis of Usage in the Literature

This section is devoted to a study of the use of the terms for disciple as they occurred in Jewish literature from the close of the Old Testament canon to the collections of rabbinic literature. Each major literature group will be analyzed in its chronological order. The specific purpose is to examine the above terms for disciple as they appear in the literature in order to understand their use by the author in the various contextual relations.

A) Septuagint (c. 250-150 B.C.)[14]

The term μαθητής does not occur in the accepted tradition of the Septuagint. It is found only in alternate readings of Jer 13:21, 20:11, and 26:9, and these so weakly attested that Rengstorf concludes that they arose with Christianity.[15] The closest approximation to the term is in I Chron 25:8 where the participle μανθανόντων translates the noun *talmîdh*. There is no technical, student concept associated with the participle. The participle suggests that this is an apprentice, one who is engaged in learning the musical trade from a master musician.[16]

---

[14] These are the generally accepted dates for the bulk of the translation, with the Pentateuch translated by 250 B.C., the rest of the Old Testament by 150 B.C., most of the Apocrypha also by 150 B.C., but some of it not until 50 B.C. (cf. Donald E. Gowan, *Bridge Between the Testaments: A Reappraisal of Judaism from the Exile to the Birth of Christianity*, Pittsburgh Theological Monograph Series, No. 14, ed. Dikran Hadidian (1976; 2d. ed.; Pittsburgh: Pickwick, 1980), pp. 307-310, 342-378.

[15] Rengstorf, p. 426, notes 83-88 for a textual discussion.

[16] R. N. Whybray, *The Intellectual Tradition in the Old Testament*, Beiheft zur Zeitschrift für die alttestamentliche Wissenschaft, 135, ed. G. Fohrer (Berlin: Walter de Gruyter, 1974), p. 37.

B) Apocrypha[17] (c. 250-50 B.C.)

The Apocryphal literature as a whole provides no examples of the use of μαθητής in the extant Greek translations.[18] Semantically associated terms such as scholar, student, apprentice, or rabbi do not occur either, but the term "scribe" (γραμματεύς) is found in several places (e.g., I Esdras 2:17, 25, 30; 8:3; Sirach 10:5; 38:24; I Macc 5:42; 7:12; 2 Macc 6:18), as are words of education such as "teach" (διδάσκω, Sir 9:1; 22:7; 4 Macc 5:24; 18:10), "learn" (μανθάνω, Baruch 3:14; Sir. 8:8, 9; παιδεύω, Sir 42:8), "learning, instruction" (παιδεία, Sir 30:17; 51:28), and "school" (bêth midhrash, Sir 51:23). The term "son" (τέκνον) is the normal designation in Sirach and Maccabees for one engaged in the learning process (e.g. Sir 2:1; 3:12, 17; 4:1, 10; 6:18, 23, 32, etc; 1 Macc 2:50, 64; 2 Macc 7:28; 4 Macc 15:1), while "servant" (normally δοῦλος) is a common term for one engaged in service of the Lord or a human master (Judith 5:5; 6:3, 7, 10, 11, etc.; Wisdom of Solomon 18:11, 21; Song of the Three Young Men 1:10, 12, 20, 63; Susannah 1:27; 1 Macc 4:30; 2 Macc 1:2; 7:6, 33; 8:29).

The Apocryphal literature therefore reveals nothing directly about the use of μαθητής / talmídh. It may be that these terms were not significant at this time, or it may be that these particular writers did not feel the term was appropriate for their subject matter. Until all of the data are examined it would be unwise at this point to advance an argument from silence.

This literature does reveal some interesting related facts. The special category of "scribes" (γραμματεις / sophᵉrîm?) is found in Sir 38:25-39:11,[19] although as far back as the captivity Ezra the priest was called a "scribe" (sophèr) skilled in the law of Moses (Ezra 7:6, 11, 12 ff.), and even earlier sophèr was used of various persons: leaders of Israel (Judg

---

[17] For a reference point those documents set out in the *Oxford Annotated Apocrypha, Expanded Edition containing the Third and Fourth Books of the Maccabees and Psalm 151*, ed. Bruce Metzger (New York: Oxford, 1977), will be referred to in this paper as the "Apocrypha." Normally 3 and 4 Maccabees and Ps. 151 are considered under Pseudepigrapha, but for convenience will be considered here.

[18] The closest form to the noun found in the Apocrypha is in the Wisdom of Solomon 6:9, where the second aorist subjunctive verbal form μάθητε occurs (*TLG*, University of California, Irvine); cf. also Lester T. Whitelocke, *An Analytical Concordance of the Books of the Apocrypha*, 2 vols. (Washington, D.C.: University Press of America, 1978). It should also be kept in mind that many of these works were originally written in Hebrew or Aramaic, and there are only fragments of some from Qumran in the original languages. The Greek translations were for the most part not completed until 150 B.C., but some not until 50 B.C. (cf. George W. E. Nicklesburg, *Jewish Literature Between the Bible and Mishnah: An Historical and Literary Introduction* (Philadelphia: Fortress, 1981) and Gowan, *Bridge Between the Testaments*, pp. 342-378).

[19] Cf. Rengstorf, "μαθητής," p. 438.

5:14), secretaries (2 Sam 8:17) and a professional class of learned men able to read and write (Jer 8:8; 36:23, 26, 32). The scribal category in Sirach implies a rigorous schooling in writing, making copies of the Scriptures, and interpretation of Scripture and oral tradition.[20] The "ode" to the "perfect scribe" (Sir 38:24-39:11), and the reference to Sirach's "school" (Sir 51:23), "confirms the picture of a scribe as one schooled in the law and religious wisdom, understanding the implications of both the written law and oral traditions."[21] The books of Maccabees (1 Macc 1:14f; 2 Macc 4:9-14) record that a Hellenistic "gymnasium" was built in Jerusalem at about the same time as Sirach recorded his reflections on the developing Jewish scribal school, i.e., around 175 B.C.[22] Therefore, even though μαθητής does not appear in the Apocrypha, both the Jewish and Hellenistic school system makes an appearance in Israel in the record of the Apocrypha, a fact which is important for understanding later Rabbinical usage.

C) Pseudepigrapha (c. 200 B.C.- A.D. 150)[23]

The pseudepigraphal literature is vast and varied. Much of it has been collected in a new English edition by James H. Charlesworth, ed.,[24] but only those works which are basically "intertestamental" are pertinent for this study. Most of these works are found in Greek manuscripts, and have been checked for the occurrence of μαθητής. At this time no occurrence of the term has been found.[25] Again, the subject material (such as apocalyptic literature and testaments) may not readily lend itself to the use of the term, or it may be that as these writers looked back on their Jewish heritage "discipleship" as expressed through the term μαθητής was not a key concern for them.

---

[20] Sir. 39:1-3 refers to the three-fold division of Scripture (v. 1) and the oral tradition of the sages (vv. 2-3); cf. Metzger, *Apocrypha*, p. 179, notes on 39:1 and 2-3; Ephraim Urbach, *The Sages: Their Concepts and Beliefs*, tr. Israel Abrahams (2d. ed.; Jerusalem: Magnes Press, 1979), pp. 568-569.

[21] Anson F. Rainey, "Scribe, Scribes," *The Zondervan Pictorial Encyclopedia of the Bible*, ed. Merrill C. Tenney, (Grand Rapids: Zondervan, 1975), V, 301.

[22] Martin Hengel, *Judaism and Hellenism: Studies in their Encounter in Palestine during the Early Hellenistic Period*, trans. from the 2d German ed. by John Bowden (Philadelphia: Fortress, 1974), I, 70.

[23] For dating see Gowan, *Bridge*, pp. 342-379.

[24] James H. Charlesworth, *The Old Testament Pseudepigrapha*, 2 vols. (Garden City, N.Y.: Doubleday, 1983-1985).

[25] Most of the pseudepigraphal literature has been entered into the *TLG* computer data base at the University of California, Irvine, but at this time no occurrence of the term has been found.

D) Qumran literature (c. 150 B.C.- A.D. 70)

The Qumran community produced a significant body of literature, much of which has been closely scrutinized. The concordances to the available literature list no occurrences of either *talmîdh* or *sheᵉwalyàʾ*.[26] Related terms are found in 1QH 2, 17 where *talmidu*[27] is a verbal construction meaning "you have taught,"[28] and in 4QpNah 2, 8 *talmud*[29] means "teaching"[30] (the origin of "Talmud").

Although the terms for "disciple" are not found in the Qumran literature, the organization of this sect may offer some help. The community at Qumran was a sect of Judaism which saw itself as a righteous remnant of Israel.[31] The Teacher of Righteousness was the founder / organizer of the Qumran community (CD 1:10-11), and it developed into a cloistered, communal, brotherhood in the desert. Admission to the community is detailed in 1QS 6:13-23: first there was examination by an official; then one entered into agreement with the "Covenant"; then examination by the "Many"; then an investigation of the person's spirit and work by the Community for a year, with an examination of his understanding of Torah at the end of that year; then one yielded his possessions after that examination; then a second trial year came with an examination for final admission following the second year. A second group of "physical" qualifications for entrance into the "Assembly" are delineated in 1QSa 1:19-21; 2:3-9. CD 14:3-6 sets out an order of precedence or rank within the community, and the life of the community was governed by this order. Spiritual qualifications were the basic

---

[26] Karl Georg Kuhn, ed., *Konkordanz zu den Qumrantexten* (Göttingen: Vandenhoeck and Ruprecht, 1960); Karl Georg Kuhn, "Nachträge zur *Konkordanz zu den Qumrantexten*," *RQ* 4 (1963-1964), pp. 163-234; Jean Carmignac, "Concordance hébraïque de le 'Röegle de la Gyerre,'" *RQ* 1(1958), pp. 7-49; Hubert Lignée, "Concordance de '1 Q Genesis Apocryphon,'" *RQ* 1 (1958), pp. 163-186; A. M. Habermann, *Megilloth Midbar Yehudah: The Scrolls from the Judean Desert, Edited with Vocalization, Introduction, Notes, and Concordance* (Tel Aviv: Machbaroth Lesifruth, 1957).

[27] Kuhn, *Konkordanz*, p. 233.

[28] This is the translation given by Geza Vermes, *The Dead Sea Scrolls in English* (1962; 2d. ed.; New York: Penguin, 1975), p. 154.

[29] Kuhn, "Nachträge," p. 234.

[30] Vermes, *Dead Sea Scrolls in English*, p. 233.

[31] The extensive discussion as to the identity of this sect, especially as it relates to the Essenes does not significantly affect this study. Those favoring an identification of the Essenes and the people of Qumran are in the majority; cf. the discussion and bibliographies in Geza Vermes, Fergus Millar, and Matthew Black, eds., A New English Version, Revised and Edited, of Emil Schürer's, *The History of the Jewish People in the Age of Jesus Christ (175 B.C.-A.D. 135)*, 3 vols., (1885; rev. ed.; Edinburgh: T. & T. Clarke, 1979), II, pp. 575-590. For a discussion of the minority position, which sees the Essenes and Qumran community as separate movements, cf. William S. LaSor, *The Dead Sea Scrolls and the New Testament* (Grand Rapids: Eerdmans, 1972), pp. 131-141.

criteria for advancement up the hierarchical order, and advancement was a desirable objective (cf. 1QS 2:22-23; 6:3-4).[32]

The essential points for this study are first, this was a community gathered out from the rest of Judaism for a communal life of strict dedication to the study of Torah and obedience to God, and second, God had sent the Teacher of Righteousness to guide the community's study and discovery of the true meaning of Torah (cf. 1QS 8:10-16; 1:1-2). The lack of any technical terminology for ''disciple'' indicates that all were part of one brotherhood. The various classifications were functionally and spiritually oriented to help carry out their life of obedience to God as prescribed in Torah. For example, Culpepper suggests that there was a school at Qumran within the community.[33] This school interpreted Scripture and tradition according to the precepts of its revered Teacher of Righteousness and wrote down its interpretation in order to guide the life of the community.[34] If there was such a school the members were not set aside in the literature as the true ''disciples'' in distinction from the rest of the brotherhood. Discipleship for Qumran was not a scribal or academic or philosophical pursuit, but rather was expressed in imitation and community conviction (CD 4:19).[35] The shared communal lifestyle and commitment to the interpretations of the revered Teacher made the community one brotherhood, and made them distinct within Israel. Indeed, as the remnant of Israel the Qumran community saw itself as the true people of God; all in the brotherhood were the true disciples of God. In this sense they saw themselves not as a movement *within* Israel, but as *the* Israel.[36]

Again, the absence of ''disciple'' terminology is problematic, but perhaps it is best to see that discipleship for Qumran was understood as communal isolation for practical devotion to God and Torah as interpreted by the Teacher of Righteousness. Therefore, Qumran appears similar to the Old Testament organization. Primary discipleship was given to Yahweh, but they had social structures which could be described as master-disciple relationships. This community appears strongly in line with the Old Testament picture.

---

[32] Othmar Schilling, ''Amt und Nachfolge im Alten Testament und in Qumran,'' *Volk Gottes: zum Kirchenverständnis der Katholischen, Evangelischen, und Anglikanischen Theologie. Festgabe für Josef Höfer*, ed. Remigius Bäumer und Heimo Dolch (Freiberg: Herder, 1967), pp. 211-212.

[33] R. Alan Culpepper, *The Johannine School: An Evaluation of the Johannine-School Hypothesis Based on an Investigation of the Nature of Ancient Schools*. SBL Dissertation Series, No. 26. (Missoula: Scholars, 1975), pp. 156-170.

[34] Ibid., p. 170.

[35] Schilling (''Amt und Nachfolge,'' p. 211) suggests that ''*Nachahmung und Gesinnungsgemeinschaft*'' is the essence of discipleship for Qumran.

[36] Urbach, *Sages*, pp. 584-585.

E) Philo (c. 25 B.C.- A.D. 50)[37]

The voluminous writings of Philo Judaeus of Alexandria are significant for New Testament study because the environment, language, and
culture are in many ways similar for both Philo and New Testament
Palestine.[38] Philo's writings are particularly important for the present
study because he is the first Jewish author whose writings are extant to
use the Greek term μαθητής, and because his works show how the term
was used by a Jewish author contemporary with Jesus. The term is found
fourteen times scattered throughout his writings.[39] While Philo's usage
is not extensive it is varied enough to show nuances of application.

1. Types of usage

a) General transparent usage

Philo's uses μαθητής in a variety of ways which are reflected in the
types of persons he calls μαθητής. First, Philo uses μαθητής to refer to a
"learner." This reflects the most basic sense of the term. In *Special Laws*
II, 227:4, Philo describes the relationship of parent and child as that of
instructor and learner (ὑφηγητής ... μαθητής). In *Special Laws* IV 140:3 the
μαθηταί are placed on a par with γνώριμοι (pupils) and contrasted with
ὑφηγηταί and διδάσκαλοι (instructors and teachers). The one who is called
μαθητής here is instructed by a teacher in discourses and doctrines until
such a time as he advances to be a "perfect man," (τέλειος ἀνήρ), one who
has advanced to the highest degree in the enlightened understanding of
justice and righteousness. The μαθητής is in the process of moving on to
be such a person. This is the most basic sense of μαθητής: one engaged
in learning.

b) Advanced learner who teaches the masses

Philo also uses the term of a more advanced learner, one who is above
the masses but below the perfect. In *The Worse Attacks the Better* 134:7, the

---

[37] Dates and general introduction to Philo have basically been taken from Samuel
Sandmel, *Philo of Alexandria: An Introduction* (Oxford: Oxford University Press, 1979) and
Peder Borgen, "Philo of Alexander," *Jewish Writings of the Second Temple Period*, ed. M.
E. Stone, *Compendia Rerum Iudaicarum ad Novum Testamentum*, II (Assen / Philadelphia:
Van Gorcum / Fortress, 1984), pp. 233-282. Greek text and English translation are from
Philo, with an introduction and English translation by G. H. Whitaker and F. H. Colson,
11 vols., *LCL* (Cambridge, Mass.: Harvard, 1929).

[38] Sandmel, *Philo*, pp. 3-4.

[39] *TLG*, University of California, Irvine. *Sacrifices of Abel and Cain* 7:4; 64:10; 79:10;
The Worse Attacks the Better 66:1; 134:7; *The Posterity and Exile of Cain* 132:2; 136:4; 147:1;
On the Unchangeableness of God 5:1; *On Husbandry* 55:1; *On the Change of Names* 270:5 (twice);
The Special Laws II, 227:4; IV, 140:3.

term is used for one who heeds the words of instruction from another and then reproduces those words. The implication is that one must have a life that is unblemished in order to be fit to be called a μαθητής. In an allegorical commentary on the story of Rebecca and the servant (Gen 24), Philo discusses virtue and the imparting of wisdom (*Posterity and Exile of Cain* 132:2). Rebecca is the virtuous teacher personified, who waters (instructs) her μαθητής (the servant) with perfect wisdom and virtue. As the story unfolds Rebecca holds out teaching which the servant (μαθητής) is able to receive (*Post* 147:1). In *The Worse Attacks the Better* (66:1) Philo makes an allegorical distinction between the twenty-five year old Levite, who is to work in the Temple, and the fifty year old who is to cease from work (Num 8:24-26). The fifty year old is perfect, a guardian and steward of virtue. The twenty-five year old is the μαθητής, only half perfect, and ministers to those who are seeking education, going over with them the doctrines and principles of wisdom. The μαθητής is advanced in learning: not perfect, but advanced enough to teach the seekers. Philo here reveals a hierarchy:

Perfect guardian of wisdom and virtue
Half-perfect disciple (μαθητής) who teaches the people
The people who are seeking education

c) One taught directly by God himself

The third type of use of the term sees the μαθητής as one who has dispensed with the instruction of men, is taught by God himself, and is now fully perfect. This is the most frequently used sense of μαθητής in Philo's writings, occurring at least six times in this manner. In *Sacrifices of Cain and Abel* 7:4 Philo retains the same hierarchical conception by clarifying that the common "people" learn by hearing and instruction. Μαθηταί are a "*genus*" (Gr. γένος) who are above the people, have advanced to perfection, have dispensed with the instruction of men, and have become "apt pupils of God" (μαθηταὶ δὲ εὐφυεῖς θεοῦ), receiving free unlabored knowledge. Those above the μαθηταί are advanced there by God and are stationed there by God himself. These advanced ones are ones such as Moses. In *Sacrifices* 79:10 Philo says that at a certain point in one's maturity, one must no longer just learn from others, but must progress to where God will cause self-inspired wisdom to spring up within the soul. Importantly, Philo here shows that this level is not exclusively designated by the term μαθητής alone, because he equates μαθητής with other terms: "God's scholar (φοιτητήν), God's pupil (γνώριμον), God's disciple (μαθητήν), call him whatever name you will, cannot any more suffer the guidance of men." Rengstorf says that this concept of one who has self-inspired wisdom from God "materially leads to Philo's mysticism."[40] The same basic thought is also found in *On the Unchangeableness of God* 5:1 and *On Husbandry* 55:1. The technical sense to μαθητής is found in *Sacrifices* 64:10. Philo contrasts "learners" (μανθανοῦσι), who have to take a long time in the educational process, with "disciples" (μαθηταί), to whom God can immediately impart knowledge without the need for time of learning. Here μαθητής is detached from the verb μανθάνω and stands more for the technical category of one taught by God without need of human instruction.[41]

d) Direct disciple of God

The fourth category of persons called μαθηταί at first seems to conflict with the above hierarchy of knowledge. In the allegorical discussion of Rebecca and the servant, Rebecca was the personification of the virtuous teacher and the servant was the μαθητής (cf. *Posterity* 132:2; 147:1). But as his commentary unfolds, Philo starts to refer to *Rebecca* as a μαθητής. The difference is that here she is a μαθητής of God. By this, Philo shows that the perfect teacher is also a μαθητής of God. An inherent characteristic of the μαθητής is lack of self-conceit, or true humility; this implies the ability to learn from God himself without recourse to external instruction (Moses is described this way as well; cf. *Sacrifices* 8-9).

Here μαθητής essentially refers to a *category of persons* who have advanced as students to a point where they can teach others and be taught by God himself. But Philo also uses μαθητής in a way which shows it is still a morphological transparency for μανθάνω because at times it signifies more of the *concept* of learning than of the *category* of student.

2. *Formative influences*

As in most every area of Philonic studies, the question of cultural, philosophical and religious influences on Philo's use of μαθητής needs to be raised. "As a legatee of both Jewish and Greek culture, Philo reflects so much of what he inherited that the question has been raised as to how much of the abundance he wrote is original, or else, how valuable it is."[42] How much of Philo's use of μαθητής is original, and further, how valuable is his understanding of the μαθητής? A few observations may show his distinctive use.

---

[40] Rengstorf, "μαθητής," p. 441.
[41] Rengstorf notes this as well; cf. ibid.
[42] Sandmel, *Philo*, p. 4.

Philo uses μαθητής in the common, general sense of a "learner," but he also has a distinctively Jewish philosophical or religious use. Philo was especially an exegete of Scripture, and however much influenced by Greek philosophical thought and methodology (i.e., Platonic and Stoic philosophy and allegorical interpretation),[43] he continued to recognize the supreme place of God in Israel. The true disciple is not a disciple of a human master, but is one who is taught by God himself. Philo does speak of master-disciple relationships, but the special category in which he places disciples removes them from human instruction so that they are learning directly from God (cf. *Sacrifices* 7:4; 64:10; 79:10). God teaching the μαθητής directly reflects more of the Old Testament Jewish influence than it does the Greek. The predominant use of μαθητής in classical or Hellenistic Greek necessitated contact with a human master (living or dead),[44] but for Philo the true disciple is one who has no need of a human instructor once he has matured in the process of gaining wisdom and virtue.

The influence is not derived totally from Old Testament Judaism however. The "inner instruction" for the initiate gives the impression of pre-Gnostic and/or mystery cult influences.[45] The knowledge which God imparts to the μαθητής is not for the masses of people. Instead, it is for those who have entered the realm of knowledge introduced by teachers, but given fully only by God himself to those ready for it.

The synagogue also influenced Philo's use of μαθητής. Synagogues apparently flourished in diaspora Egypt at the time of Philo. Philo was actively involved in the Jewish community,[46] and appeared to be involved in education in the synagogue (*On the Life of Moses* II, 215-216). Culpepper suggests that the synagogue was the place where Philo taught the allegorical interpretation of Scripture to a select group of initiates.[47] If this is true, then it was in the synagogue that Philo combined his Greek philosophical background, his interest in Jewish life and groups such as the Therapeutae and Essenes,[48] and his influence from the Gnostic / mystery cults: "...He stood within and contributed to the scholastic tradition of an Alexandrian synagogue in which both Jews and Gentile

---

[43] Culpepper, *Johannine School*, pp. 200-201.

[44] The only exception to this is those places where discipleship to gods such as Zeus is mentioned, but these references usually allude to mythological relationships.

[45] Cf. Culpepper's discussion, *Johannine School*, pp. 200-201, 207-209.

[46] Sandmel, *Philo*, pp. 3-16.

[47] Culpepper, *Johannine School*, p. 211.

[48] On the relationship of these groups see Philo, *On the Contemplative Life*; Geza Vermes, "Essenes-Therapeutai-Qumran," *Durham University Journal*, LII (June, 1960), pp. 97-115; Schürer, rev. by Vermes, et. al., *History*, I, 591-597.

'god-fearers' sought the vision of the true philosophy, which was attainable only through the proper (allegorical) interpretation of Scripture.''[49]

This is the milieu of Philo's μαθητής. In a general sense he is a learner, but in the more categorical sense he is an advanced learner who has been introduced to the mysteries of Scripture and now is taught directly by God himself. He is above the "crowds" (ὄχλοι), of whom Philo speaks with disdain,[50] and has advanced into the higher realms of direct discipleship to God.

F) Other Disciples in the Gospels (c. A.D. 30-90)

Most of the discussion of the use of μαθητής in the gospels occurs elsewhere in this dissertation,[51] but the use of the term with respect to disciples of persons (or groups) other than Jesus will be considered in this section. This use of the term is significant because it shows parallel applications by the same authors who wrote about Jesus' disciples.

1. Types of Disciples

Four groups of μαθηταί will be considered here: the disciples of John the Baptist, the disciples of the Pharisees, the disciples of Moses, and early followers of Jesus who left him.

a) Disciples of John the Baptist

Very little is known about how John gathered his disciples around him.[52] His message of repentance was known to be intended for all of Israel, and people from all parts of Israel came to be baptized by him.[53] His disciples first appeared in the Gospels at the baptism of Jesus (Jn 1:35-37), and some became the first disciples of Jesus. They next appeared in a controversy with a Jew about purification, most likely having to do with John's (and Jesus') practice of baptism (Jn 3:22-26). At the reception of Matthew Levi, the disciples of John came with the

---

[49] Culpepper, *Johannine School*, p. 212.

[50] Sandmel, *Philo*, p. 13.

[51] Cf. Chapter Four, "Matthew's use of μαθητής." All occurrences of the term in the gospels are analyzed in light of Jesus' disciples found in Matthew.

[52] Cf. Poul Nepper-Christensen, "Die Taufe im Matthèusevangelium," *NTS* 31 (1985), 189-207.

[53] Jn. 1:9-34, esp. v. 31; cf. also Mt. 3:1-12 (esp. vv. 1-5); Mk. 1:2-8; Lk. 3:3 ff. See also Josephus, *Antiquities* 18:117, who notes that John commended the Jews as a whole to exercise virtue.

disciples of the Pharisees and asked why Jesus' disciples were not fasting ("and praying" in Lk) as they were (Mt 9:14; Mk 2:18; Lk 5:33). While he was in prison John sent his disciples to ask about Jesus' messianic identity (Mt 11:2; Lk 7:18, 19), and John's own disciples buried his body (Mt 14:12; Mk 6:29). After John's death they continued with the prayer he had taught them (Lk 11:1), and many continued for years as his disciples, scattered to such distant places as Alexandria (cf. Acts 18:24-25[54]) and Ephesus (Acts 19:1-3).

The circle of disciples around John did not include all those who came for baptism, but may have initially been a group who assisted him in baptizing the crowds, similar to the way Jesus' disciples assisted him (Jn 4:1-2). There is no mention of John's expounding Scripture to his disciples,[55] but only of teaching his disciples a special prayer (Lk 5:33; 11:1) and of them having their own fasting practices (Mt 9:14; Mk 2:18). His disciples centered their lives on the practice of piety as had John.[56] The prophetic and eschatological form of his activity was the purest expression of ancient Judaism, especially in distinction from the Pharisaic and scribal activity.[57] Since John was preparing the way for Jesus and the messianic age, Bornkamm is correct in stressing that the disciples of John represent the closest analogy to the disciples of Jesus, even though they are not exactly parallel.[58]

The evidence indicates that the disciples of John continued as a movement within Judaism after his death. Although John did not consider himself anything other than the forerunner of messiah,[59] he appeared near his death to have some personal confusion about Jesus' role. This confusion quite likely passed on to certain disciples who continued his ministry as a movement.[60] John's disciples were a unique sort of μαθηταί within Judaism. They were fully committed to John as a person, but primarily as John led the way to repentance and Messiah. Their activities

---

[54] Rengstorf notes that "this account shows that the preaching of the Baptist had spread to the Egyptian *diaspora*...;" Rengstorf, "μαθητής," p. 456 n. 271. Josephus (*Ant*18:118-119) notes the great influence John had over the crowds.

[55] Although his disciples did call him rabbi at least once (Jn 3:26), and John teaches the multitudes in Lk 3:10ff.

[56] Martin Hengel, *The Charismatic Leader and His Followers*, trans. James Greig (1968; New York: Crossroad, 1981), pp. 35-37.

[57] Ibid., p. 37.

[58] Günther Bornkamm, *Jesus of Nazareth*, (1959; ET; London: Hodder and Stoughton, 1960), p. 145.

[59] Contra Hengel, *Charismatic Leader*, p. 36.

[60] Rengstorf, "μαθητής," pp. 456-457. Rengstorf rightly points out that even though the relation of John to Jesus might not have always been clear in the minds of his followers, men like Apollos and the disciples at Ephesus were easily able to turn to Jesus because John's way of preparation for the soon-coming Messiah remained central in the movement.

did not center on intellectual and scribal pursuits, but on righteousness and piety toward God. These activities appear to be dichotomized in their thinking,[61] something not envisioned in rabbinic Judaism. Even their disputations with the Jews (Jn 3:25) and Jesus' disciples (Mt 9:14 par.) concerned pietistic practices, not interpretation of Scripture or tradition. They were adherents of a movement, not members of a religious institution.[62]

b) Disciples of the Pharisees

The group known as the "disciples (μαθηταί) of the Pharisees" appears in the Gospels in Mk 2:18 (par.) and Mt 22:16 (par.). An interesting parallel is found in Josephus, who alludes to John Hyrcanus as a μαθητής of the Pharisees (*Ant* 13:289). This construction in the gospels most likely reflects an early usage, because after the fall of Jerusalem and the beginning of Jamnia as the rabbinic headquarters, the normal phrase is "disciple of the wise" (*talmîdh chàkhàm*) or disciple of the rabbi (*talmîdh ràbh*). A decided shift occurred in the rabbinic literature toward deemphasis of the term "Pharisee," because Pharisaism was no longer a sect of Judaism after Jamnia, but rather became synonymous with Judaism.[63] "Disciples of the Pharisees" in the gospels indicates "those who were being instructed in, and who were assimilating, the teachings and practices of the Pharisees."[64]

These disciples, and those of John, were concerned about the question of fasting (Mk 2:18 par.). Mt 22:16 also mentions these disciples involved in a dispute about an important Pharisaic issue: paying taxes to Caesar.[65] These passages accentuate the key ingredients of Pharisaism. The Pharisees were committed to an intense study of the Scriptures, and uniquely the oral tradition, but they were also fully committed to living out the Law and the tradition. D. Hagner suggests that, "Pharisaism was at heart, though tragically miscarried, a movement for righteousness. It was this concern for righteousness that drove the Pharisees to their legalism with such a passion."[66] All through the gospels

---

[61] See the interesting comment to this effect by Josephus, *Ant* 18:117.

[62] Müller, "μαθητής," p. 488.

[63] Cf. Donald A. Hagner, "Pharisees," *ZPEB*, IV, pp. 745-752; Samuel Sandmel, *The First Christian Century in Judaism and Christianity: Certainties and Uncertainties* (New York: Oxford, 1969), pp. 25-27, 58-59. This early usage is stressed because many (e.g., Müller, "μαθητής," p. 488) tend to read the post-Jamnian usage back into New Testament times.

[64] W. F. Albright and C. S. Mann, *Matthew*, AB, vol. 26 (Garden City, New York: Doubleday, 1971), p. LXXVI.

[65] See TB *Pesahim* 112b and *Babba Kamma* 113a-b and 114a. See David Hill, *The Gospel of Matthew*, NCB (London: Marshall, Morgan and Scott, 1972), p. 304.

[66] Hagner, "Pharisees," p. 752.

the Pharisees are concerned with fidelity to the Scripture, the traditions, and the the unblemished practice of both. Therefore it would be expected that their μαθηταί were students of the Law and tradition, and were practitioners of legalistic adherence to both.

An interesting contrast is found in Mk 2:16, where the "scribes" (γραμματεῖς) of the Pharisees are mentioned. The scribes were the official interpreters of the Law within the Pharisaic party,[67] whereas the μαθηταί of the Pharisees were followers outside of the party. Lane raises a pertinent point when he stresses that although γραμματεὺς was a specialized term for interpreter of the Law in New Testament times, "μαθητής of the Pharisees" was not specialized. By "specialized" he means that μαθητής does not necessarily signify an "institutionalized disciple" in the rabbinical-scholar sense, but rather a follower of a certain sect.[68] If one were a μαθητής of a scribe then that one would be undertaking formal education and training in scribal techniques and interpretations. But if one were a μαθητής of John the Baptist then that one would be involved in the practices and goals of the Baptist. If one were a μαθητής of the Pharisees then that one would be an adherent of the teachings of the Pharisees, and possibly be in training to become a part of that sect. The usage of the term with respect to John and the Pharisees shows that there is no specialized, restricted association as yet. Μαθητής signifies an intimate follower of a person or teaching—one who has moved into a vital, committed association; but that association varies with each group.

c) Disciples of Moses

The "Jews"[69] who questioned the parents of the man born blind (Jn 9:18ff.) attempted to scorn the man by saying that although he was a

---

[67] Schürer, ed. Vermes, *History*, p. 329.

[68] William L. Lane, *The Gospel According to Mark*, NIC (Grand Rapids: Eerdmans, 1974), p. 108. Lane actually uses the term "technical," not "specialized." In order to retain uniformity in this dissertation I have reserved "technical" to mean, as does Rengstorf (or better Bromiley, in his translation), an accepted connotation associated with a certain term. The technical connotation of μαθητής implies a master / disciple or teacher / pupil relationship (cf. Rengstorf, "μαθητής," p. 416). This is the normal use of "technical" (cf. Silva, *Biblical Words and Their Meaning*, esp. pp. 159-169). In this dissertation I will reserve "technical" for that sense, and "restricted" or "specialized," for the sense of confined, isolated, limited to only one particular group; e.g., "scribes," meaning a professional class of writer / interpreters, or μαθητής becoming "restricted" when it is used only of Jesus' followers, or *talmîdh* of rabbinical students.

[69] The consensus in Johannine studies is that οἱ Ἰουδαῖοι stands for the religious leaders of Judaism; see C. K. Barrett, *The Gospel According to St. John* (1955; 2d. ed.; Philadelphia: Westminster, 1978), pp. 171-172; Leon Morris, *The Gospel According to John*, NIC (Grand Rapids: Eerdmans, 1971), pp. 130-132. The only real question is whether the Pharisees (Jn. 9:16) were included in the leadership group in 9:18. Tenney says "yes" (Merrill C.

disciple of Jesus, *they* were disciples of Moses (Jn 9:28). Their claim was
to a direct line with the revelation of God to Moses (cf. v. 29). This is
similar to Greek use (e.g., "disciples of Socrates," who lived long after
his death), and a later specialized rabbinic use.[70] In this context, however, there is no specialized use of the term, but rather an emphasis upon
following a type of teaching: i. e., following a person known to receive
a revelation of God (Moses), or one who claims it (Jesus). Here
discipleship is a personal commitment to a type of teaching as
represented in a person, but only in a general sense of a follower. This
actually may be the most general use of these four, because any true Jew
would have called himself a "disciple of Moses" in this sense, regardless
of any secondary sectarian commitments (i.e. to John, the Pharisees,
Sadducees, Essenes, Qumran, etc.). The later rabbinic specialized use is
not the same as this general use in Jn 9:28.

d) Early disciples of Jesus who left him

   In John's gospel there is a unique record of μαθηταί who had followed
Jesus for some period of time, but after a discourse by Jesus which they
found particularly hard to accept (Jn 6:60), John says "As a result of this
many of his disciples (μαθηταί) went away to the things they left behind,
and were no longer walking with him" (Jn 6:66).[71] The expressions
"going away to the things left behind" and "no longer walking with
him" are Hebraic[72] and mark the return of these μαθηταί to their old lives
before they had begun to follow Jesus.[73] The expressions may reflect
merely a literal "following around," but in John's usage most likely
indicate that these μαθηταί were followers of Jesus because he was an
exciting new miracle-worker and teacher (cf. Jn 2:23-25).[74] There is no
indication of a specialized, restricted use of μαθηταί here, neither in the
Jewish scribal sense nor Greek school sense. The μαθηταί were simply

---

Tenney, "The Gospel of John," *The Expositor's Bible Commentary*, Vol. 9 (Grand Rapids:
Zondervan, 1981), p. 104), as does Brown (Raymond E. Brown, *The Gospel According to
John* (I-XII), AB, vol. 29 (Garden City, N.Y.: Doubleday, 1966), p. 373. See Barrett
(ibid., pp. 360) and Morris (ibid., pp. 485-487, 496-497) for the supposed division in the
Pharisees of Jn. 9:40.

   [70] See Rengstorf ("μαθητής," p. 437) for examples. The rabbinic use became
specialized because it signified a rabbinic-type study of the Law of Moses and the oral
tradition concerning it.

   [71] Ἐκ τούτου πολλοὶ [ἐκ] τῶν μαθητῶν αὐτοῦ ἀπῆλθον εἰς τὰ ὀπίσω καὶ οὐκέτι μετ' αὐτοῦ
περιεπάτουν.

   [72] See Hengel, *Charismatic Leader*, pp. 16-18; Barrett, *John*, p. 306; Brown, *John* (I-XII),
p. 297.

   [73] Morris, *John*, p. 387 n. 154.

   [74] Jn. 2:23-25 is determinative for the reaction of people observing Jesus' ministry.

people who had made some kind of a commitment to Jesus, and when they encountered teaching which disturbed them they left. This is simply a loose attachment to a movement.[75]

2. Significant features

The first significant feature that results from the examination of these groups is that μαθητής is not used in a specialized sense. The term does not have specialized connotations associated with it, but rather is used in a general sense for a follower.

Second, this general use is non-specific enough to be used for a variety of types of disciples. The type of disciple is designated by an associative or possessive genitive: e.g., disciple *of Moses, of John, of the Pharisees, of Jesus*. This is noteworthy because later use in the gospels deletes this genitive and οἱ μαθηταί becomes a specialized designation for the disciples of Jesus only.[76] Likewise, *talmîdh* alone later signified a rabbinic disciple, and a qualifier specifed the rabbi to whom the *talmîdh* was attached. Therefore the general usage at this point in the gospels shows a non-specialized use for the term which makes μαθητής non-specific enough to be used of different types of disciples.

Third, these groups of disciples show a ''non-institutionalized'' character. They were followers of a movement or teaching prevalent in Judaism, not participants in a rigidly structured organization. The emphasis is more upon a life-commitment of an individual to a teacher / master or type of belief system. Specific lifestyle changes are associated with each μαθητής, and each change results in certain expectations of how a true disciple should conduct himself (e.g., the questions about fasting brought on by the disciples of John and the Pharisees), but the emphasis is not upon structured requirements for *all* disciples in every group (e.g. entrance requirements, instructional methodology and content, advancement).

Fourth, the general, non-specialized use of μαθητής suggests similar characteristics for the Aramaic / Hebrew substratum. The particular type of discipleship was not associated with the *term* μαθητής, but with the qualifying genitive. T. W. Manson suggests that Jesus chose *sheʷalyàʾ* to designate his followers, instead of the more common word *talmîdh*. Manson suggests that Jesus was indicating by his choice of terms that

---

[75] As John's gospel unfolds Jesus makes the definition of discipleship explicit so that anyone following would know what was expected of a true disciple (see Jn. 8:31-32; Jn. 13:34-35; Jn. 15:8). This defining process indicates movement toward a ''specialized'' use of disciple, as does the movement from the use of οἱ μαθηταί αὐτοῦ to οἱ μαθηταί (Leon Morris, *Studies in the Fourth Gospel* [Grand Rapids: Eerdmans, 1969], p. 142).

discipleship was not a theoretical life of scholarship, but a practical task of labor in God's vineyard or harvest field.

> ...Jesus was their Master not so much as a teacher of right doctrine, but rather as a master-craftsman whom they were to follow and imitate. Discipleship was not matriculation in a Rabbinical College, but apprenticeship to the work of the Kingdom.[77]

Manson implies that by the time of Jesus the term *talmîdh* had become a fixed designation for a rabbinical student. Manson's reluctance to see *talmîdh* behind μαθητής, and his suggestion that *sheʷwalyàʾ*, "apprentice," was used for Jesus' disciples, appears to stem from the differences he observes in the types of discipleship between these groups. Since μαθητής was sufficiently broad in concept throughout its history to designate both a student (*talmîdh*) and an apprentice (*sheʷwalyàʾ*),[78] and since there is some later papyri evidence for its use as an apprentice (*Oxyrhynchus* IV 724 [c. 155 A.D.]),[79] Manson's proposal, that μαθητής was used to render both Hebrew / Aramaic terms, appears attractive.

But the terms in the substratum do not appear to be different for these various disciples. For example, in the "fasting" dispute (Mk 2:18 par.) the synoptic writers do not hesitate to use μαθητής to designate the followers of John the Baptist, the followers of the Pharisees, *and* the followers of Jesus. According to Manson's proposal *talmîdh* would have been the term spoken for the disciples of the Pharisees, *sheʷwalyàʾ* for the disciples of Jesus, and *sheʷwalyàʾ* also for John's (since they were not rabbinic scholars). Yet when it came to writing a Greek account μαθητής was used for all. It is unlikely that the synoptic writers would have been so insensitive to such a distinction of terms in the substratum, especially Matthew, who is well aware of many subtleties within Judaism, and who appears to write with a Jewish audience in mind.[80] An immediate linguistic association is promoted by using μαθητής for all three groups of disciples, and this association implies that these groups were called by the same name in the substratum. The disciples of John and the Pharisees were united as disciples, and the dispute with Jesus' followers

---

[76] See the preceding note. See also C. H. Turner, "Markan Usage: V. The Movements of Jesus and His Disciples and the Crowd," *JTS* 26 (1925), pp. 225-240, esp. 235 ff.

[77] Manson, *Teaching*, pp. 239-240.

[78] This was demonstrated above in chapter two.

[79] James H. Moulton and George Milligan, *The Vocabulary of the Greek New Testament, Illustrated from the Papyri and other Non-Literary Sources* (1930; rpt. London: Hodder and Stoughton, 1957), p. 385.

[80] For the most recent discussion of the these features in Mt, and its *Sitz im Leben*, cf. Donald A. Hagner, "The *Sitz im Leben* of the Gospel of Matthew," *SBLSPS* 24 (Atlanta: Scholars Press, 1985), esp. pp. 254-259.

was based on their identity as "disciples" as well. Had Jesus' followers been so distinctively called "apprentices," and not "disciples," the dispute never would have arisen. On the contrary, it appears that the common substratum term for each group led to the dispute.

A further, and crucial, difficulty with Manson's proposal is that there is no attested use of *sh^ewalyà*ʾ in Palestinian Aramaic.[81] This absence suggests that the term *sh^ewalyà*ʾ was not used because there was no need for it. *Talmîdh* was broad enough to describe various types of disciples prior to Jamnia. After Jamnia, when *talmîdh* became a specialized term for a rabbinical student, *sh^ewalyà*ʾ came into use to designate an apprentice in distinction from a rabbinic student. An interesting sidelight to this is a *baraitha* in TB *Sanhedrin* (43a) which refers to the followers of Jesus as *talmîdhîm*. This could show the actual historical circumstance, or it could be a rabbinic reflection, but at any rate, as the only extant early writing in Hebrew mentioning Jesus' followers, the *baraitha* favors *talmîdh* as the substratum term for the μαθητής of Jesus, not *sh^ewalyà*ʾ.[82]

Therefore, as attractive as Manson's proposal may be for making Jesus' disciples distinctive,[83] the distinction is precariously based if it rests on the use of *sh^ewalyà*ʾ.[84] Rather, even as μαθητής was sufficiently broad to designate diverse types of disciples, so *talmîdh*, prior to Jamnia, was sufficiently broad.

G) Josephus (c. A.D. 37-110)

Josephus is another significant source for the Jewish use of μαθητής. Much as Philo, Josephus is a voluminous writer but his uses of μαθητής are relatively few. He uses the term fifteen times and these are scattered throughout his writings.[85]

---

[81] John James Vincent, *Disciple and Lord: The Historical and Theological Significance of Discipleship in the Synoptic Gospels*, Dissertation zur Erlangung der Doktorwuerde der Theologischen Fakultaet der Universitaet Basel (1960; Sheffield: Academy, 1976), p. 31. Manson draws his support exclusively from the Babylonian Talmud and the Mandaic *Qolasta* (cf. *Teaching*, p. 238).

[82] See F. F. Bruce, *Jesus and Christian Origins Outside the New Testament* (Grand Rapids: Eerdmans, 1974), pp. 54-65, for a discussion of some of the historical difficulties with using this *baraitha*, as well as the one preceding it about Jesus' crucifixion.

[83] In this case Manson's efforts to reconstruct the supposed "Q" source of Lk. 6:40; Mt. 10:24f and Lk. 14:26f; Mt. 10:37f. (*Teaching*, pp. 237-240) are unnecessary.

[84] Vincent, *Disciple and Lord*, p. 31.

[85] *Jewish Antiquities* 1:200; 6:84; 8:354; 9:28, 33, 68, 106; 10:158, 178; 13:289; 15:3; 17:334; *Against Apion* 1:14, 176; 2:295. Cf. Karl Heinrich Rengstorf, ed., *A Complete Concordance to Flavius Josephus*, Vol. III L-P (Leiden: E. J. Brill, 1979), p. 50. The Greek text and English translation are from *Josephus*, with an English translation by H. St. J. Thackeray and Ralph Marcus, 9 vols., *LCL* (Cambridge, Mass.: Harvard University Press, 1926).

1. Types of usage

Josephus uses μαθητής in a variety of ways. His distinctive characteristics can be recognized most clearly by grouping the occurrences according to type of usage. The significant feature with respect to Josephus' use of the term is that he was born and raised during the formative years of the early church. His use of μαθητής reflects a common cultural and linguistic milieu as the time shortly after Jesus' earthly life, the growth of the church, the time during which the gospel writers wrote their gospels, and the rise of the rabbinical schools at Jamnia. Μαθητής appears in *The Antiquities of the Jews*, dating from approximately A.D. 93-94, and *Against Apion*, approximately A.D. 100-105.[86]

a) General transparent usage

Μαθητής exhibits its general transparent relationship to μανθάνω in Antiquities 1:200, where Josephus comments on the kindness of Lot to strangers, and how he had learned this kindness from Abraham. The phrase literally reads that Lot was a "disciple" (μαθητής) of Abraham's kindness.[87] The disciple is one who learns from another and follows his example. This same type of usage is found in *Ant*17:334, where a young man was taught by an older, court-wise, Jew how to try to deceive the Emperor. The older man is called διδάσκαλος ("teacher") and the younger man μαθητής. In essence, the older man is the leader, because Josephus says he pushed the young man into the scheme, and was then put to death for it (*Ant* 17:337). The younger man was the disciple who was being led on the way toward a common goal.

b) Master-disciple relationship

Josephus also carries over the technical use of the term, which signifies an intimate relationship of an accomplished master / teacher and one who is attached to him in a common cause or lifelong pursuit. In *Ant* 6:84 Moses is the leader of the people, and Josephus calls Joshua the μαθητής of Moses. Joshua is being groomed by Moses to take over leadership of Israel once Moses is gone, and the style of leadership is assured of being

[86] Harold W. Attridge, "Josephus and His Works," *Jewish Writings of the Second Temple Period*, ed. Michael E. Stone, *Compendia Rerum Iudaicarum ad Novum Testamentum*, II (Assen / Philadelphia: Van Gorcum / Fortress, 1984), pp. 185ff.

[87] "μαθητὴς τῆς Ἀβράμου χρηστότητος." Thackeray translates it "he had learnt well the lesson of Abraham's kindness" (*Josephus*, vol. IV, p. 99), and Whiston, "one that had learned to imitate the goodness of Abraham," (*The Works of Flavius Josephus*, trans. by William Whiston, 4 vols. (n.d.; rpt.; Grand Rapids: Baker, 1974), II, 93.

THE INTERTESTAMENTAL BACKGROUND 113

the same, since Joshua is the μαθητής of Moses. In *Ant* 8:354; 9:28 and 9:33, Josephus describes Elisha as the μαθητής of Elijah, and in *Ant* 10:158 and 178, Baruch is called the μαθητής of Jeremiah. The LXX does not use μαθητής with reference to these individuals, so Josephus has interpreted the relationships to be that between a master and disciple. Rengstorf declares that Josephus here transported the Greek idea into the context,[88] but the Old Testament Israel exhibits several master-disciple relationships which do not show Greek influence. Josephus may be influenced by the Greek model here, but his interpretation of these relationships is in line with other Old Testament examples.[89] Elisha is never strictly a disciple; he is also a servant, which is the typical Old Testament signification for a man of God.[90] Josephus reflects many Jewish elements in these uses.

c) Philosophical / intellectual follower

The three occurrences of μαθητής in *Against Apion* share a similar usage. Each indicates a person or a group who follows the teachings of another person or group, for the most part quite removed in time. In *Apion* 1:14 Josephus calls certain Greek intellectuals the μαθηταί of the Egyptians and Chaldeans. This approximates a negative use, implying that the Greek authors were not original thinkers. In *Apion* 1:176 the writer Clearchus is called a μαθητής of Aristotle in a positive sense, even though quite removed in time. He is a disciple in that he follows Aristotle's teaching. In *Apion* 2:295 Josephus remarks that had the precepts of Jewish laws been either committed to writing or more consistently observed by others before him: "we should have owed them a debt of gratitude as their disciples (μαθηταί)." This reflects a sense of intellectual fellowship and adherence, even though the disciple is separated by time and distance from the master.

d) Member of a school

Closely related to the disciple as a philosophical / intellectual follower and a follower of a particular master is the concept of the disciple as a member of a school. *A member of a school* could signify either the member of a particular individual's school, or it could mean a school in the

---

[88] Rengstorf, "μαθητής," pp. 439-440.

[89] Cf. chapter two above.

[90] Rengstorf ("μαθητής," pp. 439-440) is probably too narrow in saying that when Josephus links μαθητής καὶ διάκονος (Ant. 8:354) he is reserving μαθητής for the Greek concept. More likely these are supplementary terms.

broader sense of a movement. Josephus speaks of Elisha sitting in his own house with his disciples. This is typical "school" terminology from the rabbinic model,[91] and especially interesting because in the Hebrew text (2 Kings 6:32) these "disciples" are instead called "the elders" (*hazqēnim*). His use of the term possibly represents a misinterpretation of the text, in which case he may regard the prophets as participating in a discipleship fellowship with Elisha, or he may be revealing a bias toward a school orientation in his usage. A similar situation is found in *Ant* 9:106. The biblical account speaks of "one of the sons of the prophets" (2 Kings 9:1), but Josephus calls him one of Elisha's "disciples." Josephus sees in the sons of the prophets a "school" of the prophet Elisha. In *Ant* 10:158 Josephus calls Baruch a μαθητής of Jeremiah. Josephus may have interpreted this relationship to be similar to that found in Moses-Joshua and Elijah-Elisha, or he may have seen here a scribal school relationship (note the scribal emphasis in the context (cf. Jer. 36:9-19).

In *Ant* 13:289 Josephus mentions the Pharisees, one of the Jewish sects he discussed in 13:171-173, and says that John Hyrcanus was their μαθητής.[92] Here Josephus refers to Hyrcanus as an adherent of an organization or a follower of an organization's way of thinking. While Hyrcanus is not actually a member of the Pharisees, he is their disciple since, like the crowds, he is influenced by their teaching.

The final occurrence is the only explicit reference of the μαθητής in the school setting of the Pharisees (*Ant* 15:3). The reference is to the Pharisee Pollion and his μαθητής Samaias. Since they eventually worked together in a scheme on behalf of Herod, they were spoken of as being honored together. In *Ant* 15:370 other followers are attached to them both. This reflects the school setting of the Pharisees, but also shows two individuals, one senior to the other, who are linked together in a project. This is typical Greek school thought.[93]

2. Formative influences

The striking feature in Josephus' use of μαθητής is the Greek influence. He has paralleled the common Greek usage, ranging from the learner, to the master-disciple, to the intellectual fellowship, to the school. His is

---

[91] Nathan Drazin, *History of Jewish Education from 515 B.C.E. to 220 C.E. (During the Periods of the Second Commonwealth and the Tannaim)*, (Baltimore: Johns Hopkins, 1940), pp. 105-116.

[92] The parallel passage in TB *Qiddushim* 66a does not use the term *talmidh*, and neither does the book of Maccabees.

[93] Cf. Culpepper, *Johannine School*, pp. 39ff.

not a pure Greek concept, though, because definite traces of Jewish emphasis occur, ranging from Old Testament "fellowship" concepts, to scribal activities, to Pharisaic practices. Significantly, Josephus did not find any related term for μαθητής in the sources he used (whether the Hebrew Old Testament, LXX, or Apocrypha). Josephus may be imposing his own personal Hellenistic use of μαθητής, but more likely he reflects the situation in Judaism as a whole. About the comparison Josephus makes between the Jewish sects and the Greek philosophical schools (*Wars* 2:19; *Ant* 18:11), Hengel says,

> . . . the comparison between the Jewish sects and the Greek philosophical schools in Josephus is not completely unjustified. Even the master-pupil relationship in the Rabbinate, bound up with the principle of tradition, has its model less in the Old Testament, where is was not known in this strict form, than in Greece. The διδάσκαλος corresponds to the *rabh* and the *talmidh* to the μαθητής.[94]

Josephus was a product of his time. As a member of the Jewish aristocracy he received a sound education in the Jewish traditions. Although he had been removed from Israel for some time, and had certain apologetic purposes in mind,[95] he still appears to write with an understanding of μαθητής that was current in Judaism. Judaism as a whole appears to be influenced by Hellenism with regard to the master-disciple relationship. Gerhardsson rightly points out that the Jewish educational institution had been growing in Israel for many years relatively independent of the Greek influence,[96] but once Hellenism became a force in Palestine the Jewish educational institution was permanently affected by it.

Josephus reflects the developing use of μαθητής / *talmidh* in Jewish circles. The Hellenistic influence is strongly noticeable in his writings, especially with respect to the master-disciple—teacher-student relationship. Josephus interprets several Old Testament relationships to be of a Greek master-disciple nature, but even though he displays this technical association in his writings, *talmidh* is not used in a specialized or restricted sense. One may be a disciple in a variety of fashions, depending on the person or group one is following. Josephus' usage is still fairly broad, and reflects the general Palestinian usage as Hellenistically influenced. There

---

[94] Hengel, *Judaism and Hellenism*, I, 81.
[95] Attridge, "Josephus and His Works," pp. 184ff.; cf. André Paul, "Flavius Josephus' 'Antiquities of the Jews': An Anti-Christian Manifesto," *NTS* 31 (1985), 473-480.
[96] Birger Gerhardsson, *Memory and Manuscript: Oral Tradition and Written Transmission in Rabbinic Judaism and Early Christianity*, trans. Eric Sharpe (Lund: C. W. K. Gleerup, 1961), p. 89. See the evidence in chapter two above for the growth of scribal and wisdom practices in Old Testament Israel.

are definite intellectual overtones, more than in the preceding New Testament use, but he does not center on the intellectual nature of the relationship. The commitment to a specific person's or group's goals is quite pronounced, sometimes even more than the intellectual relationship.

H) Rabbinic Literature (compiled c. A.D. 200-500)

The extant rabbinic literature, in comparison to all prior Jewish literature, is massively voluminous and complex. This type of literature[97] normally refers to the Targums, Mishnah, Tosephta, Talmud, and Midrash, and within each of these categories there are specialized studies and issues. Although the rabbinic literature is so complex, and the use of "disciple" so extensive that an entire essay (or dissertation!)[98] could be written on this material alone, the attempt here will be to derive general features of the *talmîdh* in this literature. The rabbinic literature was not put into written form until some time after the first Christian century,[99] yet there is often a backward look to the first century and earlier which assumes an earlier practice. The assumption that the rabbinic literature accurately reflects earlier practice has been strongly challenged in recent decades and will be briefly examined below. Nonetheless, this literature was compiled by rabbis who post-date Christian origins, who often portray activites prior to the compilation.

These latter features point out major difficulties for this study. This literature is called "rabbinic" literature, but to an almost exclusive degree these rabbis were of only one school within the scribal spectrum of Judaism. The "scribes" were a professional class within Judaism, and each of the sects had their own scribes (Qumran [Essenes?], Sadducees, Pharisees, non-affiliated?). After A.D. 70 the rabbinic traditions tend to lean more toward the Pharisaic (and within that, the Hillelite) persuasion, because the major training school was located at Jamnia (Yavneh), which was strongly Pharisaic. This line of rabbis became fairly well syn-

---

[97] I.e., the writings compiled by the rabbis. For a general breakdown see Sandmel, *Judaism and Christian Beginnings*, pp. 103-128.

[98] E.g., see the paper by Aberbach which considers the Talmudic student, and that essentially in the TB. He does not attempt an exhaustive, nor comparative, nor critical study, yet it runs twenty-four single spaced pages: M. Aberbach, "The Relations Between Master and Disciple in the Talmudic Age," *Essays Presented to Chief Rabbi Israel Brodie on the Occasion of His Seventieth Birthday*, ed. H. J. Zimmels, J. Rabbinowitz, and I. Finestein, Vol. I, Jews' College Publications New Series, No. 3 (London: Soncino, 1967), pp. 1-24.

[99] The only real exceptions are the targums of Job and Leviticus found at Qumran, which antedate the first century A.D.

onymous with Judaism after A.D. 70.[100] To gain a more rounded picture of Judaism one needs to examine all the other extant Jewish literature, especially those writings prior to the influence of Jamnia.[101] Therefore the rabbinic literature is considered in light of the preceding Jewish literature in this study.

The late date of the composition of the rabbinic literature presents another difficulty, and the difficulty is two-fold. First, the relatively late date of these writings in comparison to the time of Jesus calls for some caution concerning the reliability of the historical reflections. The Palestinian and Onkelos Targums may be older than the Mishnah,[102] but almost certainly the Mishnah was not compiled until around A.D. 200, the Tosephta and Midrashim by A.D. 300, and the Palestinian and Babylonian Talmuds not until around A.D. 500.[103] The critical analysis of the historicity of the rabbinic writings has been a major study in recent years,[104] and the master-disciple relationship has been a central issue. The major concern is that the rabbinic writers were recording an oral tradition that had been influenced by the conditions after Jamnia, and the discussion concerns the degree to which that tradition was influenced.[105] This study will proceed on the basis of a comparative / historical control, which means comparing the rabbinic statements with other, more ancient Jewish writings and subjecting those findings to analysis in the light of the historical conditions. But further, undue skepticism can be avoided by heeding Longenecker's positive reminder:

---

[100] Neusner suggests caution with repect to the danger of equating the Mishnaic picture with Judaism, since the Mishnaic is only one part of the rabbinic world between A.D. 70 - 200 (Jacob Neusner, *Judaism: The Evidence of the Mishnah* [Chicago: University of Chicago, 1981], pp. 1-5). I would suggest that many of his cautions could be applied to post A.D. 70 rabbinic writings as a whole. See Neusner himself on this kind of rabbinic Judaism in *Judaism*, pp. x-xi.

[101] Josephus is prior to Jamnian influence since he was removed from Jewish influence (and was under Roman) after the war of A.D. 70 (cf. *Life*, 423-430).

[102] For the difficulties in dating the Targums see the bibliographies and discussion in J. T. Forestell, *Targumic Traditions and the New Testament: An Annotated Bibliography with a New Testament Index*, SBLAS 4 (Missoula: Scholars, 1979), pp. 1-15 and bibliographies, pp. 17-69.

[103] These are generally accepted dates. For discussion see Sandmel, *Judaism and Christian Beginnings*, pp. 103-128; also Jacob Neusner, *Invitation to the Talmud: A Teaching Book* (New York: Harper, 1973), passim, who discusses the majority of the rabbinic writings in relation to the Talmud, and gives good insights on the literary relationships in the light of their date of composition.

[104] For a general survey of this discussion, especially as it concerns New Testament research, see George Wesley Buchanan, "The Use of Rabbinic Literature for New Testament Research," *BTB* 7 (1977), 110-112.

[105] An example of extreme skepticism is Jacob Neusner's, *The Rabbinic Traditions about the Pharisees Before 70 A.D.*, 3 vols. (Leiden: E. J. Brill, 1971); an example of moderate skepticism is Pierre Lénhardt, "Voies de la continuité juive: Aspects de la relation maître-disciple d'après la littérature rabbinique ancienne," *RSR* 66 (1978), 489-516; and an example of slight skepticism is Gerhardsson, *Memory and Manuscript*.

A major problem in the use of rabbinic materials for the elucidation of first-century practice is, of course, the lateness of the codifications. Yet we are dealing with a religious mentality that took great pride in the preservation of the traditional; and while changes due to development or differing circumstances cannot be denied, this desire to preserve the traditional—barring other considerations—minimizes the severity of the problem.[106]

Second, the late date of composition needs to be kept in mind in order to avoid anachronistic conclusions about the disciples. This is a common fault of many who compare the disciples of Jesus with the picture of the disciples found in the rabbinic writings.[107] There may be similarities in the rabbinic picture and the actual facts of the time of Jesus, but careful comparative / historical analysis must precede any conclusions about those similarities.

With these comments in mind, a general look at the rabbinic use of *talmídh* can proceed. The intention here will not be to give an exhaustive treatment of the rabbinic *talmídh*, but to try to ascertain those elements which most reflect the conditions at the time of Jesus. Those elements are less than clearly understood in modern research. Was there a school-concept fully developed in Judaism at the time of Jesus? Was there a master-disciple relationship fully developed in Judaism, either within or outside of a school? What was the impact of Hellenism on a developing master-disciple relationship? These are the questions which will guide this analysis.

1. General use of talmídh

a) Professional student of written and oral Torah

The basic use of *talmídh* in the rabbinic writings is to denote a person engaged in the pursuit of becoming a professional student of Torah: "...[*talmídh*] is used exclusively for the one who gives himself (as a learner) to Scripture and to the religious tradition of Israel."[108] The ideal of Judaism was that every Israelite was a *talmídh* to the Torah.[109] *Aboth* 1:1 attributes a saying to the Great Synagogue which became a standard

[106] Richard Longenecker, *Biblical Exegesis in the Apostolic Period* (Grand Rapids: Eerdmans, 1975), pp. 24-25.

[107] E. g., Anselm Schulz, *Nachfolgen und Nachahmen: Studien über das Verhältnis der neutestamentlichen Jüngerschaft zur urchristlichen Vorbildethik* (München: Kösel-Verlag, 1962), pp. 19-66. Also, in spite of the careful scholarship of Rengstorf and Müller they at times compare the discipleship of Jesus with that found in the rabbinic writings as though all that is found in those writings was in practice in Jesus' day (e.g., Rengstorf, "μαθητής," pp. 444 ff.; and Müller, "μαθητής," p. 488). This anachronistic comparison is oftentimes a fault of those injudiciously using Strack and Billerbeck's *Kommentar*, (cf. the general criticism of Samuel Sandmel, "Parallelomania," *JBL* 81 (1962), pp. 1-13).

[108] Rengstorf, "μαθητής," pp. 431-432.

[109] Schürer, rev. Vermes, *History*, I, 332.

of Israel, "Be patient in [the administration of] justice, rear many disciples (*talmidhim*), and make a fence round the Torah." Many youths would eagerly gather around the more popular rabbis to study. Josephus mentions that there were so many "young men" gathering in Herod's day that they were like an army (*Wars*, I, 33:2), and Gamaliel II (100-130 A.D.) is said to have had a thousand *talmidhim* at one time (*Sotah* 49b). In the rabbinic literature the *talmidhim* characteristically directed their study toward mastering the complex and extensive oral Torah.[110] Since all of Israel had the Pentateuch and the rest of Scripture regularly read to them in the synagogue, the common people had an extensive knowledge of religious observances. Thus, what separated the *talmidhim* and the rabbis from the people was knowledge of the oral Torah.[111] As Schürer states,

> Instruction consisted in a continuous exercise of the memory. For since the aim was to imprint on the pupil's mind the whole subject, in all its countless details, and since moreover the oral Torah was not to be written down, one lesson could never suffice. The teacher had to repeat his material with his pupils over and over again.[112]

The master-disciple institution, therefore, owes its development, to a large degree, to the development of the oral law.

b) Followers of a cause

While the common use of *talmidh* designated a professional student of Torah, it was not used *exclusively* in this manner. Jesus' followers were called *talmidhim* even though he was not called "*Rabh*" in the context. On the contrary, he was described as practicing sorcery and enticing Israel to apostasy (*San* 43a). Each of his *talmidhim* are ridiculed in the text, in no way elevated as exemplars. Also, in two other rabbinic sources, *talmidhim* are equipped as soldiers and do battle (Midrash *Shir Hashirim Zuta*).[113] One reads, "In the time of Menahem and Hillel, when a dissension arose between them, and Menahem left together with eight hundred *talmidhim* who were dressed in golden scale armor." *Talmidhim* dressed in armor is not the usual sense of pupils, even though they are connected with the house of Hillel. The other reads, "Eleazar and the *talmidhim* arose and killed Elhanan and cut him in pieces. At that time the Romans

---

[110] Ibid., pp. 332-333.
[111] Neusner, *Invitation to the Talmud*, p. 13.
[112] Schürer, rev. Vermes, *History*, p. 333.
[113] See in Saul Lieberman, *Greek in Jewish Palestine: Studies in the Life and Manners of Jewish Palestine in the II-IV Centuries C.E.* (New York: Jewish Theological Seminary of America, 1942), pp. 179-183.

went and encamped in Jerusalem where they defiled all the women. Eleazar and the *talmidhim* arose and brought the soldiers down from the camp.'' These *talmidhim* are the ''Idumeans'' to whom Josephus refers (*Wars* 4.5.2), and to whom an old Tannaitic source (*Sifre Zuta*) refers as Idumean *talmidhim*.[114] Here, then, are those *talmidhim* who were involved in warfare, not in discussions of Torah. Furthermore, they are Idumeans, and in Josephus they are said to be associated with Zealots. Lastly, there are instances in the Targums where *talmidh* connotes a sense other than ''scholar.'' For example, ''brood of sinners'' (Num. 32:14), ''families'' (2 Chron. 2:53, 55), and ''sons of the prophets'' are all rendered *talmidhaʾ* (or related Aramaic forms).[115]

While these examples are not numerous, they each share a striking feature: they refer to individuals at a time period prior to Jamnia. The *talmidhim* in *San* 43a and the Midrash cited above specify persons fully committed to a personal leader and a cause. The occurrences in the targums cited refer to *talmidhim* not connected with rabbinical schools. Even though the general sense of *talmidh* is a pupil studying Torah, prior to A.D. 70 *talmidhim* can specify other kinds of followers engaged in various causes.

2. Characteristics of the talmidh

There are several characteristics of the *talmidh* which may be identified, but the caution raised earlier concerning anachronistic displacement is vital here. While there are references to *talmidhim* who lived prior to A.D. 70,[116] most references are to *talmidhim* of the later Tannaim.[117] The references to the earlier *talmidhim* are usually historical allusions. An illuminating example of rabbinic anachronisim is found in *Shabbath* 136-146. The Mishnah passage refers to the ''*béth Shammai* and *béth Hillel*,'' but the Gemara on it refers to the ''*talmidh* of Shammai and Hillel.'' Although the marginal note in the Soncino edition suggests that *talmidh* is implied by the mention of ''*béth*,''[118] the historical allusion is to a time *after* the death of Hillel and Shammai; therefore these disciples were not personal disciples of Hillel or Shammai. The historical allusion most

---

[114] See Lieberman for text and translation; ibid., pp. 182-183 n. 199.

[115] See Rengstorf, ''μαθητής,'' p. 434.

[116] E.g., the reference to *talmidhim* in the statement of the Great Synagogue in Aboth 1:1, the references to the *talmidhim* of Shammai (*Oslah* 2:5, 12) and Hillel (*Shabbath* 14b; Tosephta *Sota* 13:4 speaks of a *talmidh* removed in time).

[117] E.g., Rabban Yohanan ben Zakkai (*Aboth* 2:8), Gamaliel II (*Berachoth* 16b; *Sotah* 49b), Eliezer (*Erubin* 23a), Ishmael (*Erubin* 11b) and Akiba (*Niddah* 58b).

[118] *Shabbath* 14b (p. 59).

likely refers to a time setting just prior to A.D. 70.[119] This is an example of a rabbinic anachronistic practice, but the further caution concerns modern anachronistic practice. Characteristics of rabbinic disciples are often listed generally, without paying attention to the historical setting of each particular disciple. Since the historical allusions may range from disciples living anywhere between 100 B.C. and A.D. 500, it is vital to differentiate between the practices of disciples living at different times. The attempt here will be to try to identify those characteristics which were true of disciples of rabbis at the time of Jesus.

a) Student of Torah

The central issue for the *talmîdh* was the study of Torah, especially Oral Torah. The original scribes, beginning with Ezra the priest-scribe, are the first examples of a professional class in Israel devoted to a service of Torah. The service of Torah was not intended to be self-serving, but was designed to bestow a thorough knowledge and practice of Torah on all of the nation. The scribal tradition is noted in 1 Macc 7:12, where a "group of scribes" appears, most likely a permanent group within Israel.[120] It is not until the time of Hillel and Shammai that there are regular references to *talmîdhîm* who study the law as apprentices to being skilled in Torah. An incident is recorded in *Shabbath* 31a which may reflect an important development at this time. A heathen became a proselyte of Hillel and, "On the first day he [Hillel] taught him, *Alef, beth, gimmel, daleth*; the second day he reversed [them] to him. 'But yesterday you did not teach them to me thus,' he protested. 'Must you then not rely upon me? Then rely upon me with respect to the Oral [Torah] too'." The dependency of the *talmîdh* on the master for knowledge of Oral Torah is at the heart of the activities of the master-disciple relationship. The evidence is strong for the establishment of "schools" of interpretation by Hillel and Shammai at this time, in which the "disciples" were taught methods of interpreting Scripture by oral *halakhôth*.[121] The controversy between the Pharisees and Sadducees was centered in the issue of the addition of this Oral Law, but once the Temple was destroyed, with its attendant cult and sacrifices and practices, the Sadducees lost most of their influence, and Torah was all that was left to

[119] See note 1 on p. 54 of the Soncino ed.
[120] Gowan, *Bridge Between the Testaments*, p. 302.
[121] S. K. Mirsky, "The Schools of Hillel, R. Ishmael, and R. Akiba in Pentateuchal Interpretation," *Essays Presented to Chief Rabbi Israel Brodie on the Occasion of His Seventieth Birthday*, ed. Zimmels, Rabbinowitz, Finestein (London: Soncino, 1967), I, 291-299. See Culpepper, *Johannine School*, pp. 171-195, for an excellent discussion of the controversy concerning the existence of Hillel's school.

Israel.[122] It was out of this central, absolute need for Torah that the Pharisaic claim that the Oral Torah was needed to interpret the written Torah won out, and with the central place of Oral Torah came the necessity for an institutionalized master-disciple relationship. As Lénhardt correctly states, "If the Word of God was limited to Scripture, as the Sadducees maintained it, it would not have been necessary to institute the master-disciple relationship in order to transmit it [i.e., the Oral Torah]."[123] He further notes the central place Jamnia had in establishing the master-disciple form which would become an institution in Israel.[124] Prior to Jamnia the master-disciple relationship can be implied as a part of professional scribal training. The developing importance of Oral Torah also implies master-disciple relationships among the Pharisees. Prior to A.D. 70 the master-disciple institution was in its formative stages, but with the establishment of the central place of the study and transmission of the Oral Torah at Jamnia, the master-disciple institution was established as a centrally important institution in Judaism. In fact, Tannaim are not even mentioned prior to Akiba; the teachers came into prominence when oral Law became an established part of Torah, and this was after Jamnia.[125]

b) Further characteristics

All other characteristics of the *talmîdhîm* are actually only further descriptions of the Torah-centered *talmîdh*. *Shimmush*, for example, which is the secondary qualification of the *talmîdhîm*, means "attending upon and coming under the personal influence of the teacher and learning from his deportment."[126] But *shimmush* itself was a study of Torah, because the rabbi's life was to be an embodiment of Torah.[127] Conse-

---

[122] Eduard Lohse, *The New Testament Environment*, trans. John E. Steely (rev. ed., 1974; Nashville, Tennessee: Abingdon, 1976), pp. 51-52. Lohse also discusses the incorporation of parts of the temple liturgy into the synagogue worship at this time, another indication of the way in which scribal Pharisaism took over leadership of most every area of the national life (pp. 51, 160ff.).

[123] Lénhardt, "Voies de la continuité juive," pp. 492-493: *"si la Parole de Dieu se limitait à lÉcriture, comme le prétendaient les Sadducéens, il ne serait pas nécessaire d'instituer la relation maîtres-disciples pour la transmettre."*

[124] Ibid., pp. 493 ff.

[125] Cf. Culpepper, *Johannine School*, pp. 180-183. Obvious precursors of this movement are already reflected in the activities of the Pharisees and scribes during the ministry of Jesus (e.g., Mk7), but it remained for the events of A.D. 70 and following for teaching of the oral Law to take central prominence.

[126] Louis Isaac Rabinowitz, "Talmid Hakham," *Encyclopedia Judaica*, 16 Vols., (Jerusalem: MacMillan, 1971), 15, 746.

[127] Aberbach, "Relations between Master and Disciple in the Talmudic Age," pp. 2-7.

quently, the rabbinic *talmîdh* was essentially a Torah-centered student. The emphasis was upon the acquisition of oral Torah so that written Torah might be fully understood, but the entire life was to be brought into alignment with the precepts of Torah. These essential characteristics were also prevalent, at least in formative stages, at the time of Jesus.[128]

3. Levels of talmîdhîm

The rabbinic literature identifies several levels of students of Torah. The lowest level is the *talmîdh*, a beginner in the study of scribal materials and the first step toward becoming a rabbi. The next level of student is the *talmîdh watiq*, a "distinguished student," who could begin taking an independent line in his approach to *halakhic* questioning.[129] A senior student is called *talmîdh hàbhèr*, a "disciple-associate," indicating the status position when a student stood beside or immediately behind the rabbi during prayer-time.[130] The highest level of student is the *talmîdh chàkhàm*, a disciple qualified to become the intellectual equal of his teacher.[131] *Talmîdh chàkhàm* means "disciple of the wise," and in its later use designated a student who had completed his formal education and who, once he received ordination, would be received into the ranks of the rabbis. A more technical use of *talmîdh chàkhàm* is also found in the rabbinic writings. Instead of referring to the immediate rabbi one studied under, *chàkhàm* referred to mastery of all known rabbinic traditions, *halakhic* as well as *haggadic*. In this sense the *talmîdh chàkhàm* is an independent scholar among the wise men of Israel, an ideal scholar. *Talmîdh chàkhàm* is reserved for very few: only those such as R. Zakkai and Akiba.[132]

---

[128] For further specific characteristics, too numerous and some too uncertain in dating to discuss here, see Aberbach, "Relations between Master and Disciple in the Talmudic Age," passim; Hengel, *Charismatic Leaders*, pp. 50-57.

[129] Aberbach, "Relations between Master and Disciple in the Talmudic Age," pp. 19-20. Jastrow (*Dictionary of the Targumim, the Talmud Babli and Yersushalmi, and the Midrashic Literature*) lists this as an Arabic loan word, which would most likely put it at c. A.D. 400.

[130] Aberbach, "Relations between Master and Disciple in the Talmudic Age," pp. 12, 15. *Hàbhèr* is the term used to describe the associates of the Pharisaic sect at the time of Jesus (cf. Schürer, rev. Vermes, *History*, pp. 386-388, 398-403; G. R. Driver, *The Judean Scrolls* (Oxford: Basil Blackwell, 1965), pp. 95 ff; Urbach, *Sages*, pp. 583-589).

[131] Aberbach, "Relations between Master and Disciple in the Talmudic Age," p. 11; Rabinowitz, "Talmid Hakham," p. 746.

[132] See Gerhardsson, *Memory*, pp. 108-109 for this special use. For the more common use, see J. Goldin, "Several Sidelights of a Torah Education in Tannaite and Early Amorical Times," *Ex Orbe Religionum: Studia Geo Widengren*, Pars Prior, Studies in the History of Religions (Supplements to *Numen*) XXI (Leiden: E. J. Brill, 1972), pp. 185-186; Jeremias, *Jerusalem*, pp. 235-236. See Strack and Billerbeck for examples in the rabbinic writings (*Kommentar*, pp. 496-498).

The use of these terms appears to be quite late. There is limited evidence for *talmîdh* appearing prior to A.D. 70, but virtually none for the compound forms. The most that should be ventured is that prior to A.D. 70 *talmîdh* described one who was an apprentice scribe, who, once he had finished his course, was "ordained"[133] as a scribe or rabbi.

4. Summary

The rabbinic literature has an extensive use of *talmîdh*. Most of it reflects a practice later than the time of Jesus, and that later practice almost exclusively gives the sense of a person in training to be a rabbi. The later use indicates an institutionalized form of discipleship, where the student centers his studies on learning and practicing Torah. His studies especially center on Oral Torah, because he had to spend much time hearing it from his master in order to become proficient in its use. Therefore, the rabbinic *talmîdh* is primarily a student of Oral Torah.

The earlier uses of *talmîdh* do not reflect this specialized form of discipleship. In the Targums *talmîdhâʾ* denoted various kinds of followers, ranging from a brood of vipers, to families, to sons of the prophets. In two early midrashim *talmîdh* denoted followers who went into battle, and there were connections with radical groups such as the Zealots. Followers of Jesus were also called *talmîdhîm*.

The use of *talmîdh* prior to Jamnia appears to denote a follower of a person or movement in general. He could be a Zealot, or an apprentice, or a follower of a certain influential person or new movement. After Jamnia the term came to denote a specialized student of the written and oral Torah, but the temptation to read post-Jamnian practices back into the time of Jesus should be resisted.

IV. CONCLUDING OBSERVATIONS

The first striking feature of the use of the terms μαθητής / *talmîdh* is the absence from the oldest Jewish literature. *Talmîdh* appears only once in the Old Testament (1 Chron 25:8) and there for an apprentice. The terms do not appear in any extant Jewish literature until the time of Philo, at approximately the same time as Jesus. Philo is instructive in his use of μαθητής, because he uses it with the general sense of a "learner," and with the technical sense of a committed follower. He reveals a blend of Greek / Jewish thought by using μαθητής in the sense of a disciple of

---

[133] See Jeremias, *Jerusalem*, pp. 235-236, for a discussion of the antiquity of "ordination."

God himself: the μαθητής must not remain in subservience to any teacher, because true virtue and wisdom come only from God. By the time of the New Testament and Josephus, μαθητής carried the general / technical associations of follower, with the type of discipleship determined by the one leading. There were no specialized connotations associated with the use of the term as there were in the days of Socrates and the Sophists.

Μαθητής became a convenient vehicle to carry Jesus' concept of vital attachment to himself personally. He was his disciples' supreme teacher and leader (Mt. 23:7-10). They were not to be disciples of any other person, and were never to advance to being called rabbi. They were to make disciples of all the nations, but all new disciples were to be taught what Jesus had previouly taught them (Mt 28:18-20). Μαθητής was able to become a specialized term for Jesus' followers because the common usage was general enough to hold the specialized connotations the Christian community appended to it. The same could be said of the substratum term *talmîdh*.

The linguistic history of *talmîdh* is not as well documented as is that of μαθητής, but specialized connotations do not appear to be associated with the term prior to Jamnia. The *talmîdh* was a learner who had banded together with other learners under a leader / teacher. At the time of Jesus the type of *talmîdh* was determined by the one doing the leading and/or teaching. *Talmîdh* became a specialized term in the rabbinic literature for the student of Torah . The oral Torah became the focal point of study, although the ultimate goal was to follow Yahweh through written and oral Torah.

Μαθητής and *talmîdh* appear to be equivalent terms. They were popular terms at the time of Jesus to designate a follower who was vitally committed to a teacher / leader and/or movement. The terms themselves did not determine the type of discipleship; the type of discipleship was determined by the type of leader or movement or teaching to which the disciple was committed. The types of discipleship covered the spectrum from philosophical (Philo) to technical (scribes) to sectarian (Pharisees) to revolutionary (Zealots and Menahem) to eschatological (John the Baptist). The terms were general enough to be used for all of the above. It remained for Jesus and Jamnia to make these terms specialized.

CHAPTER FOUR

MATTHEW'S USE OF THE TERM ΜΑΘΗΤΗΣ

I. INTRODUCTION

This chapter is devoted to isolating Matthew's[1] unique use of μαθητής, and although it builds on the prior chapters, it is central to the dissertation. It is central because the purpose is to examine every occurrence of μαθητής, categorize the usage in its context, and then attempt to delineate Matthean distinctives in his use of the term. A comparative methodology will be employed which is almost standard in Matthean studies for ascertaining Matthew's theological perspective (i.e., examining the inclusions, unique material, expansions, alterations, and omissions). This methodology will isolate Matthew's distinctive portrait of the disciples. The portrait of the disciples will then be compared with other "characters" (Jesus, the named disciples, and the crowds) in order to define the distinctive role of the disciples in Matthew's gospel.

This proposed methodological approach to ascertaining the theological persective of the disciples in Matthew's gospel has recently been rejected[2] because of two related concerns. The first concern is directed toward the use of statistical analysis of the sources. The concern here is that since data have to be interpreted, they can become more of a reflection of the *interpreter's theological perspective* than an accurate understanding of the *author's intent*.[3] R. Gundry's attempt to clarify Matthew's theological intention through statistical analysis of redacted passages[4] has been accused of this very feature.[5] The second concern is directed toward an overemphasis of statistical data in which the composition of the gospel as

---

[1] The "author" of the gospel which is traditionally named after the apostle Matthew will be designated by "Matthew" in this paper, and reference to the gospel itself will be designated by "Mt."

[2] E.g., Richard W. Edwards, "Uncertain Faith: Matthew's Portait of the Disciples," in *Discipleship in the New Testament*, ed. F. F. Segovia (Philadelphia: Fortress, 1985), p. 48.

[3] Cf. the discussion in Johannes H. Friedrich, "Wortstatistik als Methode am Beispiel der Frage einer Sonderquelle im Matthäusevangelium," *ZNW* 76, No. 1 & 2 (1985), 29ff.

[4] Robert H. Gundry, *Matthew: A Commentary on His Literary and Theological Art* (Grand Rapids: Eerdmans, 1982), pp. 1-11.

[5] Cf. Donald A. Carson, "Gundry on Matthew: A Critical Review," *TrinJ* NS 3 (1982), 71-91; Philip Barton Payne, "Midrash and History in the Gospels with Special Reference to R. H. Gundry's Matthew," in *Gospel Perspectives, Vol. 3: Studies in Midrash and Historiography*, ed. R. T. France and D. Wenham (Sheffield: JSOT, 1983, pp. 177-215.

a whole is ignored. R. Edwards instead argues for a reader-response critical methodology by which the narrative of the gospel is analyzed for clues to the author's intent. He contends that the author manipulates or guides the reader through the narrative sections over a period of time and in a definite sequence in order to arrive at the cumulative intent. He suggests that "the best way to pinpoint Matthew's understanding of discipleship is to concentrate on the distribution of the narrative material rather than its total effect."[6] The reader-response approach is gaining significant attention[7] for the reason that it attempts to let the gospel speak for itself as a self-standing entity.

Both of these concerns voice helpful cautions. The study here will attempt to avoid these concerns by emphasizing a statistical analysis of Matthean distinctives in conjuction with an attempt to view Matthew's gospel as an independent literary entity. The first concern is not only directed toward the methodology employed here. Almost any methodology in biblical research has the potential danger of reading one's own perspective into the data. Therefore, the concern will be heeded by making an exhaustive study of the use of the term, but to analyze its contextual relationship as well. The cumulative weight of regular usage will alleviate this first area of concern. The second concern is helpful, but the weakness of Edward's view is that if one merely progressed through the gospel of Matthew attempting to "feel" the effect of the author's manipulation there is no objective control to distinguish distinct Matthean features from those features which are common to the gospel story and which Matthew has also included. To reverse an old cliche, one might say that Edwards view has the potential of missing the trees for the sake of the forest. Therefore, this study will attempt to isolate distintive Matthean features through a comparative study with the sources, but will also try to gain a perspective of the disciples as the gospel unfolds.[8]

II. Comparison of the Use of the Term ΜΑΘΗΤΗΣ

Matthew has a special interest in the term μαθητής. Second only to the gospel of John, he uses it more than either of the other two Synoptic

---

[6] Edwards, "Uncertain Faith: Matthew's Portait of the Disciples," p. 48.

[7] E.g., one of the most recent issues of *Semeia* is devoted to applications of reader-response criticism, and three of the chapters were devoted exclusively to this approach in Matthew; Robert Detweiler, ed., *Reader-Response Approaches to Biblical and Secular Texts*, *Semeia* 31 (1985), cf. esp. pp. 71-138. See there for bibliographies to the literature dealing with this approach, which is becoming quite extensive.

[8] J. D. Kingsbury expresses the same desire to balance these various methods in his attempt to get at the heart of the Matthean message; cf. the discussion below of Matthean Christology, and Jack Dean Kingsbury, "The Figure of Jesus in Matthew's Story: A Rejoiner to David Hill," *JSNT* 25 (1985), 61-81, esp. pp. 61-63.

gospels (Mt-73; Mk-46; Lk-37; Jn-78; Acts-28).[9] Curiously, the term is not found at all in the epistles or Revelation.[10] It will be seen that μαθητής is a favorite term of Matthew, as are the related verbs μανθάνω and μαθητεύω. Matthew regularly employs the plural form of the noun (μαθηταί), employing the singular (μαθητής) only three times (10:24, 25, 42).

If the "two-source theory" is accepted as a methodological starting point,[11] one notices that Matthew has used Markan material almost exclusively for his source of material. In fact, Matthew draws on "Q" for μαθητής material only at 10:24, 25 (cf. Lk 6:40), 11:2 (cf. Lk 7:18, 19),[12] and most likely at 5:2 (cf. Lk 6:20). Μαθητής occurs quite rarely in Q material[13] as a whole, though, being found only eight times (Lu 6:20, 40; 7:18, 19; 10:23; 12:22; 14:26, 27). This is in line with the fact that the term is hardly ever found on the lips of Jesus himself.[14] The common occurrence, therefore, is in narrative material, which makes it readily available for use as an interpretive medium for the evangelists. Such is the case for the writer of the first gospel.

The attempt to understand Matthew's use of μαθητής must employ both horizontal and vertical means of investigation. William Thompson has observed that most redaction critics adopt a "horizontal methodology" of comparing the gospel with its parallel sources in order to identify redactional material, but oftentimes a "vertical analysis" is missing, where the gospel is understood in relation to itself in order to identify the evangelist's interpretation.[15] Thompson urges that a vertical

---

[9] Robert Morgenthaler, *Statistik des Neutestamentlichen Wortschatzes* (Frankfurt am Main: Gotthelf-Verlag Zürich, 1958), p. 118.

[10] Ibid.

[11] This theory, that Matthew used Mark and some body of material called Q (here implying only those places where Mt and Lk share material not found in Mk), is the most widely accepted today among students of the gospels, but the questioning of it by some scholars should at least suggest that methodologies in gospel research need not be based upon any one theory. This chapter will use the majority position as a starting point, but the methodology will attempt to be broad enough to accommodate other theories. In essense this is a *comparative* study; therefore the conclusions would fit with most source theories even though the terminology of the two-source theory is adopted for the sake of convenience.

[12] Richard Alan Edwards, *A Concordance to Q,* Sources for Biblical Study 7 (Missoula, Montana: Scholars, 1975), p. 46.

[13] This is using the common formulation of Q material in Lk and Mt as stated in Werner Georg Kümmel, *Introduction to the New Testament*, trans. Howard Clark Kee (17th. rev. ed.; Nashville, Tennessee: Abingdon, 1975), pp. 65-66.

[14] The only occurrences are: 1) Mt 26:18, Mk 14:14, Lk 22:11; source is Mk; 2) Mt 10:24f., Lk 6:40, source is Q; 3) Lk 14:26f. (cf. Mt 10:37f.), source is Q; 4) Lk 14:33, source is L; 5) Mt 10:42 (cf. Mk 9:41), source is Mt's interpretation of Mk 10. Cf. T. W. Manson, *The Teaching of Jesus*, (2nd ed.; Cambridge: Cambridge University Press, 1935), p. 237.

[15] William G. Thompson, *Matthew's Advice to a Divided Community: Mt 17:22-18:35* (Rome: Biblical Institute Press, 1970) pp. 7-12.

analysis be used first, then a horizontal comparison,[16] but since it is hard to see how one can isolate Matthean vocabulary, style, and interpretation without first doing a comparison with the parallels, this study will reverse his order. The present section will be devoted to a study of the term μαθητής in comparison with the parallel sources. The related μαθ-stem verbs μανθάνω and μαθητεύω will also be examined.

Matthew uses μαθητής seventy-three times, and of these approximately thirty-one are shared with Mk or Q, four (or five) are expanded from references in the source context, four (to six) are occurrences in unique Matthean material, and thirty-three (or thirty-four) are inclusions[17] in Matthew's sources (either Mk or Q).[18] Taken inversely, these occurrences provide the outline for the following analysis.

A) Inclusions in parallel sections

Pierre Bonnard describes Matthew's, or his community's, reinterpretation of Mark as "the Matthean genuis" (le genie matthean).[19] Matthew, he maintains, "makes Mark clearer, more explicit, more pedagogical and easier to memorize."[20] The adjective explicit is important because with it Bonnard emphasizes a significant characteristic of Matthew's inclusions. Matthew is a skillful author who, at many points, makes explicit through inclusions how he interprets his source material. Matthew often includes a word not found in his source material, and by the inclusion he makes more explicit to whom or what he believed the source was referring. An example of this is seen in 7:28 (cf. Mk 1:21) where, as Gundry notes, "characteristically, Matthew includes the name of Jesus to clarify the subject."[21] Gundry points out that Matthew includes the name "Jesus" for this clarifying purpose some eighty times.[22]

---

[16] Ibid., p. 12.

[17] "Inclusion" designates the phenomenon where μαθητής occurs in a section parallel to the other gospels. This term is more neutral than the designation "insertion" which is often used to describe the same phenomenon. Inclusion was preferred because of the desire to employ a methodology that is flexible enough to be of value to varying source theories (cf. n. 11 above), and because its use connotes incorporating new elements to form to a larger whole. One recent criticism of redaction critical studies is that they tend to focus on bits of evidence at the expense of the larger whole; the term "insertion" tends to perpetuate that focus. By the use of "inclusion" we hope to give the impression that these "bits" of Matthean literary touches are a part of a larger whole.

[18] Cf. Appendix B. These statistics were derived by this writer from an analysis of each pericope as divided in Aland's Synopsis (Kurt Aland, ed., Synopsis Quattor Evangeliorum [9th ed.; Stuttgart, Germany: Deutsche Bibelstiftung Stuttgart, 1976]).

[19] Pierre Bonnard, Évangile selon Saint Matthieu (2nd ed.; Paris: Delachaux et Niestle, 1970), p. 8.

[20] "Mat ... le rendant plus clair, plus explicite, plus pédagogique, plus facile à mémoriser" (ibid).

[21] Gundry, Matthew, p. 136.

[22] Ibid.

Matthew follows this same pattern in his use of the term μαθητής. At least thirty-three of the seventy-three occurrences of the term in Mt can be characterized as an attempt to clarify the characters in the story. Examples of this tendency are found in 8:23 (Mk 4:36) where Matthew makes explicit that it is the μαθηταί who followed Jesus into the boat; in 12:2 (Mk 2:24) the μαθηταί are explicitly accused by the Pharisees; in 14:26 (Mk 6:49) Matthew makes it explicitly clear that the μαθηταί are afraid; in 16:21 (Mk 8:31) the μαθηταί are said to be the explicit objects of the passion prediction; in 17:10 (Mk 9:10-11) the μαθηταί ask the question about the scribal interpretation of Elijah; in 26:40, 45 (Mk 14:37, 41) Matthew makes it clear that the μαθηταί were asleep while Jesus was praying in the Garden. Other general examples are 8:21 (Lk 9:59); 16:20 (Mk 8:30); 19:25 (Mk 10:26); and 21:6 (Mk 11:4).[23] Matthew advances grammatical specificity by identifying the characters in his story through the inclusion of μαθητής.

But what is the significance of these inclusions? Are they merely a stylistic trait of Matthew as a precise author? Or might there be some other specific purpose in Matthew's inclusions? Bultmann says no: "It is obviously of no significance that Matthew often expressly mentions the μαθηταί where their presence is only presupposed in the Mark text."[24] But a close examination of the inclusions reveals some patterns that may indicate otherwise.

1. Purposeful identification

In several inclusions Matthew has purposely identified as μαθηταί those who were unidentified in his tradition. In 8:21 Matthew identifies as ἕτερος τῶν μαθητῶν one who was only ἕτερος in Q (Lk 9:59). Two verses later Matthew specifies that it is the μαθηταί who follow Jesus in the boat, whereas Mk has "*they* took Him with them in the boat." Bornkamm, an early pioneer in redaction-critical studies in Matthew, asserts that 8:18-27 was a "miracle" story interpreted by Matthew to be a "discipleship" story.[25] The inclusion of μαθηταί in vv. 21 and 23 specifically identifies the characters involved as disciples, and the catchword ἀκολουθεῖν serves

---

[23] A complete listing of Matthew's thirty-three (or thirty-four) insertions occurs in Appendix B.

[24] Rudolf Bultmann, *The History of the Synoptic Tradition*, trans. John Marsh (rev. ed.; New York: Harper and Row, 1963), p. 356.

[25] Günther Bornkamm, "The Stilling of the Storm in Matthew," *Tradition and Interpretation in Matthew*, trans. Percy Scott (Philadelphia: Westminster, 1963), pp. 52-57. Bornkamm's article on the "stilling" was originally published in German in 1948 (cf. "Preface" to *Tradition*); the significance of his work is illustrated by the fact that students of Matthew still "respond" (?!) to Bornkamm thirty-five years after his article was published!!: cf. Paul Frederick Feiler, "The Stilling of the Storm in Matthew: A Response to Günther Bornkamm," *JETS* 26/4 (1983), 399-406.

to link the pericopes together (8:19, 22, 23), so that the entire section stresses a teaching on discipleship along with the miracle working power of Jesus.[26] Matthew specifies for his readers that those involved in this incident were μαθηταί.

Mark records a passage dealing with the rewards of discipleship, and in it occurs a statement in which Jesus refers to his follower as "one who bears the name of Christ" (ἐν ὀνόματι ὅτι Χριστοῦ ἐστε) (Mk 9:41). If this is a parallel to Mt 10:42 as Aland suggests,[27] Matthew records Jesus' statement to include a reference to Jesus' followers as "little ones" (μικρῶν), with the further specificity that the follower of Jesus bears the name "disciple" (εἰς ὄνομα μαθητής). Maintaining that this is an inclusion which also draws upon Mk 9:42, Beare states that it reflects the "Matthean tendency to interpret references to 'children' or 'little ones' as meaning disciples."[28] The important point is that Matthew uses μαθητής to make the identification of the μικρῶν specific.

Matthew gives a conspicuous perspective to his understanding of μαθητής in 22:16. Whereas Mk speaks of "some" (τινες) of the Pharisees and Herodians who were sent to entrap Jesus, Matthew speaks of the μαθητάς of the Pharisees. Gundry argues that by including the term in 22:16 Matthew has made the Pharisees the subject of "send," while Mark has the chief priests, scribes, and elders sending the Pharisees (cf. Mk 11:27 with 21:23). In this way, he points out, Matthew casts the Pharisees in a worse light than Mark did, portraying them as the instigators who send out their own disciples.[29] However, the anti-Pharisaic element is not a foregone conclusion since the Pharisees were comprised of many scribes and elders.[30] The interesting points are first, that Matthew has no problem designating those who plot against Jesus as μαθηταί, and second, that μαθητής is used to designate those followers of the Pharisees who were called talmidhim in the rabbinic writings. As was shown in the preceding chapter, neither μαθητής, nor the substratum talmidh were technical terms at this time for any one particular type of follower. He was a follower here of an official leader of the Jews as well as a follower of an itinerant preacher.[31]

---

[26] Bornkamm underemphasizes the miraculous element; cf. ibid., p. 54.

[27] Aland, *Synopsis*, p. 149, sec. 104. Schweizer believes this to be pre-Markan material; Eduard Schweizer, *The Good News According to Matthew*, trans. David E. Green (Atlanta: John Knox, 1975), pp. 252-253.

[28] Francis Wright Beare, *The Gospel According to Matthew* (San Francisco: Harper and Row, 1981), p. 251.

[29] Gundry, *Matthew*, p. 441.

[30] Donald A. Carson, "Matthew," in *The Expositor's Bible Commentary*, ed. Frank E. Gaebelein, vol. 8 (Grand Rapids: Zondervan, 1984), p. 458.

[31] Cf. the related discussion of the socio-political interactions of the movement of Jesus on the Jewish establishment in Gerd Theissen, *Sociology of Early Palestinian Christianity*, trans. John Bowden (1977; Philadelphia: Fortress, 1978), pp. 59-76.

While Mark says that "some" (τινες, Mk 14:4) were indignant over the anointing of Jesus with costly ointment, Matthew identifies them as the μαθηταί (26:8). Senior recognizes the typical Matthean tendency to give a specific identification to Markan subjects, and suggests that this tendency has moved Matthew to specify the vague τινες of Mk, but suggests that the identification has an ecclesiastical purpose here. He proposes that Matthew was seeking to resolve the traditional discussion about the relative merits of *Almosen* and *Liebeswerk* in rabbinic circles.[32] Whether or not this is the intention of the story, Matthew does seem to have some purpose in mind besides specifying a vague subject. Indeed, his purpose includes specifying the μαθηταί as those complaining. Perhaps Hill's suggestion that Matthew "is applying the lesson of the story to the Christian community he knows" hints at Matthew's purpose.[33]

At the humiliating scene in the garden when Mark says that "they all forsook" Jesus and fled (ἀφέντες αὐτὸν ἔφυγον πάντες, Mk 14:50), Matthew specifies that "the disciples forsook him and fled" (οἱ μαθηταὶ πάντες ἀφέντες αὐτὸν ἔφυγον, 26:56). This inclusion of μαθητής makes the subject of fleeing more explicit, but something more may have been in Matthew's mind as well. The fact that Matthew also includes an explicit mention of the μαθηταί agreeing with Peter that they would never deny Jesus (26:35 cf. Mk 14:31), makes it quite possible that Matthew is stressing the ironic and lamentable nature of the disciples' ill-founded confidence.[34]

2. Οἱ δώδεκα completed

The description οἱ δώδεκα appears eleven times in Mk as a designation for the disciples of Jesus.[35] The pre-Matthean tradition, especially Mk, reveals a tendency to identify the circle of disciples with the Twelve.[36] Therefore, Matthew had a fixed title in his tradition which he accepted as an identification of the followers of Jesus. Matthew accepts this identification without making any special effort to establish it further.[37] In

---

[32] Donald P. Senior, *The Passion Narrative According to Matthew: A Redactional Study*, Bibliotheca Ephemeridum Theologicarum, 39 (Louvain, Belgium: Leuven University Press, 1975), pp. 32-33. So also Bonnard, *Matthieu*, p. 372.

[33] David Hill, *The Gospel of Matthew, New Century Bible* (London: Marshall, Morgan and Scott, 1972), p. 333.

[34] Cf. Gundry, *Matthew*, p. 540; Senior, *Passion*, p. 155.

[35] Robert P. Meye, *Jesus and the Twelve* (Grand Rapids: Eerdmans, 1968), p. 98.

[36] Bultmann, *History of the Synoptic Tradition*, pp. 344-346.

[37] Ulrich Luz, "Die Jünger im Matthäusevangelium," *ZNW* 62 (1971), pp. 142-143. Contra Georg Strecker, *Der Weg der Gerechtigkeit* (Göttingen: Vandenhoeck und Ruprecht, 1962), pp. 191-198, who sees Matthew making a conscious effort to make the identifica-

fact, Matthew has fewer occurrences of οἱ δώδεκα (Mt 8 times; Mk 11 times) and never writes οἱ δώδεκα *simpliciter*.[38] As an accepted identification Matthew could replace the Markan οἱ δώδεκα with οἱ μαθηταί (13:10 cf. Mk 4:10; 18:1 cf. Mk 9:35), editorially speak of τοῖς δώδεκα μαθηταῖς αὐτοῦ (11:1), and occasionally complete the title οἱ δώδεκα with μαθηταί (cf. 10:1; 20:17; 26:20). Indeed, exactly because the identification is so complete Matthew is able to be free with the title.[39] Matthew's longer title, οἱ δώδεκα μαθηταί, assumes an identification of οἱ δώδεκα with οἱ μαθηταί.

3. Inclusions of unique Matthean material

At various points in the narrative Matthew includes unique material containing the term μαθητής which is not found in his sources (Mt 15:23, 16:25; 17:6; 17:13; 18:1; 19:10). In Mark's story of the Syrophoenician woman, Matthew gives additional information. The disciples come to Jesus and beg Him to send the woman away (15:23). This prompts the statement from Jesus that He was sent only to the house of Israel (15:24). Both the disciples' plea and Jesus' answer are unique to Matthew. The picture of the disciples which Matthew paints is difficult to interpret, since the form of their request seems to cast them in a negative light,[40] while the answer from Jesus appears to imply that they had asked him to help her, casting them in a positive light.[41] In actuality, Matthew casts the disciples in a mixed light. As in 14:15 where the disciples want to send the crowds away (ἀπολύω in both cases), the woman appears as a problem beyond their abilities to help. One older commentator put it, "they were probably half touched and half annoyed by her loud and persistent cries,

---

tion complete. [An English translation has been made of Luz's work. The page citations in this dissertation are from the German edition, since the research was completed prior to the publication of the English translation; cf. Ulrich Luz, "The Disciples in the Gospel according to Matthew," trans. Robert Morgan, *The Interpretation of Matthew*, ed. Graham Stanton, Issues in Religion and Theology, no. 3 (London / Philadelphia: SPCK / Fortress, 1983).]

[38] J. Keith Elliott, "*Mathētēs* with a Possessive in the New Testament," *ThZ* 35 (1979), p. 304. The Matthean lack of the bare title οἱ δώδεκα leads Elliott to conclude that the longer title οἱ δώδεκα μαθηταί is the correct textual reading at 20:17 and 26:20. Cf. Appendix B, note 1, for a discussion of these texts.

[39] Luz, "Die Jünger," p. 142.

[40] Gundry, *Matthew*, p. 312 states that ἀπολύω is never used in Mt with the implication of relenting. Alan Hugh McNeile (*The Gospel According to St. Matthew* [1915, rpt.; Grand Rapids: Baker, 1980], p. 231) states that "their request may have arisen from mere annoyance or from their knowledge that He always repressed public excitement about Himself."

[41] Hill (*Matthew*, p. 254) regards the plea of the disciples as asking him to grant her request so that they could get rid of her. Jesus then informs them why he will not grant it.

and perhaps also were uneasy lest she should draw attention to them."[42] The disciples' motives are mixed, and Matthew uses them to accentuate the salvation-historical saying of Jesus[43] and the faith of the Gentile woman.[44]

The pericope at 16:5-12 includes an inclusion of the term μαθητής (v. 5) and an inclusion of a unique Matthean interpretation about the disciples (v. 12). Matthew has not included some of Jesus' harsher words to the disciples ("...or understand? Are you hearts hardened? Having eyes do you not see, and having ears do you not hear?" cf. 16:9 with Mk 8:17-18). Whereas, Mark closes the pericope with the sharp question of Jesus, "Do you not yet understand?," interestingly, Matthew closes the pericope with an interpretive statement: "Then they understood" (v. 12). While it appears that Mark's purpose is to stress the non-understanding and non-remembrance of the disciples who should have given the closest attention to Jesus' authority and teaching,[45] Matthew does not leave Jesus rebuking them, but indicates that Jesus recognized their imperception (πῶς οὐ νοεῖτε, v. 11), pointed out their misunderstanding (ὅτι οὐ περὶ ἄρτων εἶπον ὑμῖν) and then stressed the correct teaching (προσέχετε δὲ ἀπὸ τῆς ζύμης τῶν Φαρισαίων καὶ Σαδδουκαίων). Instead of suggesting that Matthew "cannot say that the disciples have no συνιέναι,"[46] the differences emphasize Jesus as teacher.[47] It is a result of Jesus' teaching that Matthew can say, "then (τότε) they understood" (v.12). Although their obduracy is softened, Matthew does not whitewash the disciples. Instead, through the persistent teaching of Jesus the disciples finally understand.

Mt 17:6-7 is another unique Matthean statement containing the term μαθητής. Earlier, Matthew omitted the statement of the disciples' fear at the transfiguration of Jesus and the appearance of Moses and Elijah (cf. Mk 9:6), but in 17:6-7 he records that the disciples were fearful at the word of recognition and command from the Father. This inclusion in the Markan context once again reveals a mixed attitude toward the μαθηταί. In spite of the fact that their act of reverence is syntactically tied to the

[42] John A. Broadus, *Commentary on the Gospel of Matthew* (Valley Forge: Judson, 1886), p. 341.

[43] Thomas Walter Manson, *The Sayings of Jesus* (1937, rpt.; Grand Rapids: Eerdmans, 1979), pp. 179-180, 200-201.

[44] Gundry, *Matthew*, pp. 312-313.

[45] C. E. B. Cranfield, *The Gospel According to St. Mark, The Cambridge Greek Testament Commentary* (rev. and rpt.; Cambridge: Cambridge University, 1972), p. 262. For a discussion of this theme in Mark, cf. Ernest Best, "The Role of the Disciples in Mark," *NTS* 23 (1977), 377-401.

[46] Gerhard Barth, "Matthew's Understanding of the Law," *Tradition and Interpretation in Matthew*, trans. Percy Scott (Philadelphia: Westminster, 1963), p. 114.

Father's command (ἀκούετε αὐτοῦ ... καὶ ἀκούσαντες οἱ μαθηταὶ ἔπεσαν ἐπὶ πρόσωπον αὐτῶν) their condition of fear caused their worship to be imperfect.[48] Although fear is a common element in revelation-accounts (e.g., Ex 34:30; Gen 15:1ff; Ex 20:18; Jer 1:8; Dan 10:12; Lk 24:37; Acts 10:4; Rev. 1:17)[49] Matthew does not connect fear with reverence.[50] Jesus typically admonished them not to fear (10:26, 28, 31; 14:27; 28:5, 10), but the mention of the "touch" of Jesus carries overtones of commissioning and empowering.[51] Matthew has included a section which portrays the disciples as reverent yet still fearful. They form a backdrop against which the figure of Jesus is accentuated in authority and compassion.[52]

The pericope immediately following the Transfiguration concerns the coming of Elijah (17:10-13; cf. Mk 9:11-13), and here the teaching of Jesus is accentuated through the inclusion of μαθητής material unique to Mt. Matthew states explicitly that it is the μαθηταί who ask about Elijah (v. 10) and who understand about the prophecies of his relationship to John the Baptist (v. 13). Mark does not mention the understanding. The emphasis in Mark is on the disciples' obeying Jesus' injunction to keep silent concerning the Transfiguration scene (v. 10) and then discussing among themselves the meaning (v. 10b), which gives rise to the question about the scribal interpretations of Elijah's coming (v. 11). Matthew omits the keeping silent and the discussion, and has them asking the question more abruptly. Matthew also makes the "explanation" of Jesus clearer. In Mt Jesus states explicitly that Elijah has already come "but they did know him," and a parallel situation will be the cause of the suffering of the Son of Man.[53] Because of this clearer explanation by Jesus, Matthew can record that "then" (τότε) the disciples understood. The inclusion of μαθηταί in v. 10 made it a discipleship pericope, and the clarified teaching of Jesus is the cause (cf. τότε, v. 13) of the disciples' understanding. As in 16:5-12 the disciples' understood because of the teaching of Jesus.

---

[47] Sjef van Tilborg, *The Jewish Leaders in Matthew* (Leiden: E. J. Brill, 1972), p. 109.

[48] Thomas F. Best, "Transfiguration and Discipleship in Matthew" (unpublished Ph.D. dissertation, Graduate Theological Union, Berkeley, Calif. 1974), pp. 146-148.

[49] Ibid., pp. 146-147.

[50] On φοβέομαι, the term used in this passage, cf. the following: 1:20; 2:22; 10:26, 28, 31, 14:5, 27, 30; 17:6, 7, 21, 26, 46; 25:25; 27:54; 28:5,10. Cf. also Horst Balz, "φοβέω," *TDNT*, Vol. IX (Grand Rapids: Eerdmans, 1974), pp. 208, 212. For φόβος in Mt, cf. 14:26; 28:4, 8.

[51] Cf. T. Best's discussion of ἅπτω ("Transfiguration," pp. 148-156).

[52] R. V. G. Tasker, *The Gospel According to St. Matthew, Tyndale New Testament Commentaries* (rpt; Grand Rapids: Eerdmans, 1973), pp. 164-165.

[53] Vincent Taylor, *The Gospel According to St. Mark* (2nd ed.; rpt.; Grand Rapids: Baker, 1981), pp. 394-39.

Matthew also has a somewhat softened portrait of the disciples' jockeying for position in the kingdom of heaven. Mt 18:1-5 is a discussion of true greatness in the kingdom of heaven. Matthew makes explicit that the disciples are the ones asking the question, "who is the greatest in the kingdom of heaven." The introduction differs from Mk 9:33-34, where an indefinite "they" discussed with one another who was the greatest. Matthew has none of the material concerning the disciples' jockeying for personal priority; he has only a general, almost academic, question of greatness in the kingdom. This question leaves the disciples innocent with regard to the issue, and they become a neutral backdrop to accentuate the teaching of Jesus concerning entrance into the kingdom.[54] Although the ignorance of Mark's account is softened and redirected, Matthew indicates that the disciples do not have complete understanding and so must still question and be taught by Jesus.[55]

In the passage where Jesus discusses with the Pharisees the question of divorce (Mt 19:3-12), Matthew acknowledges the imperfect understanding of the disciples, yet his inclusion of more unique material containing μαθητής redirects the focus. Matthew omits Mark's narrative allusion to a question the disciples ask about divorce (Mk 10:10), yet retains the answer (19:9). Matthew's unique material has the disciples not questioning, but making an interpretive statement (v. 10) with which Jesus partially agrees (vv. 11-12). Thus, Matthew has disciples who do not have to ask a clarifying question, but who at least partially understand and react because of their understanding. The difficulty of the passage[56] is diminished if the understanding of the disciples is indeed seen as partial. The disciples react to Jesus' teaching with an extremist conclusion: if there is such a strict law of Christ concerning divorce and marriage, then it is better never to marry. The disciples understood Jesus' strict interpretation, but they carried it to an unwarranted, extreme conclusion. Jesus corrects their partial, incorrect interpretation by linking to it a teaching on abstention from marriage. Marriage remains the normal state, divorce and remarriage remain strictly interpreted, and celibacy is accepted only by those called to it. The imperfect understanding of the

---

[54] Beare, *Matthew*, p. 375.

[55] W. F. Albright and C. S. Mann, *Matthew, The Anchor Bible*, Vol. 26 (Garden City, New York: Doubleday, 1971), p. 126.

[56] The central difficulty lies in the exception clause in 19:9. The difficulty for this study lies in the differing actions of the disciples in Mk and Mt. For recent discussions of the larger problem of the the exception clause see G. J. Wenham, "Matthew and Divorce: An Old Crux Revisited," *JSNT* 22 (1984), 95-107; Ben Witherington, "Matthew 5:32 and 19:9—Exception or Exceptional Situation?," *NTS* 31 (1985), 571-576.

disciples is positively accepted but corrected by the teaching of Jesus.[57] The inclusion of μαθητής becomes another backdrop for focusing on the advanced teaching of Jesus.

The analysis of these inclusions of unique material containing μαθητής demonstrate similarities among them: Matthew does not completely eliminate, but he does soften the obduracy and ignorance of the Markan disciples. The Matthean disciples are somewhat mixed in their understanding: they partially do and partially do not understand the teaching of Jesus. Furthermore, the disciples become a backdrop for advanced teaching by Jesus; through Jesus' further teaching the disciples come to understand.

4. Defining the relationship to οἱ ὄχλοι

Matthew includes μαθητής in several places where the ὄχλοι as a group are in evidence. These inclusions tell us something about Matthew's view of the relationship between the two groups. The first example is 9:19. As Jesus goes to care for the ruler's daughter, Matthew says, "And rising, Jesus followed him and His disciples." The mention of οἱ μαθηταὶ αὐτοῦ differs from Mark, who says, "And he went with him; and a great multitude was following him and pressing in on him" (Mk 5:24). Most commentators simply pass over this change from Mk, but Gundry states, "Mark's large crowd does not quite disappear, however, for Matthew characteristically identifies them as Jesus' disciples."[58] In this passage Gundry's thesis, that Matthew intends to identify the μαθηταί with the ὄχλοι, is difficult to maintain. That Mark does not intend to equate the crowd with the disciples in this passage is evident because he distinguishes between them in Mk 5:24 and 31. Ernest Best draws attention to the crowd's "following" Jesus in Mk 5:24, noting that a following in discipleship is not intended, but simply a description of movement.[59]

---

[57] This interpretation would help explain what is for Davies a "confused and confusing" addition. By making the disciples the ones who are confused in their interpretation, the advanced teaching of Jesus is directed to their confused interpretation and not his own teaching (cf. W. D. Davies, *The Setting of the Sermon on the Mount* (Cambridge: Cambridge University Press, 1964), pp. 393-395). This would also satisfy Gundry's desire for maintaining Jesus' positive attitude toward marriage. In his interpretation of the addition, Gundry basically regards the disciples as having a correct understanding of Jesus' teaching, but their statement concerns re-marriage (notice v. 9 has γαμήσῃ ἄλλην while v. 10 has γαμῆσαι without ἄλλος). Perhaps the interpretation advanced above best explains the data.

[58] Gundry, *Matthew*, pp. 172-173.

[59] Ernest Best, *Following Jesus : Discipleship in the Gospel of Mark*, JSNT Supp. Ser. no. 4 (Sheffield: JSOT, 1981), p. 36. Matthew carries over the non-discipleship connotation of ἀκολουθέω in this passage, but with him it is *Jesus* who follows the ruler (cf. Bonnard, *Matthieu*, p. 135; Gundry, *Matthew*, p. 173).

Matthew does not make a new identification, that the crowd in Mk was actually a group of disciples, because to do so he would have had to lose all distinctions between the μαθηταί and the ὄχλοι. That he does not do so is seen in the same narrative, when Jesus puts the crowd outside because they were making a showy uproar. Matthew's purpose for including μαθηταί in 9:19 is to focus on them as Jesus' lone companions. He has already omitted reference to the great crowd in v. 18 (cf. Mk 5:21) and has emphasized that the setting was more intimate than Mk's seashore panorama would suggest, having the ruler "come in" (εἰς ἐλθών).[60] Matthew has emphasized the figure of Jesus in the passage by focusing on the intimacy of the setting and his companions in ministry (οἱ μαθηταὶ αὐτοῦ), instead of the public ministry and public response in Mk.[61]

The fellow-worker motif is also accentuated by Matthew in the passage which marks a transition from the miracle stories in ch. 8-9 to the commissioning in ch. 10.[62] According to the two-source scheme, Mt 9:36-37 is a conflation of Mk (6:34) and Q (Lk 10:2). A significant change from Mk is that Matthew omits the story of Jesus' teaching the crowd in response to seeing their need, and instead he includes a reference to Jesus' telling the μαθηταί to pray for laborers. Taking it one step further, Matthew has Jesus calling the disciples (10:1) and sending them out to the lost sheep (cf. "sheep" in 9:36) of the house of Israel (10:6). Matthew makes a definite distinction between the μαθηταί and the ὄχλοι,[63] and illustrates the relationship between them. Mark has Jesus ministering directly to the crowd through teaching, but in Mt "teaching" drops out and Jesus, the Lord of the harvest, ministers to the crowd through the disciples. Hengel observes that the μαθηταί are thus Jesus' fellow-workers, and they are being sent out to the mission-harvest from which would come more followers of Jesus.[64] Through Matthew's inclusion of the term in 9:37, the μαθηταί are identified as Jesus' fellow-workers, and the ὄχλοι are the object of Jesus' ministry through the μαθηταί.[65]

---

[60] Cf. Bonnard, *Matthieu*, p. 135.

[61] Gundry notes the emphasis Matthew gives to the person of Jesus in several places (*Matthew*, pp. 172-176).

[62] A recent study which parallels the structure of ch. 8-9 with the structure of ch. 5-7 overlooks the transitional nature of 9:35-38 to the commissioning in ch. 10; cf. Jeremy Moiser, "The Structure of Matthew 8—9: A Suggestion," *ZNW* 76 (1985), 117-118. Schuyler Brown rightly includes 9:35-38 in his study of the commissioning, and ties the fellow-worker motif to the development of the overall structure of Mt; cf. Schuyler Brown, "The Mission to Israel in Matthew's Central Section (Mt 9:35—11:1)," *ZNW* 69 (1977), 73-90.

[63] Even Gundry notices this distinction (cf., *Matthew*, p. 181).

[64] Martin Hengel, *The Charismatic Leader and His Followers*, trans. James Greig (1968; New York: Crossroad, 1981), p. 75.

[65] Paul S. Minear, "The Disciples and the Crowds in the Gospel of Matthew," *ATR*, Supp. Ser. no. 3 (1974), 32-34.

Mt 12:46-50 contains another inclusion of μαθητής which clarifies the relationship between the μαθηταί and ὄχλοι. While Minear holds to a general Matthean editorial distinction between the two groups, he admits that the distinction is somewhat blurred in 12:46-50.[66] Mark refers to "those sitting around him" as the ones who are the mother and brothers of Jesus (cf. 12:49; Mk 3:34) but Matthew refers to the same group with the statement that Jesus stretched out his hand "toward his disciples" (τοὺς μαθητὰς αὐτοῦ). Since Mark says that the "crowd" was sitting about Jesus earlier (v. 32), there is a tendency to equate the crowd of v. 32 with the group of v. 34, and thus the crowd would be the object of Jesus' statement about being his family. Mark is quite vague at this point, but Meye believes that the inference should be made that Mark was referring to *disciples* in v. 34.[67] He demonstrates that the phrase "those about Him" always refers to disciples when unqualified in Mk.[68] Therefore, Mk already has two groups in the pericope, the μαθηταί and the ὄχλοι. Matthew simply carries over both groups, but includes the term μαθητής as an audience identifier. More difficult is what Matthew meant by his specific inclusion of the term in relationship to ὄχλοι. Did he mean to identify the ὄχλοι as the μαθηταί, or did he mean to make a distinction between them? While it is possible to understand that Matthew makes an intentional equation of the two groups,[69] the earlier (9:36-37) and the later distinctions (13:2, 10, 34, 36) Matthew makes between the groups argue for an intentional distinction in 12:46-50. Matthew has recorded a scene that highlights Jesus' teaching on discipleship. The crowd represents those who listen to the teaching of Jesus, the "someone" of v. 47 is one coming out from among the crowd who occasions the specific teaching on discipleship,[70] and the μαθηταί are those who exemplify what Jesus requires of anyone desiring a relationship with him.[71] Matthew specifies the μαθηταί as those who exemplarily do the will of the Father.[72] In this way the μαθηταί are held up as models for what the ὄχλοι should

---

[66] Ibid., p. 38.

[67] Meye, *Twelve*, pp. 150-151.

[68] Cf. esp. ibid., pp. 148-156. Meye's conclusion that the phrase τοὺς περὶ αὐτόν always indicates disciples in Mk should be given due consideration. His conclusion in Mk 4:10, that it signifies a smaller group within the Twelve, need not be accepted or detract from the basic promise that Mark is speaking of disciples (cf. pp. 152-156).

[69] Gundry, *Matthew*, pp. 248-250.

[70] For a discussion of the textual problems in 12:47, see Bruce M. Metzger, *A Textual Commentary on the Greek New Testament* (3d. ed.; New York: United Bible Society, 1971), p. 32.

[71] Van Tilborg, *Jewish Leaders*, p. 161.

[72] J. Dupont, "Le point de vue de Matthieu dans le chapitre des paraboles," *L'Évangile selon Matthieu: Rédaction et théologie*, ed. M. Didier (Gemblou: J. Duculot, 1972), pp. 239-40, 249-50.

become.[73] D. Carson suggests that the Matthean passage is "a statement about what it really means to be a disciple of Jesus and to be totally committed to him."[74] The crowds will recognize in the example of the μαθηταί that to be a "disciple" of Jesus is to be gathered around him and to do the will of the Father.

The inclusion of μαθητής in 13:10 not only shows the distinction between the crowds and the disciples, but also acts as a Matthean interpretation of their spiritual status.[75] Matthew opens the parabolic discourse (13:1) with a narrative description situating Jesus among the crowd and offers a seemingly bland observation: "And he told them many things in parables." The significance of this observation in v. 3 is recognized when the disciples come forward with a question in v. 10. The question of the disciples is not so much a request for an interpretation of the parable as a request for an explanation of the reason for speaking to the crowds in parables. This prompts an interpretation which is two-fold: a blessing on the disciples and a curse on the crowds.[76] Significantly, Mk 4:10 has οἱ περὶ αὐτὸν σὺν τοῖς δώδεκα and Matthew changes this to the simple οἱ μαθηταί. While the inference is that Matthew's disciples are co-extensive with Mk's group, what is important here is that they are drawn up against a separate group, "them" (v. 10b), who are the "crowds" of 13:2.[77] Luz observes that the crowds, because they do not understand (13:13), are a *Folie* of the disciples who understand and hear all of Jesus' teachings.[78] This should not be seen as an idealization of disciples, but rather as a contrast between disciples who learn through the teaching of Jesus and crowds who become hardened.[79] More will be said later about the portrait of the disciples in ch. 13, but everywhere in this chapter Matthew keeps the disciples and crowds separate, the latter enhancing the former's understanding through their ignorance.

Mt 23:1 is also an introductory narrative by Matthew in which he identifies the audience of the the following discourse. Mark identifies the audience of the discourse with the general πολὺς ὄχλος (Mk 12:37b), but Matthew specifies that the discourse is directed τοῖς ὄχλοις καὶ τοῖς μαθηταῖς

[73] Van Tilborg, *Jewish Leaders*, p. 161.

[74] Carson, "Matthew," p. 299.

[75] For a complex reader-response analysis of Mt 13 see Gary A. Phillips, "History and Text: The Reader in Context in Matthew's Parables Discourse," *Semeia* 31 (1985), 111-138.

[76] Ibid., pp. 121-122.77. J. D. Kingsbury, *The Parables of Jesus in Matthew 13: A Study in Redaction-Criticism* (London: SPCK, 1969), p. 24. Kingsbury notes that the antecedent of the pronoun αὐτοῖς in ch. 13 is the crowds exclusive of the disciples (cf. 13:3,10,13,24 [31,33] 34) (pp. 24-25).

[78] Luz, "Die Jünger," p. 151.

[79] David Wenham, "The Structure of Matthew XIII," *NTS* 25 (1979), 516-522.

αὐτοῦ (23:1).[80] Matthew appears to be aligning the μαθηταί and ὄχλοι on one side against the scribes and Pharisees on the other (23:2). Both the μαθηταί and ὄχλοι have something to learn from Jesus' scathing denunciation of the scribes and Pharisees, so the discourse is addressed to both of them. This helps clarify that even though the crowds are distinct from the disciples, they are at least on this occasion placed together with them in a category. Because the discourse is a denunciation of the foes of Jesus, the scribes and Pharisees, the implication is that the category which here includes the disciples and the crowds is some kind of openness to instruction from Jesus.[81]

The following observations about the relationship between the μαθηταί and the ὄχλοι in Mt can be drawn from the analysis of these inclusions. On several occasions Matthew uses the term to make the μαθηταί distinct from the ὄχλοι. The μαθηταί were seen as a more intimate group of companions in Jesus' ministry (9:19), and were also his fellow-workers in the ministry of caring for the ὄχλοι (9:36-37). The μαθηταί were purposely held up as an example to the ὄχλοι (12:49) and were on opposite ends of the spectrum of spiritual understanding (13:10). Finally, as separate groups, they were aligned together against the scribes and Pharisees in Jesus' denunciation of the latter (23:11).

5. Defining the relationship to Peter

Matthew includes μαθητής in several contexts where Peter is prominent, and through the inclusion he clarifies and interprets the source relationship between the μαθηταί and Peter. The next chapter will explore the full Matthean understanding of Peter, so only provisional conclusions will be offered in this chapter where Peter is considered.

The pericope of the withered fig tree includes a unique Matthean record of μαθηταί who marveled at the incident and then asked a question (21:20). In Mk Peter makes an exclamatory statement about the tree (Mk 11:21) and Jesus' response is not limited to Peter, but was addressed to a plural group (ὁ Ἰησοῦς λέγει αὐτοῖς. ἔχετε πίστιν θεοῦ) (Mk 11:22). Matthew states explicitly what was implied in Mark. Peter's remarks are the remarks of all the disciples. Once again, the inclusion of the term becomes a natural backdrop for teaching on discipleship (21:21-22). Matthew may be either making an identification or making a distinction

---

[80] Cf. the excellent discussion of the audience-identifier in David E. Garland, *The Intention of Matthew 23, NovT Sup*, vol. LII (Leiden: E. J. Brill, 1979), pp. 34-41.

[81] Carson, "Matthew," p. 471. G. Stanton would agree with this basic thesis, but he finds the significance of the audience-identification strictly in the Matthean church; cf. Graham N. Stanton, "The Gospel of Matthew and Judaism," *BJRL* 66 (1984), 273-274.

between the μαθηταί and Peter, but the plural response of Jesus to Peter's remark in Mark implies what is for Matthew an explicit identification of Peter and οἱ μαθηταί.

In another situation, Mark's narrative has not only Peter, but also James and John and Andrew with him, asking a question of Jesus (Mk 13:3), whereas in Mt the group of named disciples became οἱ μαθηταί (24:3). Bultmann declares that Matthew "seems to have forgotten" that the eschatological discourse was given to the four privileged ones.[82] Rather than accusing Matthew of such clumsiness, another explanation suggests just the opposite. Perhaps Matthew has intentionally used the term μαθητής instead of using the names of the four disciples because he has specific literary and theological purposes in mind. When it is observed that Matthew has already eliminated reference to εἷς τῶν μαθητῶν and has οἱ μαθηταὶ αὐτοῦ as a group approach Jesus in 24:1 (cf. Mk 13:1), and when in each major discourse he has the disciples as a group for an audience,[83] it must be concluded that Matthew has intentionally generalized the named disciples of Mark to οἱ μαθηταί. As was the case in 21:20, the question on the lips of named disciples in Mk is identified with the inclusion of the general term μαθητής in Mt. The action of the named individual is identified with the term μαθητής.

In another context involving Peter, Mark states that when Peter declared he would not deny Jesus, "they all said the same thing" (Mk 14:31). Matthew includes the term μαθητής and states that, πάντες οἱ μαθηταὶ εἶπον (26:35). Matthew also specifically includes the name ὁ Πέτρος (v. 35a) which Mark did not have (Mk 14:31). This again reveals Matthew's preference for grammatical specificity, but may also point to an intentional explicit identification of οἱ μαθηταί with the statement of Peter.[84]

Matthew records that in the garden of Gethsemane Jesus came to οἱ μαθηταί and found them sleeping (26:40), while Mk has Jesus coming and finding αὐτούς asleep (Mk 14:37). This Matthean inclusion explicitly identifies οἱ μαθηταί as sleeping (cf. 26:45). When Jesus addresses Peter, instead of the singular reference as would be expected and which is found in Mk 14:37, Matthew has a plural verb (ἰσχύσατε). Matthew's widening of the admonishment to Peter through the use of the plural verb has allowed him to include the explicitly mentioned μαθηταί (v. 40) in the admonishment. In the next verse Mark widens the exhortation by using a plural verb (Mk 14:38), and Mt follows this (26:41), but through the

---

[82] Bultmann, *History of the Synoptic Tradition*, p. 356.

[83] Cf. 5:1; 10:1; 13:10, 36; 18:1; 23:1; 24:1-3. The specific function of the disciples as Matthew's audience will be examined in a later section.

[84] Gundry, *Matthew*, p. 531.

inclusion in 26:40a and the change to a plural verb in 26:40b, Matthew once again purposely identifies the μαθηταί with Peter.

The inclusions of μαθητής in contexts involving Peter (cf. also 16:20, 21; 17:6) show a Matthean preference for the term in certain instances where disciples are named. Μαθητής acts as a backdrop for teaching on discipleship (21:20) and as an audience-identifier for discourses (24:1, 3). Matthew reveals a desire to identify the μαθηταί with Peter's addressing Jesus (21:20; 24:3), rashly declaring never to deny Jesus (26:35), and being asleep in the garden, and therefore receiving a rebuke from Jesus (26:40, 45).

6. Summary

The inclusions of μαθητής in Mt reveal several literary and theological purposes. First, the inclusions reveal a desire for grammatical specificity. Mt tightens up references to specific individuals in his own text and sources by including the term μαθητής. Matthew is a very precise author; one commentator refers to him as "meticulous Matthew."[85] Matthew carries this specificity forward one step as he makes purposeful identifications in his interpretation of Mark's text. This results in both positive (obedient, 21:6) and negative (obtusely complaining, 26:8) connotations. Second, Matthew completes the title οἱ δώδεκα by adding μαθηταί. An identification is specifically drawn between "the twelve" and "the disciples." Third, Matthew includes unique material containing μαθητής in his sources which cast the disciples as both positive and negative (15:23), worshiping yet fearful (17:6-7), and understanding, yet understanding only because of Jesus' teaching (16:5-12; 17:10-13; 18:1-5; 19:3-12). Matthew softens the obduracy and ignorance of Mark's disciples, but he has done so by accentuating the teaching of Jesus as the means by which the disciples gain further understanding. The inclusion of this material about the disciples provides a backdrop against which Jesus teaches on discipleship. Fourth, Matthew draws a distinction between the μαθηταί and the ὄχλοι. Matthew can show that the μαθηταί are Jesus' companions in ministry (9:19), fellow-workers in ministering to the ὄχλοι (9:36-37), examples to the ὄχλοι (12:46-50), Jesus' true family (12:49), those who truly understand (13:2, 10), and those who are aligned on one side with the ὄχλοι against the scribes and Pharisees (23:1). Fifth, Matthew includes the term μαθητής to make an identification between Peter and the disciples. In this way Matthew specifies that

[85] Peter F. Ellis, *Matthew: His Mind and His Message* (Collegeville, Minn.: Liturgical Press, 1974), pp. 27 ff.

all of the disciples are with Peter addressing Jesus (21:20; 24:3), rashly declaring they will not deny him (26:35), sleeping in the garden and receiving a rebuke from Jesus (26:40, 45).

B) Occurrences in Unique Material

The term μαθητής occurs a few times in material that is unique to Matthew (11:1; 26:1; 27:64; 28:13; 28:16).[86] Two of these are connected with the stereotyped Matthean formula which concludes Matthew's major discourses: καὶ ἐγένετο ὅτε ἐτέλεσεν ὁ 'Ιησοῦς (7:28; 11:1; 13:53; 19:1; 26:1). Matthew always directs each discourse, at least in part, to the μαθηταί,[87] so it is not surprising to find the term connected with this formula which serves to terminate the discourses.

Two other occurrences are found in the unique Matthean records about the setting of the guard for Jesus' tomb (27:62-66) and the reporting of the guards after the resurrection (28:11-15). The first mentions the Jewish leaders' fear of the disciples' stealing the body of Jesus lest someone think he had been raised, and the second record tells how they planned to circulate a story about the disciples' stealing the body. These records serve an apologetic purpose for the resurrection of Jesus and the integrity of the disciples.[88]

The final use of μαθητής in unique Matthean material appears in 28:16-20, the "Great Commission." Here Matthew writes, οἱ δὲ ἕνδεκα μαθηταί... (28:16). This is the first and only time Matthew speaks of the "eleven disciples," and it represents the official group who have been established by Jesus (10:1) and known prior to this by the title "the twelve disciples" (cf.. 10:1; 11:1; 20:17; 26:20). This official group proceeds to Galilee in response to Jesus' directive (cf. 28:7) and receives the commission. Matthew includes a statement of the doubt of "some"[89] while the rest worshiped (28:17). This either refers to some others besides the Eleven who doubted[90] or some of the Eleven themselves who doubted because of the epiphanic character of the situation.[91] McNeile argues for

---

[86] These differ from the "Inclusions of unique Matthean material" considered above in that here the unique material is not included in any parallel source material.

[87] Cf. Jack Dean Kingsbury, Matthew: Structure, Christology, Kingdom (Philadelphia: Fortress, 1975), pp. 5-7.

[88] Cf. Beare, Matthew, pp. 539, 543 and Schweizer, Matthew, pp. 519-521, 526-527, who accuse Matthew and his community of arrogant and thoughtless fabrication in this apology. Hill, Matthew, pp. 357-358, 360, gives a more generous treatment.

[89] οἱ δέ is best understood in this partitive sense (cf. 26:57; McNeile, St. Matthew, p. 434.

[90] Carson, "Matthew," pp. 593-594.

[91] Benjamin J. Hubbard, The Matthean Redaction of a Primitive Apostolic Commissioning: An Exegesis of Matthew 28:16-20, SBL Dissertation Series (Missoula, Montana: Scholars, 1974), p. 71; cf. also Bonnard, Matthieu, p. 418.

the former on the major contention that Matthew avoids making derogatory statements about the disciples.[92] It has already been discovered, though, that Matthew does show the weaknesses of the disciples, and it will be seen that a major Matthean theme is the littleness of their faith. Bonnard suggests that the words should be left to their plain sense: those who worshiped were not exempt from hesitation and doubt.[93] This would accord quite well with the finding in 17:5-8, where at the voice of the Father the μαθηταί had a mixture of worship and fear until Jesus alone appeared to them with a touch and word of admonishment and commission. If this is the case, in 28:17 some still had an imperfect worship, now at the appearance of Jesus, until he speaks with words of commission (vv. 18-20a) and comfort (v. 20b). Matthew again reveals a group of disciples who are obedient and who are ready to follow the commission of Christ, but who are always dependent upon Jesus.[94]

C) Expansions from Matthew's Sources

Five times Matthew uses the term μαθητής by drawing on another occurrence in the near context (10:25; 13:36; 14:19b; 15:36b; 28:8). The interpretation and context of the saying found in 10:24 and 25 differs from that in Lk 6:40 (Q). The use of μαθητής in v. 25 partially draws on the interpretation in v. 24 and the second half of the saying in Q. Placed at the center of the missions discourse, the saying enunciates a principle that is crucial to the disciples' mission: the disciples' solidarity with Jesus consists in sharing in His suffering and sharing in His authority.[95] As Jesus suffered and will suffer, so will the disciples. As Jesus exercised and will exercise authority, so will the disciples. And as Jesus ministered and will minister, so will the disciples.[96] But the disciple is always a disciple and, as Bornkamm stresses, Jesus is always Lord.[97] Thus Matthew stresses that the disciple of Jesus has an essential solidarity with Jesus, but

---

[92] McNeile, *St. Matthew*, p. 434.

[93] Bonnard, *Matthieu*, p. 418. Cf. also Jean Zumstein, *La Condition du Croyant dans L'Evangile selon Matthieu*, Orbis Biblicus et Orientalis, no. 16 (Göttingen: Vandenhoeck und Ruprecht, 1977), pp. 97, 254.

[94] A recent study by T. Donaldson focuses on the "mountain" in Mt as a location of Matthean revelation and compares the mounts of transfiguration and commission, among others; see Terence L. Donaldson, *Jesus on the Mountain: A Study in Matthean Theology*, JSNT Supp. Ser. no. 8 (Sheffield: JSOT, 1985).

[95] Brown, "The Mission to Israel in Matthew's Central Section," pp. 77-78.

[96] Cf. Brown's summaries of these comparisons (ibid., pp. 78-79).

[97] Günther Bornkamm, "End-Expectation and Church in Matthew," *Tradition and Interpretation in Matthew*, trans. Percy Scott (Philadelphia : Westminster, 1963), pp. 41-42. Bornkamm has convincingly demonstrated that κύριος in Mt is a title of deity, notwithstanding some proper amendments by Kingsbury, *Matthew*, pp. 104-113.

there is also an essential difference. The disciple of Jesus is not like the disciple of the rabbi who could himself hope to be a rabbi someday.[98] The disciple will always remain a disciple of the Lord, but will have solidarity with Jesus in mission, authority, and suffering.[99]

The occurrence of μαθητής in 13:36 shows no parallel in Aland's *Synopsis*, but it is most likely an expansion from Mk 4:34 that Matthew includes as an introduction to his unique interpretation of the parable of the tares.[100] This use of μαθητής is significant, because it reveals a programmatic distinction from the ὄχλοι. The framework of the chapter is revealed by comparing 13:1 with 13:36. In 13:1 Jesus left the house to address the crowds by the sea, and in 13:36 Jesus dismisses the crowd and goes into the house. Previously, the crowd has been a primary audience and the disciples secondary; but now the disciples are the exclusive audience. The privacy of the house signifies the exclusive nature of the teaching of the disciples, without carrying the overtones of Messianic secrecy as it may in Mark's gospel.[101] The disciples come asking for an explanation (διασάφησαν)[102] of the parable of the tares, and in so doing show that, while not perfect in their understanding, they possess the potential and desire to understand. Their "asking" prompts the explanation of the cryptic parable, and ultimately the disciples *will* understand (cf. 13:51).[103] This is greatly different from the ὄχλοι. Jesus directed the parables to them first, but their non-understanding resulted in him finally leaving them and going into the privacy of the house where the disciples become recipients (v. 36). Chapter 13 has long been recognized as a turning point in Matthew's gospel, and Jesus' leaving the crowds and going in private to the disciples may provide a clue to the turning point. Jesus leaves the unhearing and unrepentant in Israel and

---

[98] Cf. Eduard Schweizer, *Lordship and Discipleship*, Studies in Biblical Theology, No. 28 (Naperville, Ill.: Alex R. Allenson Inc., 1960), pp. 20-21; cf. also Leonhard Goppelt, *Theology of the New Testament*, trans. John E. Alsup, vol. I (Grand Rapids : Eerdmans, 1981), pp. 207-210.

[99] Hengel, *Charismatic Leader*, pp. 78-79.

[100] Joachim Jeremias (*The Parables of Jesus*, trans. S. H. Hooke [2nd. rev. ed.; New York: Charles Scribner's Sons, 1972], pp. 82-84) has demonstrated "the unique collection of the linguistic characteristics" of Matthew evident in the grammar, syntax and vocabulary of this pericope.

[101] Kingsbury (*Parables*, pp. 92-93) suggests that the "house" in Mk signifies a place for revealing the Messianic secret. In Mt no such nuance can be detected; the "house" is only a reference to the geographical home located in Capernaum.

[102] The textual difficulty of whether to read διασάφησαν (B Sin* Θ 0242^vid *pc* lat sy) or φράσον (Ψ Koine D W 30250 λ φ *pl* it) is best decided with the Nestle text in favor of διασάφησαν. This would mean that the disciples ask to have the parable "made clear" (cf. 18:31).

[103] Kingsbury, *Parables*, p. 95

now for the most part concentrates on his disciples who hear and understand.[104]

Two expansions are very similar and may be taken together. In the feedings of the five thousand (14:13-21) and four thousand (15:32-39) Matthew follows Mark in saying that the disciples were there to pass the food out to the people (14:19 cf. Mk 6:41; 15:36 cf. Mk 8:6). In both places Matthew expands the reference to the μαθηταί and says Jesus gave the bread τοῖς μαθηταῖς ... οἱ δὲ μαθηταὶ τοῖς ὄχλοις. Although Matthew's wording is not greatly different, through the double reference to the μαθηταί he has stressed the role of the disciples in feeding the crowds. Jesus had commissioned them to feed the crowds (14:16), and by mentioning them twice Matthew shows that they had fulfilled that commission.[105] Although there were great crowds in attendance, Matthew's real attention is focused on the μαθηταί as Jesus teaches and commissions them to serve the ὄχλοις.[106]

The final expansion is in 28:8. This may be designated as an expansion-conflation from the negative ending of Mk (16:8) and the charge to the women from the angel (28:7; Mk 16:7), even though Matthew may have been relying on a longer ending of Mark available to him at the time.[107] It should be noticed that the women have mixed emotions (μετὰ φόβου καὶ χαρᾶς μεγάλης) in the presence of the supernatural as had the disciples (cf. 17:6; 28:16). Matthew is thus able to drop Mk's "for they were afraid," and has them go and make the announcement to the disciples. On the basis of this command (reiterated by Jesus in v. 10) the disciples proceed to Galilee;[108] hence it is quite likely that the reference to "His disciples" meant specifically the Eleven (cf. 28:7,8,16).

Through Matthew's expansions he has given a more specific meaning to the term μαθητής. The μαθητής has solidarity with Jesus in his suffering, authority and mission, but he will always remain a disciple of the Lord (10:25). Jesus shifts his focus from the crowds to the μαθηταί since they possess the desire and potential to understand from Jesus, whereas the ὄχλοι do not (13:36). The μαθητής is designated as one who is to minister to the ὄχλοι at the commission of Jesus and through his enablement (14:19; 15:36). Finally, the μαθηταί are the ones to whom the

---

[104] Ellis, *Matthew*, pp. 59-61; Kingsbury, *Matthew*, pp. 19-25, 130-132.

[105] Heinz Joachim Held, "Matthew as Interpreter of the Miracle Stories," *Tradition and Interpretation in Matthew*, trans. Percy Scott (Philadelphia: Westminster, 1963), p. 184-186.

[106] Held, "Miracle Stories," pp. 183-184.

[107] Cf. Willoughby C. Allen, *A Critical and Exegetical Commentary on the Gospel According to S. Matthew* , The International Critical Commentary (3rd. ed.; Edinburgh: T. & T. Clark, 1912), pp. 302-304.

[108] Schweizer, *Matthew*, p. 522.

announcement of the resurrection was given and who proceed to meet Jesus in Galilee (28:8,16).

D) Parallel Occurrences with Matthew's Sources

The term μαθητής in Mt parallels occurrences in Q three times and in Mark twenty-seven times.[109] In many of these parallel occurrences Matthew simply carries over the source-material (cf. 9:11,14; 14:19a; 15:32,36a; 16:13). Matthew appears to want to be faithful to the essence of his sources' orientation, but at times he makes certain alterations which reflect his own understanding or interpretation of the μαθηταί.[110] An example of this was once thought to be Matthew's omissions of the pronoun αὐτοῦ.[111] But, as J. Elliott has shown, it was not Matthew who omitted the pronoun but the scribes. They felt that it was an otiose pronoun and not stylistically desirable, so they omitted it in their transmission.[112] Elliott demonstrates that Matthew prefers qualifying μαθητής in the same manner as Mark, and a close look at the apparatus of the text demands the longer reading in Mt.[113] But there are several alterations that Matthew makes in carrying over the term, and these deserve attention, for they help reveal Matthew's purposes in his usage.

1. Distinction between μαθηταί and ὄχλοι

Matthew has preserved or strengthened the distinction between the μαθηταί and ὄχλοι on at least nine occasions. In 14:19,22; 15:32,36 Matthew has retained Mark's distinction of two groups. Indeed, the distinction is such that a different activity is required for both groups. In 14:19 and 15:32,36, as already seen, the μαθηταί serve the ὄχλοι. In 14:22 Jesus "compelled" (ἠνάγκασεν) the disciples to get in the boat and go to the other side while he "dismissed" (ἀπολύσῃ) the crowds.[114] Matthew

---

[109] cf. Appendix B for a full listing.

[110] See the discussion of this point in Graham Stanton, "Matthew as a Creative Interpreter of the Sayings of Jesus," *Das Evangelium und die Evangelien*, ed. Peter Stuhlmacher, Wissenschaftliche Untersuchungen zum Neuen Testament, no. 28 (Tübingen: J. C. B. Mohr [Paul Siebeck], 1983), passim, but esp. pp. 273-274, 286-287.

[111] C. H. Turner, "Markan Usage: Notes, Critical and Exegetical, on the Second Gospel," *JTS* XXVI (1925), pp. 235-236. Cited in Senior, *Passion Narrative*, p. 15 n. 3.

[112] J. Keith Elliott, "Mathētēs with a Possessive in the New Testament," *ThZ* 35 (1979), p. 300.

[113] Cf. ibid., pp. 301-302 for a listing and discussion of the specifics. Some scholars have based redactional conclusions on the supposed deletions of the pronoun. An example is E. R. Martinez, "The Interpretation of οἱ μαθηταί in Matthew 18," *CBQ* XXIII (1961), 281-292, who proposes two different groups, οἱ μαθηταὶ αὐτοῦ and οἱ μαθηταί.

[114] Matthew has changed the emphasis from "he himself dismissed the crowds" to "going before him" (Gundry, *Matthew*, 296), but he has retained the dismissal of the crowds and the distinction between the two groups by showing Jesus' being identified with the μαθηταί in their journey across the lake.

emphasizes Jesus' association with the disciples in distinction from the dismissed crowds.[115]

In 5:1 Matthew has altered his source by saying that not only were the μαθηταί present for the Sermon (cf. Lk 6:20), but the ὄχλοι were also present. What is the significance of the addition of the ὄχλοι? The answer to that question is best arrived at by answering another question: "What is the relationship of the μαθηταί and ὄχλοι in Matthew's view of the audience of the Sermon?" Manson states that Matthew is having Jesus avoid the crowd and only teach the disciples;[116] Gundry suggests that the two groups are interchangeable as the audience of the Sermon;[117] Bonnard says that both the disciples and crowds are addressed without distinction;[118] and Minear proposes that the disciples are primarily addressed, but the crowds are a secondary audience.[119]

A crucial clue to ascertaining Matthew's notion of the audience is found in 7:28-29, where Matthew says that the crowds respond in amazement to the Sermon because Jesus was teaching "them."[120] This rules out seeing the μαθηταί as the only audience. As has been seen, Matthew is a very explicit and specific author, and this would strongly argue against seeing the groups as interchangeable. Instead, Matthew's editorial activity in the introduction to the Sermon serves to make an explicit distinction between them. Guelich proposes that the crowds in 5:1 form the redactional bridge between 4:23-25 and the Sermon, and with the μαθηταί specified as the actual audience in the Q tradition, Matthew has explicitly brought together two different groups to make up his audience.[121] On at least three other occasions Matthew has used a verbal phrase similar to the one used in 5:1 to recognize the crowds (ἰδὼν δὲ τοὺς ὄχλους; cf. 8:18; 9:36; 14:14).[122] In two of the other occurrences there is a definite distinction between the ὄχλοι and μαθηταί; 9:36-39 and 14:14-19 are occasions for the crowds to be served by the μαθηταί. Since it would be quite difficult to make an interchange of ὄχλος in 8:18 and μαθητής in 8:21,23, Gundry's concept of interchange is quite tenuous.

---

[115] Gundry, *Matthew*, p. 296, points to the changes from Mk as evidence of the stressed identification of Jesus with the disciples; the motif suggests that "Jesus is always with His people." This motif is illustrated in the preserved distinction between the μαθηταί and the ὄχλοι.

[116] Manson, *Sayings*, p. 47.

[117] Gundry, *Matthew*, p. 66.

[118] Bonnard, *Matthieu*, p. 54.

[119] Minear, "Disciples," pp. 32-33.

[120] Gundry, *Matthew*, pp. 66, 136-137.

[121] Robert A. Guelich, *The Sermon on the Mount: A Foundation for Understanding* (Waco, Texas: Word, 1982), pp. 59-60. Cf. also Luz, "Die Jünger," p. 151.

[122] 5:1; 8:18; and 9:36 have aorist active participles (ἰδὼν), while 14:14 has an aorist active indicative (εἶδεν).

Instead, Matthew appears to be referring to two distinct groups in 5:1—
the μαθηταί and the ὄχλοι,[123] and the object of the teaching of the Sermon
is the natural antecedent of αὐτούς in 5:2: the disciples who had come to
Jesus.[124] But not just the disciples, for 7:28,29 say explicitly that the ὄχλοι
are taught by Jesus. Since the underlying Sermon tradition clearly had
the disciples as the audience (cf. Lk 6:20),[125] this writer suggests that
Matthew has maintained that tradition and has added that the crowds
were also there, but as a secondary object of teaching because of their
interest in his mission (4:23-25).

Matthew has also strengthened the traditional distinction between the
μαθηταί and ὄχλοι in 14:15 and 15:33. He has done so by adding the term
ὄχλος to heighten the distinction already found in the context. In 16:24
Matthew has deleted the term ὄχλος and has limited the saying to οἱ
μαθηταί (16:24-28). Since this saying refers to "the nature of discipleship,
not its preconditions,"[126] it is natural that the ὄχλοι would be omitted.

2. Solidarity with Jesus

As it receives a different emphasis in Mt than in Mk, the saying about
the disciples in 10:24 stresses the disciples' solidarity with Jesus in
persecution, authority and mission. In 26:19 there is a slight change, so
that instead of the disciples confirming what Jesus told them, they are
portrayed as obedient. Thus, just as Jesus is obedient to keeping his
appointed "time" (v. 18b), so the disciples are obedient in their
appointed tasks.[127] In 26:36 Matthew emphasizes that Jesus went "with
them" to Gethsemane. The Matthean motif, "Jesus, Immanuel, with
His people," underlines the bond between Jesus and his disciples (cf. also
26:38 and 40).[128]

---

[123] Gundry's own statements, that "Matthew uses 'the crowds' and 'his disciples'
interchangeably ... They were the crowds ... Therefore the disciples about to be taught
at the beginning of the Sermon must be none other than the crowds that have been taught
at the close" (*Matthew*, p. 66), do not preserve the distinction he himself later seems to
draw between the two groups. On 13:1 he says the ὄχλοι are the whole of professing
disciples, mixed of true and false, and the μαθηταί are those true believers who come out
of the crowd (p. 251). On 13:36, when Jesus leaves the crowds and teaches the disciples,
Gundry suggests that this may signify leaving false disciples (ὄχλοι) for a ministry to true
disciples (μαθηταί) (p. 271). Then on 23:1 he suggests that the ὄχλοι and μαθηταί together
are the whole professing church, but the μαθηταί are the original Jewish Christians and
the ὄχλοι are the larger body of Gentile converts (p. 453). If there is some kind of distinction drawn between the two terms in other places, it seems best to try and understand
that distinction in 5:1 as well.

[124] Guelich, *Sermon*, p. 54.

[125] Ibid., p. 59.

[126] Gundry, *Matthew*, p. 339; cf. also Luz, "Die Jünger," p. 151.

[127] Senior, *Passion Narrative*, pp. 63-65.

[128] Schweizer, *Matthew*, p. 493.

3. Different attitude toward the μαθηταί

In several parallel uses of μαθητής, Mt differs somewhat from the Markan picture (cf. 14:26; 15:12; 17:16-19; 19:13; 24:1; 26:19). Matthew preserves the Markan picture of the terror of the disciples at the appearing of Jesus walking on water in 14:26ff. In Mark the word of Jesus (Mk 6:50) and the presence of Jesus (Mk 6:51) are emphasized, with the disciples astounded (Mk 6:51b) and not understanding because of their hardened hearts (Mk 6:52). But in Mt, at the word of Jesus, Peter comes forward to exercise faith, albeit "little faith." Once back in the boat the disciples worship Jesus (14:33). Kilpatrick refers to the incident of Peter within this context as a "Petrine story," a unique Matthean story[129] Held suggests that Matthew used this Petrine story to present "a disciple on the way of discipleship."[130] Peter becomes an example of the disciple who overcomes his fear and is ready for the highest faith, able to exercise that faith by walking on water, but who then fails in his faith and falls into the sea.[131] Matthew omits Mk's reference to non-understanding and hardness of heart (Mk 6:52), and instead focuses both on Peter as an example of a disciple who has little faith and doubt, and on the worship of those in the boat. Matthew does not exonerate the disciples for their fear, but uses the story of Peter to show how they overcame their fear and were able to worship. The figure of Jesus is exalted through this incident as the only focus of faith and worship.[132]

Matthew presents a slightly different picture of the μαθηταί in 15:1-20, and clarifies the role of various figures. Mark portrays the Pharisees and scribes as hypocrites (Mk 7:1-6), the crowds are warned of the example of the Pharisees (Mk 7:14-15), and the disciples ask a question about Jesus' parable and so show that they are still without understanding (Mk 7:18). Matthew retains the same basic picture of the Pharisees and crowd but shows the disciples making an interpretive statement / question to Jesus about the reaction of the Pharisees. The disciples are cast in a more understanding light because they understand the parable and the effect it had on the Pharisees. Then a new element is portrayed. The request for the clarification of the parable which was on the lips of the disciples in Mk is found on the lips of Peter in Mt (15:15). Peter, instead of the

---

[129] G. D. Kilpatrick, *The Origins of the Gospel According to St. Matthew* (Oxford: Clarendon Press, 1950), pp. 40-41.

[130] Held, "Miracle Stories," pp. 205-206.

[131] Ibid., p. 206.

[132] C. Carlisle applies a structuralist approach to this pericope and comes to the same basic understanding of the Matthean purpose both for the disciples and for the role of Peter; Charles Richard Carlisle, "A Note on Matthew 14:22-33," *NTS* 31 (1985), 151-155.

μαθηταί, shows his ignorance by his failure to understand the parable and his request for an explanation. Peter receives the brunt of the condemnation through the inclusion of his name, but, importantly, in Jesus' response to Peter he involves the disciples in the condemnation for not understanding. That they are involved is indicated by the plural address Jesus gives in response to Peter (15:16-17). Matthew reveals his attitude toward each participant by his account in 15:1-20. The Pharisees are willfully blind, and because of this are hypocritical (15:7,13,14). The ὄχ-λοι are exhorted to hear and understand, and if they do so they will become disciples, but if not they will be like the Pharisees, because now they have heard the message. The μαθηταί have partial understanding and perception (15:12) and so can learn from Jesus' warning about the Pharisees (15:13-14); but they are also non-understanding (15:16-17), which will be corrected through further teaching by Jesus (15:17-20). Peter is the scapegoat for the bulk of the accusation of non-understanding (15:15).

Through two parallel occurrences of μαθητής in 17:16-19, Matthew emphasizes that the disciples lack faith, but that through the teaching of Jesus they can use even what they have for greater accomplishments. In Mark's episode the faith of the father and the faith building of Jesus is emphasized (cf. Mk 9:22-24), but in Mt the whole story is condensed and the faith of the disciples is scrutinized under the light of their failure to "heal" the epileptic boy. Matthew carries over the Markan cry of the frustrated Jesus who is "a visitant from a higher realm who feels that his presence among human beings is an ordeal."[133] The cry of anguish is directed to "this generation," and in this way Matthew agrees that the people, the boy's father, the hard-hearted Jews and crowds, and even the disciples were, in their own way, "without faith" (ἄπιστος).[134] The exalted Jesus simply rebukes the demon and the boy is cured, and then the disciples are told why *they* could not cast it out: it was because of their "little faith" (17:20). In Mk the anguished cry of Jesus points to help for the "unfaith" ἀπιστία of the father (Mk 9:24), but in Mt it points toward the "little faith" ὀλιγοπιστίαν of the disciples.[135] As usual, Matthew does not leave the disciples on a negative note, but uses their lack of faith as an opportunity to highlight the teaching of Jesus. Through his teaching the disciples can exercise even the littlest of faith and "be able" to do

[133] Beare, *Matthew*, p. 369.
[134] Cf. McNeile, *St. Matthew*, p. 255; Beare, *Matthew*, 369; Floyd F. Filson, *The Gospel According to St. Matthew*, Black's New Testament Commentaries (2nd ed.; London: Black, 1971), p. 194; Held, "Miracle Stories," p. 191-192.
[135] Cf. Held, "Miracle Stories," pp. 191-192; Hill, *Matthew*, p. 270, McNeile, *St. Matthew*, p. 255.

anything (cf. ἠδυνήθησαν, 17:16; οὐδὲν ἀδυνατήσει, 17:20). Matthew emphasizes that the disciples are lacking faith, but shows that through the teaching of Jesus they can use even what they have for greater accomplishments.

Matthew also portrays the disciples in their faultiness in 19:13-15, but once again the scene becomes an occasion to clarify the means for advancing in discipleship. The disciples were upset by the bringing of children to Jesus, and so rebuked them. Jesus corrects the disciples, and what is revealed in the disciples is *"une incompréhension fondamentale du ministere de Jesus."*[136] Matthew agrees with Mark that the disciples' annoyance at this seeming interruption on the way to Jerusalem[137] reveals that did not truly understand the essence of his ministry. But Matthew softens the reply of Jesus by deleting reference to his indignancy (cf. 17:14; Mk 10:14). Matthew includes enough to carry on the tradition but he does not care to belabor the point. The faultiness of μαθηταί is not occasion for more criticism, but an opportunity for clarification and advanced teaching on discipleship (17:14-15).

4. General reference to μαθηταί

On several occasions Matthew reveals a tendency to focus on a generalized group of disciples instead of specifically named individuals. It was noticed earlier that in 24:1 Matthew omits the reference to "one" of the disciples in Mk 13:1, and instead has a general reference to "disciples." In the same context (24:3) Matthew prefers the general term μαθηταί over the proper names of Peter, James, John and Andrew (Mk 13:3). In similar fashion, but concerning the disciples of John the Baptist, Matthew records that John the Baptist sent word to Jesus by "his disciples" (11:2), whereas Mark speaks of "two of his disciples." Finally, in 28:7 Matthew deletes the angel's request that the women were also to tell "Peter" about the resurrection. Peter's name is swallowed up in the general reference, "go tell his disciples."[138] These examples reveal a Matthean tendency to focus on a generalized group of disciples instead of specifically named individuals (cf. also 20:20; Mk 10:35 and 26:37; Mk 14:33).

---

[136] Bonnard, *Matthieu*, p. 285; so also Hill, *Matthew*, p. 282, Filson, *St. Matthew*, pp 207-208.

[137] Suggested by Gundry, *Matthew*, p. 384.

[138] Gundry, ibid., p. 589, suggests Peter's name is deleted because he has apostasized. This and other views will be examined in the next chapter, "Matthew's Theological Understanding of Simon Peter."

5. Summary

Matthew remains faithful to his tradition, but at points he differs from his source material in order to reflect his own understanding of the μαθηταί. In the first place, Matthew preserves and strengthens the distinction between the ὄχλοι and μαθηταί through these alterations. The μαθηταί serve the ὄχλοι (14:19; 15:36) and become separate from the ὄχλοι to be with Jesus alone (14:22). Both groups are explicitly stated to be the audience of the Sermon on the Mount, but the μαθηταί are the primary audience and the ὄχλοι the secondary audience. Through adding reference to the ὄχλοι in 14:15 and 15:33 Matthew has further strengthened the contextual distinction between them and the μαθηταί. By omitting reference to the ὄχλοι in 16:24, he limits the saying about the nature of discipleship to its proper audience, the μαθηταί. In the second place, various passages stress the essential solidarity of the μαθηταί with Jesus in persecution, authority and mission (10:24), obedience to appointed tasks (26:19) and being "with" Jesus (26:36,38,40). Thirdly, Matthew reveals a unique attitude toward the μαθηταί by specifying Peter as an example (14:26ff) and scapegoat (15:1-20); but even in the example of Peter the μαθηταί are recognized to have imperfect faith and partial understanding. In the fourth place, the disciples are portayed in various imperfections, but the means to advance in discipleship are also portrayed. On one occasion the μαθηταί are singled out for their little faith and how they might use that little faith (17:16-19). In 19:13-15 the disciples do not fully comprehend Jesus' ministry, and so have to be taught by Jesus what is really important in discipleship. Finally, Matthew has a tendency to refer to a general group of disciples instead of singling out individuals (cf. 14:1,3; 11:2; 20:20; and 26:37).

E) Matthew's Omissions of Μαθητής

Matthew not only *includes* occurrences of the term μαθητής which are not found in the parallel sources, but he also *omits* several occurrences of the term which are found in the tradition. Mark uses μαθητής forty-six times, and Matthew omits approximately eighteen of those in writing his gospel.[139] One type of omission is when Matthew omits an entire Markan pericope that contained the term (cf. Mk 12:41-44, esp. v. 43). Another type is when Matthew omits part of a pericope (e.g. 9:21-22 cf. Mk 5:29-33; 12:15 cf. Mk 3:9-11; 15:1 cf. Mk 7:2-4; 26:18 cf. Mk 14:13-14). And then there are many times when Matthew simply omits the term itself

---

[139] See Appendix C for a complete listing of the occurrences of the term in Mk and the omissions in Mt.

(e.g. 9:14 cf. Mk 2:18; 13:54 cf. Mk 6:1; 15:39 cf. Mk 8:10, etc.). Of the eight occurrences of μαθητής in "Q" material, Matthew omits five (6:25 cf. Lk 12:22; 10:37, 38 cf. Lk 14:26, 27; 11:2 cf. Lk 7:18; 13:16 cf. Lk 10:23), but it should be noted that the occurrences in Lk 10:23 and 12:22 are most likely Lukan introductory statements.[140]

Several omissions do not reveal any significant Matthean purposes. These are a general type of omission in which Matthew merely makes some kind of change of reference. For example, in 9:14b (cf. Mk 2:18b) Matthew omits μαθητής as a qualifier of the Pharisees; in 11:2 Matthew omits the reference to the μαθηταί of John the Baptist telling him about the deeds of Christ (cf. Lk 7:18); in 17:14 Matthew says Jesus and the three disciples came to the crowd, but in Mk 9:14 they came to the disciples and saw a great crowd; in 16:18 Matthew omits Mark's reference (Mk 14:13) to Jesus' sending two disciples, and instead has "the disciples" being sent.

Beyond this general type of omission, Matthew also reveals certain purposes in his omissions of μαθητής. They exhibit many of the same theological tendencies which are revealed in the occurrences of the term.

1. Jesus alone

The most striking type of omission is Matthew's tendency to omit references to the disciples so that the focus is on Jesus alone. In 12:15f. Matthew omits the reference to Jesus being accompanied by μαθηταί and followed by a "great crowd" (Mk 3:7), and instead says, "many followed him." In the same context Matthew omits reference to the disciples being ordered to prepare a boat to escape the crowd's crush, and instead focuses on Jesus being alone and healing "them all" (cf. Mk 3:9). The focus is upon Jesus as the one who has fulfilled the role of the Servant in Isaiah and who despises popularity[141] but who is the Spirit-endowed hope of mankind. The omission of the μαθηταί (and ὄχλοι) has caused the focus to be on Jesus alone.

Several other passages also omit reference to the disciples so that attention is focused on Jesus alone. Mt 13:54 has Jesus alone going to his own country, while in Mk 6:1 the disciples accompanied him. In 15:39 Jesus sends the crowds away and then got into a boat and went away, but in Mk 8:10 the disciples accompanied him. Matthew focuses upon Jesus alone, and later refers to the disciples' coming (16:5). Matthew does not

---

[140] See Appendix D for the occurrences of μαθητής in "Q".

[141] Robert H. Gundry, *The Use of the Old Testament in St. Matthew's Gospel: With Special Reference to the Messianic Hope*, NovT Supp, vol. XVIII (Leiden: E. J. Brill, 1967), p. 209.

mean to say that the disciples are not there (cf. 16:13a); instead Jesus is focused upon more clearly when other people, including the μαθηταί, are not mentioned. In 16:13a, Matthew says, "Now when Jesus came into the district," but Mark has him accompanied by the μαθηταί (Mk 8:27). Similarly, Matthew concentrates on Jesus alone coming into the district of Caesarea Phillipi, heightening the effect of his question to the disciples about the identity of the Son of Man (16:13b). In the passion prediction the nearest antecedent to 17:22 assumes that Jesus is addressing the μαθηταί, but through the absence of an audience-identifier (cf. Mk 9:31), the focus is upon Jesus alone. This further emphasizes the passion prediction; not the prediction per se, but the Son of Man's role in it. In the scene just prior to the entry into Jerusalem (Mt 20:29-34) Matthew focuses attention on Jesus again by omitting reference to the μαθηταί accompanying him (cf. Mk 10:46), and also by omitting reference to the name of the man (Bartimaeus, son of Timaeus, Mk 10:46b) (cf. 20:30). Matthew has only a nameless crowd following Jesus and nameless blind men calling out to him, accenting Jesus alone as the compassionate one who stops and heals. Matthew, therefore, in approximately half of his omissions, isolates Jesus for the purpose of giving him focused attention.

2. Different attitude toward the μαθηταί

Through various omissions, Matthew also reveals an attitude toward the μαθηταί which differs from that of the sources. The healing of the woman with the hemorrhage occurred in Matthew's source between the material of Mt 9:21 and 9:22. Within that story in the source was an incident in which the μαθηταί somewhat sarcastically reproached Jesus for asking who had touched him (cf. Mk 5:31). Matthew may have omitted this incident intentionally to protect the disciples, but more likely he was focusing on Jesus in his ministry accompanied by his μαθηταί.[142] It has already been seen that in 19:9-10 Matthew has softened the non-understanding of Mark's disciples by omitting the question in Mk 8:10 and making it Jesus' statement (19:9), then portraying the disciples as at least partially understanding.

Matthew's omissions also have a tendency to emphasize Peter in relationship to the μαθηταί. Matthew has placed the question of the μαθηταί on Peter's lips in 15:12 (cf. Mk 7:17) and made him the brunt of a reproach for not understanding. While associating the disciples with the reproach through a plural form of the rebuke from Jesus (15:16, 17),

---

[142] Since Matthew does not avoid the weaknesses of the disciples elsewhere, there is no reason to imply that he has done so here.

Peter receives most of the accusation. In 16:23, after Peter rebukes Jesus for talking about going to the cross, Matthew records Jesus' denunciation of Peter but omits Mark's phrase "but turning and seeing his disciples" (Mk 8:33). V. Taylor observes that Mark included the disciples in Peter's rebuke by this phrase,[143] so as he omits it, Matthew focuses on Peter alone.

3. Jesus and the ὄχλοι

In two significant passages Matthew omits reference to the μαθηταί and leaves Jesus alone with the ὄχλοι. In the first, Jesus comes down from the mount of Transfiguration with the three disciples, and instead of coming to the μαθηταί who had a great crowd around while they argued with the scribes (Mk 9:14), Matthew says that they came to the "crowd" (17:14). In this way Matthew has reduced Mark's complicated scene to the principal figures of the account.[144] The principal characters are Jesus, a man from the crowd, and the disciples. Matthew simplifies the scene so that the teaching on faith becomes a means of drawing the man further from the crowd and encouraging the disciples to use their faith more effectively. Matthew also refines the picture in the second passage (20:29-34) by omitting several details and concentrating on the essentials of the narrative. He omits the term μαθηταί because the disciples are not one of the principal groups in the narrative.[145] The emphasis is upon Jesus and the crowd following him (v. 29b). The crowd rebukes the blind men much as the disciples have done before (15:23; 19:13), but here it does not result in a clarification of the objective of Jesus' ministry as it did there (15:24; 19:24). Jesus corrected the disciples on those other occasions through teaching, and then he performed the requested service. But here there is no teaching, only fulfilling the request. Jesus does not rebuke the crowd because as non-disciples they cannot be expected to "understand" (cf. 13:10ff.) the ministry of Jesus.

In another quite interesting omission of μαθητής (10:37-38), Matthew again reveals the way in which discipleship teaching is reserved for disciples. Manson suggests that the saying came from some Q source,[146] but in Matthew's gospel it has received a completely different emphasis. In Lk 14:25-27 Jesus issues the saying as a challenge to the crowd to *become* disciples, but in Mt it comes within the context of a discourse *to*

---

[143] V. Taylor, *St. Mark*, p. 379.
[144] Bonnard, *Matthieu*, p. 259.
[145] They are not left out completely though, because the antecedent of the plural pronoun (αὐτῶν) in 20:29 is the twelve disciples in 20:17ff.
[146] Manson, *Sayings*, p. 131.

disciples (cf. 10:5). Matthew omits the term μαθητής since Jesus is addressing disciples, and instead writes "worthy" (ἄξιος). In this way, instead of speaking of the conditions for taking up discipleship, Jesus is speaking of the risk of danger as a *proof of the genuineness* of the professed discipleship, the "worth" of the discipleship.[147] Matthew reserves teaching on growth in discipleship for the disciples, and challenges to take up discipleship for the crowds.

4. Summary

Matthew omits approximately eighteen of the forty-six occurrences of μαθητής in Mark and five of the eight occurrences in Q. A general type of omission occurs when Matthew makes some kind of change of reference from his source. Matthew also demonstrates literary purposes in three other types of omissions. The first type is the striking way Matthew omits references to μαθηταί and other groups in order to give attention to Jesus alone. The second type demonstrates the difference of Matthew's attitude from the sources toward the μαθηταί. This is especially indicated by the way in which he transfers various attitudes to Peter which belonged to the disciples as a whole in the tradition. The third type of omisson involves the relationship Jesus and the ὄχλοι. Jesus directed an appeal to faith to the ὄχλοι (17:14) and they were a group who followed him (20:17), but when the ὄχλοι rebuked a seeker, they were not corrected by Jesus through teaching about his ministry, because teaching on growth in discipleship is primarily directed to disciples.

F) Matthew's Use of Μανθάνω and Μαθητεύω

Matthew's preference for μαθητής and his unique use of the term also affects his use of two other μαθ-stem words, μανθάνω and μαθητεύω.

1. Μανθάνω

The verb μανθάνω is found infrequently in the Gospels, but most often in Mt (Mt-3; Mk-1; Lk-0; Jn-2; Acts-1).[148] The occurrences in Mt are 9:13; 11:29; and 24:32. This statistical scarcity of μανθάνω in the Gospels is quite out of balance in comparison with the frequency of μαθητής. Since the original definition of μαθητής was "learner" or "student," Rengstorf

[147] Gundry, *Matthew*, p. 200.
[148] Morgenthaler, *Statistik*, p. 118.

finds the scarcity of μανθάνω in the Gospels instructive for understanding the relationship of the μαθητής to Jesus. He suggests that Jesus' concern was "not to impart information, nor to deepen an existing attitude, but to awaken unconditional commitment to himself." Rengstorf suggests that Jesus did this through establishing ἀκολουθεῖν rather than μανθανεῖν as "the true mark of the μαθητής."[149] Rengstorf correctly stresses the aspect of personal commitment to Jesus, but in the way Matthew uses μανθανεῖν there is still a trace of "learning" as a characteristic of the μαθητής. This is especially recognized when one remembers that Matthew emphasizes the "understanding" of the true disciples.

The first occurrence of μανθάνω in Mt (9:13) stresses learning as a key to discovering the will of God. Jesus is in a disputation with the Pharisees and says "Go and learn..." (πορευθέντες δὲ μάθετε). Only Matthew has these additional words, and being addressed to Jesus' opponents they signify a challenge for them to truly understand the will of God. Once they have "learned" what the will of God entails, they will see that Jesus is the embodiment of the will of God and they too should be with Jesus as are the disciples, tax-gatherers, and sinners.[150] A key step to becoming a disciple is to go and *learn* that the will of God centers in Jesus and his teaching and ministry.

The second occurrence of μανθάνω also comes in a context of non-believers (Mt 11:29). Jesus speaks to the crowds about John the Baptist (11:7) and then turns and condemns the generation (11:18), the Pharisees (11:19 cf. 9:34) and the non-repentant cities (11:20-23). But in his prayer Jesus extends an offer (to the crowds of 11:7?) to come to him, take his yoke, and "learn" from him (11:29). Jesus thus contrasts himself with the scribes and their assertion that they alone can expound Scripture. As it is expressed by Jesus, true rest and joy are found in learning and obeying the will of God.[151]

The third occurrence of μανθάνω differs from the other two in that this saying of Jesus is spoken to the μαθηταί (Mt 24:32, cf. 24:3). The fact that it is spoken to disciples confirms what is found elsewhere (cf. Mt 13): only the μαθηταί can understand parables, and here Jesus says "learn the parable" (μάθετε τὴν παραβολήν). By their ability to learn from and understand the parable they show that they truly are μαθηταί. The parable fully understood will allow the disciples to know the will of God as spoken by Jesus and to be ready for his coming (24:33).

---

[149] Karl H. Rengstorf, "μανθάνω," *TDNT*, IV (ET; Grand Rapids: Eerdmans, 1967), p. 406.

[150] Dietrich Müller, "μαθητής; μανθάνω," *New International Dictionary of New Testament Theology*, trans. and ed. Colin Brown, vol. 1 (Grand Rapids: Zondervan, 1975), p. 486.

[151] Rengstorf, "μανθάνω," p. 409; Müller, "μαθητής," p. 486.

Since Matthew employed the aorist imperative in each use of μανθάνω, "learning" was not to be a casual, academic exercise. It demanded personal decision and commitment to the will of God as centered in Jesus.

2. Μαθητεύω

The verb μαθητεύω is also rarely found in the Gospels, but unlike μανθάνω, which is found eighteen times in the Epistles, μαθητεύω is absent from the Epistles (Mt-3; Mk-0; Lk-0; Jn-0; Acts-1).[152] As can be seen, the only other occurrence of the verb in the New Testament outside Mt is the one in Acts. The occurrences in Mt are at 13:52; 27:57; and 28:19; the Acts occurrence is at 14:21. Μαθητεύω is constructed from μαθητής, and in Greek usage meant intransitively "to be" or "to become" a pupil. A transitive use of μαθητεύω occurs in the New Testament which is different from non-New Testament usage. This peculiar New Testament usage means "to make disciples" (cf. 27:19; Acts 14:21).[153]

Scholars have debated whether μαθητευθείς in 13:52 is an intransitive deponent according to the classical Greek usage,[154] or whether it acquires the peculiar New Testament usage as a transitive passive.[155] Gundry observes that "it would be wrong to separate becoming a disciple (μαθητεύομαι as a deponent) from being instructed as a disciple (μαθητεύομαι as a true passive),"[156] hence the meaning would not be greatly altered either way. But since Jesus is speaking to μαθηταί about the consequence of their understanding (cf. διὰ τοῦτο),[157] it seems best to interpret this as a transitive passive in the sense of being instructed.[158] Nevertheless, the peculiar New Testament emphasis in the verb should not be lost in the translation. McNeile suggests that it should be rendered "has been instructed [as a disciple]" in order to draw fully on the Matthean emphasis.[159] A more ambiguous but accurate rendering might be "having been discipled," if one understands that "knowledge may be

[152] Morgenthaler, *Statistik*, p. 118.
[153] Cf. the entry "μαθητεύω," col. 915, and Poul Nepper-Christensen, "μαθητής," in *Exegetisches Wörterbuch zum Neuen Testament*, ed. Horst Balz and Gerhard Schneider, vol II (Stuttgart: W. Kohlhammer, 1982), col. 915-921.
[154] F. Blass and A. Debrunner, *A Greek Grammar of the New Testament and other Early Christian Literature*, trans. and rev., Robert W. Funk (9th-10th German ed.; Chicago: University of Chicago Press, 1961), p. 82 (no. 148[3]).
[155] A. T. Robertson, *A Grammar of the Greek New Testament in the Light of Historical Research* (4th ed.; Nashville, Tenn.: Broadman Press, 1934), pp. 475, 800.
[156] Gundry, *Matthew*, p. 281.
[157] Bonnard, *Matthieu*, p. 210.
[158] Kingsbury, *Parables*, pp. 126-127; McNeile, *St. Matthew*, p. 205; Tasker, *St. Matthew*, p. 140.
[159] McNeile, *St. Matthew*, p. 205.

usefully united with discipleship.''[160] The meaning is that every scribe
who has been discipled, i.e., every scribe who is truly a disciple and has
been instructed in discipleship ''concerning''[161] the kingdom of heaven
will be fully equipped for interpreting and serving in the new age. Connected with the use of μανθάνω in 11:29, the disciples who truly understand are the new scribes of the kingdom of heaven because they have
learned through being discipled by Jesus.[162]

The use in 27:57 has also been debated as to its form. The marginal
reading has the intransitive active sense of the non-New Testament
Greek usage (ἐμαθήτευσεν[163]) while the text reading in Nestle is the transitive passive (ἐμαθητεύθη[164]). The stronger reading requires the acceptance of the transitive passive form, so that much the same meaning as
was found in 13:52 accrues to the term here. Albright and Mann suggest
that Matthew intentionally avoided μαθητής by using μαθητεύω because
he did not want to imply that Joseph of Arimethea was a ''disciple,'' but
only that he had been ''taught by Jesus.''[165] But when it is recognized
that Matthew used μαθητεύω instead of Mk's reference to Joseph being
one who was looking for the kingdom, Matthew may be saying that the
acceptance of the kingdom reposes in ἐμαθητεύθη τῷ 'Ιησοῦ.[166] Matthew
does not try to draw a distinction between the noun μαθητής and the verb
μαθητεύω.[167] Instead, as Przybylski says, they both refer to a single concept: ''Just as in some cases the noun is definitely used to refer to the
disciples in a very inclusive sense, so the verb shows that disciples are
people in general who have accepted (13:52; 27:57), or will accept
(28:19), the teaching of Jesus.''[168] Therefore, as in 13:52, the sense is
that Joseph ''was discipled'' by Jesus; that is, he was a true disciple who
had been taught by Jesus concerning the kingdom.

The final occurrence of μαθητεύω is in Mt 28:19. The essential
''discipleship'' orientation of the verb is especially observed in this
pericope. If the μαθηταί were simply to ''teach all nations,''[169] the

[160] A. B. Bruce, ''The Synoptic Gospels,'' *The Expositor's Greek Testament*, vol. I (n.d.,
rpt.; Grand Rapids: Eerdmans, 1976), p. 204.
[161] The dative should be construed as a dative of ''respect;'' so Kingsbury, *Parables*,
p. 127.
[162] Cf. Gundry, *Matthew*, pp. 281-282; Kingsbury, *Parables*, p. 126; Luz, ''Die
Jünger,'' p. 158.
[163] B Koine A L W Γ Δ Φ *pm*.
[164] Sin C D Θ λ 33. 700. 892 *pc*.
[165] Albright and Mann, *Matthew*, p. LXXVII.
[166] Luz, ''Die Jünger,'' p. 157.
[167] So says Strecker, *Weg*, pp. 192f; Albright and Mann, *Matthew*, LXXVIII..
[168] Benno Przybylski, *Righteousness in Matthew and his World of Thought*, SNTSMS, no.
41 (Cambridge: Cambridge University Press, 1980), p. 110.
[169] Albright and Mann, *Matthew*, p. LXXVIII..

explicative διδάσκοντες in v. 20 would be superfluous. Indeed, the conjunction of the two verbs makes it impossible for μαθητεύω to refer to teaching.[170] Instead, as Jesus addresses the μαθηταί and commands[171] them to "make disciples of all the nations" (μαθητεύσατε πάντα τὰ ἔθνη) he is telling them to make more of what they are themselves. "Matthew's use of the term implies much more than our usual concept of evangelism; the term means both the call to and process of becoming a disciple."[172] The disciples obviously knew the process through which Jesus had taken them, and what he had taught them, but if the open-ended nature of the commission was to retain its force (ἕως τῆς συντελείας τοῦ αἰῶνος) then a manual on discipleship was needed for other μαθηταί to carry out the mandate. Placed at this climactic conclusion to his gospel, the mandate could very well be an indication of a central purpose in Matthew's *Tendenz*.[173] If one of Matthew's purposes in writing his gospel is to provide such a manual on discipleship, then all of his various purposes in the use of the term μαθητής are subsidiary to and supportive of that broader purpose.[174] Therefore, the goal of the next section will be to tie the comparative analysis together with a literary and theological analysis in order to ascertain Matthew's overall purpose in his use of the term μαθητής.

3. Summary

Although the verbs μανθάνω and μαθητεύω are not found in the abundance that belongs to the noun μαθητής, Matthew does use them more than any other gospel writer. Even in his relatively scarce use of the terms, Matthew reveals his purpose. Although μανθανεῖν cannot be said to be the most distinguishing mark of the μαθητής, and appears to follow ἀκολουθεῖν in importance, the "learning" element is still a part of Matthew's discipleship. In two passages in which Jesus interacts with the

---

[170] Przybylski, *Righteousness*, p. 110.

[171] Μαθητεύω occurs as an aorist active imperative.

[172] Grant R. Osborne, *The Resurrection Narratives: A Redactional Study*, (Grand Rapids: Baker, 1984), p. 91. Matthean contextual usage points to this conclusion, rather than theologizing based on the occurrence of the transitive verb; cf. the note in Moisés Silva, "New Lexical Semitisms?," *ZNTW* 69 (1978), p. 256 n. 9.

[173] Cf. Wolfgang Trilling, *Das Wahre Israel: Studien zur Theologie des Matthäus-Evangeliums* (3d. Auflage; München: Kösel-Verlag, 1964), pp. 21ff., whose study of Matthew's theology uses the Great Commission as a starting point.

[174] Hubbard suggests that one purpose of the commission was to act as a literary conclusion in which Matthew pulls together the principal themes of his gospel; Hubbard, *Matthean Redaction of a Primitive Apostolic Commissioning*, pp. 90, 98; cf. also E. P. Blair, *Jesus in the Gospel of Matthew: A Reappraisal of the Distinctive Elements of Matthew's Christology*, (Nashville: Abingdon, 1960), pp. 45ff.

non-believer, *learning* the will of God means centering on Jesus and his teaching (9:13; 11:29). The authenticity of an individual's discipleship is gauged by the disciples' ability to "learn" from a parable (24:32), an impossibility for one of the crowd. The use of the verb μαθητεύω indicates that being instructed as a disciple is a mark of a true disciple. To "be discipled" means that one who is a disciple continues to learn from Jesus about the kingdom of heaven (13:52; 27:57). Therefore, when Matthew concludes his gospel with the commission to "make disciples," he may be revealing a determinative *Tendenz* of his gospel.

IV. Comparison of Various Characters

The linguistic analysis of the term μαθητής as used by Matthew has yielded a great deal of information, but no attempt has yet been made to give a unified statement of Matthew's purpose in his use of the term. Matthew's purpose appears to be many faceted. For instance, he has a purpose in including the term so that disciples are specified as being with Jesus (9:19), but at times he specifically excluded them from being with Jesus (12:15). At times Matthew purposely projects a very positive attitude about the μαθηταί through including the term (12:49), but at other times he includes the term in a way that the μαθηταί are singled out for negative associations (26:56). At times Matthew omits reference to them sharing guilt with Peter (16:23), yet they are also on other occasions singled out and specified as sharing in his guilt (14:31). At times it appears that Matthew has purposely carried forward the traditional association of the term μαθηταί with the apostolic title οἱ δώδεκα (10:1), but on other occasions he has implied a wider circle of disciples (8:21; 27:57).

The divergent uses of the term must really be seen as subsidiary and complementary to Matthew's overall use and purpose. Luz has rightly criticized Strecker for following one treatment of Matthew's use of the term without full recognition of other uses. To see only one Matthean use of the term obscures the overall Matthean purpose.[175] The tendency to follow one theme in Matthew's gospel to the exclusion of others regularly occurs in Matthean studies, most often because paradoxical teaching is inherent to this gospel. The classic illustration is in Matthew's particularism and universalism. On the one hand Matthew restricts the gospel to Israel (10:5-6; 15:24), while on the other hand he extends the

---

[175] Luz, "Die Jünger," pp. 142-149. Luz confronts Strecker at this very point, because Strecker followed one basic theme and ended with a "historicization" of the μαθηταί (Strecker, *Weg*). Luz argues that Strecker did not have a broad enough understanding of Matthew's treatment of the term.

gospel to the entire world (21:43; 28:19). The resolution of these elements still occupies the attention of Matthean scholars today,[176] and gives hope for the resolution of some of the themes surrounding Matthew's use of μαθητής. This writer suggests that some of these divergent themes can be reconciled through a comparison of various characters in Matthew's gospel with his use of μαθητής. For example, what relationship does Matthew portray the μαθηταί sustaining to other characters and character groups in Mt? How has Matthew used the term in association with these other characters? These relationships reveal different emphases, and help greatly in understanding Matthew's gospel as a whole. The characters to be analyzed are Jesus, the Twelve, Peter and other named disciples (in the next chapter in full), and the crowds. Some time ago T. W. Manson contended that the teaching of Jesus was conditioned by the nature of its audience. He identified types of teaching for three audiences: scribes and Pharisees, disciples, and the general public. Whereas Manson basically applied this scheme to an analysis of the λογία, the present study will attempt to define the nature of the groups in relationship to each other.[177]

A) The Μαθηταί and Jesus

A renewed emphasis in recent Matthean studies has been to recognize that the gospel of Matthew is primarily a Christological document.[178] The preceding comparison of Matthew's use of μαθητής tends to support the Christological nature of Mt. If one major generalization is to be

---

[176] The most recent, extended discussion of this issue is by Donald A. Hagner, "The Sitz im Leben of the Gospel of Matthew," SBLSP no. 24 (Atlanta, Georgia: Scholars, 1985), 243-269.

[177] Manson, Teaching, pp. 19-21. J. Zumstein focuses upon the paradigmatic function which he says Matthew attributes to various groups. Although he has given these groups careful attention, he appears to go too far in his characterizations (Zumstein, La Condition du croyant dans l'évangile selon Matthieu, p. 81). This present study will attempt to avoid his over-characterizations.

[178] E.g., E. P. Blair, Jesus in the Gospel of Matthew: A Reappraisal of the Distinctive Elements of Matthew's Christology (Nashville: Abingdon, 1960); cf. David Hill, "Some Recent Trends in Matthean Studies" Ir BibSt 1 (1979), pp. 143-145; Graham Stanton, "The Origin and Purpose of Matthew's Gospel: Matthean Scholarship from 1945-1980," Aufstieg und Niedergang der Römischen Welt, II, 25, 3, ed. H. Temporini and W. Haase (Berlin: Walter de Gruyter, 1985), pp. 1922-1925. J. D. Kingsbury has been at the heart of the Christological discussion in Matthew, and the discussion has recently been revived: cf. Jack Dean Kingsbury, "The Figure of Jesus in Matthew's Story: A Literary-Critical Probe," JSNT 21 (1984), 1-36; David Hill, "The Figure of Jesus in Matthew's Story: A Response to Professor Kingsbury's Literary-Critical Probe," JSNT 21 (1984), 37-52; Jack Dean Kingsbury, "The Figure of Jesus in Matthew's Story: A Rejoiner to David Hill," JSNT 25 (1985), 61-81.

drawn from this study, it is that Matthew has arranged his μαθητής material in order to accentuate the figure of Jesus Christ.

Matthew's accentuation of Jesus is especially evident in Matthew's omissions of μαθητής from his sources. In at least eight out of eighteen omissions the term was omitted from a specific mention in Mk or Q in such a way that the focus in Mt is on Jesus alone.[179] Matthew's intention was not to suggest that the disciples were not there, but that they have receded into the background in order that Jesus should be given primary attention.

One of the most significant Christological contributions was in the development of the discipleship-teaching pericopae. Bornkamm establishes that by the inclusion of μαθητής in 8:21,23, the entire pericope was to be considered a "discipleship story,"[180] and if that perspective is kept in mind, one can see that Matthew has transformed many teaching segments into explicit discipleship-teaching pericopae. In approximately seventeen of Matthew's thirty-four inclusions, the term μαθητής is a signal word to note discipleship instruction.[181] The typical format is for Matthew to mention explicitly the disciples saying something or asking something, and then to describe the instruction on the nature of discipleship that Jesus gives in response. As is the case in at least three situations, the teaching of Jesus leads to an explicit statement that the disciples understand (16:12; 17:13; 13:52), entirely different from Mark's gospel where the disciples are said to not understand (cf. 6:52; 8:21; 9:10,32). Some scholars have taken this contrast between the "understanding" of the disciples in Mt and the "non-understanding" in Mk to mean that Matthew has tried to "idealize" the μαθηταί; "that he smooths away anything derogatory to the disciples."[182] On the contrary, although he does not focus on the disciples' failure (e.g., 8:25; 13:16; 14:23), Matthew explicitly tells about their deficient faith (14:31; 16:8, 22f.; 17:20), and presents negative aspects of the μαθηταί (e.g., 26:8,56).[183] Instead of an idealization of the μαθηταί, the "understanding" of the disciples accentuates Jesus and his teaching. It is because of Jesus that the disciples move to understanding. In actuality the disciples are presented in various ways by Matthew (negative, mixed,

---

[179] 12:15,16; 13:54; 15:39; 16:13a; 17:22; 20:29; 20:29.

[180] Bornkamm, "Stilling," pp. 54-57.

[181] 8:21,23; 9:27; 10:42; 12:49; 13:10; 15:23; 16:5 17:6; 17:10; 18:1; 19:10; 21:20; 24:3; 26:8,40,45.

[182] T. Francis Glasson, "Anti-Pharisaism in St. Matthew," *JQR* 51 (1960-1961), p. 136; cf. also Allen, *St. Matthew*, p. xxxiiii f.; Erich Klostermann, *Das Matthäusevangelium, Handbuch zum Neuen Testament*, 4 (1909; 4th ed; Tübingen: J. C. B. Mohr, 1971), p. 21.

[183] Cf. G. Osborne, *The Resurrection Narratives*, p. 91 n. 28.

neutral, and positive), but in each, Matthew emphasizes that Jesus instructs them in the way of discipleship. In some of these the source already had Jesus teaching, and even some reference to the μαθηταί, but Matthew's inclusions specifically designated the passage as discipleship-instruction. Jesus is explicitly accentuated as the effective Teacher of his disciples.

The emphasis on Jesus as Teacher was also seen in the use of the verbs μανθάνω and μαθητεύω. In disputation with the Pharisees and scribes, Jesus says that the process of knowing the will of God is found as one learns from Jesus and his embodiment of the will of God (9:13; 11:29). The true disciple is the one who is able to "learn" from parables through Jesus (24:32) and who is "discipled" by Jesus in the ways of the kingdom (13:52; 27:57).

As Matthew depicts Jesus caring for the ὄχλοι, he accents Jesus' care even more in his sovereign choice of the disciples to serve the crowds (9:36,37; 14:19; 15:36). The disciples will serve the crowds, but the "Lord" serves the ὄχλοι through the disciples.

These are the significant ways in which Matthew has highlighted the Christology of his gospel through the disciples. In the true sense that Mt is a "gospel," the author has incorporated "a paradigmatic history angled to set forth the fulfillment of God's redeeming motive and activity in Jesus."[184] Matthew's *angle* is especially apparent in his use of μαθητής. While they should not be relegated to *extras*, as Conzelmann does,[185] the μαθηταί serve a primary purpose in Matthew's gospel of accentuating Jesus in his words and deeds.[186]

B) The Μαθηταί and the Twelve

Matthew explicitly identified Mark's οἱ δώδεκα with the μαθηταί when he created the longer title, "οἱ δώδεκα μαθηταί."

1. Matthew carries forward the traditional identification

The majority of modern scholarship accepts the thesis that at least from Mk 3:13 on Mark identified the terms μαθητής and οἱ δώδεκα with one another.[187] As Meye contends, "Mark describes Jesus' ministry con-

[184] Ralph P. Martin, *New Testament Foundations: A Guide for Christian Students*, vol. 1 (Grand Rapids: Eerdmans, 1975), p. 23.
[185] Hans Conzelmann, *Jesus* (1959; E.T.; Philadelphia: Fortress, 1973), p. 34.
[186] Hengel, *Charismatic Leader*, p. 79.
[187] Cf., Bultmann, *History of the Synoptic Tradition*, p. 67; Taylor, *St. Mark*, pp. 229-230; Meye, *The Twelve*, pp. 98-140, 228-230; Luz, "Die Jünger," p. 142; Goppelt, *Theology*, I, 210. That this is not a consensus is observed in Hengel, *Charismatic Leader*, pp. 81-82 n. 163.

sistently with only the Twelve in view as the disciples of Jesus.''[188] Therefore, when Matthew worked with Mk, he did not have to make that identification; it was already there in the tradition and he perpetuated it.[189] All that Matthew does is make the identification more explicit. Therefore, Matthew has faithfully carried forward his tradition concerning οἱ δώδεκα μαθηταί.

2. Matthew identifies but does not exclude

If Matthew did indeed pass on this traditional identification, did he mean that he intentionally limited the μαθηταί to the Twelve in his literary scheme? Strecker claims that in Mt μαθητής has become practically a technical term referring strictly to the Twelve.[190] Albright and Mann contend that Matthew never refers to a wider group of disciples than the Twelve,[191] and Pesch states that even in the replacement of "Levi" (Mk 2:14) with "Matthew" (9:9; cf. 10:3), Matthew has intentionally drawn a strict equation of the μαθηταί and δώδεκα.[192]

While it may be accepted that Mark and Matthew generally identified the terms, it is questionable whether they intended to limit the term μαθητής exclusively to the Twelve. Hengel argues that there are signs of other disciples than the Twelve in Mk,[193] and Przybylski shows convincingly that Matthew specifically speaks of disciples other than the Twelve (8:19, 21), that he indicates a wider circle of disciples (10:24,25,42), and that he acknowledges through a related verb the existence of a named disciple, Joseph of Arimethea, other than the Twelve (27:57).[194] Matthew has a literary and theological purpose for generally identifying the μαθηταί and δώδεκα, but he does not exclude the existence of other disciples. As Kingsbury notes, the term μαθητής, where it refers to followers of Jesus, "is synonymous with those who are otherwise familiar to us as the Twelve ... In those cases where Matthew employs 'disciple' [otherwise], he regularly makes this clear."[195] Therefore, unless Matthew states otherwise, he refers to the Twelve when he refers to the μαθηταί, but he does not mean to imply that Jesus has no other disciples.

---

[188] Meye, The Twelve, p. 210.
[189] Luz, "Die Jünger," pp. 142-143.
[190] Strecker, Weg, pp. 191-192.
[191] Albright and Mann, Matthew, p. LXXVII.
[192] R. Pesch, "Levi-Mätthaus (Mc 2:14/Mt 9:9; 10:3). Ein Beitrag zur Lösung eines alten Problems," ZNW 59(1968), pp. 40-56.
[193] Hengel, Charismatic Leader, pp. 81-82 n. 163.
[194] Przybylski, Righteousness, pp. 108-110.
[195] Kingsbury, Parables, p. 41.

3. Matthew's understanding of the identification

J. J. Vincent cogently argues that to understand fully the Synoptic discipleship sayings one must keep two moments before him: "(a) the moment within the early life of Jesus in which the radical summons is made, and (b) the moment within the Church's life when the would-be disciple is tested."[196] Instead of keeping *both* moments in mind, some scholars have concentrated on one to the exclusion of the other. For instance, Strecker places the disciples strictly within the moment of the earthly life of Jesus, thus idealizing the disciples.[197] On the other hand, Frankemölle almost completely rejects any historical orientation in Mt, and contends that Matthew has constructed a document that is not truly interested in what happened to the disciples "then," only what they mean for the church "now."[198] Vincent's suggestion keeps the interpreter of Matthew from either one of these extremes. Matthew had a desire to pass his tradition on faithfully, but he also had a desire to interpret that history from his own perspective for the needs of his church.[199] An approximation of this balanced view occurs in Guelich's statement: "the evangelist's genuine interest in the past, as seen by his consistent use of the disciples as the Twelve, has a present application. The past tradition is not merely preserved; rather, it is used in terms of the context and concerns of the present situation."[200]

With these two moments before us, a significant question arises: How did Matthew mean his church to understand his use of the μαθηταί? Are the μαθηταί an embodiment of the church,[201] a symbol for Christians,[202] an idealization as a paradigm of disciples,[203] representatives of Christians or the church,[204] a transparency for the church,[205] prototypes of pastors in the church,[206] or a transparency for church leaders?[207] Many concepts

---

[196] John J. Vincent, "Discipleship and Synoptic Studies," *ThZ* 16 (1960), p. 464.

[197] Strecker, *Weg*, pp. 86ff, 191ff.

[198] Hubert Frankemölle, *Jahwebund und Kirche Christi. Studien zur Form- und Traditionsgeschichte des Evangeliums nach Matthäus*, NT Abh 10 (Münster: Verlag Aschendorff, 1974), esp. pp. 366-368.

[199] An excellent discussion of this issue for the interpretation of Matthew as a whole is to be found in Stanton, "Matthew as Creative Interpreter of the Sayings of Jesus," passim.

[200] Guelich, *Sermon*, p. 53. Cf. also Przybylski, *Righteousness*, p. 109; Schuyler Brown, " The Mission to Israel in Matthew's Central Section (Mt 9:35-11:1)," *ZNW* 69 (1977), pp. 74-75.

[201] Barth, "Understanding," p. 100 n. 2; Frankemölle, *Jahwebund und Kirche Christi*.

[202] Davies, *Setting*, pp. 93-94.

[203] Trilling, *Israel*, pp. 50, 159, 213; Zumstein, *La Croyant*, p. 81.

[204] Kingsbury, *Matthew*, pp. 33-34; *Parables*, p. 42.

[205] Luz, "Die Jünger," cf. pp. 159-165.

[206] R. Thysman, *Communauté et directives éthiques: la catéchèse de Matthieu*, Recherches et Synthèses: Section d'exégèse, no. 1 (Gembloux: Duculot, 1974).

[207] Paul S. Minear, "The Disciples and the Crowds in the Gospel of Matthew,"

overlap from each of these Matthean models; so to clarify what this writer has discovered from this analysis, instead of choosing one or the other model, a new model is chosen. The proposal is that Matthew sets forth disciples as "examples." Hopefully this is not semantic fussiness. What is meant is the following: Matthew has anchored the disciples in history through a "faithful" interpretation of his tradition. He has passed on the traditional story of Jesus and his disciples but has interpreted it to meet the needs of his particular community. This is not to say that Matthew intends to read his own situation back into the historical setting of Jesus and the Twelve, rather, just the opposite. He selects the historical data that will best speak to his church. He portrays the disciples as they really were so that they can be an example of what his church should be. Not that he has intended an idealistic paradigm. Matthew shows both the positive and negative. The positive is to show what will happen to true disciples who fully obey and follow Jesus (especially presented in the discipleship teachings). The negative shows what can happen to disciples who do not identify with Jesus in his obedience to the will of the Father (fleeing, 26:56; sleeping, 26:40,45; brash boldness, 26:35). Portrayed both positively and negatively (15:23; 16:5-12; 17:6,7; 16:19; 19:13-15) the disciples become examples of imperfect followers of Jesus, who are taught and who advance to understanding and solidarity with Jesus. And, as an example, they become a very practical and realistic display of what one must be to be called a disciple (28:16, 18).

C) The Μαθηταί and Named Disciples

Since the next chapter will explore the realm of the named disciples, especially the figure of Peter, in Matthew's gospel, it will suffice to note here that Matthew often intentionally omits reference to specifically named disciples (e.g. 20:20-28; 24:3; 26:37) or categories in the disciples (e.g. 24:1; 26:18,19), in order to present the disciples as a unified, nameless group. This Matthean tendency is in line with what Conzelmann states is the tradition's tendency to view the disciples as a collective unity,[208] but interestingly, Matthew stresses this even more so than Mark. Paradoxically though, along with his stress on a nameless, faceless entity, Matthew brings Peter into more prominence, both positively (e.g. 16:15-19) and negatively (16:23—Matthew omits "seeing disciples").

Anglican Theological Review, Supplemental Series, III (March, 1974), 31ff.; Mark Sheridan, "Disciples and Discipleship in Matthew and Luke," *Biblical Theology Bulletin*, III (1973), 237ff.

[208] Hans Conzelmann, *History of Primitive Christianity*, trans. John E. Steely (Nashville: Abingdon, 1973), p. 149.

Matthew appears to concentrate on the disciples as an exemplary group and Peter as a "typical" individual.[209] While both the group of disciples and Peter were real in the past, they hold permanent value for the present. The church as a whole can identify with the group of disciples, while the individual and individual leader within the church can learn from Peter.

D) The Μαθηταί and the Ὄχλοι

One major conclusion of the comparative study was that Matthew made a definite distinction between the μαθηταί and the ὄχλοι. But two questions have yet to be answered. First, what is the identity of οἱ ὄχλοι? Second, what is the relationship between οἱ μαθηταί and οἱ ὄχλοι? In an attempt to answer to the first question, Baird presents an audience analysis, but his conclusions include a mixture of several other terms besides ὄχλος and do not recognize a unified purpose in Matthean usage.[210] There are at least three major views of the identity of οἱ ὄχλοι in Matthew's gospel: 1) The crowd is a basically neutral, though curious group who were not attached in any serious way to Jesus, and who were at various times either positively or negatively oriented toward Jesus;[211] 2) The crowd is a very positively viewed group; in fact, they are representative of believers, the church, although it is a mixed group of true and false believers;[212] 3) The crowd represents the ordinary believer, lay Christians.[213]

The first view appears to be most plausible, because although they follow Jesus, the ὄχλοι never exhibit the twin prerequisites of discipleship: cost and commitment. They "follow" only in a literal sense, never in the metaphysical sense of "accompaniment as one's disciple."[214] The ὄχλοι are in Mt a basically neutral group who are the object of Jesus' ministry. Jesus preaches and teaches and heals them, but they nowhere exercise faith in him.[215] They follow him (4:25), appeal for healing (15:29-31), give acclaim to him (7:28; 21:9,10), but at times laugh

---

[209] Jack Dean Kingsbury, "The Figure of Peter in Matthew's Gospel as a Theological Problem," *JBL* 98 (1979), p. 78.

[210] J. Arthur Baird, *Audience Criticism and the Historical Jesus* (Philadelphia: Westminster, 1969), cf. pp. 37-46.

[211] Manson, *Teaching*, p. 19.

[212] Gundry, *Matthew*, p. 65.

[213] Minear, "Disciples and Crowds," pp. 30-32, 40-42.

[214] Jack Dean Kingsbury, "The Verb AKOLOUTHEIN ("To Follow") as an Index of Matthew's View of His Community," *JBL* 97 (1978), p. 61

[215] Cf. Kingsbury, "AKOLOUTHEIN," p. 61; Albright and Mann, *Matthew*, p. LXXVII.

at him (9:23-25), come to arrest him (26:47), are influenced by the chief priests and elders (27:20), and are reponsible for the blood of Jesus (27:24). The objective of Jesus' ministry among the crowds is to make them disciples, and, as he teaches and preaches, the sign of faith is when one comes out of the crowd and calls Jesus "Lord" (cf. 8:18,21; 17:14,15).[216] As an individual comes out of the crowd, he chooses either to exercise faith and become a believer, or chooses not to believe (cf. 19:16-22). Therefore, the crowd is a neutral group, out of which come those who will become disciples of Jesus, and those who will· decide against Jesus. The crowd was the object of Jesus' ministry in Israel (9:35-38), yet remains so among the nations (28:18).

As to the second question, the relationship of the μαθηταί to the ὄχλοι was established by Jesus himself. The μαθηταί are not true, as opposed to false, believers in the church,[217] or idealized believers who rise above the masses in the church,[218] or the priestly class in the church serving the lay people.[219] Rather, the crowd is the mass of people who are the object of Jesus' saving ministry. In his earthly ministry he went to them himself and prepared his disciples to go to them (9:35-10:5); he taught and healed and preached to them, and he prepared his disciples to minister to them (10:5ff; 14:14-19; 15:29-36). In his ascended ministry Jesus sends the disciples to a larger crowd, the nations, to make disciples of them, but Jesus still ministers through the disciples (28:16-20).

V. Summary and Concluding Observations

The relationship of the μαθηταί to various characters in Mt shows that Matthew has used the term with both literary and theological purposes in mind. One significant use of the term was to accentuate his Christology. Jesus is often considered alone in order to accentuate various aspects of his life and ministry. The term μαθητής also becomes a signal word to specify a certain teaching as a discipleship teaching. Matthew has created a literary device to show the way Jesus taught his disciples and to show how that teaching can relate to his church.

Matthew has basically intended μαθητής to be linked with οἱ δώδεκα. With both the moment of the historical disciples and the moment of the church before the reader, one is able to see that Matthew's portrait of the disciples both passes on the tradition about the Twelve, and at the same

---

[216] Bornkamm, "End Expectation," pp. 40-41.
[217] Gundry, *Matthew*, p. 271.
[218] Benjamin W. Bacon, *Studies in Matthew* (New York: Henry Holt, 1930), pp. 87-89, 240.
[219] Minear, "Disciples and Crowds," pp. 31-32, 40-42.

time presents an example of discipleship for his church. The disciples are a positive example of what Matthew expects from his church, a negative example of warning, and a mixed group who are able to overcome their lack through the teaching of Jesus. The historical disciples become a means of encouragement, warning, and instruction as examples.

As a nameless, faceless group, the disciples are for Matthew a means of accentuating not only Jesus, but also the figure of Peter. If the church as a whole can learn from the example of the disciples, the individual believer and leader in Matthew's church is able to learn from the example of Peter.

The ὄχλοι are a basically neutral, though curious group who are at times seen negatively, and at times positively. They are the people of Israel of Jesus' day who are the object of Jesus' ministry. They flocked to him for healing and teaching, but could not understand (13:10ff) because they were not truly believers. They were amazed at his teaching and shouted "Hosanna!" at his entry into Jerusalem, but they were finally led astray by the leaders of Israel. While the crowd never exercises faith in Jesus, true believers are those who come out and call Jesus "Lord." As a mixed body of those truly interested and not interested in Jesus, the crowd is now the object of the disciples' ministry. It was the disciples' responsibility to go among the crowds of Israel, and always will be their responsibility among the nations of the earth. The objective of the disciples is to "make disciples" of the nations.

This study of Matthew's use of μαθητής has revealed his special interest in the disciples as a literary figure. In the process of handing on his tradition concerning them, Matthew, through inclusions, unique tradition, expansions, alterations, and omissions, has exalted Jesus as the supreme Lord and Teacher of the historical disciples and the post-resurrection community. Matthew has emphasized the goal of the believers' life of faith through the discipleship stories directed to the μαθηταί. Matthew's gospel is at least in part a manual on discipleship. With all of the major discourses directed at least in part to the μαθηταί, with the term arranged in such a way that most sayings directed to the disciples have become teachings on discipleship, with the positive yet realistic enhancement of the picture of the disciples, and with disciples called and trained and commissioned to carry out the climactic mandate to "make disciples" in the conclusion of the gospel, Matthew has constructed a gospel that will equip the disciples in the making of disciples.

CHAPTER FIVE

MATTHEW'S THEOLOGICAL UNDERSTANDING
OF SIMON PETER

I. INTRODUCTION

Throughout the history of the Church the apostle Peter has been recognized to have a special place in the gospel of Matthew.[1] The purpose
of this chapter is to examine the role of Peter in this gospel in order to
isolate special Matthean distinctives and theological perspectives surrounding Peter. It is hoped that through an understanding of the role of
Peter Matthew's concept or theology of the *disciples as a group* will be
clarified. The dissertation topic concerns Matthew's theological and
literary purpose in the disciples, therefore, this study of the disciple /
apostle Peter is vital to the overall dissertation.

The chapter is divided into two parts. The first part is an analysis of
the texts where Peter occurs in Mt, and is exegetical in nature. It involves
a study of the Matthean text in relationship to the sources and an isolation of Matthean theological elements. The second part is theological in
nature. It takes the theological elements and establishes how they contribute to Matthew's *Tendenz* concerning Peter. The goal is to come to
some conclusions as to the relationship between the disciples as a group
and the role of Peter in the gospel of Matthew.

II. GENERAL OBSERVATIONS

The name of Peter, the disciple of Jesus, occurs about the same
number of times in each of the synoptics (Mt - 25 times, Mk - 24 times,
Lk - 29 times), and is found most frequently in the gospel of John (36
times) (cf. Appendix E). If the basic "two-source theory" of gospel
interdependency is accepted as a methodological starting point,[2] Mk and
Lk both have unique information about Peter, and, as is normal, John
has very few parallels with the synoptics; most of John's information

---

[1] See, e.g., Oscar Cullmann, *Peter: Disciple—Apostle—Martyr. A Historical and
Theological Essay*, trans. Floyd V. Filson (2nd ed.; Philadelphia: Westminster, 1962), pp.
161ff.; J. A. Burgess, *A History of the Exegesis of Matthew 16:17-19 from 1781 to 1965* (Ann
Arbor: Edwards Brothers, 1976), pp. 1-30.

[2] The same methodological guidelines will be followed for the research here as were
followed in chapter four.

about Peter is unique to his gospel (cf. Appendix E). Peter's name normally occurs in narrative material, found on the lips of persons only twelve times in all the gospels (cf. Appendix E). Most likely because the gospel writers were associated with him, Peter is normally referred to as 'Peter' in narrative materials. Matthew regularly calls him Peter; he refers to him as "Simon, called Peter" only in 4:18 and 10:2, and "Simon Peter" only in 16:16. In all other places Matthew refers to him as "Peter." Mark consistently refers to him as "Simon" before the appointment of the Twelve (Mk 3:16), and "Peter" after the appointment. Luke follows Mark's lead.

Four different appellations are used for this disciple in the New Testament: Συμεών (Simeon - Acts 15:14), Σίμων (Simon - Mk 1:16), Κηφᾶς (Cephas - Jn 1:42), and Πέτρος (Peter - Jn 1:42). Συμέων is found only in Acts 15:14 and in some MSS in 2 Pet 1:1. This is the Greek transliteration of the Semitic name Shim⁽ôn, which was probably the name given to him at birth.[3] Σίμων is a Greek name which sounds quite similar to Shim⁽ôn. It is possible that at birth he was given both names since he grew up in Bethsaida, a Hebrew town with Greek influence; or it is possible that when one was speaking Greek one would have used the Greek name as a sort of translated equivalent to the like-sounding Semitic Shim⁽ôn.[4] In the Greek New Testament Σίμων is the normal appellation for the disciple prior to his renaming by Jesus.

Κηφᾶς is the term normally used by Paul as a reference to the apostle. It is apparent that by the time of Paul, the term Κηφᾶς had become a proper name. But prior to that, was it given to Simon by Jesus as a proper name or as a descriptive title? For quite some time the opinion has been that since there is no evidence for the Semitic kêphà⁾ (the Gr. χηφᾶς is the equivalent, with a grecized nominative -ς added) being used as a proper name, then Jesus was not giving a name to Simon, but a descriptive title: Shim⁽ôn Kêphà⁾ or, "Simon Rock."[5] Recently, though, evidence has been set forth that kph⁾ was used as an Aramaic proper name, related to the Hebrew kêph ("rock") and the Aramaic kêphà⁾ ("rock").[6] This evidence suggests that Jesus was giving a new proper name to Simon, Kêphà⁾, "Rock," intending it as a hypocoristicon, playing upon the common noun for rock. This would have been quite similar

---

[3] Oscar Cullmann, "Πέτρος, Κηφᾶς," *TDNT*, VI, trans. G. W. Bromiley (Grand Rapids: Eerdmans, 1968), p. 100.

[4] Ibid.; see also Cullmann, *Peter*, p. 19; Joseph Fitzmyer, "Aramaic *Kêphà⁾* and Peter's Name in the New Testament," *To Advance the Gospel* (New York: Crossroad, 1981), pp. 112, 113.

[5] Cullmann, *Peter*, pp. 18-20; Peter Lampe, "Das Spiel mit dem Petrusnamen—Matt. XVI. 18" *NTS* 25 (1979), p. 229.

[6] Fitzmyer, "*Kêphà⁾*," pp. 116-118.

to the way in which one of the sons of Jeiel and Maacah of Gibeon (1 Chron 8:30; 9:36) and one of the princes of Midian (Num 25:15; 31:8; Josh 13:21) were called *Tsûr* (Zur) from the Hebrew noun *tsûr*, meaning "rock, cliff."[7] This seems to be the likely situation.

The final appellation for this disciple found in the New Testament is Πέτρος. Πέτρος is the Greek translation of *kêphà* (cf. Jn 1:42). There is no extant occurrence of Πέτρος in secular Greek as a proper name prior to its occurrence for Simon in the New Testament.[8] Although the Aramaic form is feminine, when referring to Simon it would naturally be given a masculine form and rendered Πέτρος instead of Πέτρα (the feminine form). At a later point in this chapter the possibility of a word play in Mt 16:16 between Πέτρος ... Πέτρα will be examined. Although πέτρος can mean a detached stone and πέτρα a mass of "living" rock, the terms could be used interchangeably.[9] But at no point would it have been appropriate to call Simon the feminine πέτρα! The natural way to render the Aramic *kêphà* would have been by Πέτρος.

III. COMPARISON OF THE USE OF PETRINE MATERIAL

The purpose of this section is to isolate Matthew's distinctive interpretation of the material concerning Peter. This will be done first through a horizontal analysis of Mt and its sources. The horizontal analysis will entail examining Matthew's inclusions, unique material, shared material, and omissions from his sources. Once this is accomplished a vertical analysis can be undertaken, where the distinctly Matthean material will be examined in light of the gospel of Matthew itself.[10] The goal is to understand Matthew's purpose as an author and theologian in his own right; one who desired to pass on the tradition, but who also has given his own unique perspective to the tradition.[11]

According to the two-source theory, Matthew started with the tradition about Peter found in the gospel of Mark and some body of tradition

---

[7] Ibid., p. 118; Francis Brown, S. R. Driver, C. A. Briggs, *A Hebrew and English Lexicon of the Old Testament* (1907, E. T.; rpt.; Oxford: Clarendon, 1974), p. 849.

[8] Fitzmyer, "*Kêphà*," pp. 119-120.

[9] Colin Brown, "πέτρα," *NIDNTT*, Vol. 3, trans. and ed. by Colin Brown (Grand Rapids: Zondervan, 1978), p. 386; Cullmann, *Peter*, p. 17.

[10] This methodological distinction of the horizontal and vertical has been strongly advocated for Matthean studies by William Thompson, *Matthew's Advice to a Divided Community: Mt 17.22-18.35* (Rome: Biblical Institute Press, 1970), pp. 7-12. Thompson urges a "vertical" approach first, but since it is almost impossible to isolate Matthean vocabulary, style, and interpretation without first doing a "horizontal" analysis, the horizontal will be undertaken first in this chapter.

[11] See the introduction and chapter four above for a more extended discussion of these issues.

referred to as "Q". Of the twenty-five occurrences of the name Peter in Mt (cf. Appendix E), or, of the nineteen pericopes concerning Peter (cf. Appendix F), all are related to the Markan source except one. The one exception is Mt 18:21, but there Mt adds a reference to Peter not found in Q (cf. Lk 17:4). Indeed, the body of sayings designated Q does not at any time refer to Peter.[12] Matthew shares fourteen pericopes with Mk, omitting six of Mark's but including five references to Peter not found in the equivalent Markan pericope (cf. Appendix F). What this shows is that Matthew used Mark for his primary references to Peter but, as now will be seen, gave a unique perspective and interpretation to the Markan picture.

A) Inclusions of Name

Four times (4:18; 8:14; 16:16; 26:35) Matthew records the same basic tradition as Mark, but in his account Matthew becomes more explicit about Peter by including the name of the disciple.

4:18

Matthew introduces Peter in this passage by saying, "Σίμωνα τὸν λεγόμενον Πέτρον" (4:18), whereas Mark has only the simple designation Σίμωνα (Mk 1:16). The inclusion of the explanatory phrase in Mt is best understood as Matthew's way of identifying 'Simon' to his readers as the one who was commonly known to them as 'Peter.'[13] Simon was probably well-known to Matthew's community by 'Peter,' which was by this time his primary name. In fact, in distinction from the other synoptics (and John's gospel to a degree), Matthew prefers to call the disciple 'Peter.' Mark, like Luke following him, consistently calls him 'Simon' up to the commissioning of the twelve (the actual naming?), and thereafter consistently calls him 'Peter.' Matthew, on the other hand, introduces his audience to "Simon, who is called Peter," and thereafter consistently calls him 'Peter' (cf. Appendix E).[14] or immediately connects 'Simon' with 'Peter' (4:18, 10:2; 16:16-18; 17:24-25—notice also that in 16:17

---

[12] Cf. Raymond E. Brown, Karl P. Donfried, John Reumann, eds., *Peter in the New Testament* (Minneapolis / New York: Augsburg / Paulist, 1973), pp. 13 n. 27; 77-79 n. 179; 113-114.

[13] Eduard Schweizer, *The Good News According to Matthew*, trans. David E. Green (Atlanta: John Knox, 1975), p. 75; Brown, Donfried, Reumann, *Peter*, p. 76 n. 172; Walter Grundmann, *Das Evangelium nach Matthäus, Theologischer Handkommentar zum Neuen Testament*, I (Berlin: Evangelische Verlagsanstalt, 1968), p. 110.

[14] Cf. the tabulation of the names of the disciple in Appendix E; and Brown, Donfried, Reumann, *Peter*, pp. 58 n. 129; 76 n. 172.

and 17:25 Jesus calls him Simon, not Matthew).[15] Through the addition of the explanatory phrase Matthew clarifies that for him and his community Simon is Peter.

But this is not to suggest that 4:18 is the actual event of the naming. Some scholars say that the participle λεγόμενον indicates that for Matthew the historical event of the naming had passed,[16] while others say the participle indicates that the name 'Peter' was given at a historical point later in the gospel.[17] Rather, the present passive more naturally suggests that 'Peter' was the common name among Matthew's readers, as indicated above, for the one who was at the time of the narrative called 'Simon.'[18] The participle plus the name 'Peter' serves as an identifier for Matthew's readers, and through the additional replacement of Mark's τὸν ἀδελφὸν Σίμωνος" with τὸν ἀδελφὸν αὐτοῦ, the emphasis stays on the name 'Peter.'[19]

8:14

On the second appearance of Simon Peter in this gospel, Matthew once again prefers to refer to him as 'Peter' (Mark has 'Simon;' Mk 1:29). Matthew has already made an effort to identify him as 'Peter' (4:18), and he continues here to show his preference for 'Peter' over 'Simon.'[20]

Matthew, in a characteristic manner,[21] abbreviates the scene. Mention of the other disciples is left out in order to focus on Jesus as the healer.[22]

---

[15] Cf. Appendix E; also Jack Dean Kingsbury, "The Figure of Peter in Matthew's Gospel as a Theological Problem," *JBL* 98 (1979), p. 69.

[16] R. C. H. Lenski, *The Interpretation of St. Matthew's Gospel* (1943; rpt; Minneapolis: Augsburg, 1961), p. 169.

[17] The following suggest that the name-giving was at 16:18: Krister Stendahl, "Matthew," *Peake's Commentary on the Bible*, ed. Matthew Black (1962; Middlesex: Thomas Nelson and Sons, 1976), p. 774; David Hill, *The Gospel of Matthew*, NCB (1972; rpt; London: Oliphants, 1977), p. 105; Brown, Donfried, Reumann, *Peter*, p. 90 n. 210.

[18] Alfred Plummer, *An Exegetical Commentary on the Gospel according to St. Matthew* (1915; rpt; Grand Rapids: Baker, 1982), p. 49, hints at this when he says "Mt does not mean that Simon on this occasion received the name of Peter (18), but that Simon is the same disciple who was afterwards famous as Peter; comp. x. 2."

[19] Robert H. Gundry, *Matthew: A Commentary on His Literary and Theological Art* (Grand Rapids: Eerdmans, 1982), p. 63.

[20] Grundmann, *Matthäus*, p. 255. McNeile mentions a comment by Spitta that the Simon mentioned here was, in the original tradition, not Peter (Alan Hugh McNeile, *The Gospel According to St. Matthew* (1915; rpt.; Grand Rapids: Baker, 1980), p.[106]); but the reference in Mk to "the house of Simon *and Andrew*" affirms this to be Simon Peter (cf. Mt 10:2; Jn 1:40-42).

[21] Cf. Plummer, *Matthew*, pp. xii-xiii; Hill, *Matthew*, p. 38.

[22] Francis Wright Beare, *The Gospel According to Matthew* (San Francisco: Harper & Row, 1981), p. 210; Heinz Joachim Held, "Matthew as Interpreter of the Miracle Stories," *Tradition and Interpretation in Matthew*, trans. Percy Scott (Philadelphia; Westminster, 1963), pp. 169-171.

The focus on Jesus is almost certainly Matthew's primary aim, but a subsidiary purpose may also be found in the omission of the mention of Andrew, James, and John (Mk 1:29). Gundry suggests that the names of Andrew, James, and John withdraw before Peter's name and thus "Matthew begins to establish a representative role for Peter."[23] This suggestion must be tested against the rest of Matthew's usage.

16:16[24]

When Peter steps forward to answer the question about Jesus' identity, Matthew uses the full name "Simon Peter" (16:16), whereas Mark (8:29) and Luke (9:20) have only "Peter." In Mark's narrative the change from "Simon" to "Peter" occurred at the commissioning of the twelve apostles (3:16), so he continues to use the simple "Peter" here. Matthew normally calls him "Peter"; therefore, it is striking that he includes "Simon" to form the full name. Even more striking is the fact that this is the only place where Matthew has the full "Simon Peter"; Mark never uses it, Luke only at 5:8, but John regularly uses the full name. It may also be important to note that in the rest of the New Testament the full name only occurs in some MSS in 2 Pet 1:1.

Why does Matthew use the full name here? One suggestion is that Matthew uses the double name as a solemn introduction to this special occasion.[25] Taking this one step further, others submit that Matthew uses the double name to provide not only a syntactical link to the passage but also to stress the *person* who is so important in the immediately following context. This person confesses, is blessed by Jesus, is the subject of a prophetic statement by Jesus, and later is a stumbling block.[26] The latter

---

[23] Gundry, *Matthew*, p. 148.

[24] This section is only one of three treatments of Mt 16:16-23. Because of the methodology adopted, this passage is first examined from the point of view as an inclusion of a name (16:16a), secondly from the point of view as an inclusion of material (16:16b-19), and finally as material shared with Mark (16:22-23). The passage may at first appear to be treated in a fragmented manner, so the reader is asked to keep this methodology in mind. The purpose is to attend the varied emphases given to the passage by Matthew.

[25] Floyd V. Filson, *The Gospel According to St. Matthew*, Black's New Testament Commentaries (1960; 1971; rpt.; London: Adam and Charles Black, 1977), p. 185; William Hendricksen, *Exposition of the Gospel According to Matthew*, New Testament Commentary (Grand Rapids: Baker, 1973), p. 643; Lenski, *Matthew*, p. 620.

[26] Beare, *Matthew*, p. 352; Gundry, *Matthew*, p. 330; Pierre Bonnard, *L'Evangile selon Saint Matthieu, Commentaire du Nouveau Testament*, I (1963; 2d. ed.; Neuchâtel: Delachaux, & Niestlé, 1970), p. 244; Kingsbury, "Figure of Peter," pp. 74-76. For a similar use in Lk 5:8, which stresses the person of Peter, cf. W. Dietrich, *Das Petrusbild der lukanischen Schriften* (Stuttgart: Katholisches Bibelwerk, 1972), pp. 44-45, and I. Howard Marshall, *The Gospel of Luke*, NIGTC (Grand Rapids: Eerdmans, 1978), p. 204.

view rightly recognizes that Matthew lays emphasis upon the identity of the person who is to have a special place in the following passage, and who is also specified as the spokesman for the group of disciples. Indeed, the question posed by Jesus was directed to the disciples as a group (cf. Mt 16:13, 15; Mk 8:27, 29), and in the tradition Peter functions as their spokesman; nevertheless, with the double name Matthew stresses more strongly the identity of Simon Peter as the spokesman, and at the same time stresses the key figure in the context to follow.[27]

26:35

The inclusion of the name Peter in 26:35 conforms to Matthew's preference for grammatical specificity. Matthew likes to make explicit what is in his source implied.[28] Matthew follows Mark as he introduces Peter in the pericope (Mt 26:30 cf. Mk 14:29), but when Mark later refers to the disciple it is with the third person singular verb (ἐλάλει, Mk 14:31),[29] while Matthew explicitly refers to him as ὁ Πέτρος (26:35). Matthew makes explicit that *Peter* declares he will even die with Jesus rather than deny him. In the same verse Matthew makes explicit that οἱ μαθηταί say the same thing as Peter (Mark has a plural pronoun and verb). Matthew stresses that Peter is the spokesman for the group of the disciples, but here it is a negative example rather than the positive representation demonstrated in 16:16ff.[30]

B) Inclusions of Material

Matthew not only gives his personal perpective to his sources through the inclusion of Peter's name, but also through the inclusion of material about Peter. There are four of these latter inclusions: three in the Markan source (Mt 14:28-29; 15:15; 16:17-19) and one in Q (Mt 18:21).

14:28-31

In the larger context of 14:22-33, Matthew has taken over a Markan passage but has given his own perspective to it.[31] Matthew preserves the

---

[27] This is almost a consensus among commentators: Beare, *Matthew*, p. 352; John A. Broadus, *Commentary on the Gospel of Matthew, An American Commentary on the New Testament* (1886; rpt.; Valley Forge: Judson, n.d.), p. 353; Bonnard, *Matthieu*, p. 244; Grundmann, *Matthäus*, p. 386; Gundry, *Matthew*, p. 330; Hendricksen, *Matthew*, p. 643; Lenski, *Matthew*, p. 620; McNeile, *Matthew*, p. 239; Plummer, *Matthew*, p. 225.

[28] Cf. Bonnard, *Matthieu*, p. 8.

[29] The inclusion of Πέτρος in Mk 14:31 in the MSS (C A G N W θ φ λ pm sy^s.h sa^pt) is most likely because of the influence of the reading in Mt.

[30] Grundmann, *Matthäus*, p. 538; Gundry, *Matthew*, p. 531.

[31] E.g., the omission of "meant to pass them by" of Mk 6:48; the addition of "worship" in Mt 14:33; and the omission of non-understanding and hardness of heart of Mk 6:52.

Markan picture of the disciples' terror at the appearance of Jesus walking on the water, but then introduces a narrative about Peter (14:28-31) found nowhere else in the gospels. The form[32] and source[33] backgrounds to this pericope have received a wide variety of interpretations, but perhaps it is best to say, for the purposes of this study, that Matthew has included a story about Peter not found in his tradition for which he makes no historical apology, and which functions as a sort of paradigm for this discipleship context.[34] The important point to discover is how this Peter-pericope functions as a paradigm. Does Matthew point to the

---

[32] The theories of the form background of this pericope range from nature "miracle story" (Rudolf Bultmann, *History of the Synoptic Tradition*, trans. John Marsh (rev. ed. 1963; New York: Harper & Row, 1976), p. 237-238), to "legend" (Martin Dibelius, *From Tradition to Gospel*, trans. Bertram Woolf (rev. 2d ed; Greenwood, S.C.: Attic, 1971, p. 116), to "post-resurrection allegory" (Brown, Donfried, Reumann, *Peter*, p. 81; Beare, *Matthew*, p. 330; Schweizer, *Matthew*, p. 321), to "haggadic midrash" (Gundry, *Matthew*, p. 300; Michael D. Goulder, *Midrash and Lection in Matthew*, [London: SPCK, 1974], p. 377), to "historical occurrence" (Plummer, *Matthew*, p. 209; Hendricksen, *Matthew*, p. 601-602). If it was a historical occurrence it was used by Matthew as a "paradigm" (cf. Held, "Miracle Stories," pp. 245-246) in the historical narrative.

[33] The source background theories are as varied as the form. They range from "reliance on a Buddhist parallel" (cf. Bultmann, *Synoptic Tradition*, p. 237; Dibelius, *Tradition to Gospel*, p. 116), to "allegorization of the post-resurrection tradition about Peter's confession-denial-restoration" (Schweizer, *Matthew*, p. 321), to "oral Petrine stories" (George D. Kilpatrick, *The Origins of the Gospel According to St. Matthew* [Oxford: Clarendon, 1946], p. 41), to "independent narrative accounts" (John M. Rist, *On the Independence of Matthew and Mark*, SNTSMS no. 32 [Cambridge: University Press, 1978], p. 71), to pure "fiction" (Beare, *Matthew*, p. 330), to "haggadic midrash" (Gundry, *Matthew*, p. 300; Goulder, *Midrash*, p. 377), to a "tradition based on the recollection of the disciples who were present with Peter" (Plummer, *Matthew*, p. 208). The question as to why, if Mark's gospel is based to a great degree on the reminiscences of Peter (according to Papias via Eusebius), Mark did not include such a dramatic story, is perplexing. R. V. G. Tasker (*The Gospel According to St. Matthew*, TNTC (1961; rpt.; Grand Rapids: Eerdmans, 1976)) suggests that the humility which Peter learned later prevented him from alluding to this incident (p. 146). Did this also prevent him from referring to the other Petrine stories unique to Mt (cf. 15:15; 16:17-19; 17:24-26; 18:21)?

[34] Held ("Miracle Stories," pp. 168, 245-246) has made a strong case for the paradigmatic nature of this story for discipleship, but does not conceive of it as a historical occurrence. But the way in which Matthew introduces the story into the larger context implies an actual connection. Matthew does not give any kind of parabolic or allegoric disclaimer (such as Jesus did in his teaching with the statement "listen to the parable", cf. 21:33, or with some grammatical signal: e.g., "compared to" found in 22:2; or "it is just like" found in 25:14). Jesus went out of his way to specify parabolic or allegorical material, and even Matthew tried to make it clear in his narrative when he was introducing a section on Jesus' parables (cf. 22:1). It is hard to see how on the one hand Jesus (in his teaching) and Matthew (in his narrative) would try to be so clear in their use of figurative material and then Matthew be so clumsy (deceptive?) in his historical narrative. As a hermeneutical practice it is this writer's opinion that one should look for literary clues to a passage being non-historical before one determines it to be such.

primacy or preeminence of Peter,[35] or view him as an example for the leaders or teachers of Matthew's church?[36] Does he see him as a representative spokesman for the disciples,[37] understand him as 'typical' of discipleship,[38] or see him as an example of one confusing pretentious enthusiasm with faith?[39]

Matthew's intent appears to include several of the above elements; the following points show how Peter functions as both a positive and negative example: First, *Peter advances from the group of disciples*. The disciples as a group were frightened, and at the word of Jesus which would give an object of faith ("it is I") Peter confesses him as "Lord" and attempts to exercise his faith by going to Jesus on the water. Through his action Peter is set apart from the disciples. Second, *Peter's walk is a real attempt at faith*. Jesus does not rebuke Peter for asking permission to walk on the water. He says only, "Come." The chiding comes from Jesus only when Peter begins to fail. Jesus seems to indicate that "having heart" and overcoming "fear" are accomplished through recognizing that Jesus himself is with them ("it is I"). Peter seeks confirmation through a command from Jesus and then in obedience walks on the water "to Jesus." Peter's actions are a real attempt at faith as delineated by Jesus.[40] Additionally, *Peter fails in his faith by looking away from Jesus*. Once on the water Peter sees the wind, becomes afraid, and begins to sink. The failure of his faith makes him at that moment a man of "little faith" (ὀλιγόπιστε). The theme of "little faith" is a favorite of Matthew; it is found only in Luke

---

[35] P. Benoit, "Matthieu" fascicle, Bible de Jérusalem (Paris: Cerf, 1961), p. 10 (cited in Bonnard, *Matthieu*, p. 223); Reinhart Hummel, *Die Auseinandersetzung zwischen Kirche und Judentum im Matthäusevangelium* (München: Chr. Kaiser, 1963), pp. 59ff.; Christoph Kähler, "Zur Form- und Traditionsgeschichte von Matth. XVI. 17-19," *NTS* 23 (1977), 41f.

[36] Hubert Frankemölle, "Amtskritik im Matthäus-Evangelium?," *Biblica* 54 (1973), pp. 257ff.; Paul Minear, *Matthew : The Teacher's Gospel* (New York: Pilgrim Press, 1982), p. 90.

[37] Cullmann, *Peter*, pp. 23f.

[38] Bultmann, *History*, 216; Held "Miracle Stories," pp. 204-206; Georg Strecker, *Der Weg der Gerechtigkeit: Untersuchung zur Theologie des Matthäus* (1962; 3d. ed.; rpt.; Göttingen: Vandenhoeck & Rupprecht, 1971), pp. 198f., 203-206; J. Kahmann, "Die Verheissung an Petrus: Mt. XVI, 18-19 im Zusammenhang des Matthäusevangeliums," *L'Evangile selon Matthieu: rédaction et théologie*, M. Didier, ed. (Gembloux [Belgique]: Duculot, 1972), p. 270; Goulder, *Midrash*, p. 378; Hill, *Matthew*, p. 248; Beare, *Matthew*, p. 330; Gundry, *Matthew*, pp. 299f.

[39] An interpretation presented, but not accepted, by Brown, Donfried, Reumann, *Peter*, p. 81.

[40] Held, "Miracle Stories," pp. 205f.; Goulder, *Midrash*, p. 377; Gundry, *Matthew*, p. 299. "Faith," described as 'focusing on the person and presence of Jesus,' is to be preferred to that suggested by Sheridan, as "... reliance on the fatherly goodness of God who cares for his creatures" (Mark Sheridan, "Disciples and Discipleship in Matthew and Luke," (*Bib Th Bul* 3 [1973], p. 247).

12:28 outside of Mt (cf. 6:30; 8:26; 14:31; 16:8; 17:20). In Matthew's use the expression should not be understood so much as indicating having a "little" faith, as referring to one who has in the past exercised faith and now no longer uses it; it is rather a faith which has failed or is bankrupt.[41] Faith is then an either / or matter. Focused on Jesus it is effective, once turned away from Jesus it is ineffective. Peter has ineffective faith, but is not a total failure because he cries out to Jesus for help. He is a disciple who has exercised his faith, but who can also fail.[42] Fourthly, *Peter's step of faith and failure results in worship of Jesus by all of the disciples.* Mark focuses on the astonishment and non-understanding of the disciples (Mk 6:51-52), but Matthew tells his readers that once Jesus rescued Peter, they got into the boat, the wind ceased, and those in the boat worshiped Jesus, and confessed, "Truly you are the Son of God" (14:33).

Therefore, Matthew's picture of Peter is neither all good (i.e., that Peter holds a position of primacy or preeminence) nor all bad (i.e., that Peter has mere enthusiasm, not faith). Matthew's use of the incident allows Peter to function as a positive example of faith as well as a negative example of how not to cause one's faith to be rendered ineffective. Jesus is the central figure, the focus of faith and worship; Peter is the representative, imperfect disciple who illustrates how the disciples can go from fear to faith to worship. Peter *is* singled out, but it is not clear that he is placed above the disciples because of his step of faith. Actually, being chided by Jesus for his lapse of faith tends to show that he is not above them. The focus moves from Peter to the worship of Jesus by "those" in the boat, almost as if as soon as Peter fulfills his function as an example he blends into the disciples as a whole, allowing the focus to center on Jesus.

The Petrine emphases are especially striking when one compares the scene in 14:28-31 to an earlier incident in Mt.[43] In 8:23-27 the disciples as a whole did not demonstrate faith (8:26; ὀλιγόπιστοι again), but once Jesus calmed the sea they "marveled" (8:27; not "worshiped"). Similarly, in 14:22ff. the disciples as a group do not recognize the

---

[41] Cf. Bonnard's comments on 17:20, where faith the size of a mustard seed is little, but effective. For Matthew, ὀλιγοπιστία signifies that the disciples do not have even the smallest amount of faith: "*il illustre seulement le minimum de foi que les disciples n'ont même pas*" (*Matthieu*, p. 261). See also Carson's comments on the use of this term as it relates to 8:26 (D. A. Carson, "Gundry on Matthew: A Critical Review," *TrinJ* 3 NS (1982), p. 80.

[42] John P. Meier, *The Vision of Matthew: Christ, Church and Morality in the First Gospel* (New York: Paulist, 1979), p. 101; Beare, *Matthew*, p. 330.

[43] Cf. Donald A. Carson, "Matthew," *The Expositor's Bible Commentary*, vol. 8, ed. Frank E. Gaebelein (Grand Rapids: Zondervan, 1984), pp. 344-346.

significance of Jesus (cf. 8:27 and 14:26) until Peter, at the word from Jesus, leads the way to worship through his example of faith. The failure of Peter's faith shows that in spite of his advance of faith he is as personally dependent on Jesus as were the group of disciples (cf. "Lord save me," 14:30; "save us Lord," 8:25). This indicates that Peter is not above or outside the circle of disciples,[44] but rather that he is a leader in the way of faith, and here his leadership is one of example within the group.

Matthew's readers would be able to identify with Peter because he is a recognizable person among the more remote group of disciples and because he is a "normal" person with strengths and weaknesses. This personal identification would enable Peter to serve as an example of faith, and the failure of faith, in the life of discipleship, and would ultimately exalt Jesus as the object of faith and worship for all disciples.

15:15

Matthew also includes material about Peter in the Markan context at 15:15 (cf. Mk 7:17), when the Pharisees criticize the disciples of Jesus for not following a tradition of washing their hands (15:1-2). Jesus rebuffs their criticism by showing their hypocrisy (15:3-9) and then warns the crowds about the example of the Pharisees (15:10-12). At this point Matthew has unique material: the disciples come and tell Jesus that the Pharisees were offended by his statements, and Jesus then instructs and warns the disciples further about the Pharisees (15:13-14). In Mk 17:17 *the disciples* come asking a question about the parable, but in Mt 15:15 *Peter* requests an explanation. What does Matthew intend by this change?

Matthew is introducing nothing new to the tradition concerning Peter. Peter is already the spokesman for the Twelve in the tradition[45] and Matthew tends to carry on that tradition and support it more strongly.[46] Matthew merely states that on this occasion it was Peter who asked this question for the disciples. Matthew has once again become more explicit.

Matthean interpreters have suggested, however, that Matthew has revealed a theological purpose in this pericope. Matthew is either raising Peter to a position of eminence,[47] establishing him as an ecclesiastical figure,[48] or else merely clarifying that he is the spokesman for the

---

[44] Kingsbury, "Figure of Peter," pp. 72f.

[45] Mk 1:36; 8:29, 32; 9:2ff.; 10:28; 11:21.

[46] Cf. Mt 8:14; 16:16; 26:35; 14:28; and the discussion of these passages above..

[47] W. F. Albright and C. S. Mann, *Matthew, The Anchor Bible*, vol. 26 (Garden City: Doubleday and Company, 1971), p. 185.

[48] Kilpatrick, *Origins*, pp. 38f., 43; Eduard Schweizer, *Matthäus und seine Gemeinde*, Stuttgarter Bibelstudien 71 (Stuttgart: Katholisches Bibelwerk, 1974), p. 327; Grundmann, *Matthäus*, p. 373; John P. Meier, *Matthew* (Wilmington: Glazier, 1980), p. 169.

disciples.[49] On the one hand, too much stress on the eminence of Peter may be misleading, because Matthew has focused the bulk of Jesus' accusation of non-understanding on Peter. Specifically, the addition of the statement of the disciples in 15:12 lessens their non-understanding as a group, Peter asks the question instead of the disciples (cf. 15:15; Mk 7:17), and the note of rebuke in Mt 15:16 is prompted by Peter's question. On the other hand, the same criticism might be leveled against the view that Matthew includes Peter's question for the purpose of establishing him as an ecclesiastical figure. Grundmann stresses that the mention of Peter is quite in line with his later importance in the decisions about Judaism (cf. Acts 10; 11:5; 15:7-11), and that Matthew is establishing that Peter's teaching has always been received directly from Jesus himself.[50] Grundmann's deductive reasoning is difficult to support from the text itself. The more direct inference from the text is that Matthew specifies that Peter is the obtuse one who brings on Jesus' rebuke. Matthew appears to be indicating that Peter is the spokesman for the disciples, but here his representative spokesmanship is basically negative. Peter's negative spokesmanship role is shown by the following: First, Matthew makes it explicit that the question which induces an accusation of non-understanding is asked by Peter, so that the focus is on him. Second, Peter is not just asking for himself, because he asks, "Explain the parable *to us*" (ἡμῖν). Third, Jesus' rebuke of their non-understanding is in response to Peter's request for clarification, but it is directed toward the larger group of disciples as well (note the plural pronoun ὑμεῖς and plural verb ἐστε).[51] Fourth, the rebuke is intensified by the inclusion of the adverbial accusative ἀκμήν, "even yet": "All of you, who have been associated with me for so long and closely, 'even yet' at this crucial juncture are you without understanding as are even the Pharisees and crowds?"[52]

Through the inclusion of this special material concerning Peter (and also that concerning the disciples as a whole, cf. 15:12-14), Matthew has softened, not deleted, the rebuke of the disciples by making them more

---

[49] Strecker, *Weg*, p. 203; Fenton, *Matthew*, p. 253; Brown, Donfried, Reumann, *Peter*, pp. 77-78; Beare, *Matthew*, p. 339.

[50] Grundmann, *Matthäus*, p. 373.

[51] Schweizer, *Gemeinde*, p. 153.

[52] Cf. Carson, "Matthew," p. 351; Hill, *Matthew*, p. 252; Tasker, *Matthew*, p. 149. The adverb stresses the present lack that is inexcusable in light of their past association and instruction from Jesus. The emphasis is upon rebuke for not having progressed in understanding as they should have. It is possible that the similar request posed by the *disciples themselves* in 13:36, and the resulting instruction by Jesus, should have made them sufficiently equipped to understand Jesus' future parables, and so would explain the ἀκμήν here (contra Gundry, *Matthew*, p. 308, who places the stress on a temporary lack that Jesus will not rectify through instruction).

understanding (15:12) and making Peter responsible for asking for clarification of Jesus' parable. Even as Peter represents the disciples in this request, he becomes their scapegoat in the rebuke. Therefore, Peter receives prominence as the representative for the disciples, but it is a negative prominence.

16:17-19

This next inclusion of Petrine material is crucial, because it contains a unique statement of Jesus about the role of Peter in the church and the kingdom of heaven. The purpose here is not to do an exhaustive study of the pericope,[53] but to try to understand Matthew's purpose in the inclusion and to try to understand how he perceives and portrays Peter's role in relation to the other disciples.

This pericope is another striking example of Matthew including significant material to which Mark does not even make allusion. Mark records the confession of Peter, "You are the Christ," and then records that Jesus responded to the confession by charging the disciples to tell no one about him. It is a very simple record, in which Peter functions as spokesman for the disciples and Jesus acknowledges the confession, but he wants it to be kept from the crowd. Matthew takes over the same basic tradition,[54] but includes an expansion of the confession (v. 16b), a blessing on Peter for making the confession (v. 17) and a pronouncement about Peter's role in the church and kingdom (vv. 18-19). For some time critical opinion has regarded this unique material about Peter as a Matthean creation,[55] but B. Meyer has recently challenged this opinion and

---

[53] Among the most important recent works on this passage are: G. Bornkamm, "The Authority to 'Bind' and 'Loose' in the Church in Matthew's Gospel," (ET, 1970); Brown, Donfried, Reumann, *Peter*, pp. 83-101; Burgess, *A History of the Exegesis of Matthew 16:17-19 from 1781 to 1965* (1976); Cullmann, *Peter* (2d. ed., 1962), pp. 155-238; Paul Hoffmann, "Der Petrus-Primat im Matthäusevangelium," *Neues Testament Und Kirche*, für Rudolf Schnackenburg, ed. Joachim Gnilka (Freiburg: Herder, 1974) , pp. 94-114; Kähler, "Matth. XVI. 17-19" (1977); J. D. Kingsbury, "The Figure of Peter in Matthew's Gospel As a Theological Problem," (1979); Peter Lampe, "Das Spiel mit dem Petrusnamen—Matt. XVI. 18," *NTS* 25 (1979), pp. 227-245; Ben F. Meyer, *The Aims of Jesus* (London: SCM, 1979), pp. 185-197; Max Wilcox, "Peter and the Rock: A Fresh Look at Matthew XVI. 17-19," *NTS* 22 (1976), pp. 73-88.

[54] Suggested by Günther Bornkamm, "End-Expectation and Church in Matthew," *Tradition and Interpretation in Matthew*, trans, Percy Scott (Philadelphia: Westminster, 1963), p. 47, and Reginald Fuller, *The Foundations of New Testament Christology* (New York: Scribner's, 1965), p. 109.

[55] Many hold to the general position that this pericope is a Matthean creation, but there are several variations in the understanding of this general position. E.g., *it is a Matthean midrashic embroidery* (Beare, *Matthew*, 353-354; Goulder, *Midrash*, pp. 386f.; Gundry, *Matthew*, p. 330); *it is a legend or tradition created by the Matthean church to counter-act a Pauline party* (T. W. Manson, *The Sayings of Jesus* [1937; new ed.; Grand Rapids: Eerdmans,

concludes that the material is historical.[56] His arguments are quite convincing, and if valid, are important for the Matthean picture of Peter,[57] and would mean that Matthew is not *creating* a role for Peter in 16:17-19,[58] but rather is *reflecting* the role given by Jesus. Either way though, Matthew has included the pericope and it is a crucial statement of his view of Peter.[59]

The meaning of the pericope is most clearly comprehended through its apparent parallelism. There are three parallel tristichs, with the first line of each unit setting the theme or making a statement about Peter, and the second and third line of each (composed in antithetic parallelism) forming an explanation or consequence of the respective first line:

(1) Blessed are you, Simon Bar-Jona;

For flesh and blood has not revealed this to you,

But my Father who is in heaven.

(2) And I tell you, you are Peter

And on this rock I will build my church,

And the gates of Hades will not overpower it.

1979], pp. 203-204) *or to oppose a party dedicated to James* (W. D. Davies, *The Setting of the Sermon on the Mount* [1964; new ed.; Cambridge: University Press, 1977], pp. 338-339); *it is a Matthean redaction finding its source in the traditions of the post-resurrectional appearances to Peter* (Brown, Donfried, Reumann, *Peter*, p. 85; Werner Georg Kümmel, *The Theology of the New Testament*, trans. John E. Steely [Nashville: Abingdon, 1973], p. 129; Kilpatrick, *Origins*, pp. 39-40; Meier, *Vision*, p. 107; Goppelt, *New Testament Theology*, I, 213); *it is a Matthean creation exalting Peter after his death* (Bornkamm, "End-Expectation," pp. 47-48; Hans Conzelmann, *History of Primitive Christianity*, trans. John Steely [Nashville: Abingdon, 1973], p. 155).

[56] Ben F. Meyer, *The Aims of Jesus* (London: SCM, 1979), pp. 185-197. Cf. also Carson, "Matthew," pp. 366f.; Karl L. Schmidt, "ἐκκλησία," *TDNT* III, trans. Geoffrey W. Bromiley (Grand Rapids: Eerdmans, 1965), pp. 518-526; Mundle, "πέτρος," p. 384; Plummer, *Matthew*, p. 227. Cullmann also holds to the historicity of the logion, but proposes that the words were originally spoken at the Last Supper in conjunction with the Lucan words "Simon, Simon, behold, Satan has demanded permission to sift you like wheat...." (Lk 22:31ff.) (*Peter*, pp. 190ff.).

[57] An important question raised is, if Mk is earlier, why would he not include such a significant incident, especially if he had special information from Peter himself (Brown, Donfried, Reumann, *Peter*, p. 85)? Meyer answers that Mark himself most likely "...omitted the response of Jesus to Simon in favour of making Simon's confession...strictly functional to the central theme of his gospel, namely, entry into the messianic mystery of the Son of man's death and resurrection." (*Aims*, p. 189).

[58] For a sampling of opinions about what Matthew might have intended through this creative activity, see the note above on this saying as a Matthean creation.

[59] Bonnard (*Matthieu*, p. 242) does not feel it is as important to establish the documentary authenticity of the pericope as to answer whether the evangelist is faithful to the person and work of Christ. While not declaring that he accepts the authenticity of these verses he does suggest rhetorically that they: 1) cohere to the totality of the Matthean Christ; 2) are confirmed by the role which Peter plays in the first days of the Christian community; and 3) can demand that their content be applied to the Christ of the gospels. Bonnard's suggestions, along with Meyer's discussion, give significant weight to the argument for the historicity of this pericope. This is Jesus' own pronouncement about Peter, but Matthew uses it as a central statement of his theology as well.

(3) I will give you the keys of the kingdom of heaven,
 And whatever you bind on earth shall be bound in heaven,
 And whatever you loose on earth shall be loosed in heaven.[60]
The first line of each tristich focuses the reader upon Matthew's under-
standing of the role of Peter, and then the second and third lines enun-
ciate the respective role.

1. Peter as the recipient of blessing (16:17)

In the first line of the initial tristich, Peter is the recipient of blessing.
Once Peter made his confession Jesus responds and says to him, "Blessed
are you Simon Bar-Jona." This statement of Jesus may carry some overtones of a *conferral* of blessing (cf. Mk 10:16), and if so would be the only
instance of an individual in the gospels who is the named recipient of a
dominical blessing.[61] But Jesus' statement appears to be more of an
acknowledgement that Peter has been blessed by a revelation from God. The
ὅτι clause is an explanation of Jesus' statement, and is similar to other
statements in Mt (cf. 5:3-11; 11:6; 13:16; 24:46). Jesus may be blessing
Peter for the statement, but more importantly is acknowledging Peter's
blessed condition which resulted from the privilege of receiving revelation from the father.[62]

Peter functions in his normal spokesman role as he makes his confession, but Jesus' response is not directed to the group as a whole (as it was
in 15:16). Jesus addresses Peter personally (notice the personal address,
verbal and pronoun forms): "Jesus said to *him* (αὐτῷ), 'Blessed are *you*
(εἶ) Simon Bar-Jona;[63] for flesh and blood has not revealed this to *you*
(σοι), but my Father in heaven." Peter is the *personal* recipient of revelation from the father, and *personally* blessed because of it. The personal
address, blessing, and revelation, raise the question of Peter's relation-

---

[60] Grundmann, *Matthäus*, pp. 384-385; Gundry, *Matthew*, p. 331; George W. E.
Nicklesburg, "Enoch, Levi, and Peter: Recipients of Revelation in Upper Galilee," *JBL*
100 (1981), p. 591.
 [61] Plummer, *Matthew*, p. 228; Brown, Donfried, Reumann, *Peter*, p. 89; Kähler,
"Matth. XVI 17-19," pp. 55-56.
 [62] Cf. Bonnard, *Matthieu*, p. 244.
 [63] The etymological difficulties of βαριωνᾶ are quite pronounced, but the best answer
seems to be that of Hill, who says "Bar-Jona ('son of Jonah') can with some difficulty
be made to mean 'son of John' (bar-Johanan)" (*Matthew*, p. 260. This is similar to a
statement made by Bonnard, *Matthieu*, p. 245; cf. also Schweizer, *Matthew*, p. 341; Carson, "Matthew," p. 375 n. 17). The point of the full name would be to emphasize the
'humanness' of the speaker (with his natural father) as opposed to the 'supernaturalness'
of the revelation-inspired confession. The suggestion of Goulder (*Midrash*, p. 387) and
Gundry (*Matthew*, pp. 332-333), that the name is a midrashic creation of Matthew to
make Simon a spiritual son of the prophet Jonah, seems a bit removed from the context.

ship to the other disciples. One view is that Peter is here exalted to a place above and apart from the other disciples.[64] The revelation was given only to him, his confession was personal, not representative, and the blessed condition is said to be his and his alone. Kähler suggests that Jesus' blessing is an official "investiture" of Peter as the "guarantor of the true tradition of the revelation."[65] A second view is that Peter continues to act as the spokesman for the disciples, but the revelation and associated blessing give him a special place. Peter, therefore, is not just a spokesman, but is distinguished from the other disciples and given a leadership position among them.[66] A third view is that Peter functions only as a spokesman and representative of the other disciples, and therefore the other disciples were included in the revelation and blessing.[67] Peter is here confessing what the other disciples had already confessed (cf. 14:33), and once Jesus recognizes the source of Peter's confession, Jesus turns and includes all the disciples (cf. 16:15, 20).[68]

Each view stresses important features. The second person singular verbal form and personal pronouns, plus the specification of his human name, indicate quite definitely that the stress is on Peter as a person. To go so far as Kähler, who says these personal forms indicate "investiture," strains their normal meaning,[69] but the emphasis on Peter as a person cannot be denied. This emphasis carries through the rest of the pericope and seems to isolate Peter in a unique way:

16:18: "I tell *you* (σοι), that *you* are Peter (σὺ εἶ Πέτρος)...;"
16:19: "I will give *you* (σοι) ... whatever *you* bind (δήσῃς) ... whatever *you* loose" (λύσῃς).

On the other hand, what Peter confesses has already been confessed by all the disciples (cf. 14:33),[70] and the expression of blessedness is similar

---

[64] E. Haenchen, *Der Weg Jesu* (Berlin: Töpelmann, 1966), p. 301; Hummel, *Auseindersetzung*, pp. 59ff.; Kähler, "Matth. XVI 17-19," pp. 55ff.; Beare, *Matthew*, p. 354; Manson, *Sayings*, 204; Davies, *Setting*, 338-339.

[65] Kähler, "Matth. XVI 17-19," pp. 55-56: "...*Garant der treuen Überlieferung der Offenbarung.*"

[66] Brown, Donfried, Reumann, *Peter*, p. 87; Filson, *Matthew*, p. 186; Meier, *Vision*, p. 111; Broadus, *Matthew*, p. 354.

[67] Hoffmann, "Petrus-Primat," pp. 108-109; Kingsbury, "Figure of Peter," pp. 74ff.; Strecker, *Weg*, pp. 201ff.; Goulder, *Midrash*, pp. 389ff.; Walker, *Heilsgeschichte*, p. 118.

[68] Kingsbury, "Figure of Peter," p. 75.

[69] Kähler, "Matth. XVI 17-19," pp. 55-56; cf. the arguments against Kähler's thesis by Kingsbury, "Figure of Peter," p. 75 n. 26.

[70] Most commentators agree that the significant feature of the Christological statement concerned the confession of Jesus as "Son of God," which is the similar confession of 14:33 and 16:16; cf. Kingsbury, "Figure of Peter," p. 74 n. 25, and Jack Dean Kingsbury, *Matthew: Structure, Christology, Kingdom* (Philadelphia: Fortress, 1975), pp. 78-83; Carson, "Matthew," p. 367; Gundry, *Matthew*, p. 330; Schweizer, *Matthew*, p. 340; Hill, *Matthew*, p. 260; Tasker, *Matthew*, p. 159.

to that already attributed to all the disciples, who had received a revelation of the mysteries of the kingdom of heaven (cf. 13:11,16).[71] Peter is obviously singled out, but he is still within the circle of disciples. His blessing and revelation are personal, but not so out of the ordinary as to set him apart from the rest of the disciples. Indeed, as a spokesman he represents the common view of the group, and the blessing and revelation may be obliquely directed to the group as well. His confession is an answer *for* the disciples (16:15,16) and provokes a charge *to* all the disciples (16:20). Perhaps it is best to say that Peter is individually singled out for his act of leadership in making the confession, yet his leadership role is from *within* the circle of disciples. He is blessed personally, yet representationally as well.

2. Peter as Πέτρος (16:18)

The second tristich begins with the statement: "And I say to you, you are Peter." The words "κἀγὼ δέ σοι λέγω" carry a tone of 'consequence' stemming from the prior statement of Peter.[72] Peter made an extremely important confession about Jesus, and in response to this Jesus makes a pronouncement about Peter. Jesus' response is "σὺ εἶ Πέτρος." This is understood by some to be the occasion of the giving of the name Πέτρος to the heretofore named 'Simon,'[73] but it is more likely a pronouncement prompted by the confession of the one who already bore the name.[74] Matthew does not seem to concern himself with specifying the actual occasion of the naming, but in every place merely assumes the readers understand that at some point the naming occurred.[75]

The meaning of the pronouncement is found in the second line of the tristich: "and on this rock I will build my church." In the Greek text there is an obvious wordplay between Πέτρος ... πέτρα. But does the Greek wordplay represent the original intent? For those who understand

---

[71] Goulder, *Midrash*, p. 387.

[72] Cf. William F. Arndt and F. Wilbur Gingrich, "κἀγώ," *A Greek-English Lexicon of the New Testament and Other Early Christian Literature* (4th. ed., 1952; rpt.; Chicago: University of Chicago Press, 1974), pp. 386-387. McNeile (*Matthew*, p. 241) says this is a revelatory statement of Jesus in addition to the revelation from the Father. But the emphatic position of σοι...σύ make it a response to Peter.

[73] Schweizer (*Matthew*, 341) calls this the Matthean bestowal of the name. Cf. also Kilpatrick, *Origins*, p. 39; Brown, Donfried, Reumann, *Peter*, p. 90 n. 210; Cullmann, *Peter*, pp. 20-21, 177.

[74] Cf. Mundle, "πέτρα," p. 383; Goulder, *Midrash*, pp. 392-393; Josef Blank, "The Person and Office of Peter in the New Testament," trans. Erika Young, *Truth and Certainty*, ed. Edward Schillebeeckx and Bas van Iersel, Concilium, Vol. 83 (New York: Herder and Herder, 1973) p. 50.

[75] See above on 4:18 below on 10:2.

the saying to be a creation of Matthew who wrote in Greek, the answer is yes: Matthew intended to contrast the "small stone" (Πέτρος) with the "large bedrock" (πέτρα).[76] For those who suggest that Jesus actually spoke in Greek on this occasion,[77] the intent is similarly to be found in the distinction between the Greek terms. But the Aramaic linguistic character of the section points to an *Aramaic* source for the wordplay,[78] whether it originated in the pre-Matthean tradition[79] or in an Aramaic saying of Jesus himself. Since Simon's Aramaic name was *kêphāʾ*,[80] the conclusion is that the Aramaic substatum of the wordplay was *kêphāʾ* ... *kêphāʾ*.[81] Therefore, the meaning of the wordplay must be sought in the use of the same Aramaic word in both halves instead of a different Greek word in each. As a common noun in Aramaic texts found in the Qumran caves, *kêphāʾ* has the meaning of 'rock' or 'crag,' "a part of a mountainous or hilly region."[82] With the same Aramaic word used in both halves of the wordplay, the meaning would be, "You are Rock, and on this rock I will build my church." Translating the wordplay into Greek, Matthew most naturally would have used the feminine noun πέτρα, because it is the most common and closest equivalent to *kêphāʾ*. But when it came to making the wordplay Matthew was required to use the less common πέτρος in the first half because it is a masculine noun.[83] The use of the two different Greek words would not change the meaning of the

---

[76] Gundry, *Matthew*, pp. 333-334; Peter Lampe, "Das Spiel mit dem Petrusnamen—Matt. XVI. 18," *NTS* 25 (1979), pp. 229, 242-245; Max Wilcox, "Peter and the Rock: A Fresh Look at Matthew XVI. 17-19," *NTS* 22 (1976), pp. 87-88. Gundry, especially, makes quite a point about being "no longer shackled by the need to suppose an Aramaic substratum" (Matthew, p. 334). His "unshackling" is through proposing that Matthew composed this section in Greek. He seems to want to avoid the natural wordplay suggested with Πέτρος, because he goes to some lengths to make an association of "this rock" with "these my words" (7:24). In his desire to avoid the difficulties of the passage he has passed over the immediate association in favor of an association that is much more distantly removed.

[77] Philip Edgcumbe Hughes, "The Languages Spoken By Jesus," *New Dimensions in New Testament Study*, ed. Richard N. Longenecker and Merrill C. Tenney (Grand Rapids: Zondervan, 1974), p. 141. Lenski (*Matthew*, p. 627) argues against using an Aramaic substratum we know so little about.

[78] Brown, Donfried, Reumann, *Peter*, pp. 90-91, esp. note 212; Cullmann, *Peter*, p. 185; Beare, *Matthew*, p. 354; Manson, *Sayings*, pp. 202-205. The Aramaic character is noted in such expressions as "Blessed are you," "Simon Bar-jona," "flesh and blood," "Father in the heavens," "church" (as a reflection of the ancient Messianic community), "gates of Hades," "Keys of the Kingdom of Heaven." Cf. also Bonnard, *Matthieu*, pp. 244-246; Albright and Mann, *Matthew*, pp. 195-197.

[79] Fitzmyer, "*Kêphāʾ*," p. 123 n. 40; Brown, Donfried, Reumann, *Peter*, pp. 91-92.

[80] See Cullmann, *Peter*, pp. 18-20; Lampe, "Das Spiel Mit Dem Petrusnamen," p. 229; Fitzmyer, "*Kêphāʾ*," pp. 116-118.

[81] Fitzmyer, "*Kêphāʾ*," p. 118.

[82] Ibid., p. 115.

[83] Cullmann, *Peter*, pp. 18-19; Mundle, πέτρα, p. 383.

wordplay though, because πέτρος and πέτρα were at times used inter-changeably.[84] The natural wordplay in Aramaic, using one word, is best served in Greek by the two different words, because the masculine form would lend itself as a more likely designation of a *person*, and the feminine form (a literary variant) for a *feature* suggested by the sense of *kêphaʾ*.[85]

The establishment of the Aramaic substratum is helpful for under-standing the meaning of the wordplay. The centuries-old discussion of the meaning[86] is centered in the identification of "this rock" (ταύτῃ τῇ πέτρᾳ). While there are variations of each, there are three basic inter-pretations of "this rock." The first view suggests that ταύτῃ τῇ πέτρᾳ refers to *Peter*.[87] Drawing upon the close syntactical and morphological relation-ship of the terms in both Aramaic and Greek, this view stresses that the most obvious intent of the wordplay is to refer to Peter. The second inter-pretation suggests that ταύτῃ τῇ πέτρᾳ refers to the *confession*.[88] This view emphasizes that the Greek wordplay makes a distinction between Πέτρος and πέτρα, and therefore the intent of the wordplay is something other than the identification of Peter and "this rock." Those who hold to this view underscore that the demonstrative pronoun ταύτῃ points away from Peter as a person and specifies an *aspect* of Peter. In this case it is the truth of the confession, or the faith[89] of Peter expressed in the confession. A third view suggests that ταύτῃ τῇ πέτρᾳ refers to *Christ*. This view generally goes outside the passage to find support in other New Testa-ment passages where Christ is referred to as the "rock" (e. g., Mt 21:42,

---

[84] C. Brown, πέτρα, p. 386.

[85] Fitzmyer suggests that *kêphaʾ* may have nuances which are reflected in the Greek terms. This would not mean the stark differences of "stone" and "bedrock", but subtle differences, like the man himself and "an aspect of him that was to be played upon" (*Kêphaʾ*," p. 119). This specific nuance remains to be tested, but his suggestion is appealing.

[86] See Cullmann (*Peter*, pp. 155-170) and Burgess (*History of the Exegesis*, passim), for an overview of the history of this discussion.

[87] This was the interpretation of most of the early church fathers, although very early many fought against its use for establishing any kind of papacy (e.g. Ignatius, Justin, Origen, Tertullian, Cyprian, Firmilian; see Cullmann, *Peter*, pp. 159-162). This became the view of the Roman Catholic Church, and is held today by scholars such as those represented in Brown, Donfried, Reumann, *Peter*, pp. 92-93; and those of a broader con-fessional background, such as Albright, Mann, *Matthew*, p. 647; Stendahl, "Matthew," p. 787.

[88] This view was held early in church history by John Chrysostom, and attested to by Origen, Eusebius, Ambrose, and Theodore of Mopsuestia (cf. Cullmann, *Peter*, p. 162; Brown, Donfried, Reumann, *Peter*, p. 93 and note 216). Recently this has been proposed by Allen, *Matthew*, p. 176; McNeile, *Matthew*, p. 241; Mundle, πέτρα, pp. 384-385.

[89] This is a view held by Luther (cited in Cullmann, *Peter*, p. 162), and early this cen-tury by Alexander B. Bruce, "The Synoptic Gospels: TO ΚΑΤΑ ΜΑΤΘΑΙΟΝ," *The Expositor's Greek Testament* (n.d.; rpt.; Grand Rapids: Eerdmans, 1976), p. 224; cf. also Tasker, *Matthew*, p. 162.

but the term used is λίθος; 1 Cor 10:4, where the term used is πέτρᾳ), and the "foundation" (e.g. 1 Cor 3:11; 1 Pet 2:4-8). Those advocating this interpretation strongly emphasize a contrastive element in the Greek terms and the copulative καί.[90]

Several considerations combine to point to Peter as the intended antecedent to "this rock." First, Jesus' pronouncement is directed toward Peter personally, both before and after the wordplay, and it is unlikely that a change of reference would have been made without some explicit indication.[91] Second, the copulative καί more naturally signals *identification* of the halves of the wordplay than *contrast*; contrast is necessary if the saying pointed to the confession or Christ. Third, Πέτρος is the nearest antecedent, and the nearest antecedent is preferred over a more distant unless something in the context specifies another referent. No other referent is specified in the passage. Fourth, the Aramaic substratum almost certainly identifies Peter as the intended antecedent (as does the interchangeability of the terms πέτρος and πέτρα). Arguing from the substratum is arguing from silence, but the likelihood of Jesus speaking Aramaic on this occasion, particularly so since recent studies show the possibility of such a wordplay existing in common Aramaic, makes such a substratum wordplay likely.[92]

The wordplay indicates that Peter will be the rock upon which Jesus will build his church, a notion consistent with the special attention given to Peter in Mt and with the way in which even from the beginning he was spokesman and leader of the Twelve. The leadership role he was beginning to assume at the time of the confession is recognized by Jesus and is promised to be extended in the laying of the foundation of the church. This is borne out in the historical record. Jesus appeared to Peter after the resurrection and gave him special encouragement to feed Jesus' sheep (Jn 21). Peter held a leadership position among the disciples prior to Pentecost (Acts 1:15ff) and was the leading figure / preacher at

---

[90] This view was held as early as Origen and Augustine (cf. Cullmann, *Peter*, p. 162; Brown, Donfried, Reumann, *Peter*, p. 93 n. 216). This was also the major view of Luther, Calvin, and many of the Reformers (cf. Cullmann, *Peter*, pp. 162-163). Recently some redaction critics, holding to the Matthean creation of the passage in Greek, have also proposed that the reference is to Christ and/or his words (e.g. Wilcox, "Peter," pp. 87-88; Gundry, *Matthew*, p. 334).

[91] Some, such as Gundry (*Matthew*, p. 334), say that the demonstrative points away from Peter to some other focus of address. He contends that if the demonstrative pointed to Peter, the saying would have been, "You are Rock, and on you...." Gundry's suggestion negates the point of using a word play. A wordplay naturally plays upon the word to which it is most similar; here, one word for rock plays upon another word for rock. The demonstrative ταύτα specifies the wordplay: "You are Peter, and upon this one functioning as Peter, I will build my church."

[92] See Carson, "Matthew," pp. 367-369 for other valuable support.

Pentecost and beyond (cf. Acts 2:14, 37,38; 3:4,6,12; 4:8; 5:3ff.; 8:14, 18ff.; 9:32ff.; 10:9ff,; 11:2ff.; 12:3ff.; 15:6ff.). Peter is given a unique function and position in the foundation of the church. This does not mean that Peter builds the church (Jesus says "I will build My church"), but that he is important in the first days of foundation. Actually he disappears from the narrative of Acts after the foundation is laid (Acts 16 and on).[93]

But even though Peter appears to be the antecedent to "this rock," the reference should not be understood too narrowly. The purpose of a wordplay is to accent specific characteristics between like sounding, or meaning, words. In this situation the person alone is not accented, otherwise the wordplay would have been unnecessary. Rather, the use of the name Πέτρος suggests that more than just the person is played upon. Those characteristics which make Simon a "rocky ledge," πέτρα, comprise the elements which make for the wordplay. The demonstrative ταύτῃ accents this even more: Peter, as the one who is now functioning as the rock, *this* is the rock upon which Jesus will build his church. And what is *this*? *This rock* is everything that Peter is at this very moment. *This rock* includes Peter as the courageous confessor who steps forward, Peter as the representative spokesman for the disciples, Peter as the blessed recipient of revelation, Peter as the first individual to make a public confession of Christ, and Peter as the one who leads the disciples forward into realms of expression of faith. Upon *this Peter* Jesus will build his church. If Simon functions in this way he is the rock; if he does not he can become a stumbling stone (16:23).

On the other hand, Jesus' pronouncement is not a conferral of unique, individual supremacy. Peter is given a special recognition for all he is and is to be, but he is never placed above or apart from the disciples. This is also borne out in New Testament church history. Although crucial in New Testament church history, Peter is almost always together with other disciples. Early in Acts he appears as the recognized leader (Acts 2,3,5,8), but at the Jerusalem council James shares the leadership (cf. Acts 15:13ff.). Thereafter Peter disappears from the narrative and Paul is the one who is given special notice for his work of continuing the work of the church. Peter is crucial for his role in the foundation of the church, but he is not the only part of the foundation (cf. Eph 2:19; Rev. 21:14).

To sum up,[94] Peter is the rock in four ways. *Positionally*, he is *primus inter pares*. He is specially recognized for all he has said and done for his

---

[93] Cf. Oscar Cullmann, "πέτρος," *TDNT*, VI (Grand Rapids: Eerdmans, 1968), p. 108.

[94] There are many other features of this tristich that could be examined, but this study has been limited to those features which directly impact upon the development of the

leadership among the disciples, but he is never said to rise above them. He has a special place in the foundation of the church, but the other disciples are a part of the foundation as well. *Representationally*, Peter is the spokesman for all the disciples. This representation goes both ways. He represents all the disciples in his confession, and represents them in receiving blessing and honor. *Functionally*, Peter is used by Christ to establish the church. As the confessor Peter declares truth about Jesus that will be part of the creation of the church, and is the tool Jesus uses to lay the foundation work. Peter, and all he represents, functions as the foundation of the church. *Chronologically*, Peter's role is a temporary one: a foundation is laid only one time, and once laid is no longer seen. Peter's role is limited to the foundational time of the church, and therefore, to his own lifetime.[95]

3. Peter and the keys (16:19)

The building metaphor of the preceding tristich leads naturally to a discussion of 'keys' in this third and final tristich. The first line sets the theme, and once again, Jesus makes a pronouncement about Peter: "I will give you the keys of the kingdom of heaven." The second and third lines explicate the theme: "and whatever you bind on earth shall be bound in heaven, and whatever you loose on earth shall be loosed in heaven."

The meaning of the "keys" further clarifies the portrait of Peter. At a future time Jesus will give ($\delta\omega\sigma\omega$) to Peter ($\sigma\omicron\iota$) the keys of the kingdom

---

Matthean Petrine figure in relation to the disciples. The discussion of matters such as the authenticity of ἐκκλησία, Jesus' meaning by it, and the importance of the "gates of Hades" statement do not directly contribute to this topic.

[95] The whole question of papal succession from Peter has not been raised, but the following observations are significant. Papal succession from Peter is clearly not a position derived from exegesis of this text, but arrived at through confessional eisegesis; cf. Cullmann, *Peter*, pp. 214ff.; Colin Brown, "The Teaching Office of the Church," *The Churchman* 83 (1969), pp. 187ff. Many Roman Catholic scholars understand the "gates of Hades" saying as a promise to Peter that hell and death will not overcome the church, which has been used by church tradition as an inference that Peter will never be defeated by Satan, hell, or death (e.g., Meier, *Vision*, pp. 112-113). But this position reads too much theology into the saying. A more satisfying interpretation of the saying of hell and earth not overcoming the church understands it as the original enigmatic form of the passion prediction, and through it Jesus gives a promise to Peter that even though he (Jesus) must go through death ("gates of hades"), this will not be the end. This interpretation was first suggested to me by Professor Colin Brown in a private conversation in his office at Fuller Theological Seminary, Pasadena, California, on September 22, 1982; this interpretation is also hinted by Cullmann, *Peter*, p. 209 [1st ed.]: "The content of the next sentence, the giving to Peter of the keys ... also refers to the future. In this case, however, the reference is not to an unlimited future, but to the death *of Jesus*" [his emphasis]; cf. also McNeile, *Matthew*, p. 242, who develops this.

of heaven. The metaphor could point to a "generic power" given to Peter alone,[96] or to his "authority" over the house of God,[97] or to a power to open or shut the doors to the kingdom.[98] The building metaphor is most closely aligned with the latter, entrance into the kingdom, but authority is not too far removed: Peter is given the authority to admit entrance into the kingdom.[99] In this way Peter is contrasted to the scribes and Pharisees who shut off entrance to the kingdom and who do not enter in themselves (23:13; cf. a similar saying in Lk 11:52, where Jesus charges the scribes and Pharisees with taking away the "keys of knowledge").[100] The Pharisees compassed land and sea to make proselytes (23:15), and Peter also has a mission to carry out to give men access to the kingdom, and this mission specially involves his preaching of the gospel.[101] Peter, as the representative disciple who gives the first personal declaration of the Messiah's identity, is the one in the book of Acts who opens the door of the kingdom to all peoples. Through his authoritative preaching and presence, the kingdom was opened to Jews (Acts 2), Samaritans (Acts 8), and Gentiles (Acts 10).[102] The entrance image is foremost in view, and therefore "the keys refer to the fact that chronologically Peter, acting as the representative of Jesus, was the first to announce the message."[103] Peter was the special medium through whom the proclamation of the gospel was first made, which opened the kingdom to all peoples.

---

[96] Brown, Donfried, Reumann, *Peter*, pp. 96, 100-101.

[97] Hummel, *Auseinandersetzung*, pp. 62-63; Blank, "Peter," p. 51; Manson, *Sayings*, p. 205; Stendahl, "Matthew," p. 787.

[98] Bonnard, *Matthieu*, p. 246; Grundmann, *Matthäus*, p. 391; Hoffmann, "Petrus-Primat," pp. 98-99, 101; Kingsbury, "Peter," p. 76 n. 27; Nicklesburg, "Enoch, Levi and Peter," p. 593.

[99] This is preferred to the view which sees Peter as a chief rabbi exercising discipline over the established community. Beare (*Matthew*, p. 355) suggests that the saying indicates "...the bundle of keys carried by the chief steward, for the opening of rooms and storechambers within the house—symbols of responsibility to be exercised within the house of God." This interpretation draws too much on the rabbinic model and not enough on the context of the saying, which relates to recognition of the Son of Man and how this recognition results in blessing and the *establishment* of the church. The tenor of the passage is establishment and entrance to the new, not regulation of the already established.

[100] Dietrich Müller, Colin Brown, "κλείς," *NIDNTT*, II, trans. and ed. Colin Brown (1969; Grand Rapids: Zondervan, 1976), p. 732; Donald Guthrie, *New Testament Theology* (Downers Grove: Intervarsity, 1981), p. 714; Bonnard, *Matthieu*, p. 246; Grundmann, *Matthäus*, p. 391.

[101] Müller, Brown, "κλείς," p. 732.

[102] Even though the Samaritans had 'believed' through the preaching of Philip (Acts 8:4-13), it was necessary for Peter and John to go there in order for them to receive the Holy Spirit (Acts 8:14ff.). Cf., ibid.; Guthrie, *Theology*, p. 714.

[103] Guthrie, *Theology*, p. 714.

Since the second and third lines of the tristich continue and elucidate the theme found in the first line, the theme of entrance to the kingdom suggested by the image of keys in the first line is continued by the image of "binding and loosing" found in the second and third lines.[104] The rabbinic literature uses "binding and loosing" to describe the authority of the rabbis in teaching and discipline,[105] but the saying to Peter does not conceive of Peter as a "supreme rabbi" who applies *halakhoth* in the life of the church[106] or who exorcises demons.[107] Rather, the saying focuses on Peter as one who is given authority to declare the terms under which God grants entrance to the kingdom. Several considerations point in this direction.

First, the rabbinic nuance to the terms "bind and loose" which best fits the idea of entrance is that of "put under the ban" and "acquit."[108] Peter functions in such a way that people are either put under the ban, or else acquitted and allowed entrance. Two passages which help clarify the meaning are Mt 18:18 and Jn 20:22b-23. Mt 18:18 describes forgiveness or retention of sins within the church, and illustrates that the disciples as a whole have responsibility for declaring the terms under which sins are forgiven or a brother excommunicated from the local church. As parallel statements, these sayings of Jesus are the basis for entrance or banishment from the kingdom (16:19) and the local church (18:18).[109] Both sayings relate to forgiveness of sin. Jn 20:22b-23 also

[104] The logic of these tristichs demands the continuation and elucidation of the first line in the second and third, because the second and third lines are syntactically related to the first as an explanation of the theme introduced in the first. Based upon the conclusion that the keys refer to entrance, the binding and loosing must also refer to entrance. Those such as Kingsbury ("Peter," p. 73 n. 23; p. 77 n. 27), Plummer (*Matthew*, pp. 230-231) and Hendrickson (*Matthew*, pp. 650-651) miss this logical relationship and have the keys referring to entrance, and the binding and loosing referring to establishing and maintaining *halakhah*. For the view suggested in this paper, cf. Hummel, *Auseinandersetzung*, pp. 60ff.; Stehdahl. "Matthew," p. 787; Günther Bornkamm, "The Authority to 'Bind' and 'Loose' in the Church in Matthew's Gospel: The Problem of Sources in Matthew's Gospel," *Jesus and Man's Hope*, vol. I, ed. D. G. Buttrick (Pittsburgh: Pittsburgh Theological Seminary, 1970), pp. 40, 46.

[105] The Hebrew *hitîr* ... *'àsar* or the Aramaic *shᵉrà'* ... *ˣsar* of the Rabbis stand behind the δεῖν λύειν; cf. Friedrich Buchsel, "δέω (λύω)," *TDNT*, vol. II, trans. Geoffrey W. Bromiley (Grand Rapids: Eerdmans, 1964), p. 60; W. von Meding, D. Müller, "δέω," *NIDNTT*, vol. I, trans. Colin Brown (Grand Rapids: Zondervan, 1975), p. 171; Cullmann, *Peter*, pp. 204-205.

[106] E. g. Hummel, *Auseinandersetzung*, pp. 60ff.; Stendahl, "Matthew," p. 787; Beare, *Matthew*, p. 355.

[107] For this view see, Richard H. Hiers, "'Binding' and 'Loosing': The Matthean Authorizations," *JBL* 104 (1985), 233-250.

[108] Cullmann, *Peter*, pp. 204-205; Müller, Brown, "κλείς," pp. 732-733.

[109] This carries on some of the nuance of teaching and discipline from the rabbinic usage. The saying in Mt 16:18, 19 draws a distinction between the ἐκκλησία (v. 18) and the βασιλείας (v. 19). The discussion of this distinction is outside the scope of this paper, but with the inclusion of the parallel saying on binding and loosing occurring in a church discipline passage, the requirement for entrance is the same for both: forgiveness of sins.

concerns the forgiveness of sins, and is a tristich of almost identical construction to Mt 16:19. In Jn 20:22b-23 the reception of the Holy Spirit by all the disciples will enable them to forgive or retain sins. Seen in this light, the role given to Peter in Mk 16:19 of "binding and loosing" must point in the same direction: Peter is given authority to declare that sins are either forgiven or retained.[110]

Second, Peter's authority to declare the terms under which God grants entrance to the kingdom is tied directly to Peter's confession. Through the revelation of the Father and the personal confession of Jesus as the Messiah, the Son of the Living God, Peter receives blessing and becomes the foundation of the church. His confession is a condensation of the gospel, and through Peter's preaching of the gospel, and the preaching of others who followed him, sins are forgiven and entrance gained to the kingdom.

Third, Peter is an instrument through whom God the Father grants forgiveness of sin. The passives, "will have been bound" and "will have been loosed," and the phrase, "in heaven," are Semitic circumlocutions for describing the action of God.[111] Fourth, the periphrastic future perfect tense indicates that what Peter does in this present age has already been determined by God.[112] Peter is only an instrument which God uses, because God alone can grant forgiveness of sin and entrance to the kingdom.

This third tristich isolates both the unique and representative roles of Peter. Peter alone is given the keys, because once the door is unlocked there is no more need for keys to open the doors. This points to a temporally limited, functional role for Peter alone. But the authority of "binding and loosing" is shared by all the disciples (cf. 18:18; most likely Jn 20;22b-23). This is a representative role given to Peter. Therefore, the saying implies that once Peter opens the doors to Jews, Samaritans, and Gentiles, all the disciples will continue to proclaim the gospel, which will either bind people and prevent them from entering the kingdom, or loose them from their sins so that they may enter the open doors.

---

[110] Cf. Bonnard, *Matthieu*, p. 246; Carson, "Matthew," pp. 370-374; Cullmann, *Peter*, p. 205; Grundmann, *Matthäus*, p. 391; Guthrie, *Theology*, p. 714; Müller, Brown, "κλείς," p. 733; Nickelsburg, "Enoch, Levi and Peter," pp. 594-595. Guthrie (*Theology*, p. 714 points out that Peter was the first historically to proclaim a loosing from sins (Acts 2:38) and a binding (Acts 5:3).

[111] Brown, Donfried, Reumann (*Peter*, p. 96 n. 220) cite C. H. Dodd, *Historical Tradition in the Fourth Gospel* (Cambridge: Cambridge University Press, 1963), pp. 347-349. They also note that the Johannine parallel tristich (Jn 20:22b-23) has the passive tense ("are forgiven," "are held fast") which is also a circumlocution for God; cf. also Gundry, *Matthew*, p. 335.

[112] Gundry, *Matthew*, p. 335; see the excellent discussion in Carson, "Matthew," pp. 370ff.

4. Summary of and Conclusion to 16:17-19

This is by far the most important passage in the gospel of Matthew concerning the role of Peter, primarily because it contains an actual pronouncement of Jesus about the role of Peter found only in Mt. Matthew's use of the saying reveals his attitude about Peter in three ways: personally, representationally, and exemplarily.

Personally. Peter is the recipient of revelation from the Father which makes him personally blessed. He makes a personal confession which prompts a pronouncement from Jesus directed to Peter personally. Peter functions as a leader of the Twelve by acting as their spokesman in the confession, and is designated by Jesus to have a personal leadership role in the foundation of the church and the use of the keys of the kingdom. Because of the personal nature of the passage, all this directed to Peter is temporally limited to his lifetime.

Representationally. Peter acts as the spokesman for all the disciples, not just for himself. Peter acts as the representative for the disciples in the revelation, blessing and pronouncement, which therefore are at least obliquely directed to the disciples. Even though Peter is a leader, his leadership is from within; it is a *primus inter pares.* Peter later functions foundationally in the church, but shares the foundational role with the other apostles. Although Peter alone appears to receive and use the keys of the kingdom, he shares with the disciples the binding and loosing of sins for exclusion or entrance to the kingdom once the doors are opened.

Exemplarily. Peter represents all the disciples, and since the disciples in Mt are an example for all believers,[113] Peter acts as a personal example for all believers. His confession is a model confession for all believers. His courage in stepping forward is an example of boldness in the face of diverse opinions about Jesus. The way he acts as a spokesman is an example of boldness and leadership in the church. He is also an example of how entrance is made to the kingdom: confession and "loosing," or forgiveness of sin.

18:21

The final inclusion to be considered is in the context of forgiveness in the church, and the focus is on the question Peter asks of Jesus (18:21). Whereas the other inclusions of name (4:18; 8:14; 16:16; 26:33) and material (14:28-28; 15:15; 16:17-19) came in Markan material, this inclusion comes in material ascribed to Q. In the Matthean passage Peter

---

[113] This aspect of Matthean discipleship was one of the major features discovered in chapter four above, "Matthew's Use of the Term Μαθητής."

comes forward to ask a question that is suggested by Jesus' saying in
18:15. Since the context is one of church discipline (cf. vv. 16:18) some
have suggested that Peter, as the designated church leader (cf. 16:18),
asks a clarifying question about church discipline, and in return, Jesus
gives church law to Peter.[114] But this makes too much of Peter's question.
In fact, it overlooks the strong negation in Jesus' answer (οὐ placed first
for emphasis), and Jesus' correction of Peter's concept of forgiveness.
Peter sounds too much like a rabbi as he tries to ascertain delineated
limits for forgiveness. Jesus' response suggests that there are no limits to
forgiveness.[115]

Matthew records that on this occasion Peter acts in his usual
spokesman role, instead of functioning as a church leader. The group of
disciples were listening to Jesus' discourse (cf. 18:1ff.) when Peter comes
forward to ask what appears to be a question concerning himself ("sin
against me, and I forgive him"). Jesus corrects Peter ("I say to you;"
σοι), but the parable concerning forgiveness is broadened to include the
whole group again (in v. 35 the personal pronouns are plural: ὑμῖν; the
verbal forms are also plural). While Peter's question concerned himself,
in some way he was speaking for all the disciples, and Jesus directs his
teaching toward them all.[116]

Peter once again functions in his usual spokesman, representative role
in this passage, but there are negative connotations associated with his
question. Peter has gone beyond the rabbinic requirement (forgive three
times), but only quantitatively. Peter still counts, and Jesus abolishes all
limits so that Peter and all the disciples can qualitatively go beyond the
rabbis.[117] His question is a somewhat negative example, but his example
shows that all disciples must continually learn from Jesus.

C) Unique Matthean Material

The only Petrine passage that is classified here as unique Matthean
material is 17:24-27. This may be somewhat misleading, because each of
the inclusions of material (14:28-29; 15:15; 16:17-19; 18:21) are also unique to Matthew. The material in 17:24-27 is classified separately because
it is a self-contained unit; i.e., it is not part of a narrative or discourse.[118]

---

[114] Meier, *Vision*, p. 133; Goulder, *Midrash*, p. 402.

[115] Plummer, *Matthew*, p. 255; Meier, *Vision*, p. 133.

[116] Thompson, *Matthew's Advice*, pp. 207, 250-251; Bornkamm, "Bind and Loose,"
p. 47.

[117] Schweizer, *Matthew*, pp. 371f., 376f.

[118] Most synopses or harmonies of the gospels list this pericope separately. E.g., Kurt
Aland, ed., *Synopsis Quattuor Evangeliorum* (10th. ed.; Stuttgart: Biblia-Druck, 1977), p.
245.

Once again Peter is identified as the spokesman for the disciples. When the tax-collectors ask "Does not your (pl. ὑμῶν) teacher pay the tax?" (v. 24), their plural address signifies that Peter is the principal disciple outsiders approach to find out a matter about Jesus. Peter is addressed as the representative disciple and answers for them.[119] As the pericope unfolds, the focus is on Jesus and Peter alone. Some have understood this to mean that Peter is the official spokesman for Jesus, and that he has been personally instructed and supported by Jesus.[120] Although the emphasis on Peter as an individual should not be neglected, it should not be pressed too far either. Saying that Matthew intends to show that Peter now possesses authority to teach, forces an interpretation that is nowhere stated or even implied. Peter is given special attention by Matthew through the inclusion of the pericope, but the attention stems from his prominence among the disciples (the tax-collectors approach him) and the natural follow-up of Jesus. The incident becomes an opportunity for Jesus to teach about the responsibility of sons of God (pl.; "all the disciples") to the earthly temple. Therefore, Peter is more than just a paradigm of obedience,[121] because he is the prominent disciple who speaks for the disciples about Jesus. But he is not appointed to an authoritative position either, because the passage only treats his ideas as a backdrop for the teaching of Jesus himself.

Thus, as Peter is approached as the representative spokesman for the disciples he is isolated with Jesus and, therefore, is given special attention. The special attention is not for the purpose of highlighting Peter, but rather for highlighting the teaching of Jesus. Peter is given personal prominence as a leader of the disciples, and also as an example of the true disciple who learns from Jesus and is supplied by Jesus.[122]

D) Occurrences Shared With Mark

This section will consider the occurrences of Peter which are basically the same as those found in Mark. The preceding sections have been con-

---

[119] Bruce, "Synoptic Gospels," p. 234; Plummer, *Matthew*, p. 244; David Daube, "Responsibility of Master and Disciples in the Gospels," *NTS* (1972-3), 13.

[120] Meier, *Vision*, pp. 125-127; Bornkamm, "Bind and Loose," pp. 47-49; Trilling, *Israel*, p. 159.

[121] E.g., Gundry, *Matthew*, p. 356; Strecker, *Weg*, pp. 254-255.

[122] The last few words show that the στατῆρα found in the fish's mouth was for both Jesus and Peter (ἀντὶ ἐμοῦ καὶ σοῦ). The στατῆρα would have been just sufficient to pay the δίδραχμα (v. 24) for Jesus and Peter (cf. the discussion on the background and equivalences in Albright and Mann, *Matthew*, pp. 211-214). Such precision excludes overly "typifying" or "exalting" Peter. The language of the pericope suggests that Matthew expected his readers to see this in the historical framework of the gospel, and from that background learn from the story.

cerned with Matthew's striking expansions of the Markan picture of Peter. Here it will be noticed the way in which Matthew takes over the broad features of the Markan picture, but even in taking over Mark's picture Matthew gives his own perspective to the shared material.

Matthew carries over the name Peter (or Simon) from Mk sixteen times (cf. Appendix H). Two have already been discussed in other sections (4:18; 16:16), and several are in the same context and may be examined together. Seven occurrences shared with Mk are worthy of special consideration here (10:2; 16:22-23; 17:1-4; 19:27; 26:33; 26:37-40; 26:58-75).

10:2

Matthew gives a list of the Twelve in 10:2-4. As in every listing of the disciples in the New Testament, Peter's name stands at the head (cf. Mk 3:16ff.; Lk 6:14ff.; Acts 1:13ff.). In itself this fact might point to some kind of prominence among the disciples, but in addition Matthew has stated in his narrative "First, Simon, who is called Peter" (none of the parallels have the adjective πρῶτος). Matthew possibly was only stating that Peter was first in the list; in other words, that πρῶτος is hardly more than an attempt to make Mark's list concrete.[123] If Matthew had continued numbering the other disciples this might be plausible, but only Peter is given a number. Almost all commentators agree that standing at the head of the list, πρῶτος is redundant and superfluous unless it acts as a true adjective and describes Peter himself; i.e., gives him some kind of "first-place."[124]

This prominence is two-fold. First, Peter was the first-called of the disciples in Matthew's gospel. Matthew seems to emphasize the first-calling by using the same wording in 4:18 as he does in 10:2: "Simon, who is called Peter." Since Peter is the first-called he is the first in the listing of the disciples. Indeed, the wording of the calling of the first *four* disciples in Mt is exactly the order of their listing among the Twelve in Mt, unlike Mk (cf. 4:18, 20 to 10:2; Mk 1:16, 19 to Mk 3:16b-18a). Matthew seems to place an importance on the order of their calling, and since Peter is the first called, Peter's primacy in 10:2 is "salvation-historical" in nature.[125] Second, Peter's prominence comes not only from being the

---

[123] Cf. Schweizer, *Matthew*, p. 237; Strecker, *Weg*, p. 204 n. 1.
[124] Cf. Albright and Mann, *Matthew*, p. 117; Allen, *Matthew*, p. 100; A. B. Bruce, "Synoptic Gospels," p. 158; Carson, "Matthew," p. 237; Fenton, *Matthew*, p. 151-152; Grundmann, *Matthäus*, p. 287; Meier, *Matthew*, p. 104; Plummer, *Matthew*, p. 147; McNeile, *Matthew*, p. 131; Tasker, *Matthew*, p. 106.
[125] Cf. Kingsbury, "Peter," pp. 70-71; Hoffmann, "Petrus-Primat," pp. 108-110; Grundmann, *Matthäus*, p. 287.

first called, but also because he is first in terms of his leadership among the other disciples. Each of the listings of the disciples notes this by placing Peter first, but the πρῶτος in Matthew appears to be an emphasis on Peter's position of leadership. Importantly though, Peter is kept within the group of disciples. He is not separate or stated to be of a different sort. Rather, he is *primus inter pares*. Matthew recognizes Peter as the leader of the Twelve and the most prominent.[126]

As the first-called and leader of the Twelve, Peter is viewed by Matthew to have a special role. This role is specified by the rest of his use in the gospel.

16:22-23

In spite of giving a unique record of the special role of Peter as the rock of the church (16:17-19), Matthew does not downplay the scene that immediately follows, where Peter is a stumbling-stone to Jesus. In fact, Matthew has emphasized certain aspects of this negative picture of Peter.[127] For example, Matthew includes the actual words of Peter ("God forbid Lord! This shall never happen to you" 16:22), omits Mark's (Mk 8:33) reference to Jesus turning and seeing the disciples (thus focusing on Peter alone), and includes the phrase "you are a stumbling-stone to Me" (16:23). Matthew therefore records elements that show a strong contrast to the confession scene. The negative confession of v. 22 is a contrast to the positive confession of v. 16. Peter's rebuke results from following the direction of Satan (vv. 22-23), whereas his confession was a revelation of the Father (v. 17). Peter is named a 'stumbling-stone' to Jesus (v. 23), whereas he was the 'rock' earlier (v. 18). Since he is not receptive to the further revelation of Jesus about the cross, he is not on God's side (v. 23b). He is like the people who did not correctly identify the Son of Man (vv. 13ff.). As positive as was the pronouncement in 16:17-19, this statement to Peter is negative. Matthew has thus provided a positive and negative example side by side through Peter.

Peter is singled out personally as the negative example no less than he was as a positive example. This needs to be duly emphasized as a correc-

---

[126] Cf. Grundmann, *Matthäus*, p. 287; Albright and Mann, *Matthew*, p. 117; Allen, *Matthew*, p. 100; Broadus, *Matthew*, p. 213; A. B. Bruce, "Synoptic Gospels," p. 158; Fenton, *Matthew*, p. 151f.; McNeile, *Matthew*, p. 131; Plummer, *Matthew*, p. 147.

[127] Gundry (*Matthew*, p. 338) tries to show that these elements of Matthew's account soften rather than harshen the portrait of Peter. His reasoning is not convincing. Meier, (*Vision*, pp. 116-119), a Catholic scholar, has more convincingly shown that Matthew heightens the negative aspects.

tive to any tendency to exalt him above the other disciples. Peter's forcefulness of character helped make him a leader, but it also singled him out for a denunciation stronger than that aimed at any other believer in the New Testament.[128] Peter functions as a negative example of what happens when a believer, even a leader, ceases to listen to the voice of God the Father. He will be influenced by Satan to think only human thoughts of Jesus.[129] Plummer pertinently states:

> Peter's primacy is of a strangely varied character, and it is sometimes a primacy of evil rather than of good. If he is first in rank, and first in confession of faith, he is also first in tempting, and first at denying, his Master. The rock of foundation almost at once becomes a rock of offense, and that, not to the Church, but to its very Builder.[130]

Matthew, more than any other gospel writer, stresses the extremes of Peter's primacy. Peter is thus able to function as a historical person who exercises leadership, but who also exhibits the extremes of negative and positive example.

17:1, 4

Matthew (17:1-4) has almost the same material as Mark (Mk 9:1-6) concerning Peter in the Transfiguration account. Peter once again is the spokesman, here for the inner three. The portrait of Peter is both good and bad, or perhaps more accurately, "humanly foolish." Matthew's special touches have accentuated both the positive[131] and the negative,[132] but Peter is still making a basically foolish request. Whether Peter

---

[128] Other persons, both believers (Ananias, Acts 5:3) and unbelievers (Lk 22:3), are said to have had Satan enter their heart. Even the Jews who rejected Jesus through the lies of their hearts were only called sons of their father the devil (Jn 8:44). No one else is ever called "Σατανᾶς," as Peter is here. This statement is quite similar to that made by Jesus at the temptations in the desert (cf. 4:10; Lk 4:8).

[129] Cf. Bonnard, *Matthieu*, pp. 248f.; Hill, *Matthew*, pp. 263.; Plummer, *Matthew*, p. 231ff.; Schweizer, *Matthew*, pp. 344ff. An interesting comparison is to be found in two Catholic scholars who give a fair treatment of this incident: cf. Meier, *Vision*, pp. 116ff.; Hans Küng, *On Being a Christian*, trans. Edward Quinn (Garden City: Doubleday, 1976), p. 499.

[130] Plummer, *Matthew*, p. 234.

[131] E.g., χύριε (v. 4) for ῥαββί' (Mk 9:5); inserting "if you wish," as a note of seeking Jesus' will on the matter (but there is some MSS evidence that Mk also originally contained θέλεις [e.g. D θ φ 565 pc it; cf. Vincent Taylor, *The Gospel According to St. Mark* (2nd. ed.; 1966; rpt.; Grand Rapids: Baker, 1981), p. 390].

[132] E.g., omitting "for he did not know what to say, for they were afraid" (Mk 9:6), which functions as an excuse for him and the disciples (cf. Bonnard, *Matthieu*, p. 255); stressing that "I will make three booths" (v. 4) as opposed to Mk's "let us" (Mk 9:5) (but it should be noticed that the same early MSS of Mk 9:5 have the first person ποιήσω [e.g., D W it]).

thought that this was the new center of the coming kingdom,[133] wanted to care for these honorific personages,[134] wanted to prolong this scene of glory,[135] or wanted to establish new "tabernacles" for the center of communication with God,[136] he is still overlooking that Jesus must move on to the cross (cf. 16:21).

Consequently, Peter serves as an example of a very privileged disciple who reacts emotionally to a vision instead of acting with faith based on a word from Jesus (here, concerning the cross). Peter speaks foolishly, and therefore is a very real example of a human disciple who needs to learn from the Father (v. 5) and Son (vv. 5, 7, 9).[137]

19:27

Peter acts as the spokesman for the disciples in a somewhat anxious way when he says: "We have left everything and followed you" (cf. 19:27 to Mk 10:28). If anything, Matthew accentuates this anxiety by adding, "What then shall we have?"[138] This should not be seen as an overly mercenary bent in Peter, but rather an anxious question of a human disciple who has not yet fixed his eyes on the truly great benefits of being with Jesus. But nonetheless, Jesus promises a great heavenly reward for the disciples, showing he is not totally rebuking Peter (cf. v. 28). Peter is a very human disciple who has given vent to the anxious question of all the disciples. Jesus' instruction is intended to quiet their anxiety and lead them to a greater realization of spiritual truth (cf. the chiasmus of 19:30 and 20:16, and the instructive parable between). Peter is an example of a disciple experiencing anxiety, whom Jesus must correct through instruction.

26:33

Matthew carries over Peter's false declaration that he will not deny Christ, but it is an even stronger negation here, because Peter says "I will never fall away." (cf. 26:33 to Mk 14:29).[139] Peter's personal accountability is noted, because he says, "though all fall away 'because of you' (unique to Mt), I will never deny you." Peter tries to set himself

---

133 Albright, Mann, *Matthew*, p. 203; Beare, *Matthew*, p. 364.

134 Filson, *Matthew*, p. 192; Hendrickson, *Matthew*, p. 667.

135 Fenton, *Matthew*, pp. 277f.; Filson, *Matthew*, p. 192; McNeile, *Matthew*, p. 250; Plummer, *Matthew*, p. 239.

136 Bonnard, *Matthieu*, p. 255; Hill, *Matthew*, p. 268.

137 Contra, Gundry (*Matthew*, pp. 343-344), who sees Peter as a positive example here.

138 Kingsbury, "Figure of Peter," p. 70.

139 Cf. ibid.; Gundry, *Matthew*, p. 530

against the rest, but in doing so he becomes even more personally culpable. Tied together with v. 35, Peter functions as the spokesman and representative for the disciples, but he is also leading the way toward overconfidence.

26:37, 40

There is a decided accent on Peter in the garden of Gethsemane scene. Matthew omits Mark's reference to the proper names of James and John (cf. 26:37; Mk 14:33) and says, "and taking with him Peter and the two sons of Zebedee" This reflects that Matthew, unlike the other evangelists, tends not to mention specific disciples (cf. 20:20; 24:1,3; 28:7). But, in this instance Matthew excludes the names of the other disciples so that the emphasis is left on Peter (cf. 8:14). The stress on Peter's name focuses attention on Peter, the individual, as the representative disciple who goes into the garden with Jesus.[140]

In 26:40 Jesus comes back to the disciples (Mk has αὐτούς) after his time of prayer and finds them sleeping. Jesus then addresses Peter, "could you not watch with me one hour?" The interesting point here is that even though Peter is specifically addressed, the verbal form "could you [not] watch" is plural in Mt (ἰσχύσατε) but singular in Mk (ἴσχυσας, Mk 14:37). Matthew has included the other disciples in the admonishment, but since Peter is their leader and representative he is addressed. Matthew thus focuses on Peter, but reveals that Jesus intends the others as well.

26:58, 69, 73, 75

After the arrest of Jesus, Matthew similarly records that Peter follows Jesus from afar (cf. 26:58 to Mk 14:54) and ends up sitting in the courtyard of the high priest (cf. 26:69 to Mk 14:66). Then, in 26:73-75, come Peter's denials. Matthew has the same basic narrative of Mk, but there are several changes that are enlightening. In v. 70 Matthew adds that Peter denies Jesus "before all" who were in the courtyard, and, unlike Mk, makes no mention of the possible excuse that he did "not understand" the maid's accusation that he was with Jesus (cf. 26:70 to Mk 14:68). Also, in v. 72 Matthew states that the second denial is already "with an oath," and that Peter claims "I do not know the man" (cf. 26:72 to Mk 14:70).[141] Finally, in v. 75, Matthew adds that Peter went

---

[140] Cf. Kingsbury, "Figure of Peter," p. 70.
[141] Cf. ibid.

out and wept "bitterly." This is an intensification of the self-condemnation that Peter now experiences. These changes deepen the dark denial that Peter made and with which Peter has to live. This is the last time Peter is mentioned in Mt; therefore, Peter is left on a negative note.

E) Omissions of Markan Use

The name of Peter (or Simon) occurs twenty-four times in Mk. Matthew includes sixteen of those occurrences (they were all examined in the above section), but he omits eight (cf. Appendix H). Some have suggested that where Matthew omits the Markan reference to Peter no significant difference in theological outlook is revealed.[142] This certainly is the case in at least four of the omissions. In 8:14 (Mk 1:30) Matthew has merely consolidated the narrative and has omitted the name Simon. In another case Matthew does not report the incident in Mk 1:35-38 where Simon and those with him pursue Jesus to report that people were searching for him. In 26:40b (Mk 14:37b) Matthew has omitted the phrase, "Simon, are you asleep?," but this is not a crucial element. Likewise, in 26:69b (Mk 14:67) Matthew has omitted the phrase, "and seeing Peter warming himself," a change which does not appear significant.

There are four other omissions which may reveal a Matthean theological perspective. The first is found in 9:23-25 (Mk 5:37). Here Matthew has omitted reference to the inner three (Peter, James, and John) going into the house to heal the ruler Jairus' daughter. Matthew is known for occasionally abbreviating Mark's fullness of detail, and the entire passage (9:18-26) shows signs of abbreviation.[143] The focus is on Jesus alone and his compassionate healing. The exclusion does not appear to reflect on Peter.

The second is found in 21:20 (Mk 11:21). Matthew has "the disciples" asking a question about the withered fig tree, whereas in Mk it is "Peter" who speaks. Peter functions in his spokesman role in Mk (notice that Jesus responds to Peter in the plural: αὐτοῖς ... ἔχετε [Mk 11:22]), representing all the disciples, so Matthew has merely chosen to

---

[142] Brown, Donfried and Reumann, *Peter*, p. 76. I have noted more omissions than do Brown, Donfried and Reumann, because I have not only isolated "references" to Peter, but I have also tabulated all the occurrences of the proper name of the disciple (cf. Appendix H with the tabulation of Petrine passages in Brown, Donfried, and Reumann [*Peter*, pp. 58ff]). The tabulation in Appendix H includes both.

[143] Kilpatrick, *Origins*, p. 73.

let the disciples speak for themselves.[144] Matthew is consistent with the spokesman / representative role for Peter found in Mk.

The third omission that may reveal a Matthean perspective is observed in 24:3 (Mk 13:3). This is similar to 9:23-25 in that an inner group of disciples is omitted (Peter, James, John, and Andrew), but here the inner group is replaced with the generalized "disciples." Already, in a near passage, Matthew has replaced "one of his disciples" (Mk 13:1) with "his disciples" (24:1). Matthew prefers in this context to note that the *group* of disciples was present, rather than just one. As Matthew introduces the Olivet discourse he prefers to leave the disciples anonymous, making them a generalized audience of disciples, exactly like the disciple-audience of the other major discourses (cf. 5:1; 10:1; 13:10, 36; 18:1; 23:1). Matthew has intentionally generalized the named disciples to be an anonymous group, a move which specifies that the discourse is instruction for discipleship.[145]

The fourth omission of a reference to Peter which may signal a theological perspective is in 28:7 (Mk 16:7). While in Mark's account the angel at the tomb directs the women to tell the disciples and Peter that the risen Jesus was going to meet them in Galilee, Matthew omits the reference to Peter. Most commentators simply pass over this omission,[146] but those who do mention it note that the omission is surprising and strange in view of Matthew's interest in Peter elsewhere.[147] These commentators find it difficult to grasp Matthew's reason for omitting the mention of Peter. Some propose that the simplest explanation is that the mention of Peter in Mark was a later addition, and that since Matthew's tradition did not include Peter's name, he never really omitted it.[148] An intriguing scheme suggests that Matthew portrayed Peter as having forfeited his salvation at the denials, and the reason he is not mentioned in 28:7 is because Matthew typifies Peter as an apostate.[149] Since Lk

---

[144] Gundry suggests that the apparent difference between Mk and Mt of the chronology in the cursing reveals theological differences. "In Mk only Peter recalls on the next day what Jesus had said on the preceding day. In Matthew everything happens on the same day with all the disciples watching—Peter has no chance to exhibit the superiority of his memory over that of his fellows" (Matthew, p. 417). This suggestion stresses a human feature of Peter's supremacy ("memory"), whereas a divinely given feature was stressed by Jesus in the classic "appointment" passage (i.e., the divine revelation) (cf. 16:16ff.).

[145] A discussion of the role of the "crowds" in the audience of some of the discourses was discussed in chapter four.

[146] E.g., Grundmann, *Matthäus*, p. 570; Carson, "Matthew," p. 588.

[147] Fenton, *Matthew*, p. 450; Hill, *Matthew*, p. 359; McNeile, *Matthew*, p. 432; Plummer, *Matthew*, p. 421; Schweizer, *Matthew*, p. 525.

[148] Cf. McNeile, *Matthew*, p. 432; Plummer, *Matthew*, p. 421; Schweizer, *Matthew*, p. 525; Brown, Donfried, Reumann, *Peter*, pp. 77 n. 176.

[149] Gundry, *Matthew*, pp. 548ff.; 589.

24:34, 1 Cor 15:5, and Mk 16:7 all indicate a widespread tradition of an appearance to Peter, a more likely suggestion is that Peter is omitted either because he is included in the disciples, thus making any specific reference to him superfluous,[150] or because Peter was the first one to have seen the Lord and would not need telling.[151] The suggestion that Peter is omitted because he is included in the group of disciples fits best with the developing pattern in Mt. The latter three omissions of Peter (21:20; 24:3; 28:7) were for the purpose of accenting the group of disciples over named disciples. This fits with an overall tendency of Matthew to omit proper names for disciples (e.g. 8:14; 20:20,41; 26:37), and since the disciples as a group are alone with Jesus in the final scene of the gospel (cf. 28:16ff; the commissioning), perhaps Matthew's purpose was to progressively advance the group of disciples as the final focus.

IV. THEOLOGICAL ANALYSIS

The comparative, exegetical analysis of the preceding section has isolated the elements which are significant in Matthew's understanding of Peter and his role. The present section will organize those elements in order to clarify Matthew's overall theological and literary purposes involved in his understanding of Peter, and especially how those purposes relate to the disciples as a whole. Therefore, the first task is to organize the isolated exegetical emphases. Second, these emphases will be grouped according to the theological themes which Matthew used to form the Petrine model. Third, this model will be analyzed in the light of the progression in use in Mt. Fourth, and finally, the model of Peter will be compared to the role of the disciples in order to understand their theological and literary relationship.

A) Tabulation of the Exegetical Emphases

The examination of Matthew's handling of the texts concerning Peter reveals various exegetical emphases. Those emphases concerning Peter which were isolated in the preceding comparative, exegetical section may be summarized as follows:

1. *Peter is the spokesman for the disciples*
   Peter often represents all the disciples in what he says and does, both positively and negatively. While the representation was found in the tradition, it is accentuated by Matthew:

---

[150] G. Osborne, *The Resurrection Narratives*, p. 80.
[151] Goulder, *Midrash*, p. 448.

a. Positively. Peter's spokesmanship results in a favorable portrayal in 8:14; 14:28-29, 33; 16:16-19; and 17:24-27.

b. Negatively. Peter's spokesmanship results in an unfavorable portrayal in 14:30-31; 15:15; 17:4; 18:21; 19:27; and 26:37, 40.

2. *Stress is placed in the person Peter*
Peter is isolated and personal attention is focused on him. This is a favorite Matthean theme (8:14; 10:2; 14:28ff.; 15:15; 16:16, 17, 18, 19; 16:22-23; 17:4; 17:24-27; 26:33, 35, 37, 40).

3. *The disciples are a nameless entity and Peter represents them as a personal disciple* (14:26ff.; 15:15; 16:16ff.; 17:4; 18:21; 19:27; 26:35, 37, 40).

4. *Other disciples are omitted or de-emphasized in order to focus on Peter.*
a. Omitted—8:14; 16:22-23; 26:37, 40 (the latter, 16:23 and 26:40, focus on Peter in a negative fashion).

b. De-emphasized—14:28ff. (positive and negative); 16:16ff.; 17:4 (negative)

5. *Peter is viewed as a normal person with strengths and weaknesses.*
He is seen here as a very real human being (14:28ff.; 15:15; 16:16-23; 17:4; 17:24-27; 18:21; 19:27; 26:33-35,37-40).

6. *Peter functions as an example of what if means to be, or not to be, a disciple.*
a. *Positive example—14:28-29; 16:16-19; 17:24-27.*

b. *Negative example—14:30f.; 15:15; 16:22-23; 17:4; 18:21; 19:27; 26:33-35, 37-40, 69-75).*

7. *Peter functions as a leader of the disciples.*
As was the case in being their representative (2 above), Peter's leadership can be positive or negative.
a. Positive leadership—14:28-29; 10:2; 16:16, 17, 18, 19; 17:24-27.

b. Negative leadership—14:30-31; 15:15; 16:22-23; 17:4; 18:21; 19:27; 26:33-35, 37-40.

8. *Peter is specified by Matthew alone to have a unique prominence, which swings to both positive and negative extremes.*
a. Positive—10:2; 16:16-19

b. Negative—16:22-23; 26:69-75

9. *At times all named disciples (even Peter) are omitted in order to focus on the group of disciples as a whole* (9:23; 20:20, 24; 21:20; 24:1 [one of the disciples]; 24:3; 28:7).

B) Theological Purposes Reflected in Matthew's Portrait of Peter

The above exegetical emphases reveal a varied attitude toward Peter, but the same three theological purposes that were ascertained in the examination of 16:17-19 tie these elements together.

1. Personal

Matthew stresses Peter as a person. Matthew emphasizes that Peter himself is the "rock" of the church, and the one authorized to use the "keys" of the kingdom. Peter is the "first" disciple and the leader, spokesman, and representative of the disciples. Other disciples are deemphasized or omitted in order to focus on Peter. Peter is accorded a unique, personal prominence in Matthew's gospel.

But the personal stress is not all positive. He is held personally culpable for being a Satan-inspired stumbling-stone. His dark night of denial is even darker in Mt. His spokesmanship does not always receive a blessing (as it did in 16:16, 17). Various attempts at leadership as spokesman receive a negative reaction from Jesus, ranging from instructional correction (18:21; 19:27) to patient rebuke (14:31; 15:15) to a most severe denunciation (16:22-23).

On other occasions Peter is held up as a very real human disciple. He is caught with conflicting faith and lack of faith (14:28-31). He can be quite obtuse and foolish in his apprehension of Jesus' ministry (15:15; 17:4; 19:27). He can go from the highest confession to the lowest spiritual perception in one setting, and as a result receive from Jesus the greatest pronouncement or the strongest denouncement.

Matthew has portrayed a very realistic picture of the person Peter. He is not some mythical or midrashic caricature, but a very real disciple whom Jesus has personally taught, corrected, and established as a rock to carry on his work.

2. Representational

Matthew also portrays Peter as the representative of the disciples: what Peter does, he does in the name of the disciples. Peter is specified to be the spokesman for the disciples, and therefore, does not act independently from them (14:28; 15:15; 16:16; 17:4; 18:21; 19:27; 26:40). In the instances where Peter is given the greatest prominence, he is still a part of the group of disciples (10:2) and, although given a personal function, still basically represents the others (16:16-19). Several times the disciples are only a nameless entity, and then Matthew has Peter step forward to represent them in a confession of faith (14:28; 16:16) or has Peter step forward to ask Jesus a question (15:15; 18:21), or even has Jesus direct attention to Peter out of the nameless group (26:40).

That Peter is not some kind of "supreme rabbi" is indicated by the fact that he does not always represent the disciples in a positive way. His leadership and representation often is of a negative sort (e.g., 14:30; 15:15; 16:22-23; 17:4; 18:21; 26:40). Once again, Matthew portrays a very realistic Peter. He is a very human spokesman. Toward the end of Mt Peter loses the spotlight as the representational disciple and the focus shifts to the disciples as a group (cf. 21:20; 24:3; 28:7). Matthew's final emphasis and focus is on the disciples, not Peter.

3. Exemplary

Peter is both a positive and negative example of a disciple. He is a very human disciple whom Matthew has presented as a model for all disciples to follow. He is an example of exercising faith (14:28), confessing Jesus as Messiah, Son of God (16:16) and learning from Jesus (17:24-27). In even more cases he is the example of what not to do: disciples should not take their eyes off Jesus (14:30), should not be a stumbling-block (16:23), should not seek earthly rewards (19:27), and should not deny Jesus (26:69-70). Even with all the highs and lows of Peter's prominence, he is characterized by Matthew as a very real, very human, quite exemplary, disciple.

C) Progression in the Petrine figure

The portrait of Peter in Mt is one of extreme highs and extreme lows. A chronological graph of the positives and negatives of Peter (see Appendix I) shows no overall consistency in the Matthean portrait. Matthew begins by viewing Peter very positively, but ends his portrait very negatively (with the denials). No sooner does Peter achieve the heights of praise (16:16-19) than he sinks to his lowest condemnation (16:22-23). It seems like every time he reaches a high, Matthew counters with an incident underscoring his faults, which may indicate that Matthew purposely accentuated the positive-negative tension in Peter.[152]

Along with this tension, some over-all characteristics in the progression of the Petrine figure may be noted. Peter was the spokesman for the disciples in the Markan tradition (cf. Mk 1:36; 8:29,32; 9:2ff.; 10:28; 11:21), and Matthew has taken this over and expanded it. The "disciples . . . Peter" sequence appears frequently as an indication of Peter's

---

[152] A recent work by R. A Edwards recently was published which focuses on this same high-low tension in the disciples. I came to the above conclusion, based upon my own analysis of the text quite some time ago, but I am encouraged to see a like-minded conclusion in Edwards' work. Since this dissertation was in the final stages just as his essay was published, I can only give partial attention to the thesis, but it holds promise for future analysis.

spokesmanship role. "In each case, Jesus speaks to the disciples, and then Peter makes a request (14:28; 15:15), asks a further question (18:21; 19:27) or responds to the Master's words (16:16; 16:22).[153] Further, in every passage where Peter occurs from 10:2 until the denial there is some indication that he is the spokesman:[154]

10:2	πρῶτος	...10:2	Σίμων ὁ λεγόμενος Πέτρος
14:26	οἱ μαθηταί	...14:28	ὁ Πέτρος
15:12	οἱ μαθηταί	...15:15	ὁ Πέτρος
16:13	τοὺς μαθητὰς αὐτοῦ	...16:16	Σίμων Πέτρος
16:21	τοῖς μαθηταῖς αὐτοῦ	...16:22	ὁ Πέτρος
17:1	Πέτρον καὶ Ἰάκωβον καὶ Ἰωάννην	...17:4	ὁ Πέτρος
17:24	Ὁ διδάσκαλος ὑμῶν	...17:24	τῷ Πέτρῳ
18:35	ὑμῖν ... ἀφῆτε	...18:21	ὁ Πέτρος
19:27	ἡμεῖς ἀφήκαμεν	...19:27	ὁ Πέτρος
26:35	πάντες οἱ μαθηταί	...26:33, 35	ὁ Πέτρος
26:37, 40	υἱοὺς Ζεβεδαίου	...26:37, 40	τὸν Πέτρον
	...τοὺς μαθητὰς		...τῷ Πέτρῳ

Peter is accentuated as the spokesman for the twelve in all but his first two occurrences in this gospel,[155] and his last, at the denial.

A related characteristic is that Peter is advanced as a salvation-historical model.[156] He is the first disciple called (4:18), the first among the disciple / apostles (10:2), and the first member of the church (16:17-19). He is the first to go through Jesus as the bridge from Israel to the church. He is, therefore, personally prominent as a link between the OT promises of the messianic kingdom and salvation, and their fulfillment in the New Testament. Peter is an illustrative Jewish individual who has made the salvation-historical transition from Israel to the church.

Over half of the occurrences of Petrine material are in the section of Mt that reveals ecclesiastical concerns (13:53 - 18:35). Matthew exhibits a strong interest in the foundational importance of Peter to the church (perhaps an indication that Matthew is writing at an early date, clarifying Jesus' role in establishing Peter as the 'rock' of the church).

But along with the way Matthew clarifies Peter's foundational ecclesiastical and salvation-historical role, he everywhere accentuates the tension in Peter. As soon as Jesus establishes Peter's foundational role in the church (16:17-19), he immediately denounces Peter for being a

---

[153] Thompson, *Advice*, p. 205.
[154] The following tabulation combines some of Thompson's data with my own.
[155] But even in these, Matthew lists Peter first (4:18) and omits the Markan mention of Andrew, James and John in order to focus on Peter and Jesus alone (8:14).
[156] Cf. Kingsbury, "Figure of Peter," pp. 74ff.; Hoffmann, "Petrus-Primat," pp. 108f.

stumbling-stone (16:22-23). Matthew accentuates Peter's personal culpability, because he omits the Markan reference of Jesus turning and seeing the other disciples. Peter personally receives the highest pronouncement and severest denouncement. Matthew stresses this personal tension in Peter in many other places (see this graphically displayed in Appendix I). The way in which this tension fits into Matthew's scheme is clarified by two passages. In 19:27 Peter somewhat anxiously points out to Jesus, "Lo, we have left everything and followed you." Then, unique to Matthew, Peter asks, "What then shall we have?" Notice that Peter is the spokesman asking for rewards for the sacrifice of all the disciples. Then, unique to Mt, Jesus responds and tells them that in the new world they will sit on twelve thrones, judging the twelve tribes of Israel (19:28). Even though Peter is the spokesman he is in not differentiated from the other disciples. All twelve thrones will surround the "glorious throne" of the Son of Man. Only Jesus is exalted. Peter's spokesmanship is therefore only functional, not positional. He is only one of the twelve. Also, Peter's salvation-historical role is shared by the others, because they are all to share in judging Israel. The mention of the twelve tribes of Israel judged by the twelve disciples clarifies the relationship among the disciples. Even as one of the tribes of Israel functioned with special importance (e.g., Levi was the priestly tribe; Judah bore messiah) no tribe had permanent importance or preeminence. Their individual importance was functional and therfore temporally limited. So also with Peter's spokesmanship. He is personally important in function, but not continually set apart or exalted. Indeed, the two sayings which form a chiasmus (19:30 and 20:16) seem to be specifically pointed toward stopping any thoughts of personal exaltation. Only the Son of Man is to be honored and exalted.

Matthew reiterates the absence of personal exaltation in 23:7-10, attributing to Jesus a saying unique to his gospel. As important as Peter is in the foundation of the church, he can never be considered a supreme rabbi. An ideal in Israel was to be called rabbi, but Jesus said his disciples were not to be called such, because his disciples have one Teacher and they are all brothers. The disciples are not to be called father, because they have one Father in heaven. The disciples are not to be called master, for Christ alone is their Master. The greatest is to be a servant, and whoever exalts himself will be humbled, and whoever humbles himself will be exalted. The disciples are to be one brotherhood, with no one exalted above the other. If they exalt anyone, they are actually displacing God. It is significant that the next saying is a condemnation of the scribes and Pharisees for shutting off the kingdom from man; the very role Peter is now to fulfill (cf. 16:19). The Pharisees got to their point of losing the kingdom through exalting themselves as the legal experts. No disciple, Peter included, can be exalted above his brothers.

These passages, 19:27ff. and 23:7ff., help clarify the Matthean tension in the portrait of Peter. He is functionally important in Jesus' work of building his church. But nonetheless, he is still only one of the disciples; he is one of the brethren. Since Matthew has clarified Peter's unique functional role in the foundation of the church, he must make it clear that Peter is not perfect, nor exalted, nor given a special place in the coming age. In fact, once Matthew has clarified Peter's role in the church, he begins to make it explicit that he is only one of the twelve. This is done in 19:27 (as seen above), 26:33-35 (by specifying all the disciples boasted of not denying Jesus), 26:37 (by rebuking Peter with the others for sleeping), the denials, and the omission of Peter in 21:20; 24:3; 28:7. This is not to say that Peter is rejected, but rather that the focus now shifts to the disciples as a group.

A reason for this shift may be found in Matthew's concept of history. Peter's foundational role is necessary to stress for the beginning days of the church. But since his role does not go beyond the foundation, Matthew does not want to overly stess him. Instead, he appears to recognize that the age of the church will go on beyond the foundation. Matthew mentions only the group of disciples after the resurrection because the focal point is on Jesus' commission, which has to do with making disciples until the end of the age (28:16-20). Even as Peter was commissioned for his foundational work which Christ would perform through him, so all disciples are commissioned for the age-long work beyond the foundation, which again, is promised the abiding presence of Jesus.

V. Concluding Observations: The Relation of Peter to the Disciples

Now that the portrait of Peter in Matthew's gospel has been visualized, this portrait must be seen in relationship to the disciples as a whole. Matthew's use of the term μαθητής was analyzed in the previous chapter and it was discovered there that the major role of the disciples was exemplary. They function in Matthew's gospel as an example, both positively and negatively, of what it means to be a disciple. Their portrait is intended as an example to Matthew's church. The focus in Mt is upon Jesus who calls, instructs, and sends disciples out to make more of what he has made them to be. But in this process Matthew has presented the disciples as a nameless, faceless, collective unity. Against this backdrop of anonymity

Matthew also gives a portrait of Peter. Peter stands out starkly because he is the only named disciple who is emphasized.[157]

Therefore, the uniqueness of Peter is prominently visible in Mt. No other disciple has his prominence. Since he was quite likely writing to a Jewish-Christian community, Matthew emphasizes Peter as an example of salvation-historical continuity. Jesus called Peter first, established him as the first of the disciples / apostles, and set him as the rock, the first member of the church. But Peter is de-emphasized near the end of Mt because the church was not to exalt him as a supreme rabbi. Peter is only one of the group of disciples. Even though he is their leader, he is *primus inter pares* and is never detached from the group. Jesus creates a new community where all disciples are brothers, and Jesus alone is their teacher and Master. This is why the strengths and weaknesses of Peter are portrayed. Just like all the other disciples, Peter has strengths and weaknesses and is instructed by Jesus so that he can progress and understand Jesus' mission. Almost everything that is said of Peter is elsewhere said of the disciples. Peter is one of the disciples, but he also has to carry out his specific role as leader of the twelve and rock of the church. This does not exalt him or separate him; it is a functional role through which Jesus uses him. In like manner the eleven (Peter included) are given the age-long commission to make disciples. Peter is to function as the rock and user of the keys, but once his role is performed he ceases to be significant. He is like any other of the nameless disciples. This may have been Matthew's way of avoiding ongoing preeminence among the disciples. Since the nameless disciples were the ones who were given the commission, their work of making disciples can go throughout the age.

Peter also functions exemplarily in much the same way as do the group of disciples. In his strengths and in his weaknesses he can be an example to Matthew's church. This is why Matthew has accentuated the truly human element in Peter. The church would find much in common with Peter's typically human characteristics, and he would be the named example from among the disciples. He is much like any common believer with his highs and lows, and therefore, becomes an example from whom the church can learn. This may also be the case for the leaders of Matthew's church. Even as Peter had success and failure as a leader, so the leaders of the church can learn from Peter's example. Several of the questions or responses to Jesus voiced on behalf of the disciples by Peter were issues that still would speak to the church of Matthew's day (e.g., 15:15;

---

[157] This was also Mark's thrust, but Matthew accentuates it by omitting Mark's mention of other named disciples in Mk 1:29; 5:37; 9:38; 10:35,41; 13:3; 14:33. Matthew makes no attempt to name disciples other than Peter, except that he has a slightly stronger portrait of Judas than does Mark (cf. Mt 27:3-10).

17:24f.; 18:21). As Jesus instructs Peter, instruction is provided for the church. This example is a primary aim of Matthew through Peter and the disciples. The focus was to be on the Jesus who promised to Peter, "I will build My church;" who had called him and corrected him and instructed him. The focus was to be on the risen Lord Jesus who sent out the disciples and said "I am with you always, even unto the end of the age." Matthew's gospel is just that: "the good news" that Messiah has come to be with his people and will be with them always. Peter and the disciples are historical examples of what Jesus, with his people, can accomplish. The following words may very well reflect the thoughts of Matthew as he wrote his account of Peter:

> It needed the Saviour's insight to discover an Apostle in Simon Bar-jona, the fisherman; and the Saviour's patient culture to elicit the dormant qualities of his character, and fitted him to be the leader of the Primitive Church. But if the Master could do so much for him, what may He not effect, my reader, for thee and me?[158]

---

[158] The words of introduction by F. B. Meyer to his devotional work, *Peter: Fisherman, Disciple, Apostle* (n.d.; rpt.; Fort Washington, Pennsylvania: Christian Literature Crusade, 1978), p. 5.

SUMMARY AND CONCLUDING REMARKS

The methodology employed in this study accentuated both the detail and the overall effect of Matthew's artistry. The intent was, first, to clarify the existence and type of master-disciples in the milieu in which Jesus first called his disciples; second, to set that background against the type of disciples Jesus called and established; third, to compare the Matthean use of the term μαθητής with the parallels in order to identify the uniqueness of Jesus' disciples as seen through the eyes of Matthew; and fourth, to trace the development of the disciples in the gospel as a literary device.

The study of the use of μαθητής in chapter one revealed that Rengstorf overstated the Sophistic influence. While it was readily adaptable to be used to designate a Sophistic student in the classical and Hellenistic periods, μαθητής had a much wider connotation throughout its history. In the earliest written use (the early classical period) the term was used in three ways: it was used with a general sense, in morphological relation to μανθάνειν, to refer to a "learner;" it was also used quite early with a technical sense to refer to an "adherent" of a great teacher, teaching, or master; and it was also used somewhat more restrictedly by the Sophists to refer to the "institutional pupil" of the Sophists. Socrates / Plato (and those opposed to the Sophists) tended to avoid using the term to designate his followers in order to avoid Sophistic misassociations, but he used the term freely to refer to "learners" and "adherents" where there was no danger of misunderstanding.

In the late Hellenistic period μαθητής continued to be used with general connotations of a "learner" and "adherent," but it was used more regularly to refer to an "adherent." The type of adherency was determined by the master, but it ranged from being the pupil of a philosopher, to being the follower of a great thinker and master of the past, to being the devotee of a religious figure. By the time of the third century A.D. the term was used by one prolific writer to refer exclusively to an adherent. Μαθητής became a *terminus technicus* to refer to an adherent.

The progression to "adherent" in Hellenism at the time of Christ and the early church made μαθητής a convenient term to designate the followers of Jesus, because the emphasis in the common use of the term was not upon "learning," or upon being a "pupil," but upon adherence to a great master. Hence a "disciple" of Jesus, designated by the Greek term μαθητής, was one who adhered to his master, and the type of adherence was determined by the master himself. The movement toward *terminus technicus* was almost complete at the time of the gospel writers. Without specialized connotations surrounding it, μαθητής was general enough in common Greek to be used of a wide variety of types of master-disciple relationships and was still adaptable enough to be used later by the Christian church as a technical / specialized term to denote the intimate follower of Christ.

Rengstorf also addressed the issue of the striking absence of 'disciple' terminology, saying that the terms for disciple were absent because the concept of discipleship was absent. Once again, he overstated the case. Evidence for the existence of master-disciple relationships in the Old Testament is found in a limited way in the terms *talmîdh* and *limmûdh* and in the social structures of the prophets, the scribes, and the wise men.

The single occurrence of *talmîdh* in the Old Testament indicates a student or apprentice in musical instruction (1 Chron 25:8). *Talmîdh* here indicates a master-disciple relationship which centers on instruction in a skill, and therefore is a morphological transparency for the verb *lâmadh*. *Limmûdh* is also morphologically related to *lâmadh*. The *limmûdhîm* in Isa 8:16 and 50:14 were a group gathered around a master in such a way that they were referred to by a possessive ("my disciples," Isa 8:16) and their relationship was characterized by some kind of educational process which accentuated speaking and listening (Isa 50:4). The same term was also used to specify the "disciples" of Yahweh (Isa 54:13), which indicates that *limmûdhîm* could be disciples of both Yahweh and a human master. Although the occurrences of the these terms are scarce, they indicate that established master-disciple relationships are at least to be found among the musicians and writing prophets. The casual way in which the terms are used indicate an even broader usage behind these examples.

The prophets also demonstrate master-disciple relationships. Groups of prophets were found around Samuel, and he appears to exercise some kind of "mentor" authority over them. The relationship does not speak of a school setting, but rather of a "fellowship" of prophets who look to Samuel as an authority. A similar type of relationship is found with the "sons of the prophets" and Elisha. Elisha exercised leadership authority over these prophets, but, again, it is not in a school setting. The sons of the prophets were not prophets in training, but were rather gathered around Elisha for guidance in performing their own prophetic activities. This is not a master-disciple relationship of the school, but is a master-disciple relationship in mutual commitment to service of Yahweh.

The scribes also demonstrate characteristics of master-disciple relationships. Based on the nature of their profession the scribes would naturally be involved in apprentice-type training in the rudimentary skills of their trade: e.g., reading, writing, transcribing. Other skills are

also associated with the Old Testament scribes, such as political responsibilites as advisors in the royal court. After the exile Ezra's responsibilites as scribe centered on teaching the law, but such a responsibility
was also in evidence prior to the exile (cf. Jer 8:8-9). Much of the training
for these various scribal responsibilites appears to have occurred within
the family and clan, which would speak of master-disciple training in
these skills being from father to son. But as advanced training and
specialization was needed, the most likely place for this to occur would
have been within the scribal guild. Such a guild might be described as
a "fellowship of professionals." This might speak of a school for scribes,
possibly located at the court, but evidence for such a school is lacking.
Some kind of master-disciple relationship is required to account for the
continuity of the scribal arts in Israel. While there is no obvious
dependence on any Old Testament model of master-disciple relationship
within the scribes, there does appear to be a sociological development
from scribal families to a fellowship of scribes within the nation, to the
sophistication of the court, to the Torah-centered activities of Ezra, to
later rabbinic thinking. Such a development implies master-disciple relationships.

J. Crenshaw elucidates the diverse nature of "wisdom" in a three-fold
manner: wisdom is a world outlook, a teaching position, and a folk tradition.[1] Understood from this point of view, "wisdom" requires master-
disciple relationships for its acquisition and use, but the types of relationship vary in form and function. Master-disciple relationships behind the
perpetuation and dissemination of the wisdom tradition would be found
in informal father-son relationships, in training of elders for making
judicial decisions in the city gate, in the wisdom orientation of advisors
in the court, and within certain groups who specialized in wisdom and
were involved with the recording of wisdom sayings. Those specializing
in wisdom (e.g., elders and court advisors) would help regulate and fine-
tune the wisdom which was originally disseminated throughout the
cultural milieu by means of family / clan education and contextualization. A wisdom school is often suggested for this nation-wide wisdom
specialty, and evidence of wisdom emphasis at the royal court gives some
weight to this suggestion. But the absence of "school" evidence suggests
that greater potential for finding master-disciple is to be found in the
family / clan, elder / leader training, and "wise men" who were
specialists in the wisdom tradition.

In spite of the relative absence of disciple terminology and explicit
teaching on discipleship, the nature of the prophetic ministry, the writing

---

[1] Crenshaw, *Old Testament Wisdom*, pp. 17-25.

prophets, the scribes, and the wisdom tradition speak strongly of the existence of master-disciple relationships in Israel. The casual way in which the terms are used in the infrequent occurrences indicates a common usage behind the examples found in the Old Testament. The author appears to be alluding to something in the experience of his readers. While later 'discipleship' terminology was not used to designate them, relationships within the social structure of Israel indicate master-disciple relationships. The nature of these relationships assume professional training, but the Old Testament focuses on the function of these groups rather than on the process of acquiring their skills. These types of relationship are quite different than the formal, institutionalized model Rengstorf fears would preempt the place of discipleship to Yahweh. Indeed, each of these master-disciple relationships were involved in the process of the communication of the revelation of Yahweh (prophecy, law, wisdom) and the suggested intimacy of the relationship indicates mutual support in the task of revealing the word of the Lord to the nation. Such a supportive fellowship can certainly be designated "discipleship," providing examples from which the New Testament form of discipleship can learn.

The common terms for discipleship are also strikingly scarce in most of the Jewish intertestamental literature. *Talmîdh* / μαθητής do not appear in any extant Jewish literature until the time of Philo, at approximately the same time as Christ. Philo is instructive in his use of μαθητής, because he uses it with the general sense of a "learner," and with the technical sense of a committed follower. He reveals a blend of Greek / Jewish thought by using μαθητής in the sense of a disciple of God himself: the μαθητής must not remain in subservience to any teacher, because true virtue and wisdom come only from God. By the time of the New Testament and Josephus, μαθητής carried the general / technical associations of adherent, with the type of discipleship determined by the one leading. There were no specialized connotations associated with the use of the term.

The linguistic history of *talmîdh* is not as well documented as is that of μαθητής, but specialized connotations do not appear to be associated with the term prior to Jamnia. The *talmîdh* was a learner who had banded together with other learners under a leader / teacher. At the time of Jesus the type of *talmîdh* was determined by the one doing the leading and/or teaching. *Talmîdh* became a specialized term in the rabbinic literature for the student of Torah . The oral Torah became the focal point of study, although the ultimate goal was to follow Yahweh through written and oral Torah.

Μαθητής and *talmîdh* appear to be equivalent terms. They were popular terms at the time of Jesus to designate a follower who was vitally committed to a teacher / leader and/or movement. The terms themselves did not determine the type of discipleship; the type discipleship was determined by the type of leader or movement or teaching to which the disciple was committed. The types of discipleship covered the spectrum from philosophical (Philo) to technical (scribes) to sectarian (Pharisees) to revolutionary (Zealots and Menahem) to eschatological (John the Baptist). The terms were general enough to be used for all of the above. It remained for Jesus and Jamnia to make these terms specialized.

While the later terms for master-disciple relationships are relatively absent from the Jewish literature prior to the time of Christ, the structure of Jewish social phenomena once again imply master-disciple relationships. The professional scribal tradition found in Sirach, which requires master-disciple training, is implied throughout Jewish history. The education of young scholars such as Philo, the Pharisees, and Josephus is a common phenomenon and suggests rigorous training. And the existence of various social movements, such as John the Baptist, the radicals with Menahem, and the Qumran isolationaries, either explictly or implicitly speak of the intimate attachment of a group to an individual as the group carries out their perception of the will of Yahweh. The master-disciple relationship should be seen as a common phenomenon in Israel at the time of the arrival of Jesus; so common in fact that Jesus had to clarify for those who followed him his specific form of master-disciple relationship. Jesus' ideal for his disciples must be studied in its own light as a continuation of the Jewish heritage, yet as a departure from other master-disciple relationships of his day. He was his disciples' supreme teacher and leader (Mt. 23:7-10). They were not to be disciples of any other person, and were never to advance to being called rabbi. They were to make disciples of all the nations, but all new disciples were to be taught what Jesus had previouly taught them (Mt 28:18-20). This is where the concept of discipleship in Matthew becomes important for the ongoing process of making disciples.

This study of Matthew's use of μαθητής reveals his special interest in the disciples as a literary figure. In the process of handing on his tradition concerning them, Matthew, through inclusions, unique tradition, expansions, alterations, and omissions, has exalted Jesus as the supreme Lord and Teacher of the historical disciples and the post-resurrection community. Matthew has emphasized the goal of the believers' life of faith through the discipleship stories directed to the μαθηταί. Matthew's gospel is at least in part a manual on discipleship. With all of the major discourses directed to the μαθηταί, with the term arranged in such a way that most sayings directed to the disciples have become teachings on discipleship, with the positive yet realistic enhancement of the picture of the disciples, and with disciples called and trained and commissioned to carry out the climactic mandate to "make disciples" in the conclusion of the gospel, Matthew has constructed a gospel that will equip the disciples in the making of disciples.

The relationship of the μαθηταί to various characters in Mt shows that Matthew has used the term with both literary and a theological purposes. One significant use of the term was to accentuate his Christology. Jesus is often considered alone in order to accentuate various aspects of his life and ministry. The term μαθητής also becomes a signal word to specify a certain teaching as a discipleship teaching. Matthew has created a literary device to show the way Jesus taught his disciples and to show how that teaching can relate to his church.

Matthew has basically intended μαθητής to be linked with οἱ δώδεκα. With both the moment of the historical disciples and the moment of the church before the reader, one is able to see that Matthew's portrait of the disciples both passes on the tradition about the Twelve, and at the same time presents an example of discipleship for his church. The disciples are a positive example of what Matthew expects from his church, a negative example of warning, and a mixed group who are able to overcome their lackings through the teaching of Jesus. The historical disciples become a means of encouragement, warning, and instruction as examples.

The ὄχλοι are a basically neutral, though curious group who are at times seen negatively, and at times positively. They are the people of Israel of Jesus' day who are the object of Jesus' ministry. They flocked to him for healing and teaching, but could not understand (13:10ff) because they were not truly believers. They were amazed at his teaching and shouted "Hosanna!" at his entry into Jerusalem, but they were finally led astray by the leaders of Israel. While the crowd never exercises faith in Jesus, true believers are those who come out and call Jesus "Lord." As a mixed body of those truly interested and not interested in Jesus, the crowd is now the object of the disciples' ministry. It was the disciples' responsibility to go among the crowds of Israel, and always will be their responsibility among the nations of the earth. The objective of the disciples is to "make disciples" of the nations.

Since the disciples function in Matthew's gospel as an example, both positively and negatively, of what it means to be a disciple, the portrait of Peter in Matthew's gospel provides a personalized example of discipleship. The portrait is intended as an example to Matthew's church. The focus in Mt is upon Jesus who calls, instructs, and sends disciples out to make more of what he has made them to be. But in this process Matthew presents the disciples as a nameless, faceless, collective unity. Against this backdrop of anonymity Matthew gives a portrait of Peter. Peter stands out starkly because he is the only named disciple who is emphasized.

Therefore, the uniqueness of Peter is prominently visible in Mt. No other disciple has his prominence. Since he was quite likely writing to a Jewish-Christian community, Matthew emphasizes Peter as an example of salvation-historical continuity. Jesus called Peter first, established him as the first of the disciples / apostles, and set him as the rock, the first member of the church. But Peter is deemphasized near the end of Mt because the church was not to exalt him as a supreme rabbi. Peter is only one of the group of disciples. Even though he is their leader, he is *primus inter pares* and is never detached from the group. Jesus creates a new community where all disciples are brothers, and Jesus alone is their teacher and Master. This is why the strengths and weaknesses of Peter are portrayed. Just like all the other disciples, Peter has strengths and weaknesses and is instructed by Jesus so that he can progress and understand Jesus' mission. Almost everything that is said of Peter is elsewhere said of the disciples, and vice versa. Peter is one of the disciples, but he also has to carry out his specific role as leader of the twelve and rock of the church. This does not exalt him or separate him; it is a functional role through which Jesus uses him. In like manner the eleven (Peter included) are given the age-long commission to make disciples. Peter is to function as the rock and user of the keys, but once his role is performed he ceases to be significant. He is like any other of the nameless disciples. This may have been Matthew's way of avoiding ongoing preeminence among the disciples. Since the nameless disciples were the ones who were given the commission, their work of making disciples can go on throughout the age.

Peter also functions exemplarily in much the same way as do the group of disciples. In his strengths and in his weaknesses he can be an example to Matthew's church. This is why Matthew has accentuated the truly human element in Peter. The church would find much in common with Peter's typically human characteristics, and he would be the named example from among the disciples. He is much like any common believer with his highs and lows, and therefore, becomes an example from whom the church can learn. This may also be the case for the leaders of Matthew's church. Even as Peter had success and failure as a leader, so the leaders of the church can learn from Peter's example. Several of the questions or responses to Jesus voiced on behalf of the disciples by Peter were issues that still would speak to the church of Matthew's day (e.g., 15:15; 17:24f.; 18:21). As Jesus instructs Peter, instruction is provided for the church. This example is a primary aim of Matthew through Peter and the disciples. The focus was to be on the Jesus who promised to Peter, "I will build My church;" who had called him and corrected him and instructed him. The focus was to be on the risen Lord Jesus who sent out the disciples and said "I am with you always, even unto the end of the age." Matthew's gospel is just that: "the good news" that Messiah has come to be with his people and will be with them always. Peter and the disciples are historical examples of what Jesus, with his people, can accomplish. It is hoped that this message is now clearer through the study of this monograph.

EPILOGUE:
RECENT DEVELOPMENTS IN MATTHEAN DISCIPLESHIP[1]

Critical study of the disciples in Matthew's gospel is a comparatively recent phenomenon.[2] Since the completion of my initial study of the Matthean disciples nearly ten years ago, a virtual landslide of materials has appeared. In this essay we will take stock of the scholarly work, survey the most recent proposed models of the Matthean disciples, and provide an evaluation.

I. MODERN STUDY OF THE MATTHEAN DISCIPLES

When reviewing modern critical study of the Matthean disciples, we must award pride of place to the groundbreaking work of Günther Bornkamm, especially for the 1948 essay, "The Stilling of the Storm in Matthew."[3] The appearance of this essay is commonly said to mark the beginning of redaction-critical approaches to Matthean studies in general, and the Matthean disciples in particular. Bornkamm's students G. Barth and H. Held also carried out significant, exploratory, redaction-critical work on the disciples in Matthew.[4] Quickly following came the studies of W. Trilling, G. Strecker, and R. Hummel.[5] An influ-

---

[1] A first form of this chapter appeared in a paper I delivered to the Matthew Section of the Society of Biblical Literature at the annual meeting in November, 1991. The paper was published as "Named and Unnamed Disciples in Matthew: A Literary-Theological Study," *SBLSP* 30, ed. Eugene H. Lovering, Jr. (Atlanta: Scholars Press, 1991). My thanks to Scholars Press for permission to include material from that paper. I have updated the discussion for this chapter.

[2] For a variety of reasons, but especially because of the note of incomprehension found there, the spotlight focused upon the disciples in Mark's gospel for the last 25 years. For an overview, see C. Clifton Black, *The Disciples according to Mark: Markan Redaction in Current Debate*, JSNTSup 27 (Sheffield: JSOT, 1989) and Christopher D. Marshall, *Faith as a Theme in Mark's Narrative*, SNTSMS 64 (Cambridge: Cambridge University Press, 1989).

[3] Günther Bornkamm, "Die Sturmstillung im Matthäusevangelium," *Wort und Dienst*, Jahrbuch der Theologischen Schule Bethel (1948), 49-54. The real impact of Bornkamm's work was not felt in the English-speaking world until 1963 when it was translated and published along with the redaction-critical works of his students in Günther Bornkamm, Gerhard Barth, and Heinz Joachim Held, "The Stilling of the Storm in Matthew," *Tradition and Interpretation in Matthew*, trans. Percy Scott (1960; Philadelphia: Westminster, 1963), 52-57.

[4] Gerhard Barth, "Matthew's Understanding of the Law," in *Tradition and Interpretation in Matthew*, 58-164; Heinz Joachim Held, "Matthew as Interpreter of the Miracle Stories," in *Tradition and Interpretation in Matthew*, 165-299.

[5] Wolfgang Trilling, *Das Wahre Israel: Studien zur Theologie des Matthäus-Evangeliums* (3d ed.; München: Kösel-Verlag, 1964); Georg Strecker, *Der Weg der Gerechtigkeit: Untersuchung zur Theologie des Matthäus* (1962; 3d ed.; rpt. Göttingen: Vandenhoeck und Ruprecht, 1971); Reinhart Hummel, *Die Auseinandersetzung zwischen Kirche und Judentum im Matthäusevangelium* (Munich: Kaiser, 1963).

ential work focusing exclusively on the disciples in Matthew's gospel was the redaction-critical work by U. Luz, "The Disciples in the Gospel according to Matthew," first published in German in 1971.[6] Several studies followed Luz's lead.[7] R. Gundry's climactic redaction-critical study in 1982—*Matthew: A Commentary on His Literary and Theological Art*—paid special attention to the disciples.[8] The subtitle of Gundry's commentary indicated one direction in which Matthean studies would take: redaction-critical analysis would give way to literary-critical analysis of Matthew. The transition from redaction-criticism to literary-criticism was made through composition-critical analysis of the disciples, which in part characterized my own first work on Matthew's disciples, published in 1988 as—M. Wilkins, *The Concept of Disciple in Matthew's Gospel: As Reflected in the Use of the Term Μαθητής.*[9]

A significant, new direction was charted through literary-critical, especially narrative, approaches to Matthew's gospel. J. Kingsbury's pioneering work in redaction-critical study of Matthew was followed by pioneering literary-critical study in the late 1970's, 1980's and into the 1990's. He provided early narrative-critical leadership with his work on Matthew's gospel in general[10] and his study of the Matthean disciples in particular.[11] R. Edwards provided a study of the Matthean disciples in 1985 employing exclusively a literary-critical approach in "Uncertain Faith: Matthew's Portrait of the Disciples."[12] The decades of the

[6]Ulrich Luz, "Die Jünger im Matthäusevangelium," *ZNW* 62 (1971), 141-171; trans. and repr. in *The Interpretation of Matthew*, ed. G. Stanton, IRT 3 (1971; London / Philadelphia: SPCK / Fortress, 1983), 98-128 (page numbers cited in this chapter are from the German edition).

[7]E.g., Jean Zumstein, *La Condition du Croyant dans L'Evangile Selon Matthieu*, Orbis Biblicus et Orientalis 16 (Göttingen: Vandenhoeck und Ruprecht, 1977); Andrew H. Trotter, "Understanding and Stumbling: A Study of the Disciples' Understanding of Jesus and His Teaching in the Gospel of Matthew" (Ph.D. dissertation, Cambridge University, 1987).

[8]Robert H. Gundry, *Matthew: A Commentary on His Literary and Theological Art* (Grand Rapids: Eerdmans, 1982), 5-10, and throughout the commentary. Gundry recently issued a second edition of his commentary with a new subtitle: *Matthew: A Commentary on His Handbook for a Mixed Church under Persecution* (2d ed.; Grand Rapids: Eerdmans, 1994). His view of the disciples in Matthew remains basically the same as in the original commentary.

[9]My first work could be described as "composition criticism" in that, on the one hand, I tended to be more concerned with the gospel as a whole than with redactional changes, and on the other hand, with the content of theology rather than with "story." Cf. Michael J. Wilkins, *The Concept of Disciple in Matthew's Gospel: As Reflected in the Use of the Term Μαθητής*, NovTSup 59 (Leiden: E. J. Brill, 1988). For a discussion of the differences in methodologies, see Stephen D. Moore, *Literary Criticism and the Gospels: The Theoretical Challenge* (New Haven: Yale University Press, 1989), 4-7.

[10]E.g., Jack Dean Kingsbury, *Matthew: Structure, Christology, Kingdom* (1975; new ed.; Philadelphia: Fortress, 1989); *Matthew as Story* (2d ed.; rev. and enlarged; Philadelphia: Fortress, 1988).

[11]E.g., Jack Dean Kingsbury, "The Figure of Peter in Matthew's Gospel as a Theological Problem," *JBL* 98 (1979), 67-83; "The Verb AKOLOUTHEIN (To Follow) as an Index of Matthew's View of His Community," *JBL* 97 (1978), 56-73; "The Developing Conflict between Jesus and the Jewish Leaders in Matthew's Gospel: A Literary-Critical Study," *CBQ* 49 (1987), 57-73; "On Following Jesus: The 'Eager' Scribe and the 'Reluctant' Disciple (Matthew 8:18-22)," *NTS* 34 (1988), 45-59.

[12]Richard A. Edwards, "Uncertain Faith: Matthew's Portrait of the Disciples," in *Discipleship in the New Testament*, ed. Fernando F. Segovia (Philadelphia: Fortress, 1985).

1980's and early 1990's produced an increasing stream of literary studies that, at least in part, considered the disciples in Matthew.[13]

A different direction taken in the study of the Matthean disciples was stimulated by sociological and anthropological approaches to the text. In the 1970's M. Hengel and G. Theissen provided early inspiration in Germany through a study of the Jesus movement.[14] The study of the first century social/cultural setting quickly became an international concern.[15] The social dynamic of Jesus and his disciples stimulated also in the decades of the 1980's and early 1990's several exploratory studies of the Jesus movement and the Matthean community, which necessarily involved addressing the Matthean disciples.[16]

Some of the most recent studies of the Matthean disciples attempt to amend the polarization of methods by undertaking a synthesis of various critical disciplines, with special focus on combining historical/social and literary methods.[17] We will examine these attempts shortly, but first we must look at some virtually consensus features of the Matthean disciples.

II. FEATURES OF THE MATTHEAN DISCIPLES

A major result of recent studies in Matthew's gospel is that something of a consensus has been reached concerning certain features of the Matthean disciples.[18] These features gain clarity through an analysis of the disciples in

---

[13]E.g., David R. Bauer, *The Structure of Matthew's Gospel: A Study in Literary Design*, Bible and Literature Series 15 (Sheffield: Almond Press, 1988); Dorothy Jean Weaver, *Matthew's Missionary Discourse*, JSNTSup 38 (Sheffield: JSOT Press, 1990); David B. Howell, *Matthew's Inclusive Story: A Study in the Narrative Rhetoric of the First Gospel*, JSNTSup 42 (Sheffield: JSOT Press, 1990); Jack Dean Kingsbury, ed., "The Gospel of Matthew," A Special Issue of *Interpretation*, Vol. XLVI, No. 4 (October, 1992).

[14]Martin Hengel, *The Charismatic Leader and His Followers*, trans. James Greig (1968; New York: Crossroad, 1981); Gerd Theissen, *Sociology of Early Palestinian Christianity*, trans. John Bowden (1977; Philadelphia: Fortress, 1978).

[15]Cf. also John G. Gager, *Kingdom and Community: The Social World of Early Christianity* (Englewood Cliffs, New Jersey: Prentice-Hall, 1975); Bruce J. Malina, *The New Testament World: Insights from Cultural Anthropology* (Atlanta: John Knox, 1981) and *Christian Origins and Cultural Anthropology: Practical Models for Biblical Interpretation* (Atlanta: John Knox, 1986); Richard A. Horsley, *Jesus and the Spiral of Violence* (San Francisco: Harper & Row, 1987) and *Sociology and the Jesus Movement* (New York: Crossroad, 1989), 95, 137; Bengt Holmberg, *Sociology and the New Testament: An Appraisal* (Minneapolis: Fortress, 1990).

[16]E.g., Amy-Jill Levine, *The Social and Ethnic Dimensions of Matthean Salvation History* (Lewiston, N.Y.: Edwin Mellen, 1988); David E. Orton, *The Understanding Scribe: Matthew and the Apocalyptic Ideal*, JSNTSup 25 (Sheffield: Sheffield Academic Press, 1989); J. Andrew Overman, *Matthew's Gospel and Formative Judaism: The Social World of the Matthean Community* (Minneapolis: Fortress, 1990), 126-140; Anthony J. Saldarini, *Matthew's Christian-Jewish Community* (Chicago: University of Chicago Press, 1994).

[17] See n. 46 below. E.g., Warren Carter, *Households and Discipleship: A Study of Matthew 19-20*, JSNTSup 103 (Sheffield: JSOT, 1994); Stephen C. Barton, *Discipleship and Family Ties in Mark and Matthew*, SNTSMS 80 (Cambridge: Cambridge University Press, 1994); M. Eugene Boring, "The Convergence of Source Analysis, Social History, and Literary Structure in the Gospel of Matthew," SBLSP 33 (Atlanta: Scholars, 1994).

[18] These features are developed in part in the earlier chapters of this book, and receive fuller

Matthew in comparison to the disciples in the other gospel accounts, especially the other synoptics.[19]

A) The small group of disciples around Jesus

Matthew (and Mark) refers only to a small group of Jesus' disciples. This reference is different than Luke's and John's, who refer to a great crowd of Jesus' disciples (cf. Luke 6:17; 10:1; John 6:60, 66). In Matthew's gospel Jesus can meet with the disciples "in a house" (cf. 9:10-19; 9:28; 13:36ff.) and they can all travel together in a single boat (cf. 8:23; 14:22). On several occasions Matthew focuses on a small group of disciples when in Luke and even in Mark there are indications of a larger group of disciples. In Matthew's "Sermon on the Mount" the disciples come away from the crowds (5:1), whereas in Luke's "Sermon on the Plain" we find "a great multitude of His disciples" (Luke 6:17). In Matthew's account of the entry to Jerusalem a "crowd" goes before Jesus (21:9), whereas Luke speaks of a "multitude of the disciples" (Luke 19:37). Matthew, who does not record the commissioning of the twelve, speaks of Jesus summoning the twelve disciples who were also called apostles (10:1), whereas in Mark's and Luke's accounts of the commissioning these apostles were chosen from numerous other disciples (Mark 3:13-19 and Luke 6:13). Matthew tells of Jesus sending out only the twelve (10:5), but Luke speaks of Jesus sending out at another time the seventy (Luke 10:1). In his story, Matthew consistently has only a small group of disciples around Jesus.

B) The "disciples," the "Twelve," and the "apostles"

In keeping with this emphasis upon a small number of disciples, Matthew (and Mark[20]) tends to identify those individuals called "the disciples" with the

---

treatment in Michael J. Wilkins, *Following the Master: A Biblical Theology of Discipleship* (Grand Rapids: Zondervan, 1992), 176-191.

[19]Although I am philosophically in agreement with Graham Stanton (*A Gospel for a New People: Studies in Matthew* [Edinburgh: T.&T. Clark, 1991], ch. 1, 2) that "redaction-critical" work is essential as a background to literary and sociological analysis, the comparative approach I employ differs from typical (not necessarily Stanton's) redaction-critical analysis in at least four ways. First, it requires no particular form of source dependency with reference to the synoptic problem. Second, a comparative approach acknowledges as crucial to Matthew's portrait of the disciples features which are both held in common with the other gospels as well as features which differ. Third, typical redaction-critical approaches tend to focus on bits of evidence at the expense of the larger, narrative whole. Fourth, redaction-critical analysis tends to be driven by the principle of "transparency," which puts the historical-critical cart before the narrative horse. I adopted a comparative approach in my initial study of the Matthean disciples (*The Concept of Disciple in Matthew's Gospel*, 6-9, 129 n.17). Some would call this a composition-critical approach (e.g., Stephen S. Smalley, "Redaction Criticism," *New Testament Interpretation: Essays on Principles and Methods*, ed. I. Howard Marshall (Exeter, England / Grand Rapids: Paternoster / Eerdmans, 1977), 181; Moore, *Literary Criticism and the Gospels*, 4-7.

[20]Robert Meye contends, "Mark describes Jesus' ministry consistently with only the Twelve in view as the disciples of Jesus" (Robert P. Meye, *Jesus and the Twelve* [Grand Rapids: Eerdmans, 1968], 210; see also 98-140, 228-230). The majority of modern scholarship accepts the thesis that at least

titles "the Twelve" and "the apostles."[21] Although Mark refers to Jesus' disciples simply as "the Twelve" on at least eleven occasions, Matthew never uses this title by itself.[22] As an accepted identification in parallel passages, Matthew can use "the disciples" where Mark has "the Twelve" (13:10 cf. Mark 4:10; 18:1 cf. Mark 9:35), he can give a narrative reference "to his twelve disciples" (11:1), and he can occasionally complete the title "the Twelve" with "disciples" to form the longer title "the twelve disciples" (cf. 10:1; 20:17; 26:20). Only Matthew uses this longer title. R. Pesch states that the preference for the name "Matthew" (9:9; cf. 10:3) over "Levi" (Mark 2:14) is another indication that Matthew understands a strict equation of the disciples with the Twelve.[23]

In addition to this use of the title "the Twelve," Matthew and Mark use the title "apostles" only once, in each case referring to the Twelve being sent out on a mission in Palestine (10:2; Mark 6:30). Therefore, Matthew makes a very close identification of the term "disciple" with the title "the Twelve," which is immediately connected with the term "apostles."

C) Disciples, crowds, and religious leaders

Three primary character groups—Jesus' disciples, the crowds and the Jewish leaders—provide a background for Matthew's story of Jesus. The disciples are those who have made a commitment to Jesus. The crowd is the basically neutral group that is the object of Jesus' saving ministry of preaching, teaching, and healing; but as a group the crowd does not exercise faith in him. The Jewish leaders are the antagonists, those responsible for Jesus' crucifixion.[24]

The disciples were Jesus' intimate companions during his earthly ministry (9:19; 14:22) and his fellow-workers in the ministry of caring for the crowds (9:36-37; 14:13ff.; 15:32ff.). Jesus held the disciples up to the crowds as an example of his true family; i.e., those who do the will of the Father (12:49-50). The

---

from Mk 3:13 on Mark identified the terms "disciple" and "the Twelve" with one another. Cf. Rudolf Bultmann, *The History of the Synoptic Tradition*, trans. John Marsh (ET; rev. ed.; New York: Harper and Row, 1963), 344-346; Vincent Taylor, *The Gospel According to St. Mark* (2d ed.; rpt.; Grand Rapids: Baker, 1981), 229-230; Leonhard Goppelt, *Theology of the New Testament*, trans. John E. Alsup, vol. I (Grand Rapids : Eerdmans, 1981), 210; C. S. Mann, *Mark*, AB 27 (Garden City, N.Y.: Doubleday, 1986), 246-251. That this is not a consensus is observed in Hengel, *The Charismatic Leader and His Followers*, 81-82 n. 163.

[21]Luz, "Die Jünger im Matthäusevangelium," 142-143. G. Strecker (*Der Weg der Gerechtigkeit*, 191-198) somewhat differently, sees Matthew making a conscious effort to make the identification complete.

[22]J. Keith Elliott, "*Mathētēs* with a Possessive in the New Testament," *ThZ* 35 (1979), 304. The Matthean lack of the bare title οἱ δώδεκα leads Elliott to conclude that the longer title οἱ δώδεκα μαθηταί is the correct textual reading at 20:17 and 26:20. Cf. Appendix B, n. 1, for a discussion of these texts.

[23]R. Pesch, "Levi-Mätthaus (Mc 2:14/Mt 9:9; 10:3). Ein Beitrag zur Lösung eines alten Problems," *ZNW* 59 (1968), 40-56.

[24]Jack Dean Kingsbury, "The Developing Conflict between Jesus and the Jewish Leaders in Matthew's Gospel: A Literary-Critical Study," *CBQ* 49 (1987), 57-73.

"crowd" is a basically neutral, though curious, group who were not attached in a serious way to Jesus, and who were at various times either positively or negatively oriented toward him.[25] As Jesus preaches, teaches, and heals, the crowd follows him around (e.g., 4:25) but does not exhibit the twin prerequisites of discipleship: cost and commitment. The crowd follows Jesus only in a literal sense, never in the metaphysical sense of accompaniment as one's disciple.[26] The crowd follows him (4:25), appeals for healing (15:29-31), gives acclaim to him (7:28; 21:9,10); but at other times laughs at him (9:23-25), comes to arrest him (26:47), is influenced by the chief priests and elders to ask for Barabbas but to deliver over Jesus (27:20), and finally, as the "people," is responsible for the blood of Jesus (27:24). Therefore, the crowd is a neutral group, out of which come those who will become disciples of Jesus, or else those who will decide against him and ultimately be persuaded to join the religious leaders in opposing Jesus.[27]

D) The disciples understand Jesus' teaching

More than the other evangelists, Matthew emphasizes that the essence of true discipleship lies in individuals who understand and obey Jesus' teaching. On at least three occasions Matthew says that the disciples "understand" Jesus' teaching (16:12; 17:13; 13:51), whereas in parallel passages Mark indicates that the disciples do not understand (Mark 6:52; 8:21; 9:10, 32). Matthew's purpose is different than that of Mark. Mark emphasizes how difficult it was even for the disciples to comprehend the magnitude of Jesus' earthly ministry.[28] Matthew agrees, but he gives a further point: when Jesus teaches, disciples understand. Typically, Matthew shows how difficult it is to understand all that is transpiring in Jesus' earthly ministry, but after Jesus has finished teaching, the disciples finally understand.

The disciples and the crowds were at different points on the spiritual-understanding spectrum. On the occasion of the great discourse on the parables of the mystery of the kingdom, Jesus first directed parables to the crowd (13:1ff.). However, the parables revealed the hard-heartedness of the crowd: they can-

---

[25]T. W. Manson, *The Teaching of Jesus* (2d ed.; Cambridge: Cambridge University Press, 1935), 19.

[26]Kingsbury, "The Verb AKOLOUTHEIN," 61; Albright and Mann, *Matthew*, LXXVII.

[27]Cf. W. D. Davies and Dale C. Allison, *A Critical and Exegetical Commentary on The Gospel According to Saint Matthew*, 3 vols., ICC (Edinburgh: T.&T. Clark, 1988), 1:419-420. *Contra* Robert Gundry, *Matthew*, who is almost a lone voice as he continues to contend even in the second edition of his commentary that Matthew uses "the crowds" and "his disciples" interchangeably (see e.g., p. 66; p. 654 n. 46; *et passim*). See chapter four above for a complete discussion of the disciples and the crowds in Matthew.

[28]Ernest Best, *Disciples and Discipleship: Studies in the Gospel According to Mark* (Edinburgh: T.&T. Clark, 1986); Camille Focant, "L'Incompréhension des Disciples dans le deuxième Evangile," *Revue Biblique* 82 (1985), 161-185; Theodore John Weeden, Sr., *Mark—Traditions in Conflict* (Philadelphia: Fortress, 1971); Werner Heinz Kelber, "Conclusion: From Passion Narrative to Gospel," *The Passion in Mark: Studies on Mark 14-16*, ed. W. H. Kelber (Philadelphia: Fortress, 1976), 153-180.

not understand (13:10-17). As a result, Jesus leaves the crowd to go into the privacy of the house where the disciples become recipients of his teaching (13:10, 36). At the end of instruction to the disciples, they indicate that they now understand (13:51). True disciples will understand Jesus' teaching. Jesus said that knowing the will of God is found as one learns from him and his embodiment of the will of God (9:13; 11:29). The true disciple is the one who is obedient to the will of God (12:49-50), who learns from Jesus' parables (13:51; 24:32), and who is "discipled" by Jesus in the ways of the kingdom (13:52; 27:57).

The relationship between Jesus the teacher and his disciples has received increasing attention. While they should not be relegated to *extras*,[29] the disciples serve a primary purpose in Matthew's gospel of accentuating Jesus in his words and deeds. Matthew's arrangement of his story accentuates Jesus as the effective teacher of his disciples.[30] Each of the major discourses are directed primarily to the disciples (5:1; 10:1; 13:10, 36; 18:1; 23:1; 24:1-3), and teaching segments are often transformed into explicit discipleship-teaching pericopae by inclusion of the term disciple.[31] Matthew wants us to know that Jesus has come to teach the will of God, and the true disciple is the one who understands and obeys. This prepares the reader for the concluding commission, where new disciples are to be taught to obey all that Jesus had commanded the original disciples (28:16-20).

E) With Jesus or against him

Therefore, the disciples are "with Jesus," the Jewish leaders are "against Jesus," and the crowds must make a decision to be either "with him or against him."[32] At first the crowds were amazed at Jesus' teaching (7:28-29) and miracles (9:8), and received Jesus' compassionate attention (9:35-38; 14:13-14), apparently siding with him. But they increasingly demonstrate hardness of heart (cf. 13:2-3; 10-17; 34-36),[33] until at the end the Jewish leaders persuade the crowds to ask for the death of Jesus (27:15-25). From that point the crowds disappear from the narrative. Only disciples are "with Jesus" as his followers after the resurrection.

F) Simon Peter: First among equals

The focus in Matthew is upon Jesus who calls, instructs, and sends disciples out to make more of what he has made them to be. But Matthew presents the disciples as a nameless, faceless, collective unity. Matthew often omits reference

---

[29]As does Hans Conzelmann, *Jesus* (1959; ET; Philadelphia: Fortress, 1973), 34.

[30]Cf. Trotter, "Understanding and Stumbling," 280-281; Hengel, *Charismatic Leader*, 79.

[31]8:21,23; 9:27; 10:42; 12:49; 13:10; 15:23; 16:5 17:6; 17:10; 18:1; 19:10; 21:20; 24:3; 26:8,40,45.

[32]Cf. Mt 12:30; Mk 9:40; Lk 9:50—the saying in Matthew is the more restrictive. Matthew and Luke record the statement, "The one who is not with me, is against me, and the one who does not gather with me scatters" (Mt 12:30/ Lk 11:23). Mark and Luke have the reverse statement, "The one who is not against us, is for us" (cf. Mk 9:40; Lk 9:50), a saying not found in Matthew.

[33] Hence Matthew's community should expect similar kinds of responses to their message; see Warren Carter, "The Crowds in Matthew's Gospel," *CBQ* 55 (1993), 54-67.

to named disciples (e.g., 20:20-28; 24:3; 26:37) or categories in the disciples (e.g., 24:1; 26:18,19), to present the disciples as a unified, nameless group. This Matthean tendency is in line with what Conzelmann states is the tradition's tendency to view the disciples as a collective unity.[34] Interestingly, Matthew stresses this even more than Mark.

Paradoxically though, along with his stress on a nameless, faceless entity, Matthew brings Peter into more prominence, both positively (e.g., 16:15-19) and negatively (16:23—Matthew does not have "seeing disciples"). Matthew concentrates on the disciples as the group of Jesus' followers and Peter as a "typical" individual follower.[35] Against this backdrop of anonymity, Peter stands out starkly because he is the only named disciple who is emphasized. Peter functions in much the same way as do the group of disciples. In his strengths and in his weaknesses he can be an example to Matthew's readers; so, Matthew accentuates the truly human element in Peter. The readers would find much in common with Peter's typically human characteristics. He is much like any ordinary believer with his highs and lows, and, therefore, becomes an example from whom the reader can learn.[36]

This is also the case for the leaders of Matthew's church. Peter is always cast in the gospels as the leader of the disciples. But it is a leadership from within: Peter is first among equals.[37] Therefore, Peter can function as an example for the leaders of Matthew's church. Even as Peter had success and failure as a leader, so the leaders of the church can learn from Peter's experiences. Several of the questions or responses to Jesus voiced on behalf of the disciples by Peter were issues that still speak to the church of Matthew's day (e.g., 15:15; 17:24f.; 18:21).[38]

The church as a whole can identify with the group of disciples, while the individual believer and individual leader within the church can learn from Peter. As Jesus instructs Peter, instruction is provided for the church. The focus is on Jesus who promised to Peter, "I will build My church;" who had called him and corrected him and instructed him. As Jesus worked with and through Peter, so He would with the church.[39]

---

[34]Hans Conzelmann, *History of Primitive Christianity*, trans. John E. Steely (Nashville: Abingdon, 1973), 149.

[35]Jack Dean Kingsbury, "The Figure of Peter in Matthew's Gospel as a Theological Problem," *JBL* 98 (1979), 78. This in contrast to Arlo J. Nau, *Peter in Matthew: Discipleship, Diplomacy, and Dispraise* (Collegeville, MN: Liturgical, 1992), who overplays the negative portrait, the "denigration" of Peter in Matthew's purpose (e.g., 128-134).

[36] Fred W. Burnett, "Characterization and Reader Construction of Characters in the Gospels," *Semeia* 63 (1993), 3-28.

[37] *Contra* Chrys C. Caragounis, *Peter and the Rock,* Beiheft zur Zeitschrift für die neutestamentliche Wissenschaft und die Kunde der älteren Kirche, 58 (Berlin: Walter de Gruyter & Co., 1990), who suggests that πέτρα points away from πέτρος.

[38]Cf. Overman, *Matthew's Gospel and Formative Judaism,* 126-140.

[39] For the most recent discussion of the role of Peter, both historically and in Matthew's gospel, see Pheme Perkins, *Peter: Apostle for the Whole Church* (Columbia, S.C.: University of South Carolina Press, 1994). See also the helpful discussion by Ulrich Luz, "Peter: True Christian or Pope," in *Matthew in History: Interpretation, Influence, and Effects* (Minneapolis: Fortress, 1994), 57-74.

G)   Placement of the commission

The so-called "great commission" (28:16-20) that concludes this gospel encapsulates Matthew's understanding of the purpose of Jesus' ministry. In addition, the placement of the commission at the conclusion of Matthew's gospel has long been recognized as an indication of Matthew's overall purpose for writing his gospel.[40] This commission is especially crucial for our understanding of the disciples' role in Matthew's gospel. Jesus directed his earthly ministry to teaching and training his disciples; now he sends the disciples out to all the nations[41] to make more of what he has made of them.

Implied in the command is both the call to and the process of becoming a disciple.[42] As one comes out from the nations to start life as a disciple, that one grows in discipleship through baptism and through obedience to Jesus' teaching. The participle "baptizing" describes the activity by which the new disciple identifies with Jesus, [43] while the participle "teaching" (διδάσκοντες) introduces the activities by which the new disciple grows in discipleship. We should note that the process of growth does not include only instruction (διδάσκοντες). Growth in discipleship is accomplished as the new disciple obeys (τηρεῖν) what Jesus commanded (ἐνετειλάμην) the original disciples. Obedience was the hallmark of Jesus' disciples (12:49-50).

III.   THE CIRCLE OF DISCIPLES IN MATTHEW'S GOSPEL

Our understanding of the Matthean disciples has been greatly enhanced by the abundance of recent studies. This brief glimpse at the portrait of the Matthean disciples reveals a growing consensus concerning their basic features. Matthew focuses on a small circle of disciples around Jesus, composed primarily of the Twelve, separated from the religious leaders and the crowds to be with Jesus. Jesus teaches these disciples and then he sends them out to make more disciples whom they will baptize and teach.

While these characteristics of the disciples are fairly well accepted by most scholars, a central issue surprisingly remains without consensus. Who is in the circle of disciples and how are they intended to function within Matthew's gospel? The answer to that question is significant, because it provides a major key to the interpretation of Matthew's gospel.

From an historical-critical perspective and a sociological/anthropological perspective, the constitution of the circle of disciples is an important consid-

---

[40]See B. Rod Doyle, "Matthew's Intention as Discerned by His Structure," *Revue Biblique* 95 (1, 1988), 34-54; Bauer, *The Structure of Matthew's Gospel*.

[41] Wilkins, *Following the Master*, 186-191. This mission includes Jews and Gentiles; *contra* David C. Sim, "The Gospel of Matthew and the Gentiles," *JSNT* 57 (1995), 19-48, who suggests that Matthew's community goes only to the Jews.

[42]Grant R. Osborne, *The Resurrection Narratives: A Redactional Study* (Grand Rapids: Baker, 1984), 91; cf. Moisés Silva, "New Lexical Semitisms?," *ZNTW* 69 (1978), p. 256 n. 9.

[43]For discussion of the meaning of baptism as "adherence" see William B. Badke, "Was Jesus a Disciple of John?," *Evangelical Quarterly* 62 (3, 1990), 195-204.

eration because those who make up the circle of disciples provide a "window" of insight to the life and teaching of Jesus, early Christian tradition, the composition of Matthew's community, and master-disciple relationships in general in first century Judaism.

From a literary-critical perspective the constitution of the circle of disciples is important because it provides a "mirror" reflecting both the point of view of the implied author and the identification of the implied reader with characters in Matthew's story. Literary-critical approaches suggest that the implied reader is guided by the implied author to make an evaluative decision about the disciples in their role within the narrative world of the text, and so either to identify with them or not.[44]

Who, then, is in the circle of disciples in Matthew's gospel? An overview of both historical-critical and literary approaches to the Matthean disciples reveals diverse answers to that question. However, since several of these studies were published near the same time, they were not able to inform each other. This has created a wealth of data and insights, yet it has also produced narrowly focused, sometimes disparate, perspectives of the Matthean disciples. In addition, increasing specialization within these disciplines has tended to create a wedge that stifles interaction.[45]

Our purpose here is to lay out the various perspectives of the circle of disciples so that they can be analyzed in the light of one another. Historical-critical and literary-critical studies have developed somewhat independently of one another in the last two decades, yet several of the reconstructions of the circle of disciples are strikingly *similar between* disciplines, while strikingly *dissimilar within* disciplines. One of the most encouraging current movements is seeing Matthean scholars attempt a multi-disciplined approach to Matthew's gospel by combining both literary and historical-critical methods of inquiry.[46]

---

[44]The metaphor of "windows and mirrors," which attempts to describe these approaches, was made popular among literary critics by Murray Krieger, *A Window to Criticism* (Princeton: Princeton University Press, 1964), 3-70. The metaphor has also become well-known among literary critics of biblical literature, especially through the influential work by Norman R. Petersen (*Literary Criticism for New Testament Critics,* GBS, ed. Dan O. Via, Jr. [Minneapolis: Fortress, 1978], 24-25).

[45]Petersen, *Literary Criticism,* 24-25. Matthean scholars still speak of the "potential" for these approaches to be used in a complementary methodology; e.g., Mark Allan Powell, *What Is Narrative Criticism?,* GBS, ed. Dan O. Via, Jr. (Minneapolis: Fortress, 1990), 10; Howell, *Matthew's Inclusive Story,* 259; Jack Dean Kingsbury, "Analysis of a Conversation," *The Social History of the Matthean Community: Cross-Disciplinary Approaches,* ed. David L. Balch (Minneapolis: Fortress, 1991).

[46] E.g., Warren Carter, *Households and Discipleship: A Study of Matthew 19-20;* see particularly ch. 2 where Carter attempts to employ methods drawn from literary criticism (i.e., audience-oriented criticism), historical criticism, and the social sciences (pp. 30-55); so also Stephen C. Barton, *Discipleship and Family Ties in Mark and Matthew,* who aims to employ a multi-disciplinary approach to the text of Matthew's gospel—i.e., traditio-historical, literary, and sociological (cf. esp. pp. 11-22); and M. Eugene Boring, "The Convergence of Source Analysis, Social History, and Literary Structure in the Gospel of Matthew," who claims that a new methodology is needed which aims for a convergence of the disciplines specified in the title of the paper, but who focuses mostly on literary issues.

Although we cannot here develop a methodology that incorporates both disciplines,[47] hopefully this will allow greater dialogue between disciplines and a broader perspective from which further study of the Matthean disciples can proceed. After we lay out the various answers to the question of the circle of the disciples, we will provide some evaluation that will hopefully further the understanding of Jesus' disciples in Matthew's gospel.

A) Historical-critical portraits of the Matthean disciples

The Matthean disciples are said to provide a window into the world of Jesus, the early church, and/or Matthew's community. This conclusion is reached through redaction-critical analysis as well as sociological/ anthropological analyses.

1. Wandering charismatics and sympathizers

Gerd Theissen is an example of a scholar who posits a two-level system within the Jesus movement of the first century. The first level is composed of those whom he calls "sympathizers." The sympathizers were settled, local communities that were sympathetic to Jesus' ministry, but who were not truly the embodiment of Christianity because they remained entangled in the affairs of daily life, including influences from Judaistic regulations of behavior, from internal structures of authority, and from procedures for accepting and rejecting members (i.e. baptism and discipline).[48] Among those sympathizers who welcomed Jesus were Mary and Martha (Luke 10:38ff.), Simon the leper (Mark 14:3ff.) and some women who gave Jesus material support (Luke 8:2f.).

The second level is composed of those whom he calls "wandering charismatics." The wandering charismatic heeded a call to follow Jesus, which included an ethical radicalism of giving up home, family, possessions, and protection. These wanderers were not a marginal phenomenon in the Jesus movement. Rather, they were central to the synoptic presentation of the Jesus movement and formed the leading members of the early church.[49] Those included within this group Theissen calls apostles, prophets, and disciples.

---

[47]The difficulties of such a methodology are rooted especially in the problem of establishing criteria by which one moves from the text to the social situation of Matthew's gospel (cf. Kingsbury, "Analysis of a Conversation"). I have attempted a bi-focal methodology elsewhere: Michael J. Wilkins, "The Interplay of Ministry, Martyrdom, and Discipleship in Ignatius of Antioch," *Worship, Theology, and Ministry in the Early Church*, ed. M.J. Wilkins and T. Paige, JSNTSup 87 (Sheffield: JSOT Press, 1992), and *Following the Master: A Biblical Theology of Discipleship* (Grand Rapids: Zondervan, 1992).

[48]Theissen, *Sociology of Early Palestinian Christianity*, 18-21.

[49]Theissen, *Sociology of Early Palestinian Christianity*, 8-16. A variation on this theme occurs in Leif E. Vaage, *Galilean Upstarts: Jesus' First Followers According to Q* (Valley Forge, PA: Trinity Press International, 1994), who says that Jesus' earliest followers in Galilee looked very much like wandering, homeless, penniless Cynics (cf. 103-106).

The two groups within the Jesus movement had a complementary relationship.

The radical attitude of the wandering charismatics was possibly [sic.?] only on the basis of the material support offered to them by the local communities. To some degree the local communities relieved them of worries about their day-to-day existence. In turn, the local communities could allow themselves to compromise with the world around them because the wandering charismatics maintained such a clear distinction.[50]

Therefore, the first level group was less committed, and they felt free to remain in a condition of compromise with the world because they were not called to the higher level. The more committed wandering charismatics were the only ones called to such a commitment.[51]

Theissen interprets the small group of disciples around Jesus to be an indication that Matthew teaches a two-level system of ethics within the Jesus movement, because only a few can be as committed as were the disciples. Theissen suggests that the incident of the rich young ruler indicates that only through the process of accomplishing a "better righteousness" can one become a disciple. He explains,

In Matthew, the rich young ruler is first asked to observe all the commandments. Only after this is he summoned to become a disciple. His call is put in conditional, rather than apodeictic, terms: 'If you would be perfect, go, sell what you possess and give to the poor . . .' (Matt. 19.21). There are special rules for those who are perfect. The Didache puts it in a similar way: 'If you can bear the whole yoke of the Lord, you will be perfect, but if you cannot, do what you can' (Didache 6.2).[52]

Theissen suggests that traversing a graduated series of norms was necessary to pass from being a compromising local sympathizer to being a fully commit-

---

[50]Theissen, *Sociology of Early Palestinian Christianity*, 22-23.

[51]Cf. also Gerhard Lohfink, *Jesus and Community: The Social Dimension of Christian Faith* (Philadelphia: Fortress, 1984), 31-35, 39-44. Martin Hengel leans in this direction at times as well. He suggests that the "call" to discipleship in Jesus' earthly ministry was directed only to the disciples who followed him around, essentially the Twelve (cf. Hengel, *The Charismatic Leader and His Followers*, 62-63). He does acknowledge that the gospel accounts include others who are called, but says that those passages are part of a later tradition (p. 63). He could avoid this difficulty by recognizing that there is a uniform distinction between the call to the Twelve and the general call to discipleship. He himself seems to recognize this later (cf. pp. 82-83). For criticism of this position, see Richard A. Horsley, *Jesus and the Spiral of Violence: Popular Jewish Resistance in Roman Palestine* (San Francisco: Harper & Row, 1987), 209ff.

[52]Theissen, *Sociology of Early Palestinian Christianity*, 19.

ted wandering charismatic (the "perfect one" implied in 19:21). Therefore, only a small group of radically committed individuals were able to become disciples.[53]

2. Teaching ministers of the church

Several authors postulate that the disciple is a believer who has been called out from among other believers to enter into training for "ministry." Discipleship means to be with Jesus to learn from him how to serve the crowd. Focusing on the distinction between the crowds and the disciples in the gospel of Matthew, P. Minear maintains that because the crowds represent followers of Jesus, his disciples "form a much more limited and specialized group than is usually supposed. They are those chosen and trained as successors to Jesus in His role as exorcist, healer, prophet, and teacher."[54] He says elsewhere, "The author of this Gospel was a teacher who designed his work to be of maximum help to teachers in Christian congregations."[55]

This view of the disciples results from observing the close relationship of the twelve disciples with Jesus in his ministry to the crowds and the opposition to him from the religious leaders. Minear states, "We must remember that Matthew normally applied the term disciple to the twelve only, who were being trained for a special vocation, and not to all believers or followers. . . . The twelve disciples correspond to the prophets, wise men, and scribes who were leaders in the churches of the second generation. The crowds of followers match the lay members of these churches."[56]

D. Orton similarly suggests that the disciples in Matthew's gospel correspond to the "prophets, wise men, and scribes" of 23:34. These are not three separate categories within the church, but rather express various facets or modes of the "prophetic" or "charismatic" role Jesus' disciples exercise in distinction from the scribes and Pharisees of Judaism.[57] Jesus' disciples fulfill the apocalyptic portrayal of the ideal scribe who is divinely inspired to understand the mysteries of God, to be invested with divine authority, and to interpret creatively Jesus' teaching.[58] Orton does not specify the distinction between Jesus' disciples and other groups, as does Minear, but the thrust of his argumentation

---

[53]This same position was held early this century by the influential Matthean scholar, Benjamin W. Bacon, *Studies in Matthew* (New York: Henry Holt, 1930), 87-89, 240.

[54]Paul S. Minear, "The Disciples and the Crowds in the Gospel of Matthew," *Anglican Theological Review,* Supplemental Series, III (March, 1974), 31; cf. also Mark Sheridan, "Disciples and Discipleship in Matthew and Luke," *BibTheolBul* 3 (1973), 235-255; R. Thysman, *Communauté et directives éthiques: la catéchèse de Matthieu,* Recherches et Synthèses: Section d'exégèse, no. 1 (Gembloux: Duculot, 1974).

[55]Paul S. Minear, *Matthew: The Teacher's Gospel* (New York: Pilgrim, 1982), 3-28.

[56]Minear, *Matthew: The Teacher's Gospel,* 11.

[57]David E. Orton, *The Understanding Scribe: Matthew and the Apocalyptic Ideal,* JSNTSup 25 (Sheffield: Sheffield Academic Press, 1989), 155.

[58]Orton, *The Understanding Scribe,* 162-163.

implies that the disciples are those "ideal scribes" who are sent by Jesus to continue his role as Teacher and Maskil. J. Suggs, S. Love, and S. Byrskog similarly refer to the disciples as those who teach the Matthean community.[59]

These scholars suggest that the Matthean disciples are individuals who are separated from the rest of the community to carry out Jesus' role of ministering to the rest of the community, especially through some form of teaching.

3. Ideal examples for the community

An interesting reversal of this view of the disciples is offered by several authors. They suggest that the word disciple is the designation in Matthew's gospel for a Christian or true believer in the Matthean community[60] or group.[61]

Recently, A. Overman has taken the lead of some of these early redaction-critics and has noted the way in which the disciples understand Jesus' teaching. He suggests that the community as a whole, as represented by the disciples, are recipients of Jesus' teaching. The entire community is called to learn from Jesus and obey. The entire community is to be about the business of making disciples and teaching what Jesus commanded the disciples. Overman emphasizes,

> In his idealizing of the disciples and their emergence in the Gospel as followers of Jesus who truly learn, understand, and now *teach* others, Matthew provides a model for the life and behavior of the community member. While Jesus is the hero and agent of God in Matthew's story, it is really the life and ministry of the disciples, centering as it does on learning, understanding, and instruction, which constitutes the primary focus of the member's own ministry in the present. The community members are to identify and emulate the disciples of Jesus as they are portrayed in the Gospel.[62]

---

[59]M. Jack Suggs, *Wisdom, Christology, and Law in Matthew's Gospel* (Cambridge, Mass.: Harvard University Press, 1970), 120-127, who refers to the disciples as the scribes of Matthew's community. Stuart L. Love, "The Place of Women in Public Settings in Matthew's Gospel: A Sociological Inquiry," *BibTheolBull* 24 (1994), 52-65, who sees the disciples as male teachers of the Matthean community (see esp. pp. 56-58). Samuel Byrskog, *Jesus the Only Teacher: Didactic Authority and Transmission in Ancient Israel, Ancient Judaism and the Matthean Community* (Stockholm: Almqvist & Wiksell, 1994) understands the disciples to be a special group who transmit Jesus' teaching to the Matthean community (esp. pp. 234-236).

[60]Variations on this theme are advocated by Luz, "Die Jünger im Matthäusevangelium," 159-165; Hubert Frankemölle, "Amtskritik im Matthäus-Evangelium?," *Bib* 54 (1973), 247-262 and *Jahwebund und Kirche Christi: Studien zur Form- und Traditionsgeschichte des Evangeliums nach Matthäus*, NT Abh 10 (Münster: Verlag Aschendorff, 1974), esp. 84-85, 150ff.; Davies and Allison, *Saint Matthew*, 1:425.

[61] Saldarini (*Matthew's Christian-Jewish Community*) makes a technical distinction between the terms "community" and "group," but he is in line with this view of the disciples in Matthew: "the disciples serve as a transparency for the later Matthean group and symbolize their attitudes and behavior" (p. 85).

[62]Overman, *Matthew's Gospel and Formative Judaism*, 135-136. For a similar view, but without the emphasis upon teaching, see Horsley, *Jesus and the Spiral of Violence*, 231-245.

Two emphases should be noted here. First, Overman stresses the egalitarian nature of the community. Teachers and students are both called disciples within the community. All members are equal as disciples within the community, because all are called to be learners, to understand fully the teachings of Jesus and to fulfill them. Second, Overman accentuates an "idealizing" touch that Matthew has included in his portrait of the disciples. By this he means that the disciples in Matthew have become ideal types; they are prototypes for the follower of Jesus.

> The disciples do not appear to struggle and at times fail in their attempt to follow Jesus, as the Markan disciples seem to do. The disciples in Matthew lack sharp contours, with little or no personal and biographical information provided about them. The disciples are models *(Vorbild)* for the members of the community.[63]

The emphasis upon "community" is especially important for Overman's social reconstruction of the disciples.

B) Literary portraits of the Matthean disciples

Literary portraits do not reveal the same diversity, primarily because most do not go beyond the text. As we noted above, historical-critical approaches to the Matthean disciples tend to be guided by the principle of transparency as a first-line approach to the text. Literary critics, as a rule, try to understand the disciples within the developing narrative before making judgments about how the disciples would have been understood in the implied author's and/or reader's community.

Several recent literary studies of Matthew's gospel advocate portraits of the disciples that are similar, yet different, from one another. These studies are similar in that they view the disciples as the character group with which the reader can most easily identify. They also tend to view the disciples as virtually co-extensive with the Twelve. The difference lies in the way in which they understand the role of the Twelve (exemplary or not) and the identity of the implied reader.

1. Disciples as the model for teachers

A. Lincoln suggests that, although the central character of Matthew's story is Jesus, a great impact may be felt from the narrative if one focuses upon the role of the disciples.[64] Through focusing on the disciples, attention can also be

---

[63]Overman, *Matthew's Gospel and Formative Judaism,* 135. He acknowledges the influence of Frankemölle (*Jahwebund und Kirche Christi,* 256) in this direction, but several other early redaction-critics also tended toward "idealization;" e.g., Trilling, *Das Wahre Israel,* 50, 159, 213 and Zumstein, *La Condition du Croyant dans L'Evangile Selon Matthieu,* 81.

[64]Andrew T. Lincoln, "Matthew—A Story for Teachers?," *The Bible in Three Dimensions: Essays in Celebration of Forty Years of Biblical Studies in the University of Sheffield,* ed. David J. A. Clines, Stephen E. Fowl, and Stanley E. Porter, JSOT Sup 87 (Sheffield: Sheffield Academic Press, 1990),105-106.

paid to the implied readers. The implied readers' situation is most similar to that of the disciples, not to that of Jesus, although they are expected to share the point of view of Jesus. Therefore, the readers identify more with the disciples as characters in the story, whose portrayal includes development and uncertainty, than with Jesus, who is in many ways more static and fulfills his narrative role or task in a fairly straightforward and unambiguous fashion.[65]

Lincoln argues, specifically, that the story of the disciples with their developing understanding yet uncertain faith is a story of those who are being prepared to teach with authority among all nations. This perspective of the disciples is noted especially at two climactic points—the first at the close of the major period of public ministry in 16:13-20 and the second at the ending of the narrative as a whole in 28:16-20.[66] Matthew's gospel is of course a story about Jesus, but the best way to appreciate the impact of this particular story on the reader is to focus on the implied readers and their relationship to Jesus' disciples. Throughout the narrative, the implied author tells his story about Jesus in such a way as to prepare his implied readers to be missionary teachers among the nations, carrying on the task of Jesus the teacher. Lincoln states,

> In preparation for this task they have been thoroughly acquainted with Jesus' teaching, mission, and authoritative presence.... Matthew's gospel should be read as a story for would-be teachers. The implied author is in effect saying to the implied reader, 'So, you want to be a teacher? Let me tell you a story.'[67]

Therefore, Lincoln suggests that the reader is understood to be some form of "teacher."

2. Jesus as the model for discipleship

D. Howell takes a different tack toward the disciples. Howell agrees that within the narrative the disciples are a character group that is both positively and negatively oriented toward Jesus. However, he emphasizes that the implied reader is informed by other characters, minor and major, and is privy to information and teaching communicated to him/her by the implied author through the narrative, but not available to the disciples. This leads Howell to declare that

---

[65]Lincoln, "Matthew—A Story for Teachers?," 105-106.

[66]Lincoln, "Matthew—A Story for Teachers?," 106. While not emphasizing "teaching" to the same degree, the disciples function as a role model for the church leaders of Matthew's community in the view of Andries Van Aarde, *God-With-Us: The Dominant Perspective in Matthew's Story, and other Essays*, Hervormde Teologiese Studies Supplement 5 (Pretoria: Periodical Section of the Nederduitsch Hervormde Kerk van Afrika, 1994), 87-104

[67]Lincoln, "Matthew—A Story for Teachers?," 124-125. This conclusion is quite similar to the assumption Paul Minear makes about actual authors and readers in the social setting of Matthew's community; Paul S. Minear, *Matthew: The Teacher's Gospel* (New York: Pilgrim, 1982), 3-28.

the disciples as a character group in the plotted story of the Gospel must therefore not be seen as a cipher for the members of Matthew's church, for the Matthean implied reader is an entity distinct from the disciples. The disciples neither embody all the values and norms commended by the implied author, nor do they know everything about Jesus that would help the Matthean church members and other actual readers respond properly to Jesus.[68]

For Howell, discipleship does not mean membership in a character group, but concerns the values that Jesus and the implied author commend to their hearers/readers. The implied reader is able to learn from all the characters, both negatively and positively, what it means to follow Jesus.[69] Because of this, the implied reader is superior to every character in the story, and is driven to Jesus as the only worthy model for discipleship. Although both the disciples and Jesus are placed in similar circumstances, it is only Jesus who responds in a uniformly positive manner. Hence, "The parallels between Jesus and his disciples in Matthew drive the implied reader to look to Jesus and his behavior rather than to the disciples to learn what it means to live a life obedient to God. Jesus becomes a model of righteousness."[70]

3. The actual and the ideal

Another Matthean scholar who has applied literary-critical methodologies to the text of Matthew's gospel is D. Patte.[71] Patte takes special note of the small group of individuals called disciples in Matthew's gospel. That small group is what he describes as the "actual disciples" (e.g., Peter, Andrew, James, and John), who must be distinguished from the "ideal disciples" of Jesus' teaching.[72] The "actual disciples" are those who follow Jesus around and are the ones who have the responsibility to "make disciples of all nations" (28:19), yet since they are to teach these new disciples to obey all that Jesus taught them, they are making "ideal disciples," not more of what they are as "actual disciples." At times Matthew brings into the narrative characters who function as "ideal disciples" since they embody what Jesus had taught (e.g., the women who followed and served Jesus).[73] The reader is to learn from the example of the "ideal disciples" of Jesus' teaching, leading them in turn to be "scribes 'trained' for the kingdom of heaven." Patte claims that "Matthew's entire Gospel is aimed at training scribes 'for the kingdom.'"[74]

---

[68]Howell, *Matthew's Inclusive Story*, 235. Howell here follows the insightful study of the minor characters by Janice Capel Andersen, "Matthew: Gender and Reading," *Semeia* 28 (1983), 23-24.

[69]Howell, *Matthew's Inclusive Story*, 250-251.

[70]Howell, *Matthew's Inclusive Story*, 247.

[71]Daniel Patte, *The Gospel According to Matthew: A Structural Commentary on Matthew's Faith* (Philadelphia: Fortress, 1987).

[72]Patte, *The Gospel According to Matthew*, 119, 136 n. 16.

[73]Patte, *The Gospel According to Matthew*, 391ff.

[74]Patte, *The Gospel According to Matthew*, 199, 105 n. 6.

4. Examples for Christians

J. Kingsbury has long recognized the small group that constitutes the disciples in Matthew's gospel. In early redaction-critical works he suggested that Matthew generally identifies the disciples with the Twelve, although he does not exclude the existence of other disciples, and that this small group of disciples is representative of Christians or the church of Matthew's day.[75] In his later, literary-critical works Kingsbury continues to suggest that the reader identifies with the disciples and learns from them, both positively and negatively. For example, when looking at the "eager scribe" and the "reluctant disciple" in Matthew 8:18-22, Kingsbury draws "cardinal tenets of discipleship" from which the reader is to learn.[76] Kingsbury suggests that the disciples as a group are a single, primary character within Matthew's story. They are "round" because they not only possess numerous traits (like Jesus), but because they possess traits that conflict.

> Because the disciples possess conflicting traits, the reader is invited, depending on the attitude Matthew as narrator or Jesus takes toward them on any given occasion, to identify with them or to distance himself or herself from them. It is through such granting or withholding of approval on cue, therefore, that the reader becomes schooled in the values that govern the life of discipleship in Matthew's story.[77]

For Kingsbury the small group of disciples constitutes the example from which the reader learns. The reader is a member of the community.[78]

IV. NAMED AND UNNAMED DISCIPLES

A) Specificity and ambiguity

This survey of recent portraits of the disciples in Matthew's gospel underscores the obvious conclusion that the term "disciples" (μαθηταί) designates a major character group within Matthew's story. The disciples are Jesus' intimate companions (9:23), the recipients of his teaching (5:1,2), his brother, sister, and mother (12:46-50), and those who share his outreach to the crowds (9:35-38). Throughout much of Matthew's story, the spotlight focuses on the Twelve, who at many points appear to be virtually co-extensive with the character group "the disciples." The Twelve give specificity to the character group.

---

[75]Jack Dean Kingsbury, *The Parables of Jesus in Matthew 13: A Study in Redaction-Criticism* (London: SPCK, 1969), 41-43. Cf. also, Jack Dean Kingsbury, "AKOLOUTHEIN," 56-73.

[76]Kingsbury, "On Following Jesus," 57.

[77]Kingsbury, *Matthew as Story,* 13-14.

[78] So also David R. Bauer, "The Major Characters of Matthew's Story: Their Function and Significance," *Interpretation* XLVI (October, 1992), 361-363.

However, from the very first occurrence of "disciples" in Matthew's gospel (5:1), a measure of ambiguity surrounds the term. There we find Matthew stating that Jesus saw the crowd, went up on the mountain, and "his disciples came to him." Up to this point, the word 'disciple' has not been used, and only four individuals have been called to follow Jesus (4:18-22; note that they are not yet specified in the text by the term "disciples"). Moreover, at this juncture it is difficult indeed to identify the disciples with the Twelve because at least one of them, Matthew the tax-collector, does not meet Jesus until 9:9. Who then are the disciples of 5:1? Davies and Allison answer the question in this way:

> The problem of 5.1 simply warns us that our evangelist was not overly interested in informing his readers as to who exactly was on the mountain when Jesus spoke. In 5.1, the unspecified disciples, who must be a group larger than the four of 4.18-22, are—and this is the key point— contrasted with the crowd and so represent the church. The disciples, in other words, stand for the faithful; they are transparent symbols of believers. So the sermon on the mount is spoken directly to Matthew's Christian readers.[79]

We may question the validity of bringing in the issue of transparency this early in the narrative, and we may want to clarify the identification of the readers, but the emphasis upon ambiguity surrounding "the disciples" is important. While the Twelve are often assumed to be implied in the use of the term, this is not uniform. Matthew speaks specifically of disciples other than the Twelve (8:21),[80] he implies a wider circle of disciples (10:24, 25, 42),[81] and he acknowledges through a related verb the existence of a disciple other than the Twelve, Joseph of Arimathea (27:57).[82] Matthew generally identifies the disciples with the Twelve, but he does not exclude the existence of other disciples. Unless Matthew states otherwise, he refers to the Twelve when he refers to the disciples, but he does not mean to imply that Jesus has no other disciples. The ambiguity surrounding this nameless, faceless circle of disciples creates elasticity. It allows the term to function as a referent for the inner circle of Twelve, yet allows it to expand to imply a wider circle of disciples as well.

---

[79]Davies and Allison, *Saint Matthew*, 1:425.

[80]Kingsbury, "On Following Jesus," 45-59. Gundry understands this disciple to be a professing, although false disciple (Gundry, *Matthew*, 150-152; so also in his article "On True and False Disciples in Matthew 8:18-22," *NTS* 40 [1994] 433-41. For an attitude toward the scribe (Mt 8:19-20) which differs from Kingsbury, see Jarmo Kiilunen, "Der Nachfolgewillige Schriftgelehrte: Matthäus 8. 19-20 im Verständnis des Evangelisten," *NTS* 37 (1991), 268-279.

[81]Weaver, *Matthew's Missionary Discourse*, 16.

[82]Cf. Michael J. Wilkins, "Named and Unnamed Disciples in Matthew: A Literary-Theological Study," *SBLSP* 30, ed. Eugene H. Lovering, Jr. (Atlanta: Scholars Press, 1991), 432ff.; Przybylski, *Righteousness in Matthew and His World of Thought*, 108-110. So also Luz, "Die Jünger im Matthäusevangelium," 158.

B) Disciples and crowds

We saw earlier in our discussion of the features of the Matthean disciples that
Jesus' objective was to make disciples from the crowd. The sign of faith is when
one responds to Jesus' teaching by coming out of the crowd to call Jesus "Lord"
(cf. 8:18, 21; 17:14,15).[83] As an individual comes out of the crowd, he or she
chooses either to exercise faith and become a believer, or chooses not to believe
(cf. 19:16-22). The crowd is a neutral group, out of which come those who will
become disciples of Jesus, or else those who will decide against him and ultimately
be persuaded to join the religious leaders in opposing Jesus.[84] After the crowd is
persuaded by the religious leaders to call for Jesus to be crucified (27:15-24), the
crowd disappears from Matthew's narrative. Only the disciples and the religious
leaders continue to play a part in the narrative until the end of the story.

Now the character contrast between those who are either with Jesus or against
him is complete. There is no more middle ground. The introduction of the
exemplary minor characters in 27:54-61—the Roman centurion, the Galilean
women followers, the Jewish rich man Joseph of Arimathea—implies that they
are "with Jesus." These minor characters do not have the name μαθητής applied
to them, hence they stand outside of the developing plot.[85] The "disciples"
appear in contrast to the religious leaders (27:64; 28:13); the "disciples" will be
the object of the resurrection announcement by the women (28:7, 8, 9), and
as the "eleven disciples" they meet Jesus in Galilee to receive the final commission (28:16).[86] However, the appearance of these exemplary minor characters opens the way for them to be understood as models of "discipleship."
What is the relationship of the terms "disciples" and "discipleship"?

C) Disciples and discipleship

We have noted that the "disciples" are a major character group within
Matthew's story. They are Jesus' intimate companions (9:23), the recipients of
his teaching (5:1, 2), his brother, sister, and mother (12:46-50) and those who
share his outreach to the crowds (9:35-38). The Twelve normally are in view,
but we see hints of disciples other than the Twelve from the very first occurrence of the term (5:1), and at various other points within the narrative (e.g.,
8:21; 10:24, 25, 42; 13:52; 27:57). The label "the disciples" implies the Twelve,
but it has enough ambiguity so that the character group is a bit more elastic.

---

[83]Günther Bornkamm, "End-Expectation and Church in Matthew," in *Tradition and Interpretation in Matthew*, 40-41.

[84]Cf. Davies and Allison, *Saint Matthew*, 1:419-420.

[85] See Wilkins, "Named and Unnamed Disciples in Matthew," esp. 432ff.

[86]Among the evangelists, only Matthew has a nameless group of disciples in the resurrection
narrative. The women appear by first name and then as a category of unnamed, faithful minor
characters (28:1-10), but the disciples appear only as a nameless, faceless group of "disciples" (28:7,
8, 13), "brothers" (28:10), and "eleven disciples" (28:16); see Dorothy Jean Weaver, "Matthew 28:1-
10," *Interpretation* XLVI (October, 1992), 398-402.

Since the disciples represent those who have come out of the crowd to be with Jesus, they become examples for the reader. As they respond with obedience to Jesus' call (4:18-22; 9:9), as they come to him for instruction (13:10, 36), as they are rebuked for little faith (17:19-20) and self-aggrandizement (18:1-4), and as they recover from apostasy (26:56) to meet with the risen Jesus (28:16), the reader can empathize with their situation.

"Discipleship" is obviously related to the developing life of the disciples, but it is more expansive as well. Discipleship is exemplified in those who are not named as "disciples." Since the norms and values of the implied author are lodged with the narrator and Jesus, no one group embodies the author's ideology nor serves as a single role model. Not only the character group called "disciples" have come out of the crowd to be with Jesus. J. Andersen suggests,

> This is why some actual readers call characters like the Canaanite woman and women at the cross and tomb disciples. If 'discipleship' is defined as the norms and values the implied author wishes the implied reader to adopt rather than as membership in the character group, then various male and female characters embody aspects of discipleship.[87]

The reader stands in a position whereby all characters in the story are evaluated. In addition to the disciples, therefore, a variety of minor characters contribute to the reader's understanding of discipleship. The faith (8:2; 8:5-13; 9:2; 17:14), humble station (18:2; 19:13), and servanthood (26:7; 27:55-60) of various minor characters act as a foil for the disciples, which is a positive example of discipleship for the readers. The use of impersonal, indefinite, or inclusive pronouns and expressions in Jesus' teaching is another sign that Matthew extends the invitation and demands of discipleship beyond characters in the story.[88] The women at the cross and the tomb also mirror faithful discipleship and point to a significant theme of inclusion in Matthew's gospel: inclusion of poor and rich, Jew and Gentile, fisherman and tax-collector, male and female.[89]

The opposition to Jesus by the religious leaders, the rejection of Jesus by the crowds, and the apostasy of the disciples also become examples from which the implied reader is led to learn. In the end, one who comes out of the nations to be made a disciple to Jesus will be baptized and taught to obey all that Jesus has commanded (28:18-20).

> In the Great Commission the narrator and implied reader are placed in the same temporal position as the disciples; the time of mission following the resurrection and prior to the consummation of the age.... With

---

[87]Andersen, "Matthew: Gender and Reading," 23-24.

[88]Howell, *Matthew's Inclusive Story*, 221-226.

[89] Elaine Mary Wainwright, *Towards a Feminist Critical Reading of the Gospel according to Matthew*, BZNW 60 (Berlin: Walter de Gruyter, 1991), 338-339.

this backward glance at all Jesus has taught, the disciples and the implied reader are challenged to accept Jesus' call and be obedient to his teaching as it has been narrated in the Gospel.[90]

V. TENSION IN THE MATTHEAN DISCIPLES

Matthew's gospel has long been understood to operate within an inherent tension, usually noted in the particularistic/universalistic dimension.[91] Tension also characterizes Matthew's view of the disciples. The conflicting historical-critical and literary-critical portraits of the disciples described above reflect that tension. A few concluding observations may help identify some of the causes of the tensions in the disciples' portraits.

First, although Matthew's worldview tends to limit the term "disciple" to the male inner circle around Jesus, especially the Twelve, the values embodied in various minor characters and teachings strain those boundaries to include within the discipleship relationship to Jesus those not normally expected. Wealth, occupation, gender, purity, ethnicity, and family ties are less important than the stance characters take in relationship to Jesus.[92]

Second, Matthew intends his readers to understand that the Christian life is equivalent to being "with Jesus." We need to distinguish between the disciples as a character group within the narrative and the circle of disciples implied elsewhere in the minor characters and in the open-ended invitations offered to the crowds, hints and reflections of the unique form of discipleship Jesus had instituted.[93]

Third, distinctions among Jesus' followers relate to function, not spiritual standing or commitment. The either-or nature of being with Jesus or against him excludes a two-class system of believers within Matthew's gospel. All those "with Jesus" are equal in relationship to him. Therefore, disciples are equal to those minor characters who have also come out of the crowd to be with Jesus. However, Matthew does focus on the *function* of the disciples, which sets them aside for particular service. This tension is seen in the Twelve, who were called both disciples (10:1) and apostles (10:2). As disciples they were equal to others who were with Jesus, yet as apostles they had a unique salvation-historical role (10:5-6; 19:28).

Fourth, although Jesus is the ultimate model of the norms and values com-

---

[90]Howell, *Matthew's Inclusive Story*, 226.

[91]Cf., e.g., Roger Mohrlang, *Matthew and Paul: A Comparison of Ethical Perspectives*, SNTSMS 48 (Cambridge: Cambridge University Press, 1984), passim.; Ulrich Luz, *Matthew 1-7: A Commentary*, trans. W. C. Linss (1985; Minneapolis: Augsburg, 1989), 73-99.

[92]Andersen, "Matthew: Gender and Reading," 20-23; Wainwright, *Towards a Feminist Critical Reading of the Gospel according to Matthew*, 338-339; D. A. Carson, "Matthew," *EBC* 8 (Grand Rapids: Zondervan, 1984), 596-597.

[93] Leon Morris, "Disciples of Jesus," *Jesus of Nazareth: Lord and Christ. Essays on the Historical Jesus and New Testament Christology*, ed. Joel B. Green and Max Turner (Grand Rapids: Eerdmans, 1994), 125-127.

mended by the reader, the experience of the readers is closer to that of those who are with Jesus (the disciples and others who come out of the crowd). Jesus' life is uniformly obedient to God; the disciples learn how to be obedient. The stumbling disciples provide an example for the readers of how Jesus would work with them.[94]

On the one hand, discipleship does not mean membership in the character group of disciples in Matthew's gospel. Discipleship is held open for all those who come out of the crowd to be with Jesus. All character groups are evaluated by the reader (both implied and real) as to their relationship to Jesus. The climactic commission that concludes Matthew's story offers a discipleship relationship to all persons, offering wholeness and knowledge of God in the presence of Jesus.[95]

On the other hand, discipleship is understood as a priority of the kingdom of God which is not limited to any particular group—national, ethnic or familial. Rather, Jesus declares that spiritual union in the family of God takes precedence. Discipleship to Jesus relativizes all other ties of allegiance by forming an eschatological family composed of those who do the will of God (Mt 12:46-50).[96]

---

[94] Trotter, "Understanding and Stumbling," 280ff.

[95] See the chapter "The Recovery of Wholeness in Matthew" in Dan O. Via, Jr., *Self-Deception and Wholeness in Paul and Matthew* (Minneapolis: Fortress, 1990), 99-138.

[96] Michael J. Wilkins, "Brother/Brotherhood," *Anchor Bible Dictionary*, ed. David Noel Freedman (Garden City: Doubleday, 1992), I:782-783; Barton, *Discipleship and Family Ties in Mark and Matthew*, 225.

APPENDIX A

Classification of Usage of Μαθητής in Plato's Writings according to Non-Sophistic and Sophistic Material

Non-Sophistic Material			Sophistic Material		
No. of Occurrence	Work	Type of Occurrence	No. of Occurence	Work	Type of Occurence
3	*Euthyphron*	GL, TA	1	*Apology*	TS
2	*Cratylus*	L	4	*Theaetetus*	TS
1	*Symposium*	GL, TA	2	*Sophist*	TS
1	*Lysis*	GTA	6	*Euthydemus*	TS
1	*Menexenus*	TA	2	*Gorgias*	TS
2	*Republic*	GTA	6	*Meno*	TS
5	*Laws*	GTA			
3	*Epistles*	GTA			
1	*Phaedo*	GL			
2	*Phaedrus*	GL			
*1	*Laches*	GL	*1	*Laches*	TS
*2(3)	*Protagoras*	GL	*1(2)	*Protagoras*	TS
Total-24(25)			Total-23(24)		

The type of occurrence is classified according to the following usage
GL   = General, Learner
GTA = General, with leanings toward Technical, Adherent
TA   = Technical, Adherent
TS   = Technical, Sophistic pupil
   These classifications are fairly obvious from the usage in the respective contexts, but there is some overlapping from general to technical usage. The significant feature is that there is very little overlapping from Sophistic to non-Sophistic usage.
   *Works where there is a use of the term in both Sophistic and non-Sophistic contexts, but with no overlapping from one contextual use to the other.

APPENDIX B

Comparison of the Occurrences of Μαθητής in Matthew with the Sources

Μαθητής found in Mt	Inclusions in Markan tradition	Inclusions in Q (Lk) tradition	Unique Matthean material	Expansions from context and source	Shared with Q (Lk)	Shared with Mark
1) 5:1						6:20
2) 8:21		9:59				
3) 8:23	4:36					
[8:25]¹	[4:38]					
4) 9:10					2:15	
5) 9:11					2:16	
6) 9:14a					2:18a	
7) 9:14b				2:18b		
8) 9:19	5:24					
9) 9:37⁴	6:32 conflation	10:2				
10) 10:1	6:7					
11) 10:24						6:40
12) 10:25				Mt 10:24 & Lk 6:40		
13) 10:42	9:41					
14) 11:1			X			
15) 11:2						7:18
16) 12:1					2:23	
17) 12:2	2:24					
18) 12:49	3:34					
19) 13:10	4:10					
20) 13:36			X?	Mt 13:10 & Mk 4:34?		
21) 14:12					6:29	
22) 14:15					6:35	
23) 14:19a					6:41	
24) 14:19b				Mt 14:19a & Mk 6:41		
25) 14:22					6:45	
26) 14:26	6:49					
27) 15:2					7:5	

28) 15:12			7:17
29) 15:23	7:25		
30) 15:32			8:1
31) 15:33			8:4
32) 15:36a			8:6
33)15:36b		Mt 15:36a	
		& Mk 8:6	
34) 16:5	8:14		
35) 16:13			8:27
36) 16:20	8:30		
37) 16:21	8:31		
38) 16:24			8:34
39) 17:6	9:7-8		
40) 17:10	9:10-11		
41) 17:13	9:13		
42) 17:16			8:18
43) 17:19			9:28
44) 18:1	9:33-34		
45) 19:10	10:12		
46) 19:13			10:13
47) 19:23			10:23
48) 19:25	10:26		
49) 20:17[1]	10:32		
50) 21:1			11:1
51) 21:6	11:4		
52) 21:20	11:20		
53) 22:16	12:13		
54) 23:1	12:37		
55) 24:1			13:1
56) 24:3	13:3		
57) 26:1[3]	14:1?	X?	
58) 26:8	14:4		
59) 26:17			14:12
60) 26:18			14:14
61) 26:19			14:16
62) 26:20[1]	14:17		
63) 26:26	14:22		
64) 26:35	14:31		
65) 26:36			14:32
66) 26:40	14:37		
67) 26:45	14:41		
68) 26:56	14:50		
69) 27:64		X	
70) 28:7			16:7
71) 28:8		Mt 28:7	
		& Mk 16:8	

72) 28:13   X
73) 28:16   X
Totals
72-73   31-32[1,3,4]   2   4-6[2,3]   4-5[2]   27   3

Notes to Appendix B

[1] There are three questionable occurrences of μαθητής in Mt. After examination, the conclusion is that two of the three are to be accepted, giving a total of seventy-three times the term appears in Mt.

8:25 - The Nestle text excludes the term, while the apparatus shows it to be found in various texts, including the TR. οἱ μαθηταί is found in Koine φ al; οἱ μαθηταὶ αὐτοῦ in C W Θ λ pm b g' (q) sy; and the term is excluded in B Sin pc lat. The textual evidence is not strong enough to warrant inclusion of the term.

20:17 - Metzger's *Textual Commentary* judged that the term should be included in brackets, allowing for the possibilities that either the copyists added the term to the more primitive expression οἱ δώδεκα, or that the present passage was assimilated to the text of Mark (10:32) (pp. 51-52). The term is omitted in Sin D L Z Θ 1.892 pc sy[s.c.] bo, but it is included in B C Koine W 085.13.118.209pm lat sy[p] sa. Along with Matthew's characteristic addition of μαθητής to be more specific, his customary practice is to complete the Markan title οἱ δώδεκα with μαθηταί. With the majority of the UBS committee, the judgement is that the copyists assimilated the text to Mk; therefore the term should be included (cf. Gundry, *Matthew*, p. 400; Elliott, "Mathétés," p. 304).

26:20 - The external evidence weighs in favor of excluding the term in the view of Metzger's *Textual Commentary* (p. 64) (p[37]vid, 45 vid B Koine D Γ λ φ 565. 700pm sy[s]; Eus). But internal evidence, that Matthew habitually completes οἱ δώδεκα with μαθητής (10:1; 11:1; 20:17) and that Matthew always qualifies οἱ δώδεκα with a noun, possessive case, or possessive pronoun, and certain external evidence (Sin A L W Δ Θ φ (074). 33 al lat sy sa bo), have produced the conclusion in this paper that the term should be included (cf. Gundry, Ματτηεω, p. 526; Elliott, "Mathétés", p. 304).

[2] The occurrence of the term in 13:36 could conceivably be understood as an inclusion in unique Matthean material (apparently Gundry takes it as such; *Matthew*, p. 271), as is found in Aland's *Synopsis* (sec. 131, p. 183). Although the section as a whole is unparalleled, the use of the term is most likely derived from Mk 4:34 and linked with an explanatory interpretation intended for the disciples, as in 13:24-30. It is therefore classified as an "expansion."

[3] Although the occurrence of the term in 26:1 could be referred to as an insertion, it is more correctly understood as an inclusion in unique Matthean material. This is because it is a part of the stereotyped Matthean formula which is used to conclude his major discourses and introduce narrative material.

[4] The occurrence in 9:37 is counted as a Q inclusion for statistical purposes, but in reality it is a conflation of Mk 6:34 and Lk 10:2.

APPENDIX C

Comparison of the Occurrence of Μαθητής in Mark with the Parallel
Usage in Matthew

Occurrence of μαθητής in Mk	Usage in Mt
1) 2:15	9:10 included
2) 2:16	9:11 included
3) 2:18a	9:14a included, but limits to John's disciples
4) 2:18b	9:14b omitted second reference to John's disciples
5) 2:18c	9:14c omitted reference to disciples of Pharisees
6) 2:18d	9:14d included
7) 2:23	12:1 included
8) 3:7	12:15 omitted
9) 3:9	12:15 omitted - narrative section omitted
10) 4:34	13:34 expanded in 13:36
11) 5:31	9:21-22 omitted - narrative section omitted
12) 6:1	13:54 omitted
13) 6:29	14:12 included
14) 6:35	14:15 included
15) 6:41	14:19 included
16) 6:45	14:22 included
17) 7:2	15:1 omitted - narrative section omitted
18) 7:5	15:2 included
19) 7:17	15:12,15 included, but change of reference
20) 8:1	15:32 included
21) 8:4	15:33 included
22) 8:6	15:36 included
23) 8:10	15:39 omitted
24) 8:27a	16:13a omitted
25) 8:27b	16:13b included
26) 8:33	16:23 omitted
27) 8:34	16:24 included
28) 9:14	17:14 omitted

29) 9:18	17:16 included
30) 9:28	17:19 included
31) 9:31	17:22 omitted
32) 10:10	19:9 omitted; or a change of reference to 19:10
33) 10:13	19:13 included
34) 10:23	19:23 included
35) 10:24	19:23, cf. v. 25 - omitted, and change of reference
36) 10:46	20:29 omitted
37) 11:1	21:1 included
38) 11:14	21:19 transfers to v. 20, and refers to Peter
39) 12:43	pericope omitted (cf. 23:39, 24:1)
40) 13:1	24:1 included, but change of reference
41) 14:12	26:17 included
42) 14:13	26:18a omitted, then changes reference in v. 19
43) 14:14	26:18b included
44) 14:16	26:19 included
45) 14:32	26:36 included
46) 16:7	28:7 included

APPENDIX D

Comparison of the Occurrence of Μαθητής in Q-material (in Luke) with
the Parallel Usage in Matthew

Occurrence of μαθητή in Q-material in Luke	Usage in Matthew
1) 6:20	5:2 included
2) 6:40	10:24 included
3) 7:18	11:2a omitted
4) 7:19	11:26 included
5) 10:23	13:16 included
6) 12:22	6:25 omitted
7) 14:26	10:37 omitted
8) 14:27	10:38 omitted

APPENDIX E

Listing of Occurrences of the Name Peter in all Four Gospels, Showing Chronological Advancement and Parallels to Matthew

Matthew	*Mark*	*Luke*	*John*
			1:40 Simon Peter
			1:41 Simon
			1:42 Simon
			1:44 Peter
1) 4:18 Simon called Peter	1:16 Simon		
2) 8:14 Peter	1:29 Simon	4:38a Simon	
	1:30 Simon	4:38bSimon	
	1:36 Simon		
		5:3 Simon	
		5:4 Simon	
		5:5 Simon	
		5:8 Simon Peter	
		5:10a,b Simon (2x)	
3) 10:2 Simon called Peter	3:16 Simon, he surnamed Peter	6:14 Simon, also named Peter	
		7:40 Simon	
		7:43 Simon	
		7:45 Simon	
		8:45 Peter	
	5:37 Peter	8:51 Peter	
			6:8 Simon Peter
4) 14:28 Peter			
5) 14:29 Peter			
			6:68 Simon Peter
6) 15:15 Peter			
7) 16:16 Simon Peter	8:29 Peter	9:20 Peter	
8) 16:17 Simon Bar-Jona			
9) 16:18 Peter			
10) 16:22 Peter	8:32 Peter		

11) 16:23 Peter	8:33 Peter		
12) 17:1 Peter	9:2 Peter	9:28 Peter	
		9:32 Peter	
13) 17:4 Peter	9:5 Peter	9:33 Peter	
14) 17:24 Peter			
15) 17:25 Simon			
16) 18:21 Peter			
		12:41 Peter	
17) 19:27 Peter	10:28 Peter	18:28 Peter	
	11:21 Peter		
	13:3 Peter		
		22:8 Peter	
			13:6 Simon Peter
			13:6 Peter
			13:8 Peter
			13:9 Simon Peter
			13:24 Simon Peter
			13:36 Simon Peter
			13:37 Peter
18) 26:33 Peter	14:29 Peter	22:31 Simon, Simon	
19) 26:35 Peter		22:34 Peter	
20) 26:37 Peter	14:33 Peter		
21) 26:40 Peter	14:37 Peter, "Simon"		
			18:10 Simon Peter
			18:11 "Peter"
22) 26:58 Peter	14:54 Peter	22:54 Peter	18:15 Simon Peter
			18:16 Peter...Peter
			18:17 Peter
			18:18 Peter
23) 26:69 Peter	14:66 Peter	22:55 Peter	
	14:67 Peter		18:25 Simon Peter
24) 26:73 Peter	14:70 Peter	22:58 Peter	18:26 Peter
		22:60 Peter	18:27 Peter

25) 26:75 Peter   14:72 Peter   22:61
                                   Peter...Peter
                                   [22:62 Peter]
              16:7 Peter
                                              20:2 Simon Peter
                   24:12 [Peter]   20:3 Peter
                                              20:4 Peter
                                              20:6 Simon Peter

                   24:34 Simon
                                              21:2 Simon Peter
                                              21:3 Simon Peter
                                              21:7
                                              Peter...Simon
                                              Peter
                                              21:11 Simon
                                              Peter
                                              21:15 Simon
                                              Peter, "Simon"
                                              21:16 "Simon"
                                              21:17
                                              "Simon"...Peter
                                              21:20 Peter
                                              21:21 Peter

APPENDIX F

Pericopes Concerning Peter in the Four Gospels (Using Aland's *Synopsis* parallels)

	Mt	Mk	Lk	Jn
1 First followers, Peter named Cephas				1:40-44*
2 Call of first disciples	4:18	1:16-20*		
3 Mother-in-law healed	8:14	1:29-30*	4:38	
4 Informed of a larger area of ministry		1:36-38*		
5 Miraculous catch			5:1-11*	
6 Appointment of the Twelve	10:2	3:16*	6:14	
7 Hemorrhaging woman			8:45*	
8 Jesus heals Jairus' daughter		5:37*	8:51	
9 Brother of Andrew				6:8*
10 Walks on water	14:28-31*			
11 Asks for an explanation of the parable	15:15*			
12 Confession in response to defecting disciples				6:68*
13 Confession at Ceasarea Philippi	16:16	8:29*	9:20	
14 Jesus' pronouncement	16:17-19*			
15 Peter as the stumblingstone	16:22-23	8:32-33*		
16 Transfiguration	17:1	9:2*	9:28	
17 Sleeping at Transfiguration			9:32*	
18 Building tabernacles at Transfiguration	17:4	9:5*	9:33	
19 Payment of Temple tax	17:24-27*			
20 Question about forgiveness	18:21*			
21 Question about parable			12:41*	
22 Question about reward for sacrifice	19:27	10:28*	18:28	
23 Comment on cursed fig tree		11:21*		
24 Question about Temple		13:3*		
25 Prepare Passover			22:8*	
26 Jesus washes feet in Upper Room				13:6-10*
27 Request identity of betrayer				13:24ff.*
28 First prediction of denials			13:31-34*	13:36-38*
29 Second prediction of denials	26:33-35	14:29-31*		
30 Garden of Gethsemane with Jesus	26:37	14:33*		
31 Asleep in the Garden	26:40	14:37*		
32 Cuts off high priest's ear				18:10-11*
33 Follows the arrested Jesus	26:58	14:58*	22:54	18:15-16*
34 Denials	26:69-74	14:66-72*	22:55-60	18:17, 25-27*
35 Remembers prediction of denials	26:75	14:72*	22:61-62*	
36 Angel instructs women to tell Peter of resurrection		16:7*		
37 Runs to empty tomb			[24:12*]	20:2-10
38 Jesus appears to Peter			24:34*	
39 Jesus' dialogue with Peter in Galilee				21:1-25*

*Indicates the primary source for reference to Peter.

Traditions unique to each gospel:

Mt - 5 (14:28-29; 15:15; 16:17-19; 17:24-27; 18:21)

Mk - 4 (1:36; 11:21; 13:3; 16:7)

Lk - 8 or 9 (5:1-11; 8:45; 9:32; 12:41; 22:8; 22:31-34; 22:61; [24:12]; 24:34)

Jn - 8-11 (1:40-44; 6:8; 6:68; 13:6-10; 13:24ff.; 13:36-37?; 18:10-11; 18:15-16?; 18:17?; 18:25-27?; 20:2-10; 21:1-25)

Traditions shared in the Synoptics: 15

Of the 15, Mark includes all; Mt has 14; Lk has 10.

Mt and Lk never share against Mk.

Therefore, there is only one time Mt omits a Markan saying (Mk 5:37) which Lk also includes (Lk 8:51) (cf. Mt 9:22; healing Jairus' daughter).

There is no occurrence of Peter in "Q" material.

Occurrences (and Absences) of the Name Simon Peter in Matthew as Compared to the Sources

	Usage in in Mt	Inclusion of name in Mk	Inclusion of Material in Mk	Inclusion of Material in Q (Lk)	Material Unique to Matthew	Shared with Mark	Absent from Mark
1	4:18	1:16				1:16	
2	8:14	1:29					1:29
	cf. 8:17f.						1:36
	cf. 9:23f.						5:37
3	10:2					3:16	
4	14:28		6:50-51				
5	14:29-31			6:50-51			
6	15:15-16		17:17				
7	16:16	8:29				8:29	
8	16:17		8:29-30				
9	16:18-19		8:29-30				
10	16:22					8:32	
11	16:23					8:33	
12	17:1					9:2	
13	17:4					9:5	
14	17:24				X		
15	17:25				X		
16	18:21-22			X			
17	19:27f.					10:28	
	cf. 21:20					11:21	
	cf. 24:3					13:3	
18	26:33				14:29		
19	26:35	14:31					
20	26:37				14:33		
21	26:40				14:37		
	cf. 26:40b					14:37b	
22	26:58				14:54		
23	26:69				14:66		
24	26:73				14:70		
25	26:75				14:72		
	cf. 28:7						16:7

APPENDIX H

Usage of the Name Simon Peter in Mark Compared with the Usage in
Matthew

Usage in Mark	Usage in Matthew
1:16 Simon	4:18 adds "called Peter"
1:29 Simon	8:14 changes Simon to Peter
1:30 Simon	*8:14 consolidates the narrative and omits the name Simon
1:36 Simon (39 in Aland)	*Mt omits this pericope (1:35-38)
3:16 Simon he surnamed Peter	10:2 Simon, who is called Peter
5:37 Peter	*cf. 9:23-25; omits reference to Peter and others entering with Jesus
8:29 Peter	16:16 makes it the full "Simon Peter"
8:32 Peter	16:22 Peter
8:33 Peter	16:23 Peter
9:2 Peter	17:1 Peter
9:5 Peter	17:4 Peter
10:28 Peter	19:27 Peter
11:21 Peter	*cf. 21:20; reference to Peter is omitted and changed to disciples marvelling and asking
13:3 Peter	*cf. 24:3; reference to Peter, James, and Andrew omitted and changed to disciples asking
14:29 Peter	26:33 Peter
14:33 Peter	26:37 Peter, but Mt omits mention of James and John
14:37a Peter	26:40a Peter
14:37b "Simon"	*26:40b omits address to Simon
14:54 Peter	26:58 Peter
14:66 Peter	26:69 Peter
14:67 Peter	*26:69 omits mention of woman seeing Peter warming himself
14:70 Peter	26:73 Peter
14:72 Peter	26:75 Peter
16:7 Peter	*cf. 28:7; omits mention of angel specifying Peter to be told

*Indicates an omission of a reference to Peter found in Mark.

Matthew includes 16 of Mark's 24 references to Peter
Matthew omits 8 of Mark's references to Peter
 4 omissions are *incidental* (8:14 [Mk 1:30]; 8:18 [Mk 1:36]; 26:40b [Mk 14:37b]; 26:69 [Mk 14:67]).
 4 omissions are *significant* (9:23-25 [Mk 5:37]; 21:20 [Mk 11:21]; 24:3 [Mk 13:3]; 28:7 [Mk 16:7]),

Chronological Graph of Peter in Matthew:
Viewed Positively and Negatively

BIBLIOGRAPHY

Aberbach, M. *The Relations Between Master and Disciple in the Talmudic Age. Essays Presented to Chief Rabbi Israel Brodie on the Occasion of His Seventieth Birthday.* Edited by H. J. Zimmels, J. Rabbinowitz, and I. Finestein. Vol. I. Jew's College Publications New Series, No. 3. London: Soncino, 1967.

Abogunrin, S. O. "The Three Variant Accounts of Peter's Call: A Critical and Theological Examination of the Texts." *NTS* 31 (1985), 587-602.

Aland, Kurt, ed. *Synopsis Quattuor Evangeliorum.* 10th ed. Stuttgart: Biblia-Druck, 1977.

Albright, W. F. and Mann, C. S. *Matthew.* AB. Vol. 26. Garden City, N.Y.: Doubleday, 1971.

Albright, William F. *Samuel and the Beginnings of the Prophetic Movement: The Goldenson Lecture of 1961.* In *Interpreting the Prophetic Tradition: The Goldenson Lectures 1955-1966.* The Library of Biblical Studies. Edited by H. O. Orlinsky. New York: Hebrew Union College, 1969.

Alcorn, Wallace A. "Biblical Concept of Discipleship as Education for Ministry." Unpublished Ph.D. dissertation. New York University, 1974.

Allen, Willoughby C. *A Critical and Exegetical Commentary on the Gospel According to S. Matthew.* ICC. 3d ed. Edinburgh: T.&T. Clark, 1912.

Andersen, Janice Capel. "Matthew: Gender and Reading." *Semeia* 28 (1983), 23-24.

Arndt, William F. and Gingrich, F. Wilbur. *A Greek-English Lexicon of the New Testament and Other Early Christian Literature.* 4th ed.; 1952. Rpt. Chicago: University of Chicago Press, 1974.

Audet, J. P. "Origines comparées de la double tradition de la loi et de la sagesse dans le proche-orient ancien. " *International Congress of Orientalists.* Vol. I. Moscow, 1960.

Bacon, Benjamin W. *Studies in Matthew.* New York: Henry Holt, 1930.

Badke, William B. "Was Jesus a Disciple of John?" *Evangelical Quarterly* 62 (3, 1990), 195-204.

Baird, J. Arthur. *Audience Criticism and the Historical Jesus.* Philadelphia: Westminster, 1969.

Balch, David L., ed. *The Social History of the Matthean Community: Cross-Disciplinary Approaches.* Minneapolis: Fortress, 1991.

Bammel, Ernst. *Jesu Nachfolger, Nachfolgeüberlieferungen in der Zeit des frühen Christentums.* Studia Delitzschiana, Dritte Folge 1. Heidelberg: Lambert Schneider, 1988.

Banks, Robert. *Jesus and the Law in the Synoptic Tradition.* Cambridge: At the University Press, 1975.

Barr, James. *The Semantics of Biblical Language.* Oxford: Oxford University Press, 1961.

Barrett, C. K. *The Gospel According to St. John.* 1955; 2d ed. Philadelphia: Westminster, 1978.

Barth, Gerhard. "Matthew's Understanding of the Law. " *Tradition and Interpretation in Matthew.* Translated by Percy Scott. Philadelphia: Westminster, 1963.

Barton, Stephen C. *Discipleship and Family Ties in Mark and Matthew.* SNTSMS 80. Cambridge: Cambridge University Press, 1994.

Bauer, David R. *The Structure of Matthew's Gospel: A Study in Literary Design.* Bible and Literature Series 15. Sheffield: Almond Press, 1988.

Beare, Francis Wright. *The Gospel According to Matthew.* HNTC. San Francisco: Harper and Row, 1981.

Benoit, P. *Matthieu fascicule, Bible de Jérusalem.* Paris: Cerf, 1961.

Best, Ernest. *Disciples and Discipleship: Studies in the Gospel According to Mark.* Edinburgh: T.&T. Clark, 1986.

_____. *Following Jesus : Discipleship in the Gospel of Mark.* JSNTSS 4. Sheffield: JSOT Press, 1981.

_____. *Mark: The Gospel as Story.* Studies of the New Testament and Its World. Edited by John Riches. Edinburgh: T.&T. Clark, 1983.

_____. "The Role of the Disciples in Mark." *NTS* 23 (1977), 377-401.

Best, Thomas F. "Transfiguration and Discipleship in Matthew." Unpublished Ph.D. dissertation. Graduate Theological Union, Berkeley, Calif., 1974.

Betz, Hans Dieter. *Nachfolge und Nachahmung Jesu Christi im Neuen Testament.* BHT 37. Tübingen: Mohr/Siebeck, 1967.

Black , C. Clifton. *The Disciples according to Mark: Markan Redaction in Current Debate.* JSNTSup 27. Sheffield: JSOT, 1989.

Blair, E. P. *Jesus in the Gospel of Matthew: A Reappraisal of the Distinctive Elements of Matthew's Christology.* Nashville: Abingdon, 1960.

Blank, Josef. "The Person and Office of Peter in the New Testament." Translated by Erika Young. *Truth and Certainty.* Edited by Edward Schillebeeckx and Bas van Iersel, Concilium, Vol. 83. New York: Herder and Herder, 1973.

Blass, F. and Debrunner, A. *A Greek Grammar of the New Testament and Other Early Christian Literature.* Translated and revised by Robert W. Funk. 9th-10th German ed. Chicago: University of Chicago Press, 1961.

Boling, Robert G. *Judges.* AB. Vol. 6A. Garden City, N.Y.: Doubleday and Company, 1975.

Bonitz, H. *Index Aristotelicus.* 2d ed. Graz: Akademische Druck- U. Verlagsanstalt, 1955.

Bonnard, Pierre. *L'Evangile Selon Saint Matthieu.* CNT I. 1963; 2d ed. Neuchâtel: Delachaux & Niestlé, 1970.

Borg, Marcus J. *Jesus: A New Vision. Spirit, Culture, and the Life of Discipleship.* San Francisco: Harper and Row, 1987.

Borgen, Peder. "Philo of Alexandria." *Jewish Writings of the Second Temple Period.* Edited by M. E. Stone. Compendia Rerum Iudaicarum ad Novum Testamentum. Section Two. Assen/Philadelphia: Van Gorcum/Fortress, 1984.

Bornkamm, Günther. "Die Sturmstillung im Matthäusevangelium." *Wort und Dienst. Jahrbuch der Theologischen Schule Bethel* (1948), 49-54.

_____. "End-Expectation and Church in Matthew." *Tradition and Interpretation in Matthew.* Translated by Percy Scott. Philadelphia: Westminster, 1963.

_____. *Jesus of Nazareth.* 1959; ET. London: Hodder and Stoughton, 1960.

_____. "The Authority to 'Bind' and 'Loose' in the Church in Matthew's Gospel: The Problem of Sources in Matthew's Gospel." *Jesus and Man's Hope.* Vol. I. Edited by D. G. Buttrich. Pittsburgh: Pittsburgh Theological Seminary, 1970.

_____. "The Stilling of the Storm in Matthew." *Tradition and Interpretation in Matthew.* Translated by Percy Scott. Philadelphia: Westminster, 1963.

Bornkamm, Günther; Barth, Gerhard; and Held, Heinz Joachim. *Tradition and Interpretation in Matthew.* Translated by Percy Scott. 1963; rpt. Philadelphia: Westminster, n.d.

Bowersock, G. W. *Greek Sophists in the Roman Empire.* Oxford: Clarendon, 1969.

Bright, John. *Jeremiah.* AB. Vol. 21. 2d ed. Garden City, N.Y.: Doubleday and Co., 1965.

Broadus, John A. *Commentary on the Gospel of Matthew. An American Commentary on the New Testament.* 1886; rpt.; Valley Forge: Judson, n.d.

Brown, Colin. "πέτρα." *NIDNTT*. Vol. 3. Translated and edited by Colin Brown. Grand Rapids: Zondervan, 1978.

_____. "The Teaching Office of the Church." *The Churchman* 83 (1969), 184-196.

Brown, Francis S.; Driver, R.; and Briggs, Charles A. *A Hebrew and English Lexicon of the Old Testament.* ET; Oxford: Clarendon, 1974.

Brown, Raymond E. *The Gospel According to John (I-XII).* AB. Vol. 29. Garden City, N.Y.: Doubleday, 1966.

Brown, Raymond E.; Donfried, Karl P.; and Reumann, John, eds. *Peter in the New Testament.* Minneapolis: Augsburg; and New York: Paulist, 1973.

Brown, Schuyler. "The Mission to Israel in Matthew's Central Section (Mt 9:35—11:1)." *ZNW* 69 (1977), 73-90.

_____. "The Two-fold Representation of the Mission in Matthew's Gospel." *ST* 31(1977), 21-32.

Bruce, Alexander B. "The Synoptic Gospels: TO KATA MATQAION." *The Expositor's Greek Testament.* N.d.; rpt. Grand Rapids: Eerdmans, 1976.

Bruce, F. F. *Jesus and Christian Origins Outside the New Testament.* Grand Rapids: Eerdmans, 1974.

Bryce, G. E. *A Legacy of Wisdom: The Egyptian Contribution to the Wisdom of Israel.* Lewisburg: Bucknell University Press, 1979.

Buchanan, George Wesley. "The Use of Rabbinic Literature for New Testament Research." *BTB* 7 (1977), 110-112.

Buchsel, Friedrich. "δέω (λύω)." *TDNT.* Vol. II. Grand Rapids: Eerdmans, 1964.

Bultmann, Rudolf. *History of the Synoptic Tradition.* Translated by John Marsh. Rev. ed. 1963. New York: Harper & Row, 1976.

Burgess, J. A. *A History of the Exegesis of Matthew 16:17-19 from 1781 to 1965.* Ann Arbor: Edwards Brothers, 1976.

Burnett, Fred W. "Characterization and Reader Construction of Characters in the Gospels." *Semeia* 63 (1993), 3-28.

Byrskog, Samuel. *Jesus the Only Teacher: Didactic Authority and Transmission in Ancient Israel, Ancient Judaism and the Matthean Community.* Coniectanea Biblica NT Series 24. Stockholm: Almqvist & Wiksell International, 1994.

Caird, G. B. *The Language and Imagery of the Bible.* Philadelphia: Westminster, 1980.

Caragounis, Chrys C. *Peter and the Rock.* Beiheft zur Zeitschrift für die neutestamentliche Wissenschaft und die Kunde der älteren Kirche, 58. Berlin: Walter de Gruyter & Co., 1990.

Carlisle, Charles R. "Jesus' Walking on Water: A Note on Matthew 14:22-23." *NTS* 31 (1985), 151-155.

Carmignac, Jean. "Concordance hébraïque de le 'Règle de la Guerre'." *RQ* 1 (1958), 7-49.

Carson, Donald A. *Exegetical Fallacies.* Grand Rapids: Baker, 1984.

_____. "Gundry on Matthew: A Critical Review." *TrinJ* NS 3 (1982), 71-91.

_____. "Matthew." *The Expositor's Bible Commentary.* Vol. 8. Edited by Frank E. Gaebelein. Grand Rapids: Zondervan, 1984.

Carter, Warren. "The Crowds in Matthew's Gospel." *CBQ* 55 (1993), 54-67.

_____. *Households and Discipleship: A Study of Matthew 19-20.* JSNTSup 103. Sheffield: JSOT, 1994.

Charlesworth, James H. *The Old Testament Pseudepigrapha.* 2 vols. Garden City, N.Y.: Doubleday, 1983-1985.

Childs, Brevard S. *Introduction to the Old Testament as Scripture.* Philadelphia: Fortress, 1979.

Clarke, M. L. *Higher Education in the Ancient World.* Albuquerque: University of New Mexico Press, 1971.

Clements, R. E. *Prophecy and Tradition.* Atlanta: John Knox, 1975.

Conzelmann, Hans. *History of Primitive Christianity.* Translated by John E. Steely. Nashville: Abingdon, 1973.

_____. *Jesus.* 1959; ET. Philadelphia: Fortress, 1973.

Cook M. J. "Interpreting 'Pro-Jewish' Passages in Matthew". *HUCA* 54 (1983), 135-146.

Cooke, G. A. *A Critical and Exegetical Commentary on the Book of Ezekiel.* ICC. Edinburgh: T.&T. Clark, 1936.

Cope, O. Lamar. *Matthew: A Scribe Trained for the Kingdom of Heaven.* CBQMS 5. Washington, D.C.: The Catholic Biblical Association of America, 1976.

Cranfield, C. E. B. *The Gospel According to St. Mark.* The Cambridge Greek Testament Commentary. Rev. and rpt. Cambridge: Cambridge University, 1972.

Crenshaw, James L. *Old Testament Wisdom: An Introduction.* Atlanta: John Knox, 1981.

_____. "Review of Les écoles et la formation de la Bible dans l'ancien Israël, by André Lemaire." *JBL* 103 (1984), 630-632.

_____, ed. *Studies in Ancient Israelite Wisdom.* New York: KTAV, 1976.

Crosby, Michael H. *House of Disciples: Church, Economics, and Justice in Matthew.* Maryknoll: Orbis, 1988.

Cullmann, Oscar. *Peter: Disciple —Apostle —Martyr. A Historical and Theological Essay.* ET; 2d ed. Philadelphia: Westminster, 1962.

_____. "Πέτρος, Κηφᾶς," *TDNT.* Vol. VI. Grand Rapids: Eerdmans, 1968.

Culpepper, R. Alan. *The Johannine School: An Evaluation of the Johannine-School Hypothesis Based on an Investigation of the Nature of Ancient Schools.* SBLDS 26. Missoula: Scholars, 1975.

Cundall, Arthur E. *Judges: An Introduction and Commentary. In Judges, Ruth.* By Arthur E. Cundall, Leon Morris. *TOTC.* Downers Grove/London: Inter-Varsity, 1968.

Daube, David. "Responsibilities of Master and Disciples in the Gospels." *NTS* 19 (1972-3), 1-15.

Dauber, Kenneth. "The Bible as Literature: Reading Like the Rabbis." In *Reader-Response Approaches to Biblical and Secular Texts.* Edited by Robert Detweiler. *Semeia* 31 (1985), 27-47.

Davies, W. D. *The Setting of the Sermon on the Mount.* 1964; new ed. Cambridge: University Press, 1977.

Davies, W. D. and Dale C. Allison. *A Critical and Exegetical Commentary on The Gospel According to Saint Matthew.* 3 vols. ICC. Edinburgh: T.&T. Clark, 1988.

de Vaux, Roland. *Ancient Israel: Its Life and Institutions.* Translated by John McHugh. New York: McGraw-Hill, 1961.

Demsky, A. "Education (Jewish) in the Biblical Period." *Encyclopedia Judaica.* Jerusalem, 1971, VI.

Dibelius, Martin. *From Tradition to Gospel.* Translated by Bertram Woolf. Rev. 2d ed; Greenwood, S.C.: Attic, 1971.

Dietrich, W. *Das Petrusbild der lukanischen Schriften.* Stuttgart: Verlag Katholisches Bibelwerk, 1972.

Dodd, C. H. *Historical Tradition in the Fourth Gospel.* Cambridge: Cambridge University Press, 1963.

Donaldson, Terence L. *Jesus on the Mountain: A Study in Matthean Theology.* JSNTSS 8. Sheffield: JSOT, 1985.

Dover, K. J., ed. *Ancient Greek Literature.* Oxford: Oxford University Press, 1980.

————. "Comedy." In *Ancient Greek Literature.* Edited by K. J. Dover. Oxford: Oxford University Press, 1980.

Doyle, B. Rod. "Matthew's Intention as Discerned by His Structure." *Revue Biblique* 95 (1, 1988), 34-54.

Drazin, Nathan. *History of Jewish Education from 515 B.C.E. to 220 C.E. (During the Periods of the Second Commonwealth and the Tannaim).* Baltimore: Johns Hopkins, 1940.

Driver, G. R. *The Judean Scrolls.* Oxford: Basil Blackwell, 1965.

Dunn, James D. G. *Jesus and Discipleship.* Understanding Jesus Today. Edited by H. C. Kee. Cambridge, UK: Cambridge University Press, 1992.

————. "Pharisees, Sinners, and Jesus." *The Social World of Formative Christianity and Judaism.* Essays in tribute to Howard Clark Kee. Philadelphia: Fortress, 1988.

————. *Unity and Diversity in the New Testament: An Inquiry into the Character of Earliest Christianity.* 1977; 2d ed.; London/ Philadelphia: SCM/ Trinity, 1990.

Dupont, J. "Le point de vue de Matthieu dans le chapitre des paraboles." *L'Évangile selon Matthieu: Rédaction et théologie.* Edited by M. Didier. Gemblou: J. Duculot, 1972.

Edwards, Richard Alan. *A Concordance to Q.* SBLSBS 7. Missoula, Mont.: Scholars, 1975.

————. *Matthew's Story of Jesus.* Philadelphia: Fortress, 1985.

————. "Uncertain Faith: Matthew's Portrait of the Disciples." In *Discipleship in the New Testament.* Edited by Fernando F. Segovia. Philadelphia: Fortress, 1985.

Eichrodt, Walther. *Theology of the Old Testament.* 2 vols. Translated by J. A. Baker. The Old Testament Library. 6th German ed. Philadelphia: Westminster, 1961.

Elliott, J. Keith. "Mathetes with a Possessive in the New Testament." *TZ* 35 (1979), 300-304.

Ellis, Peter F. *Matthew: His Mind and His Message.* Collegeville, Minn.: Liturgical Press, 1974.

Ellison, H. L. *The Prophets of Israel: From Ahijah to Hosea.* Grand Rapids: Eerdmans, 1969.

Eppstein, V. "Was Saul Also among the Prophets?" *ZAW* 81 (1969), 287-304.

Erickson, Richard J. "Biblical Semantics, Semantic Structure, and Biblical Lexicology: A Study of Methods, with Special Reference to the Pauline Lexical Field of Cognition." Unpublished Ph.D. dissertation, Fuller Theological Seminary, 1980.

Fabry, H. J. "*chbhl.*" *TDOT.* Vol. IV. Edited by G. J. Botterweck and H. Ringgren. Translated by D. E. Green. 1975-1977. Grand Rapids: Eerdmans, 1980.

Feiler, Paul Frederick. "The Stilling of the Storm in Matthew: A Response to Günther Bornkamm." *JETS* 26 (1983), 399-406.

Feldmeier, Reinhard. "Die Darstellung des Petrus in den synoptischen Evangelien." In *Das Evangelium und die Evangelien.* Edited by Peter Stuhlmacher. WUNT 28. Tübingen: J. C. B. Mohr (Paul Siebeck), 1983.

Filson, Floyd V. *The Gospel According to St. Matthew.* Black's New Testament Commentaries. 1960; 1971; rpt. London: Adam and Charles Black, 1977.

Fitzmyer, Joseph. "Aramaic *Kepha'* and Peter's Name in the New Testament." In *To Advance the Gospel.* New York: Crossroad, 1981.

Focant, Camille. "L'Incompréhension des Disciples dans le deuxième Évangile." *Revue Biblique* 82 (1985), 161-185.

Fohrer, Georg. "σοφία." *TDNT.* Vol. VII. Grand Rapids: Eerdmans, 1971.

Forestell, J. T. *Targumic Traditions and the New Testament: An Annotated Bibliography with a New Testament Index.* SBLAS 4. Chico, Calif.: Scholars Press, 1979.

France, R. T. "Jewish Historiography, Midrash, and the Gospels." *Gospel Perspectives.* Vol. 3: Studies in Midrash and Historiography. Edited by R. T. France and D. Wenham. Sheffield: JSOT, 1983.

France, R. T. and Wenham, David, eds. *Gospel Perspectives.* 3 vols. Sheffield: JSOT, 1980-1983.

Frankemölle, Hubert. "Amtskritik im Matthäus-Evangelium?" *Bib* 54 (1973), 247-262.

_____. *Jahwebund und Kirche Christi. Studien zur Form- und Traditionsgeschichte des Evangeliums nach Matthäus.* NT Abh 10. Münster: Verlag Aschendorff, 1974.

Freeman, Hobart E. *An Introduction to the Old Testament Prophets.* Chicago: Moody, 1968.

Friedrich, Gerhard. "προφήτης." *TDNT.* Vol. VI. Grand Rapids: Eerdmans, 1968.

Friedrich, Johannes H. "Wortstatistik als Methode am Beispiel der Frage einer Sonderquelle im Matthäusevangelium." *ZNW* 76 (1985), 29-42.

Fuller, Reginald. *The Foundations of New Testament Christology.* New York: Scribner's, 1965.

Gager, John G. *Kingdom and Community: The Social World of Early Christianity.* Prentice-Hall Studies in Religion Series. Englewood Cliffs, N.J.: Prentice-Hall, 1975.

Garland, David E. *The Intention of Matthew 23.* NovTSup LII. Leiden: E. J. Brill, 1979.

Gerhardsson, Birger. *Memory and Manuscript: Oral Tradition and Written Transmission in Rabbinic Judaism and Early Christianity.* Translated by Eric Sharpe. Lund: C. W. K. Gleerup, 1961.

_____. *The Mighty Acts of Jesus According to Matthew.* Lund: C. W. K. Gleerup, 1979.

Gerstenberger, Erhard. "Covenant and Commandment." *JBL* 84 (1965), 51-65.

_____. "The Woe-Oracles of the Prophets." *JBL* 81 (1962), 249-263.

_____. *Wesen und Herkunft des 'apodiktischen' Rechts.* WMANT 20. Neukirchen-Vluyn: Neukirchener, 1965.

Glasson, T. Francis. "Anti-Pharisaism in St. Matthew." *JQR* 51 (1960-1961), 130-137.

Goldin, J. "Several Sidelights of a Torah Education in Tannaite and Early Amorical Times." In *Ex Orbe Religionum: Studia Geo Widengren. Pars Prior. Studies in the History of Religions.* Supplements to Numen. XXI. Leiden: E. J. Brill, 1972.

Goppelt, Leonhard. *Theology of the New Testament.* Vol. 1. Translated by J. A. Alsup. Edited by J. Roloff. Grand Rapids: Eerdmans, 1981.

Gottwald, Norman K. *The Hebrew Bible—A Socio-Literary Introduction.* Philadelphia: Fortress, 1985.

Goulder, Michael D. *Midrash and Lection in Matthew.* London: SPCK, 1974.

Gowan, Donald E. *Bridge Between the Testaments: A Reappraisal of Judaism from the Exile to the Birth of Christianity.* Pittsburgh Theological Monograph Series, No. 14. Edited by Dikran Hadidian. 1976; 2d ed. Pittsburgh: Pickwick, 1980.

Grant, Michael. *Saint Peter: A Biography.* New York: Scribner, 1994.

Greenberg, Moshe. *Ezekiel 1-20.* AB. Vol. 22. Garden City, N.Y.: Doubleday, 1983.

Griffiths, Michael. *The Example of Jesus.* The Jesus Library. Downers Grove, Ill.: Inter-Varsity, 1985.

Grundmann, Walter. *Das Evangelium nach Matthäus.* THKNT. Vol. I. Berlin : Evangelische Verlagsanstalt, 1968.

Guelich, Robert A. "The Gospel Genre." In *Das Evangelium und die Evangelien.* Edited by Peter Stuhlmacher. WUNT 28. Tübingen: J. C. B. Mohr (Paul Siebeck), 1983).

_____. *The Sermon on the Mount: A Foundation for Understanding.* Waco, Tex.: Word, 1982.

Gundry, Robert H. *Matthew : A Commentary on His Literary and Theological Art.* Grand Rapids: Eerdmans, 1982.

_____. *Matthew: A Commentary on His Handbook for a Mixed Church under Persecution.* 2d ed. Grand Rapids: Eerdmans, 1994.

_____. "On Interpreting Matthew's Editorial Comments." *WTJ* 47 (1985), 319-328.

_____. "On True and False Disciples in Matthew 8:18-22." *NTS* 40 (1994), 433-441.

_____. *The Use of the Old Testament in St. Matthew's Gospel: With Special Reference to the Messianic Hope.* NovT Sup XVIII. Leiden: E. J. Brill, 1967.

Guthrie, Donald. *New Testament Introduction.* 3d ed. Downers Grove: Inter-Varsity, 1970.

Haag, H. "ben." *TDOT.* Edited by G. Johannes Botterweck and Helmer Ringgren. Translated by John T. Willis. Vol. II. 1972; rev. ed. Grand Rapids: Eerdmans, 1977.

Habermann, A. M. *Megilloth Midbar Yehudah: The Scrolls from the Judean Desert.* Edited with Vocalization, Introduction, Notes, and Concordance. Tel Aviv: Machbaroth Lesifruth, 1957.

Hadas, Moses. *A History of Greek Literature.* New York: Columbia University Press, 1950.

Haenchen, E. *Der Weg Jesu.* Berlin: Töpelmann, 1966.

Hagner, Donald A. *The Jewish Reclamation of Jesus: An Analysis and Critique of Modern Jewish Study of Jesus.* Grand Rapids: Zondervan, 1984.

_____. "The Sitz im Leben of the Gospel of Matthew." *SBLSP* 24. Atlanta, Ga.: Scholars Press, 1985.

Hammond, N. G. L., and Scullard, H. H., eds. *The Oxford Classical Dictionary.* 2d ed. Oxford: Clarendon, 1970.

Hanson, Paul D. *The People Called: The Growth of Community in the Bible.* San Francisco: Harper & Row, 1986.

Harrison, R. K. *Introduction to the Old Testament.* Grand Rapids: Eerdmans, 1969.

_____. "Jeremiah." In *Jeremiah and Lamentations: An Introduction and Commentary.* TOTC. Downers Grove, Ill.: Inter-Varsity Press, 1973.

Hausman, Robert Arnold. "The Function of Elijah as a Model in Luke-Acts." Unpublished Ph.D. dissertation. University of Chicago, 1975.

Held, Heinz Joachim. "Matthew as Interpreter of the Miracle Stories." *Tradition and Interpretation in Matthew.* Translated by Percy Scott. Philadelphia : Westminster, 1963.

Hendricksen, William. *Exposition of the Gospel According to Matthew.* New Testament Commentary. Grand Rapids: Baker, 1973.

Hengel, Martin. *Judaism and Hellenism: Studies in Their Encounter in Palestine during the Early Hellenistic Period.* 2 vols. Translated by John Bowden. WUNT 10. 2d ed. Philadelphia: Fortress, 1974.

_____. *The Charismatic Leader and His Followers.* Translated by J. Greig. 1968. New York: Crossroad, 1981.

Hermisson, Hans-Jürgen. *Studien zur israelitischen Spruchweisheit.* WMANT 28. Neukirchen-Vluyn: Neukirchener Verlag, 1968.

Hiers, Richard H. "'Binding' and 'Loosing': The Matthean Authorizations." *JBL* 104 (1985), 233-250.

Hill, David. *Greek Words and Hebrew Meanings: Studies in the Semantics of Soteriological Terms.* SNTSMS 5. Cambridge: At the University Press, 1967.

_____. "Some Recent Trends in Matthean Studies." *Irish Biblical Studies* 1 (1979), 139-149.

_____. "The Figure of Jesus in Matthew's Story: A Response to Professor Kingsbury's Literary-Critical Probe." *JSNT* 21 (1984), 37-52.

_____. *The Gospel of Matthew.* NCB. 1972; rtp. London: Oliphants, 1977.

Hillyer, Norman. " sopher." *NIDNTT.* Vol. III. Grand Rapids: Zondervan, 1978.

Hoffmann, Paul. "Der Petrus-Primat im Matthäusevangelium." *Neues Testament und Kirche, für Rudolf Schnackenburg.* Edited by Joachim Gnikla. Freiburg: Herdes, 1974.

Holmberg, Bengt. *Sociology and the New Testament: An Appraisal.* Minneapolis: Fortress, 1990.

Horsley, Richard A. *Jesus and the Spiral of Violence: Popular Jewish Resistance in Roman Palestine.* San Francisco: Harper & Row, 1987.

_____. *Sociology and the Jesus Movement.* New York: Crossroad, 1989.

Howell, David B. *Matthew's Inclusive Story: A Study in the Narrative Rhetoric of the First Gospel.* JSNTSup 42. Sheffield: JSOT Press, 1990.

Hughes, Philip Edgcumbe. "The Languages Spoken by Jesus." *New Dimensions in New Testament Study.* Edited by Richard N. Longenecker and Merrill C. Tenney. Grand Rapids: Zondervan, 1974.

Hummel, Reinhart. *Die Auseinandersetzung zwischen Kirche und Judentum im Matthäusevangelium.* München: Chr. Kaiser, 1963.

Humphreys, W. Lee. "The Motif of the Wise Courtier in the Book of Proverbs." *Israelite Wisdom: Theological and Literary Essays in Honor of Samuel Terrien.* Edited by J. Gammie, W. Brueggemann, W. L. Humphreys, and J. Ward. Missoula, Mont.: Scholars Press, 1978.

Jastrow, Marcus, ed. *A Dictionary of the Targumim, the Talmud Babli and Yerushalmi, and the Midrashic Literature.* New York: Pardes, 1950.

Jenni, Ernst. "lmdh." *THAT.* Vol. II. Edited by Ernst Jenni and Claus Westermann. München: Chr. Kaiser, 1971.

Jeremias, Joachim. "γραμματεύς." *TDNT.* Vol. I. Grand Rapids: Eerdmans, 1964.

_____. *The Parables of Jesus.* Translated by S. H. Hooke. 2d rev. ed. New York: Charles Scribner's Sons, 1972.

Kähler, Christoph. "Zur Form- und Traditionsgeschichte von Matth. XVI. 17-19." *NTS* 23 (1977), 36-58.

Kahmann, J. "Die Verheissung an Petrus: Mt. XVI, 18-19 im Zusammenhang des Matthäusevangeliums." *L'Evangile selon Matthieu: rédaction et théologie.* Edited by M. Didier. Gembloux [Belgique]: Duculot, 1972.

Kaiser, Otto. *Isaiah 1-12: A Commentary.* The Old Testament Library. Edited by Peter Ackroyd, James Barr, John Bright, and G. Ernest Wright. Philadelphia: Westminster, 1972.

Kaiser, Walter C. "lamadh." *TWOT.* Edited by R. Laird Harris, Gleason L. Archer, Jr., and Bruce K. Waltke. Chicago: Moody, 1980.

Kaylor, R. David. *Jesus the Prophet: His Vision of the Kingdom on Earth.* Louisville: Westminster/John Knox, 1994.

Keil, C. F., and Delitzsch, F. *Commentary on the Old Testament in Ten Volumes.* Translated by Andrew Harper. N.d.; rpt. Grand Rapids: Eerdmans, 1975.

Kelber, Werner Heinz. "Conclusion: From Passion Narrative to Gospel." *The Passion in Mark: Studies on Mark 14-16.* Edited by W. H. Kelber. Philadelphia: Fortress, 1976.

Kidner, Derek. *Ezra and Nehemiah: An Introduction and Commentary.* TOTC. Downers Grove, Ill./London: InterVarsity, 1979.

Kiilunen, Jarmo. "Der Nachfolgewillige Schriftgelehrte: Matthäus 8. 19-20 im Verständnis des Evangelisten." *NTS* 37 (1991), 268-279.

Kilpatrick, G. D. *The Origins of the Gospel According to St. Matthew.* Oxford: Clarendon Press, 1950.

Kingsbury, Jack Dean. *Matthew: Structure, Christology, Kingdom.* Philadelphia: Fortress, 1975.

_____. *Matthew as Story.* 2d ed.; rev. and enlarged; Philadelphia: Fortress, 1988.

_____. "On Following Jesus: The 'Eager' Scribe and the 'Reluctant' Disciple (Matthew 8:18-22)." *NTS* 34 (1988), 45-59.

_____. *The Parables of Jesus in Matthew 13: A Study in Redaction-Criticism.* London: SPCK, 1969.

_____. "The Developing Conflict between Jesus and the Jewish Leaders in Matthew's Gospel: A Literary-Critical Study." *CBQ* 49 (1987), 57-73.

_____. "The Figure of Jesus in Matthew's Story: A Literary-Critical Probe." *JSNT* 21 (1984), 1-36.

_____. "The Figure of Jesus in Matthew's Story: A Rejoiner to David Hill." *JSNT* 25 (1985), 61-81.

_____. "The Figure of Peter in Matthew's Gospel as a Theological Problem." *JBL* 98 (1979), 67-83.

_____, ed. "The Gospel of Matthew." A Special Issue of *Interpretation.* Vol. XLVI, No. 4 (October 1992).

_____. "The Verb AKOLOUTHEIN (To Follow) as an Index of Matthew's View of His Community." *JBL* 97 (1978), 56-73.

Klostermann, Erich. *Das Matthäusevangelium.* HNT 4. 1909; 4th ed. Tübingen: J. C. B. Mohr, 1971.

Koch, Klaus. *The Prophets: Volume I, The Assyrian Period.* Translated by M. Kohl. Philadelphia: Fortress, 1983.

Koehler, Ludwig, and Baumgartner, Walter, eds. *Lexicon in Veteris Testamenti Libros.* Vol. I. Leiden: E. J. Brill, 1951.

Kraeling, Emil G. *Commentary on the Prophets, Vol. I: Isaiah, Jeremiah, Ezekiel.* Camden, N.J.: Thomas Nelson and Sons, 1956.

Krieger, Murray. *A Window to Criticism.* Princeton: Princeton University Press, 1964.

Kuhn, Karl Georg, ed. *Konkordanz zu den Qumrantexten.* Göttingen: Vandenhoeck und Ruprecht, 1960.

Kuhn, Karl Georg. "Nachträge zur Konkordanz zu den Qumrantexten." *RQ* 4 (1963-1964), 163-234.

Kümmel, Werner Georg. *Introduction to the New Testament.* Translated by Howard Clark Kee. 17th rev. ed. Nashville, Tenn.: Abingdon, 1975.

_____. *The Theology of the New Testament.* Translated by John E. Steely. Nashville: Abingdon, 1973.

Küng, Hans. *On Being a Christian.* Translated by Edward Quinn. Garden City: Doubleday, 1976.

Lampe, Peter. "Das Spiel Mit dem Petrusnamen—Matt. XVI. 18." *NTS* 25 (1979), 227-245.

Lane, William L. *The Gospel According to Mark.* NICNT. Grand Rapids: Eerdmans, 1974.

Lang, Bernhard. *Die weisheitliche Lehrrede: Eine Untersuchung von Sprüche 1-7.* SBS 54. Stuttgart: Kath. Bibelwerk; 1972.

_____. *Monotheism and the Prophetic Minority: An Essay in Biblical History and Sociology.* The Social World of Biblical Antiquity Series 1. Sheffield: Almond, 1983.

LaSor, William S. *The Dead Sea Scrolls and the New Testament.* Grand Rapids: Eerdmans, 1972.

Légasse, S. "Scribes et disciples de Jésus." *RB* 68 (1961), 321-345; 481-506.

Léon-Dufour, Xavier, ed. *Dictionary of Biblical Theology.* 2d ed. New York: Seabury, 1973.

Lemaire, André. *Les écoles et la formation de la Bible dans l'ancien Israël.* Fribourg/Göttingen: Universitaires/Vandenhoeck und Ruprecht, 1981.

_____. "Sagesse et ecoles." *VT* XXXIV (1984), 270-281.

Lénhardt, Pierre. "Voies de la continuité juive: Aspects de la relation maître-disciple d'après la littérature rabbinique ancienne." *RSR* 66 (1978), 489-516.

Lesky, Albin. *A History of Greek Literature.* Translated by James Willis and Cornelis de Heer. 2d ed. New York: Thomas Y. Crowell, 1966.

Levine, Amy-Jill. *The Social and Ethnic Dimensions of Matthean Salvation History.* Studies in the Bible and Early Christianity 14. Lewiston, N.Y.: Edwin Mellen, 1988.

Lieberman, Saul. *Greek in Jewish Palestine: Studies in the Life and Manners of Jewish Palestine in the II-IV Centuries C.E.* New York: Jewish Theological Seminary of America, 1942.

Lignée, Hubert. "Concordance de '1Q Genesis Apocryphon'." *RQ* 1 (1958), 163-186.

Lincoln, Andrew T. "Matthew—A Story for Teachers?" *The Bible in Three Dimensions: Essays in Celebration of Forty Years of Biblical Studies in the University of Sheffield.* Edited by David J. A. Clines, Stephen E. Fowl, and Stanley E. Porter. JSOT Sup 87. Sheffield: Sheffield Academic Press, 1990.

Lindblom, Johannes. *Prophecy in Ancient Israel.* Oxford: Blackwell, 1962.

_____. "Wisdom in the Old Testament Prophets." *Wisdom in Israel and in the Ancient Near East: Presented to Professor Harold Henry Rowley.* Edited by M. Noth and D. Winton Thomas. VTSup III. Leiden: E. J. Brill, 1955.

Lohfink, Gerhard. *Jesus and Community: The Social Dimension of Christian Faith.* Philadelphia: Fortress, 1984.

Lohse, Eduard. *The New Testament Environment.* Translated by John E. Steely. Rev. ed., 1974. Nashville, Tenn.: Abingdon, 1976.

Longenecker, Richard. *Biblical Exegesis in the Apostolic Period.* Grand Rapids: Eerdmans, 1975.

Louw, J. P. *Semantics of New Testament Greek.* SBL Semeia Studies. Philadelphia/Chico: Fortress/Scholars, 1982.

Love, Stuart L. "The Place of Women in Public Settings in Matthew's Gospel: A Sociological Inquiry." *BibTheolBull* 24 (1994), 52-65.

Luz, Ulrich. "Die Jünger im Matthäusevangelium." *ZNW* 62 (1971), 141-171.

_____. "The Disciples in the Gospel according to Matthew." Translated and edited by Graham Stanton. In *The Interpretation of Matthew.* IRT 3. 1971. London/Philadelphia: SPCK/Fortress, 1983.

_____. *Matthew 1-7: A Commentary.* Translated by W. C. Linss. 1985; Minneapolis: Augsburg, 1989.

_____. *Matthew in History: Interpretation, Influence, and Effects.* Minneapolis: Fortress, 1994.

MacKenzie, R. A. F. "Review of R. N. Whybray, *The Intellectual Tradition in the Old Testament.*" *Bib* 56 (1975), 266-268.

Malherbe, Abraham J. *Social Aspects of Early Christianity.* Baton Rouge, La.: Louisiana State University Press, 1977.

Malina, Bruce J. *Christian Origins and Cultural Anthropology: Practical Models for Biblical Interpretation.* Atlanta: John Knox, 1986.

_____. *The New Testament World: Insights from Cultural Anthropology.* Atlanta: John Knox, 1981.

Mann, C. S. *Mark.* AB 27. Garden City, N.Y.: Doubleday, 1986.

Manson, T. W. *The Sayings of Jesus.* 1937, rpt. Grand Rapids: Eerdmans, 1979.

_____. *The Teaching of Jesus: Studies of Its Form and Content.* 2d ed. Cambridge: Cambridge University Press, 1935.

Marrou, Henri I. *A History of Education in Antiquity.* Translated by George Lamb. 3d ed. New York: Sheed and Ward, 1956.

Marshall, Christopher D. *Faith as a Theme in Mark's Narrative.* SNTSMS 64. Cambridge: Cambridge University Press, 1989.

Marshall, I. Howard. *The Gospel of Luke.* NIGTC. Grand Rapids: Eerdmans, 1978.

_____, ed. *New Testament Interpretation: Essays on Principles and Methods.* Exeter, England / Grand Rapids: Paternoster / Eerdmans, 1977.

Martin, Ralph P. *New Testament Foundations: A Guide for Christian Students.* Vol. 1, The Four Gospels. Grand Rapids: Eerdmans, 1975.

_____. "St. Matthew's Gospel in Recent Study." *ExpTim* LXXX (1968-1969), 132-137.

Martinez, E. R. "The Interpretation of οἱ μαθηταί in Matthew 18." *CBQ* XXIII (1961).

McCarter, P. Kyle, Jr. *I Samuel.* AB. Vol. 8. Garden City, N.Y.: Doubleday, 1980.

McKane, William. *Prophets and Wise Men.* SBT 44. Naperville, Ill.: Alec R. Allenson,1965.

_____. "Review of R. N. Whybray, *The Intellectual Tradition in the Old Testament.*" *JSS* 20 (1975), 243-248.

McKenzie, John L. *Second Isaiah.* AB. Vol. 20. Garden City, N.Y.: Doubleday, 1968.

McNeile, Alan Hugh. *The Gospel According to St. Matthew.* 1915, rpt. Grand Rapids: Baker, 1980.

Meier, John P. *A Marginal Jew: Rethinking the Historical Jesus.* Vols. 1&2. Anchor Bible Reference Library. New York: Doubleday, 1991; 1994.

_____. *Matthew.* Wilmington: Glazier, 1980.

_____. *The Vision of Matthew: Christ, Church and Morality in the First Gospel.* New York: Paulist, 1979.

Melbourne, Bertram L. *Slow to Understand: The Disciples in Synoptic Perspective.* Lanham, Md.: University Press of America, 1988.

Mettinger, Tryggve D. *Solomonic State Officials: A Study of the Civil Government Officials of the Israelite Monarchy.* ConB OTS 5. Lund: Gleerup, 1971.

Metzger, Bruce M. *A Textual Commentary on the Greek New Testament.* 3d ed. New York: United Bible Society, 1971.

_____, ed. *Oxford Annotated Apocrypha, Expanded Edition containing the Third and Fourth Books of the Maccabees and Psalm 151.* New York: Oxford, 1977.

Meye, Robert. *Jesus and the Twelve: Discipleship and Revelation in Mark's Gospel.* Grand Rapids: Eerdmans, 1968.

Meyer, Ben F. *The Aims of Jesus.* London: SCM, 1979.

Minear, Paul. *Matthew: The Teacher's Gospel.* New York: Pilgrim Press, 1982.

_____. "The Disciples and the Crowds in the Gospel of Matthew." *ATR* Sup Ser 3 (1974), 28-44.

Mirsky, S. K. "The Schools of Hillel, R. Ishmael, and R. Akiba in Pentateuchal Interpretation." *Essays Presented to Chief Rabbi Israel Brodie on the Occasion of His Seventieth Birthday.* Edited by Zimmels, Rabbinowitz, Finestein. London: Soncino, 1967.

Mohrlang, Roger. *Matthew and Paul: A Comparison of Ethical Perspectives.* SNTSMS 48. Cambridge: Cambridge University Press, 1984.

Moiser, Jeremy. "The Structure of Matthew 8—9: A Suggestion." *ZNW* 76 (1985), 117-118.

Montgomery, James A. *A Critical and Exegetical Commentary on the Books of Kings.* Edited by Henry S. Gehman. ICC. Edinburgh: T.&T. Clark, 1951.

Moore, Stephen D. *Literary Criticism and the Gospels: The Theoretical Challenge.* New Haven: Yale University Press, 1989.

Morgenthaler, Robert. *Statistik des neutestamentlichen Wortschatzes.* Frankfurt am Main: Gotthelf-Verlag Zürich, 1958.

Morris, Leon. *The Gospel According to John.* NICNT. Grand Rapids: Eerdmans, 1971.

_____. "Disciples of Jesus." In *Jesus of Nazareth: Lord and Christ. Essays on the Historical Jesus and New Testament Christology.* Edited by Joel B. Green and Max Turner. Grand Rapids: Eerdmans, 1994.

_____. *Studies in the Fourth Gospel.* Grand Rapids: Eerdmans, 1969.

Moulton, James H. and Milligan, George. *The Vocabulary of the Greek New Testament, Illustrated from the Papyri and other Non-Literary Sources.* 1930; rpt. London: Hodder and Stoughton, 1957.

Müller, Dietrich and Brown, Colin. "κλείς." *NIDNTT.* Vol. 2. Translated and edited by Colin Brown. 1969. Grand Rapids: Zondervan, 1976.

_____. "μαθητής." Translated and edited by Colin Brown. *NIDNTT.* Vol. 1. Grand Rapids: Zondervan, 1975.

Müller, H.-P. "chakham." *TDOT.* Vol. IV. Translated by David E. Green. Grand Rapids: Eerdmans, 1980.

Müller, Mogens. "Salvation-History in the Gospel of Matthew: An Example of Biblical Theology." *New Directions in Biblical Theology: Papers of the Aarhus Conference, 16-19 September 1992.* Edited by Sigfred Pedersen. NovTSup 76 (Leiden: E. J. Brill, 1994).

Mundle, Wilhelm. "πέτρα." Translated and edited by Colin Brown. *NIDNTT.* Vol. 3. Grand Rapids: Zondervan, 1978.

Murphy, Roland E. "Assumptions and Problems in Old Testament Wisdom Research." *CBQ* 29 (1967), 101-112.

_____. *Wisdom Literature: Job, Proverbs, Ruth, Canticles, Ecclesiastes, and Esther, The Forms of the Old Testament Literature.* Vol. XIII. Grand Rapids: Eerdmans, 1981.

_____. "Wisdom—Theses and Hypotheses." *Israelite Wisdom: Theological and Literary Essays in Honor of Samuel Terrien.* Edited by J. Gammie, W. Brueggemann, W. L. Humphreys J. Ward. Missoula, Mont.: Scholars Press, 1978.

Myers, Jacob M. *1 Chronicles.* AB. Vol. 12. 1965; 2d ed. Garden City, N.Y.: Doubleday and Company, 1974.

_____. *Ezra-Nehemiah.* AB. Vol. 14. Garden City, N.Y.: Doubleday and Company, 1965.

Nau, Arlo J. *Peter in Matthew: Discipleship, Diplomacy, and Dispraise.* Collegeville, Minn.: Liturgical, 1992.

Nepper-Christensen, Poul. "Die Taufe im Matthäusevangelium." *NTS* 31 (1985), 189-207.

_____. "μαθητής." In *Exegetisches Wörterbuch zum Neuen Testament.* Vol II. Edited by Horst Balz and Gerhard Schneider. Stuttgart: W. Kohlhammer, 1982.

Neusner, Jacob. *Invitation to the Talmud: A Teaching Book.* New York: Harper, 1973.

_____. *The Rabbinic Traditions about the Pharisees Before 70.* 3 vols. Leiden: E. J. Brill, 1971.

_____. *Judaism: The Evidence of the Mishnah.* Chicago: University of Chicago, 1981.

Nicklesburg, George W. E. "Enoch, Levi, and Peter: Recipients of Revelation in Upper Galilee." *JBL* 100 (1981), 601-606.

_____. *Jewish Literature Between the Bible and Mishnah: An Historical and Literary Introduction.* Philadelphia: Fortress, 1981.

Nida, Eugene A. *Language Structure and Translation.* Essays selected and introduced by Anwar S. Dil. Stanford, Calif.: Stanford University Press, 1975.

Olivier, J. P. J. "Schools and Wisdom Literature." *JNSL* IV (1975), 49-60.

Orton, David E. *The Understanding Scribe: Matthew and the Apocalyptic Ideal.* JSNTSup 25. Sheffield: Sheffield Academic Press, 1989.

Osborne, Grant R. *The Resurrection Narratives: A Redactional Study.* Grand Rapids: Baker, 1984.

Overman, J. Andrew. *Matthew's Gospel and Formative Judaism: The Social World of the Matthean Community.* Minneapolis: Fortress, 1990.

Patte, Daniel. *The Gospel According to Matthew: A Structural Commentary on Matthew's Faith.* Philadelphia: Fortress, 1987.

Paul, André. "Flavius Josephus' 'Antiquities of the Jews': An Anti-Christian Manifesto." *NTS* 31 (1985), 473-480.

Payne, Philip Barton. "Midrash and History in the Gospels with Special Reference to R. H. Gundry's Matthew." *Gospel Perspectives.* Vol. 3: Studies in Midrash and Historiography. Edited by R. T. France and D. Wenham. Sheffield: JSOT, 1983.

Perdue, Leo G. *Wisdom and Cult: A Critical Analysis of the Views of Cult in the Wisdom Literatures of Israel and the Ancient Near East.* SBLDS 30. Missoula, Mont.: Scholars, 1977.

Perkins, Pheme. *Jesus as Teacher.* Understanding Jesus Today. Edited by H. C. Kee. Cambridge, UK: Cambridge University Press, 1990.

————. *Peter: Apostle for the Whole Church.* Studies on Personalities of the New Testament. Gen. ed. D. Moody Smith. Columbia, S.C.: University of South Carolina Press, 1994.

Pesch, R. "Levi-Mätthaus (Mc 2:14/Mt 9:9; 10:3). Ein Beitrag zur Lösung eines alten Problems." *ZNW* 59(1968), 40-56.

Petersen, Norman R. *Literary Criticism for New Testament Critics.* GBS. Edited by Dan O. Via, Jr. Minneapolis: Fortress, 1978.

Porter, J. R. "The Origins of Prophecy in Israel." In *Israel's Prophetic Tradition: Essays in Honour of Peter R. Ackroyd.* Edited by R. Coggins, A. Phillips, and M. Knibb. Cambridge: Cambridge University Press, 1982.

Powell, Mark Allan. *What Is Narrative Criticism?* GBS. Minneapolis: Fortress, 1990.

Przybylski, Benno. *Righteousness in Matthew and His World of Thought.* SNTSMS 41. Cambridge: Cambridge University Press, 1980.

Plummer, Alfred. *An Exegetical Commentary on the Gospel according to St. Matthew.* 1915; rpt. Grand Rapids: Baker, 1982.

Rabinowitz, Louis Isaac. "Talmid Hakham." *Encyclopedia Judaica.* 16 vols. Jerusalem: Macmillan, 1971.

Rainey, Anson F. "Scribe, Scribes." *ZPEB.* Edited by M. C. Tenney, 5 vols. Grand Rapids: Zondervan, 1975.

Rengstorf, Karl H. "Διδάσκω, διδάσκαλος." *TDNT.* Vol. II. Grand Rapids: Eerdmans, 1967.

————. "μαθητής." *TDNT.* Vol. IV. Grand Rapids: Eerdmans, 1967.

————. "μαθητής." *Theologisches Wörterbuch zum Neuen Testament.* Edited by Gerhard Kittel, L-N. Stuttgart: W. Kohlhammer, 1942.

————. "μανθάνω." *TDNT.* Vol. IV. Grand Rapids: Eerdmans, 1967.

————, ed. *A Complete Concordance to Flavius Josephus.* Vol. III L-P. Leiden: E. J. Brill, 1979.

Rist, John M. *On the Independence of Matthew and Mark.* SNTSMS 32. Cambridge: University Press, 1978.

Robertson, A. T. *A Grammar of the Greek New Testament in the Light of Historical Research.* 4th ed. Nashville, Tenn.: Broadman Press, 1934.

Ryken, Leland. *The Literature of the Bible.* Grand Rapids: Zondervan, 1974.

Saldarini, Anthony J. *Matthew's Christian-Jewish Community.* Chicago Studies in the History of Judaism. Chicago: University of Chicago Press, 1994.

————. *Pharisees, Scribes and Sadducees in Palestinian Society: A Sociological Approach.* Wilmington, Del.: Michael Glazier, 1988.

Sand, Alexander. *Das Gesetz und die Propheten: Untersuchungen zur Theologie des Evangeliums nach Matthäus.* Regensburg: Friedrich Pustet, 1976.

Sanders, E. P. *Jesus and Judaism.* Philadelphia: Fortress, 1985.

_____. *The Historical Figure of Jesus.* New York: Penguin, 1993.

Sandmel, Samuel. "Parallelomania." *JBL* 81 (1962), 1-13.

_____. *Philo of Alexandria: An Introduction.* Oxford: Oxford University Press, 1979.

_____. *The First Christian Century in Judaism and Christianity: Certainties and Uncertainties.* New York: Oxford, 1969.

Sawicki, Marianne. "How to Teach Christ's Disciples: John 1:19-37 and Matthew 11:2-15." *LexThQ* 21 (1, 1986), 14-26.

Schilling, Othmar. "Amt und Nachfolge im Alten Testament und in Qumran." *Volk Gottes: zum Kirchenverständnis der Katholischen, Evangelischen, und Anglikanischen Theologie.* Festgabe für Josef Höfer. Edited by Remigius Bäumer und Heimo Dolch. Freiberg: Herder, 1967.

Schmidt, Karl L. "ἐκκλησία." *TDNT.* Vol. III. Grand Rapids: Eerdmans, 1965.

Schulz, Anselm. *Nachfolgen und Nachahmen: Studien über das Verhältnis der neutestamentlichen Jüngerschaft zur urchristlichen Vorbildethik.* SANT 6. Munich: Kösel-Verlag, 1962.

Schürer, Emil. *The History of the Jewish People in the Age of Jesus Christ (175 B.C.-A.D. 135).* 3 vols. A New English Version, Revised and edited by Geza Vermes, Fergus Millar, and Matthew Black. 1885; rev. ed. Edinburgh: T.&T. Clarke, 1979.

Schweizer, Eduard. *Lordship and Discipleship.* Translated and revised by the author. SBT 28. 1955. London: SCM, 1960.

_____. *Matthäus und seine Gemeinde.* SBS 71. Stuttgart: Katholisches Bibelwerk, 1974.

_____. *The Good News According to Matthew.* Translated by David E. Green. Atlanta: John Knox, 1975.

Scott, R. B. Y. *Proverbs and Ecclesiastes.* AB. Vol. 18. 2d ed.; Garden City, N.Y., 1965.

_____. *The Way of Wisdom.* New York: Macmillan, 1971.

Seccombe, David P. "Take Up Your Cross." In *God Who is Rich in Mercy: Essays Presented to D. B. Knox.* Edited by Peter T. O'Brien and David G. Peterson. Homebush, Australia: Anzea, 1986.

Segal, Alan F. *Rebecca's Children: Judaism and Christianity in the Roman World.* Cambridge, Mass.: Harvard University Press, 1986.

Segovia, Fernando F., ed. *Discipleship in the New Testament.* Philadelphia: Fortress, 1985.

Senior, Donald P. *The Passion Narrative According to Matthew : A Redactional Study.* BETL 39. Louvain, Belgium: Leuven University Press, 1975.

Silva, Moisés. *Biblical Words and Their Meaning: An Introduction to Lexical Semantics.* Grand Rapids: Zondervan, 1983.

_____. "New Lexical Semitisms?" *ZNTW* 69 (1978), 253-257.

Sim, David C. "The Gospel of Matthew and the Gentiles." *JSNT* 57 (1995), 19-48.

Smalley, Stephen S. "Redaction Criticism." *New Testament Interpretation: Essays on Principles and Methods.* Edited by I. Howard Marshall. Exeter, England / Grand Rapids: Paternoster / Eerdmans, 1977.

Soulen, Richard N. *Handbook of Biblical Criticism.* 1976; 2d ed. Atlanta, Ga.: John Knox, 1981.

Stanton, Graham. *A Gospel for a New People: Studies in Matthew.* Edinburgh: T.&T. Clark, 1991.

_____. "Matthew as a Creative Interpreter of the Sayings of Jesus." In *Das Evangelium und die Evangelien.* Edited by Peter Stuhlmacher. WUNT 28. Tübingen: J. C. B. Mohr (Paul Siebeck), 1983.

_____. "Revisiting Matthew's Communities." *SBLSP* 33. Edited by Eugene H. Lovering, Jr. Atlanta: Scholars Press, 1994.

_____. "The Gospel of Matthew and Judaism." *BJRL* 66 (1984), 264-284.

_____. "The Origin and Purpose of Matthew's Gospel: Matthean Scholarship from 1945 to 1980." *Aufstieg und Niedergang der Römischen Welt*. II, 25, 3. Edited by H. Temporini and W. Haase. Berlin: Walter de Gruyter, 1985.

Stendahl, Krister. "Matthew." *Peake's Commentary on the Bible*. Edited by Matthew Black, 1962. Middlesex: Thomas Nelson and Sons, 1976.

Stock, Augustine. *The Method and Message of Matthew*. Collegeville, Minn.: Liturgical, 1994.

Stone, Michael E., ed. *Jewish Writings of the Second Temple Period: Apocrypha, Pseudepigrapha, Qumran Sectarian Writings, Philo, Josephus*. Vol. Two of The Literature of the Jewish People in the Period of the Second Temple and the Talmud. Section Two of Compendia Rerum Iudaicarum ad Novum Testamentum. Assem / Philadelphia: Van Gorcum / Fortress, 1984.

Strack, Hermann L. and Billerbeck, Paul. "Das Evangelium nach Matthäus Erläutert aus Talmud und Midrasch." *Kommentar Zum Neuen Testament aus Talmud und Midrasch*. München: C. H. Beck'sche, 1922-1928.

Strecker, Georg. *Der Weg der Gerechtigkeit: Untersuchung zur Theologie des Matthäus*. 1962; 3d ed.; rpt. Göttingen: Vandenhoeck & Rupprecht, 1971.

Suggs, M. Jack. *Wisdom, Christology, and Law in Matthew's Gospel*. Cambridge, Mass.: Harvard University Press, 1970.

Tagawa, Kenzo. "People and Community in the Gospel of Matthew." *NTS* 16 (1969-1970), 149-162.

Tasker, R. V. G. *The Gospel According to St. Matthew*. TNTC. 1961; rpt. Grand Rapids: Eerdmans, 1976.

Taylor, Vincent. *The Gospel According to St. Mark*. 2d ed. 1966; rpt. Grand Rapids: Baker, 1981.

Tenney, Merrill C. "The Gospel of John." *The Expositor's Bible Commentary*. Vol. 9. Grand Rapids: Zondervan, 1981.

Terrien, Samuel. "Amos and Wisdom." *Studies in Ancient Israelite Wisdom*. Edited by James L. Crenshaw. 1962; rpt. New York: KTAV, 1976.

Theissen, Gerd. *Sociology of Early Palestinian Christianity*. Translated by John Bowden. Philadelphia: Fortress, 1978.

Thompson, J. A. *The Book of Jeremiah*. NICOT. Grand Rapids: Eerdmans, 1980.

Thompson, William G. *Matthew's Advice to a Divided Community: Mt 17:22—18:35*. AnBib 44. Rome: Biblical Institute Press, 1970.

Thysman, R. *Communauté et directives éthiques: la catéchèse de Matthieu*. Recherches et Synthèses: Section d'exégèse, no. 1. Gembloux: Duculot, 1974.

Tidball, Derek. *The Social Context of the New Testament: A Sociological Analysis*. Exeter, England / Grand Rapids: Paternoster / Zondervan, 1984.

Tilborg, Sjef van. *The Jewish Leaders in Matthew*. Leiden: E. J. Brill, 1972.

Trakatellis, Demetrios. "'Ακολούθει μοι/Follow Me' (Mk 2:14): Discipleship and Priesthood." *GrOrthThR* 30 (3, 1985), 271-285.

Trilling, Wolfgang. *Das Wahre Israel: Studien zur Theologie des Matthäus-Evangeliums*. 3d ed. München: Kösel-Verlag, 1964.

Trotter, Andrew H. "Understanding and Stumbling: A Study of the Disciples' Understanding of Jesus and His Teaching in the Gospel of Matthew." Ph.D. dissertation, Cambridge University, 1987.

Turner, C. H. "Markan Usage: V. The Movements of Jesus and His Disciples and the Crowd." *JTS* 26 (1925), 225-240.

Urbach, Ephraim E. *The Sages: Their Concepts and Beliefs.* Translated by Israel Abrahams, 2 vols. 2d ed. Jerusalem: Magnes Press, 1979.

Vaage, Leif E. *Galilean Upstarts: Jesus' First Followers According to Q.* Valley Forge, PA: Trinity Press International, 1994.

Van Aarde, Andries. *God-With-Us: The Dominant Perspective in Matthew's Story, and Other Essays.* Hervormde Teologiese Studies Supplement 5. Pretoria: Periodical Section of the Nederduitsch Hervormde Kerk van Afrika, 1994.

Vermes, Geza. "Essenes-Therapeutai-Qumran." *Durham University Journal* LII (1960), 97-115.

_____. *The Dead Sea Scrolls in English.* 1962; 2d ed. New York: Penguin, 1975.

Via, Dan O. Jr. *Self-Deception and Wholeness in Paul and Matthew.* Minneapolis: Fortress, 1990.

Vincent, John James. "Disciple and Lord: The Historical and Theological Significance of Discipleship in the Synoptic Gospels." Dissertation zur Erlangung der Doktorwuerde der Theologischen Fakultaet der Universitaet Basel, 1960. Sheffield: Academy, 1976.

_____. "Discipleship and Synoptic Studies." *ThZ* 16 (1960), 456-569.

von Meding, W. and Müller, D. "δέω." *NIDNTT.* Vol. I. Translated and edited by Colin Brown. Grand Rapids: Zondervan, 1975.

von Rad, Gerhard. "The Joseph Narrative and Ancient Wisdom." *Studies in Ancient Israelite Wisdom.* Edited by James L. Crenshaw. New York: KTAV, 1976.

_____. *The Message of the Prophets.* Translated by D. M. G. Stalker. New York: Harper and Row, 1962.

_____. *Wisdom in Israel.* N.d.; ET 1972. Nashville: Abingdon, 1984.

Wainwright, Elaine Mary. *Towards a Feminist Critical Reading of the Gospel according to Matthew.* BZNW 60. Berlin: Walter de Gruyter, 1991.

Weaver, Dorothy Jean. *Matthew's Missionary Discourse.* JSNTSup 38. Sheffield: JSOT Press, 1990.

Weeden, Theodore John, Sr. *Mark—Traditions in Conflict.* Philadelphia: Fortress, 1971.

Wenham, David. "The Structure of Matthew XIII." *NTS* 25 (1979), 516-522.

Wenham, G. J. "Matthew and Divorce: An Old Crux Revisited." *JSNT* 22 (1984) 95-107.

White, L. Michael. "Shifting Sectarian Boundaries in Early Christianity." *BullJohnRylUnivLibMan* 70 (3, 1988), 7-24.

Whitelocke, Lester T. *An Analytical Concordance of the Books of the Apocrypha.* 2 vols. Washington, D.C.: University Press of America, 1978.

Whybray, R. N. *Isaiah 40-66.* NCB. London: Marshall, Morgan & Scott, 1975.

_____. *The Intellectual Tradition in the Old Testament.* BZAW 135. Berlin: Walter de Gruyter, 1974.

Wilcox, Max. "Jesus in the Light of His Jewish Environment." *Aufstieg und Niedergang der Römischen Welt.* Edited by H. Temporini and W. Haase. Berlin: Walter de Gruyter, 1982. II, 25, 1:131-195

_____. "Peter and the Rock : A Fresh Look at Matthew XVI. 17-19." *NTS* 22 (1976), 73-88.

Wilkens, W. "Die Komposition des Matthäus-Evangeliums." *NTS* 31 (1985), 24-38.

Wilkins, Michael J. *The Concept of Disciple in Matthew's Gospel: As Reflected in the Use of the Term Μαθητης.* NovTSup 59. Leiden: E. J. Brill, 1988.

_____. *Following the Master: A Biblical Theology of Discipleship.* Grand Rapids: Zondervan, 1992.

_____. "Christian;" "Belief/Believer;" "Imitate/Imitator;" "Brother/ Brotherhood;"

"Barabbas;" "Bartholemew." *Anchor Bible Dictionary*, edited by David Noel Freedman. 6 vols. Garden City: Doubleday, 1992.

_____. "Discipleship;" "Disciples;" "Sinner." *Dictionary of Jesus and the Gospels*, ed. Joel B. Green and Scot McKnight, consulting ed. I. Howard Marshall. Downers Grove: InterVarsity Press, 1992.

_____. "Named and Unnamed Disciples in Matthew: A Literary-Theological Study." *SBLSP* 30. Edited by Eugene H. Lovering, Jr. Atlanta: Scholars Press, 1991.

_____. "The Interplay of Ministry, Martyrdom, and Discipleship in Ignatius of Antioch." *Worship, Theology, and Ministry in the Early Church*. Edited by M. J. Wilkins and T. Paige. JSNTSup. 87. Sheffield: JSOT Press, 1992.

Wilkins, Michael J. and J. P. Moreland. *Jesus Under Fire: Modern Scholarship Reinvents the Historical Jesus*. Grand Rapids: Zondervan, 1995.

Wilkins, Michael J. and Terence Paige. *Worship, Theology, and Ministry in the Early Church*. JSNTSup. 87. Sheffield: JSOT Press, 1992.

Wilson, Robert R. *Prophecy and Society in Ancient Israel*. Philadelphia: Fortress, 1980.

_____. *Sociological Approaches to the Old Testament*. GBS: OT Series. Philadelphia: Fortress, 1984.

Witherington, Ben, III. "Matthew 5:32 and 19:9—Exception or Exceptional Situation?" *NTS* 31 (1985), 571-576.

_____. *The Christology of Jesus*. Minneapolis: Fortress, 1990.

Wolff, Hans Walter. *Amos the Prophet: The Man and His Background*. Translated by F. McCurley, 1964. Philadelphia: Fortress, 1973.

_____. "Micah the Moreshite—The Prophet and His Background." *Israelite Wisdom: Theological and Literary Essays in Honor of Samuel Terrien*. Edited by J. Gammie, W. Brueggemann, W. L. Humphreys, and J. Ward. Missoula, Mont.: Scholars Press, 1978.

Wood, Leon. *The Prophets of Israel*. Grand Rapids: Baker, 1979.

Wright, F. A. *A History of Later Greek Literature: From the Death of Alexander in 323 B.C. to the Death of Justinian in 565 A.D.* London: Routledge and Kegan Paul Ltd., 1932.

Young, Edward J. *The Book of Isaiah*. 3 vols. 1965; 2d ed. Grand Rapids: Eerdmans, 1972.

_____. *My Servants the Prophets*. Grand Rapids: Eerdmans, 1955.

Zumstein, Jean. *La Condition du Croyant dans L'Evangile Selon Matthieu*. Orbis Biblicus et Orientalis 16. Göttingen: Vandenhoeck und Ruprecht, 1977.

INDEX OF AUTHORS

INDEX OF REFERENCES

1. OLD TESTAMENT

NEW TESTAMENT

3. JEWISH LITERATURE

4. EARLY CHRISTIAN LITERATURE

5. CLASSICAL AND HELLENISTIC GREEK LITERATURE